TEX MORTON

TEX MORTON

From Australian Yodeler to International Showman

ANDREW K. SMITH
With Peter Burgis and Hedley Charles

THE CHARLES K. WOLFE MUSIC SERIES
Ted Olson, *Series Editor*

THE UNIVERSITY OF TENNESSEE PRESS
Knoxville

The Charles K. Wolfe Music Series was launched in honor of the late Charles K. Wolfe (1943–2006), whose pioneering work in the study of American vernacular music brought a deepened understanding of a wide range of American music to a worldwide audience. In recognition of Dr. Wolfe's approach to music scholarship, the series will include books that investigate genres of folk and popular music as broadly as possible.

Copyright © 2023 by The University of Tennessee Press / Knoxville.
All Rights Reserved. Manufactured in the United States of America.
FIRST EDITION.

Library of Congress Cataloging-in-Publication Data
Names: Smith, Andrew K., 1953- author. | Burgis, Peter, contributor. | Charles, Hedley, contributor.
Title: Tex Morton : from Australian yodeler to international showman / Andrew K. Smith, with Peter Burgis and Hedley Charles.
Description: First edition. | Knoxville : The University of Tennessee Press, 2023. | Series: The Charles K. Wolfe music series | Includes bibliographical references and index. | Summary: "Tex Morton was an early country music star in New Zealand, Australia, and, to a lesser degree, in southern Asia. In a time when the American country-music boom was just beginning to echo around the world, Morton turned his natural talent for yodeling into full-blown country music stardom, even making his way to America for a time. Andrew K. Smith's biography explores Morton's early life, his burgeoning career, his tumultuous celebrity, his final years, and his lasting place in the global phenomenon of country music"—Provided by publisher.
Identifiers: LCCN 2022042604 (print) | LCCN 2022042605 (ebook) | ISBN 9781621907763 (paperback) | ISBN 9781621907770 (pdf)
Subjects: LCSH: Morton, Tex, 1916–1983. | Country musicians—New Zealand—Biography. | Country musicians—Australia—Biography. | Hypnotists—Biography. | LCGFT: Biographies.
Classification: LCC ML420.M5679 S55 2023 (print) | LCC ML420.M5679 (ebook) | DDC 782.421642092 [B]—dc23/eng/20220906
LC record available at https://lccn.loc.gov/2022042604
LC ebook record available at https://lccn.loc.gov/2022042605

CONTENTS

FOREWORD *Ted Olson* — ix
ACKNOWLEDGMENTS — xiii
TERMINOLOGY — xvii
ABBREVIATIONS — xxi

INTRODUCTION — 1

1. New Zealand, 1916–1935 — 7
2. "The Yodelling Boundary Rider" — 18
3. The Yodeling Boundary Rider Becomes a Star — 32
4. Arch Kerr and New Hillbilly Acts — 48
5. Sister Dorrie — 57
6. The Early War Years and the Twins — 63
7. Tex Morton's Regal Zonophone Legacy — 72
8. Tex Morton's Fabulous Wild West Rodeo — 88
9. Marketing Tex Morton — 107
10. Legal Troubles — 110
11. Tex Morton's Dude Ranch — 143
12. The Tasman and Rodeo Recordings — 150

13	The Great Morton in North America	158
14	The Great Morton, Hypnotist	178
15	The Great Morton in Hollywood	188
16	Back in Australia	197
17	The Great Morton in the Far East	207
18	New Zealand, 1967–1970	217
19	Australia, 1970–1983	223

AFTERWORD	241
DISCOGRAPHY	247
NOTES	291
INDEX OF SONGS AND NARRATIONS	365
GENERAL INDEX	371

ILLUSTRATIONS

FOLLOWING PAGE 118

Teenager Bob Lane practicing in Nelson
The Lane family, late 1930s
Letter sent to Bob Lane's parents from Nelson College, 1931
Morton's fledgling band, early 1930s
The young boundary rider
Morton's first commercial recording, February 25, 1936
Morton, ca. 1938
Morton, 1940s
Buckjumping in Australia, 1940s
Lance and Violet Skuthorpe and their crew, 1940s
Tex Morton comic book
On tour in Tasmania, 1940
Unwanted publicity
Newspaper photograph of Morton and his twin sons
Morton's Wild West Rodeo, 1940s
Dunedin, New Zealand, late 1949 or early 1950
Morton with Dixie Bill Hilton
Morton performing his act, New Zealand, 1960s
Morton with Buddy Wikara at the Hawaiian Club, 1940s
The Great Morton, 1950s
Entertaining Indigenous fans in the Australian Outback

The Hamilton County Bluegrass Band
Entertaining children, 1960s
Marjorie Morton, early 1960s
The Great Morton in the USA, 1950s
The Great Morton at the Seville Theatre, Montreal, 1950s
Program for the Grand Ole Opry Tour, 1959
Kath Morton in Tex's shooting act, Canberra, 1964
Morton with Gunsynd, the champion racehorse, 1970s
Kath Morton next to the bust of Tex, July 1991
Lance Skuthorpe at the 1938 Calgary Stampede
On set with Angela Punch McGregor

FOREWORD

It is hardly surprising that Robert William Lane (1916–1983) changed his name to Tex Morton since, as a performer and as a person, he valued everything American. As a professional musician this New Zealand native modelled his persona—and to a considerable degree his sound—on that prototypically American recording artist, Jimmie Rodgers (though the New Zealander's own music lacked the instinctive influence of Black musical tradition so resonant in the music of Rodgers, a Meridian, Mississippi-native). Clearly Morton believed he could construct his life in the American mode— that is, he felt he could create his own path through the world undeterred by social conventions or cultural limitations.

While not a pioneer of country music in the strictest sense, Morton was indisputably a pioneer of the genre within New Zealand and Australia. (Another Australian musician—Art Leonard—released earlier recordings influenced by Vernon Dalhart, a multifaceted American popular recording star who made many records during the 1920s that were marketed as country music. By the mid-1930s, when Morton's first recordings were released, Rodgers was the bellwether for mainstream country music and Dalhart was considered outside the fold.)

As Andrew Smith's detailed Morton biography reveals, Morton was more than a practitioner of diasporic country music in a far-flung locale, he was a force to be reckoned with. He not only forged a profession for himself as a country music performer but also established a vital country music culture of value to others living in the English-speaking postcolonial populations in

Oceania—populations that, despite residing on the other side of the world from the prevailing country music culture, nonetheless had many social values and cultural referents in common with North American country music fans. (That genre, of course, was always an international phenomenon, having originally drawn musical and thematic elements from many world cultures.)

In an interview conducted for this essay, Smith, an Australian, explained his native country's embrace of the genre: "Australia took to country music from the start, and Australian artists developed their own style of country music while continuing to record in the 'American-style' as well. In Australia, this led to the development of the Australian bush ballad, which was essentially country music backing with singers singing about the Australian bush/country. It's a bit like Darwinian evolution: American country music found its way to Australia, where it was modified somewhat to suit local conditions."

Smith continued: "I used to swap music with U.S. collectors, and they all liked Slim Dusty's bush ballads. Slim Dusty himself was inspired and influenced by Morton, who started the ball rolling by writing and recording Australian material. Morton's 'Wrap Me Up in My Stockwhip and Blanket' certainly qualifies as the first recorded Australian bush ballad. At the same time, since authenticity is important in country music, Morton felt compelled to convince people he was the 'real thing.' A natural-born embellisher/liar, he fabricated fictitious stories about meeting Jimmie Rodgers and later Hank Williams."

Given his early embrace of the genre and his prolific performing and recording career while living in New Zealand and then Australia, Morton was dubbed "the father of Australasian/Australian country music." While Rodgers was long-ago nicknamed "the father of country music," Morton's sobriquet is more accurate, as Rodgers was preceded in North America by numerous recording artists that were the true progenitors of the genre, such as Ernest Stoneman, Uncle Dave Macon, and Vernon Dalhart.

Morton, a homegrown practitioner of country music within his native place, felt singular pressure to fairly represent another culture's musical genre while stamping upon that genre his own—his culture's own—stories and sensibilities. A devout servant of country music (a cultural force that has long governed a faithful flock), Morton made a pilgrimage to visit the sites of the Mother Church (North America, Hollywood, Nashville), trying to ingratiate himself into the country music industry. And that industry was not entirely welcoming to him, Smith observed: "I think Tex made his run in Nashville too late. By the early 1950s, country music in the U.S. was changing, with artists like Hank Williams, Lefty Frizzell, Carl Smith, and Ray Price taking center stage. But Morton's music was from an earlier era."

Morton—ever the indefatigable spirit with unquenchable thirst to perform before rapt fans—was unperturbed. Redefining himself as "the Great Morton," he became something no other country performer had the audacity or instinct to be: a music performing hypnotist. Whether truly attuned to alternative psychological states of consciousness or simply a showman who explored altered states of human perception in an on-stage laboratory, Morton was a brilliant performance artist for whom music was a mechanism for lulling audiences into a sense of togetherness in mutual celebration of country music's characteristic working-class identity. Toward that goal, Morton was partly a self-styled shaman and partly an unofficial international ambassador for the genre.

For many years Morton had been seen as a marginal figure in country music history, though more recently several North American scholars—Bill C. Malone, Ivan Tribe, Barry Mazor, and Jocelyn Neal—have acknowledged the artist's unique contributions to the genre. Australians themselves tended to marginalize Morton's achievement. According to Smith, "When he died, unlike his successors Slim Dusty and Smoky Dawson, Morton wasn't given a well-publicized funeral. There was no recognition of Morton by the Nelson Council, and his ashes are buried in a very modest grave." But throughout his lifetime the performer flourished despite being beset with hardships. He developed talents (music performance, hypnotism, and acting) and cultivated wise if quirky perspectives that resonated with country music fans around the world. As illustrated in this book, the Great Morton's real strength—in his recording and performing career as in his life—was his authoritative, fearless, and jubilant celebration of living in the margins.

TED OLSON
East Tennessee State University

ACKNOWLEDGMENTS

The author is particularly grateful to the following people:

Tex Morton's family: Barbara, Rex and Kim Lane; and Marjorie, Bob and Kath Morton—for their generous help and clarification of research findings and for photographs used in this book.

In Australia: co-authors Peter Burgis, for his knowledge of both popular and country music artists, and for his extensive archive of radio and record magazines of the 1930s and 1940s, most of which are not accessible online. Peter reissued some Tex Morton radio programs on his Kingfisher label in the 1990s. Hedley Charles, for his widespread knowledge of both Australian country music performers and country music in general. He interviewed Marjorie Morton, who told him it was the only time a researcher had spoken to her about her involvement with Tex Morton.

Discographers and collectors David Crisp and David Hardy. Without David Crisp's encyclopedic knowledge of early 78 rpm issues in both the USA and Australia, along with other information he generously provided, much of this book would not have been possible. His annotated discography of records released on the Regal Zonophone label was indispensable as was his citing of Australian releases in Tony Russell's indispensable *Country Music Records, A Discography, 1921–1942*. David Crisp, David Hardy and Hedley Charles could always be relied on to send discographical data at a moment's notice. Sadly, both Hedley Charles and David Crisp passed away before this book was published.

Australian personalities: Glenn Aird, Delores and John Balaam, Tex Banes, Tony Barry, Norbert Batchelor, Jim Bowditch, Bernie Burnett,

Arthur Bussey, Dick Carr, Buck Carson, Eric Cleburne, Peter Colman, Garry Coxhead, Tex Croft, Rex Dallas, Trevor Day, Smoky and Dot Dawson, Slim Dusty, Joe Ellul, Gene Bradley Fisk, Robert Gear, Ray Grieve, Terry Gordon, Johnny Greenwood, Lynette Guest, Ian Hands and Zeta Burns, Johnny Heap, Brian Howard, Joan Martin Hundley, Paul Kelly, Kevin King, Anne Kirkpatrick, Joy Kirkpatrick (Joy McKean), Kevin Knapp, Reg Lindsay, Colin Mackay, Athol McCoy, John Meredith, John Minson, Mike O'Malley, Colin Munro, Max Munro, Slim Newton, Dallas Nyberg, Gordon Parsons, George Payne, Neville Pellitt, Lorraine Pfitzner, Bill Robertson, Hal Saunders, Mary Schlue, Eric Watson, Llewellyn Weeding, Ron Wills, and others too numerous to list (although cited in Endnotes); Helen Harris, Karen Williams and Judy Linton for information about their fathers (Gil Harris, Buddy Williams, and Billy Blinkhorn, respectively). For **technical advice**: Lisa Featherstone, Damien Kingston and Graham Seal ; The numerous Australians who contacted me following a nationwide radio broadcast eliciting information about Tex Morton—too many to list here, but they are cited in the text; The staff of the National Library of Australia, the National Film and Sound Archive, and the Australian Country Music Hall of Fame.

In New Zealand: Chris Bourke, Peter Posa, Barry Skinner, Gordon Spittle, Joyce Stephens, Colleen and Paul Trenwith, Alan Turley, and library staff at Nelson College.

In Canada: Fred Isenor, Jack Litchfield, Rod Olstad, Keith Titterington, and library staff at McGill University.

Overseas experts and performers: Kevin Coffey, Colin Escott, Marva Felchin, Billy Garland, Paul Hazell, Dick Hill, Pee Wee King, Pete "Brother Oswald" Kirby, Barry Mazor, W. K. (Bill) McNeil, Bill Olson, Bob and Kittra Moore, Ralph Peer II, Bob Pinson, Nolan Porterfield, Ronnie Pugh, John Rumble, Tony Russell and June Webb; and library staff at UCLA.

James Akenson and Max Ellis, for their unwavering **support** from the beginning of this project.

The University of Tennessee Press: It was pleasure working with the University of Tennessee Press, in particular with Thomas Wells, for his willingness to consider this book after several Australian publishers turned it down, Kelly Gray, Jonathan Boggs, Linsey Perry, Tom Post, and Stephanie Thompson of the University of Tennessee Press, Pat Ford for her meticulous and expert editing of the original manuscript, and Ted Olson for helpful feedback and comments.

All sources quoted are cited in the notes. I would like to make particular mention of the following useful publications: Gordon Spittle's relatively brief *The Tex Morton Songbook* (GWS Publications) is the only other extant biography of Morton, and contains previously undocumented information about his career as a stage hypnotist in North America, although it also contains some misinformation about Morton's career. Such distortion abounds in numerous online articles about Morton, many of which are inaccurate and frequently repeat deep-rooted misconceptions. For a general discussion of Australian country music artists of the 1940s, see Eric Watson's *Country Music in Australia, volume 1* (Angus and Robertson, Publishers). Tony Russell's opus magnum *Country Music Records: A Discography, 1921–1942* (Oxford Press) was constantly consulted when discussing Morton's likely musical influences; David Crisp's identification of Australian releases of records, in Russell's discography and in the magazine *Country & Western Spotlight*, was invaluable, as also were his numerous comments in letters and emails.

TERMINOLOGY

CURRENCY AND UNITS OF MEASUREMENT

Prior to 1966, Australian currency was based on the British system of pounds, shillings and pence (pennies). In 1966, "decimal currency," based on dollars and cents was introduced. Generally, one pound (twenty shillings) equates to two dollars; ten shillings to one dollar; one shilling to ten cents; and one penny to about one cent. The symbol for the pound is "£" (for example, £34). "Quid" was Australian slang for one pound; its plural, "quids," referred to money in general. Currency conversions have been noted in the endnotes, but no attempt has been made to equate currency values to their modern-day equivalents.

At the time of publishing this book, one Australian dollar was worth about 67 cents in USA currency, but the exchange rate has fluctuated considerably over time. In October 2010, for example, the Australian dollar reached parity with the United States dollar.

Prior to 1983, when the Australian dollar was floated and its value varied according to market forces, the Australian Reserve Bank fixed the value of Australian currency.

The Australian measurement system was changed during the 1970s and 1980s, from the Imperial system to the Metric system. In general, one Imperial mile is equivalent to about 1.6 kilometers; one yard (about 91 centimeters, or 36 inches) is equivalent to slightly less than a meter (100 centimeters, or about 39 inches). Approximate conversions have been provided in the endnotes.

SPELLING

The American system of spelling has been used, except when particular English/Australian spellings (such as "yodeller" or "yodelling") have been cited in texts or printed on record labels.

SALES FIGURES

Australia's Columbia Graphophone Company (later part of EMI) kept, on index cards, monthly figures of record sales. Records were often kept in Columbia's catalog for twenty years or more. The figures used in this book are the total sales of discs over the time they were in the catalog. They were obtained from EMI by discographers who were given special access to them some years ago.

A review of the monthly sales over an extended period, for a small sample of discs, suggested that sales of a record peaked shortly after its release, followed by lengthy periods of negligible sales, punctuated now and then by brief periods of high sales.

HILLBILLY MUSIC

Although country music is no longer described as "hillbilly," the term has been applied in this book when referring to country music of the 1930s and 1940s, because that is what it was called at that time. And, although "hillbilly" is frequently used in a derogative manner, it can also be an adjective for "hard core" country music, as distinguished from "soft" and sometimes pop-styled incarnations. This book employs the term in the latter sense, even when describing the music prior to the time it acquired the term "hillbilly." Hence, the term "hillbilly," when used in this book, refers to a type of country music and is not pejoratively meant.

OUTDATED LANGUAGE

In some instances, this book quotes 1950s terminology like "deaf and dumb" and "crippled" for disabilities. Such terminology is no longer used in Australia.

"AUSTRALASIA"

The countries of Australia and New Zealand collectively comprise "Australasia."

The six states of Australia, with their capital cities, are: New South Wales (Sydney), Victoria (Melbourne), Queensland (Brisbane), South Australia (Adelaide), Western Australia (Perth) and the island state of Tasmania (Hobart). There are two Australian territories: the Northern Territory (Darwin), and the Australian Capital Territory (Canberra, the Australian national capital). Wellington is the capital city of New Zealand. The Tasman Sea separates Australia and New Zealand.

New Zealanders are sometimes referred to as **Kiwis**. A **Pom** is a person from England.

SOME AUSTRALIAN TERMINOLOGY

Broadly speaking, the bush is synonymous with rural areas as opposed to population centers. The outback is even more remote than the bush, and sometimes refers to Australia's arid interior.

A **boundary rider** is an employee on a sheep or **cattle station** (ranch) who maintains fences to prevent stock from straying. A **stockman** is essentially equivalent to an American cowboy. A **drover** is a stockman who moves cattle over long distances. A **stockwhip** is constructed differently from an American bullwhip, but both are used to move cattle. **Buckjumping** is a rodeo event in which a rider attempts to remain in the saddle of a bucking horse (**buckjumper**) for a specified time. A **digger** is an Australian soldier. A **duffer** is a cattle rustler. **Bushrangers** were the equivalent of American outlaws. **Ned Kelly** was an infamous bushranger who wore bullet-proof armor in a siege and shoot out with police in 1880. He was hanged later that year. To some, he was a champion of the underdog; to others, a mere thief and murderer.

A **rattler** is a train. **Jumping the rattler** means to ride on a train illegally. The terms **bagman** and **swaggie** refer to a hobo or transient laborer who carried his or her possessions in a bag.

An Australian male is frequently called a **bloke**, equivalent to "guy" in the USA, although "guy" is now used in Australia as well. Young women used to be called **sheilas**. A friend is often referred to as a **mate**. A **larrikin** is a boisterous, often badly behaved youth. A **lair** is a person who behaves in a brash and vulgar manner. A married man might refer to his wife as **the missus** (Mrs). A red-headed person might be called **Bluey**.

A **spruiker** is a person who, typically in a loud voice, tries to entice members of the public to buy tickets for a show. In the United States, such a person might be called a "barker". **Maintenance** in Australia covers both alimony and child support. To **do a runner** means to leave suddenly, often without paying rent or other debts. **Shoot through** means to leave suddenly.

Fair dinkum means "genuine", as in "He's a fair dinkum stockman", or telling the truth, as in "Are you fair dinkum?" Going **walkabout** means to go on an extended journey. It often refers to Indigenous Australians venturing into the wilderness. A **serviette** is a napkin.

Vulgarities: In 1930s Australia, **bum** was considered vulgar as it roughly translates to the American "ass." Harry McClintock's Australian Zonophone disc of "Hallelujah! I'm a 'Bum'" helpfully included this definition of the offending word on the label: "Bum is an Americanism meaning a 'tramp' or a 'ne'er do well.'" Tex Morton stated that his grandmother boxed his ears when he sang "Hallelujah! I'm a Bum" to her, and management at the ABC radio network requested Morton to sing the line "Hallelujah! I'm a Tramp" in place of "Hallelujah! I'm a Bum."

In Australia, **bastard** can be a term of endearment (as in "Come on in, you old bastard") or derision (as in "What mean bastard would do a thing like that?") **Bugger** can sometimes mean to break. **Buggered** means broken. For example: "He buggered [broke] the axle," or "the axle was buggered [broken]."

The "great Australian adjective," **bloody**, is used frequently to describe almost anything.

ABBREVIATIONS

ABC   Australian Broadcasting Corporation (prior to July 1, 1983, as Australian Broadcasting Commission). In Australia, it is commonly referred to as "the ABC."
CMA   *Country Music in Australia*
CWS   *Country & Western Spotlight*
EM   *Everybody's*
EMI   Electric and Musical Industries
MLS   "My Life Story" (series of articles, written as though by Tex Morton, in *Radio Pictorial of Australia*)
NFSA   National Film and Sound Archive (Australia); known as ScreenSound Australia, 1999–2004
NLA   National Library of Australia
PTM   Papers of Tex Morton 1937–1985, a collection of documents relating to Tex Morton, held in the National Library of Australia (Canberra, Australian Capital Territory, Australia). BIB ID 5977543; ms. No. MS Acc11.103. In the main, they comprise clippings from newspaper and magazines. They were donated to the Library by Kath Morton
RPA   *Radio Pictorial of Australia*
RZ   *Regal Zonophone (a Columbia Graphophone budget label)*
SMH   *Sydney Morning Herald*
TMS   *The Tex Morton Songbook*
Zo   *Zonophone*

PEOPLE

AS	Andrew Smith
BL	Barbara Lane (Tex Morton's sister)
CM	Colin Mackay
DC	David Crisp
EW	Eric Watson
GG	Garth Gibson
HC	Hedley Charles
JM	John Minson
JMe	John Meredith
KL	Kim Lane (Tex Morton's brother)
KM	Kath Morton (Tex Morton's partner from 1963 to 1983)
MM	Marjorie Morton (officially Tex Morton's wife from 1937 to 1979, though they were separated for most of that time)
PB	Peter Burgis
RL	Rex Lane (Tex Morton's brother)
RM	Robert ("Bob") Morton (Tex Morton's son)
RW	Rob Willis
RWI	Ron Wills
SDD	Smoky and Dot Dawson
TM	Tex Morton

INTRODUCTION

"The Big Bang of Country Music," as some have described Ralph Peer's historic 1927 recording sessions in Bristol, Tennessee,[1] reverberated not only in the United States but around the world as well, its shockwaves rippling and resounding to destinations far away in Canada, Australia, Great Britain, India, South Africa and other remote parts of the globe. In distant New Zealand, the plaintive singing and expressive yodeling of Jimmie Rodgers, one of Peer's "Big Bang" discoveries, resonated with a callow teenager who became so captivated with the "Singing Brakeman" that, much to the chagrin of his parents, he lost all interest in schoolwork and instead obsessively learned to play guitar, sing, and yodel in Rodgers's inimitable style. The youngster was Robert William Lane, who later changed his name to the more American-sounding "Tex Morton." He was the first "star" of Australian and New Zealand country music.

The history of Australian country music predated Morton, however, extending back in time to 1788, when Australia (as it was later known) was settled by the British as a penal colony, because Britain could no longer send her convicts to the United States after the American Revolution. The early settlers and convicts brought music with them from Britain and Ireland. Their songs, sometimes modified to reflect local conditions, formed the basis of Australian folk music.

During the nineteenth century, American entertainers toured Australia. Included were minstrel shows, dancers (like Lola Montez), actors (such as Edwin Booth and Laura Keene), Hawaiian musicians, and "Wild West" rodeos like those of Doc Carver. Such acts instilled in Australians a fondness for

American performers and their music. Over time, Australian music evolved to become a melting-pot of British, Irish, North American and Indigenous sources. Australia's First Peoples are the world's oldest living society, having inhabited the continent for some 60,000 years. During the twentieth century, numerous Indigenous Australians developed a passion for country music and some became well-known recording artists, performing their own songs.

The introduction of "hillbilly" recordings from the United States was what kick-started the Australian country music industry, however. At first, imported records from North America consisted mainly of what is now called "citybilly" music, chiefly among the likes of Vernon Dalhart, (whose "The Wreck on the Southern Old 97" was the first country music disc released in Australia, in early 1925),[2] Carson Robison, Frank Luther and Frankie Marvin. With their popular-song-style melodies and pleasant voices, these artists were particularly liked by Australians who bought sizeable numbers of their records, especially considering that Australia's population was only about six million in 1925.[3] From 1929 on, Jimmie Rodgers's harder-edged music was issued in Australia, where it was enormously influential. Over time, nearly all his songs were released in Australia. Rodgers inspired Tex Morton in New Zealand, and Australians like Buddy Williams and Slim Dusty. Morton later attributed the development of Australian country music directly to Rodgers. Astonishingly, the "Big Bang" had transplanted American country music to Australia.

It's tempting to speculate that several factors would explain why Australians embraced American country music. Both countries had historic ties to Great Britain, English was their main language, and by the early 1900s most of their populations lived in rural areas. Geographically, both countries are of similar size, with wide open spaces, so that songs of cowboys in the American West could easily be related to stockmen in the Australian outback.

Since country music had almost universal appeal to working-class people, with its story songs, sometimes overt sentimentality, and nostalgia for a romanticized past, it's not surprising that urban and rural dwellers in both countries took a liking to it. As Jocelyn Neal noted: "The musical evocation of wide-open spaces, rural themes, working-class identity, and even cowboy images all resonated with Australian culture, and over the span of the twentieth century, Australia developed its own robust country music scene, which parallels that in the United States."[4]

There were some differences, however. Australian country music was arguably less religious than much American country music, and there was virtually no tradition of blues music in Australia in the early 1900s, thus hardly any Australian hillbilly singers performed blues-styled songs similar to Jimmie Rodgers or Cliff Carlisle. During the 1940s, nearly all Australian country music recordings were of solo singers accompanying themselves on guitar, with yodeling, whereas American country artists frequently had full backup groups. And as American country music increasingly focused on urbanized "honky-tonk" music, Australian country music didn't make this transition until much later.

Australians were quick to emulate American country performers. Arguably, the first Australian to record country music was Len Maurice, a popular vocalist of the day, who between 1929 and 1932 recorded a handful of songs under the pseudonym of "Art Leonard"—a decidedly-citybilly clone emulating Dalhart's genteel style rather than the harder-edged music of Jimmie Rodgers. But it was Tex Morton, with his Jimmie Rodgers style singing and yodeling, that reinvigorated country music in Australia.

During the 1920s and 1930s, Australian record companies, unlike their North American counterparts, showed scant interest in local folk music. Instead, they focused on the nascent sounds of American hillbilly music, so it's not surprising that Australian country music initially was derivative of country music from the United States. But over time, performers like Morton wrote and sang about Australia within the format of the American country music genre. During the 1940s and 1950s, an overlap of contemporary country music with Australian folk music, particularly with poetry about rural areas and personalities, led to the development of a peculiarly Australian form of country music called "the Australian Bush Ballad," later exemplified by the music of Slim Dusty. Tex Morton pioneered the fusion of American country music with local themes, thus foreshadowing the Australian Bush Ballad genre.[5]

Radio was an important source of country music, too. Australian audiences listened eagerly to Tex Morton and others singing "live" over the air, and to transcriptions from America, like "Pinto Pete and His Ranch Boys." During the 1930s, however, Pinto Pete was replaced by "Wild West" transcriptions developed by local entertainer Smoky Dawson, who set them within an Australian context.

When still an ambitious teenager in New Zealand, Tex Morton ran away from home and embarked on a rags-to-riches career that he could only have dreamt of while still in school. He journeyed to Australia, performed on radio and the stage, and recorded commercially in 1936 when he was only 19. Within a few years he had emerged as the first "star" of Australian country music and would inspire other hopefuls to follow in his footsteps, like Buddy Williams and Slim Dusty (the future "king of Australian country music"). Morton was the Jimmie Rodgers of Australian country music: its influential progenitor and foremost stylist, and his early recordings established the core of Australian country music. But he was much more than a "hillbilly" singer. A world-class master showman, for the best part of a decade he toured North America as a stage hypnotist, sharpshooter, memory expert and singer. He traveled with Pee Wee King and recorded in Nashville and, on his return to Australia, made more recordings, including spoken narrations, as well as acting in television series and major movies.

In a fabulous career that lasted almost half a century, Morton created a distinctly Australian country music sound, performing original compositions with lyrics set in Australia. Although country music is popular in many nations, relatively few have adapted and modified it into their own distinct form—Australia and Canada, are two. "In Australia, . . . Tex Morton and other musicians heard American hillbilly records in the 1920s, and within a few short years had developed their own version of country music that was built on the same source material but that developed as a native Australian musical genre," wrote country-music authority Jocelyn Neal.[6]

Nearly all American writings about country music are mute on the international ramifications of the "Big Bang," and its effect on Australian country music. In his biography of Rodgers, for example, Nolan Porterfield omitted any mention of Morton, although an earlier book by Mike Paris and Chris Comber justifiably gave Rodgers credit for shaping Australian country music. Morton was briefly mentioned in books by Bill Malone, Jocelyn Neal and Ivan Tribe (who played Morton's records on his radio program in the United States during the 1980s),[7] but it wasn't until a 1995 encyclopedia of country music and Barry Mazor's book, *Meeting Jimmie Rodgers*, that he was given his full due and was favorably compared with American artists like Ernest Tubb.[8] More recently, Morton's renditions of Rodgers's recordings have appeared in international anthologies of the Singing Brakeman's songs, and in 2018, the International Country Music Conference in Nashville featured a session expressly devoted to Australian country music, in which Morton featured prominently.

Until now, Morton's career and influence have not been studied in depth and, owing to a cultural cringe, he has largely been ignored by Australian publishers who have no interest in "dead hillbillies." Instead, fans have posted stories, at times far-fetched, about him on the internet, many of which emanated from Morton himself as he habitually exaggerated and invented a halcyon past that was largely fictitious. Even his entry in *The Australian Dictionary of Biography* contains an error.[9] Separating fact from fiction was a major facet of this book, the first full-length biography of the versatile and talented entertainer.

I have endeavored to be objective throughout and, where there were conflicting accounts, I tried to include alternative points of view, appreciating all along that interviewees might disagree with some assertions made in this book. A specific challenge was checking many of Morton's claims about his academic qualifications and his accounts of appearing in American movies and television series. My recourse was to inspect lists of actors from the internet and other resources, where available. The absence of Morton's name in them, however, doesn't necessarily disprove his claims, because the lists could be incomplete. Consequently, several findings should be treated with a degree of caution where noted. In fact, some statements in this book might even be unintentionally incorrect, based only on evidence available at the time of writing. My sole intent was to disentangle fact from fiction, and to obtain firsthand reports of his life and personality, varied as they sometimes were.

Research for this book commenced in the late 1980s and continued, off and on, for the next 30 or so years. It was significantly aided by some of Morton's family members—his sister Barbara, his son Bob, his wife Marjorie, his now-deceased brothers Rex and Kim, and his long-term partner Kath. They volunteered information and corrected the manuscript without ever interfering with assertions that were critical of Morton's actions. The author was considerably assisted by co-authors Hedley Charles and Peter Burgis, and especially by discographer and collector David Crisp who, with David Hardy, compiled the discography. Australian performers, collectors and researchers, and international authorities from the United States, Great Britain and New Zealand all helped, as well.

I am particularly grateful to Thomas Wells and the team of professionals at the University of Tennessee Press for their support in the serious study of

Australian country music. It is, perhaps, appropriate that this book is part of the Charles Wolfe series, for Dr. Wolfe encouraged publication of essays about Morton and female Australian singers in books that he co-edited with Dr. James Akenson, a long-term advocate of this work and an enthusiastic ambassador for Australian country music in the United States.[10] Dr. Wolfe even played a Tex Morton album for an American old-time musician who learned to sing a ballad about Ned Kelly, Australia's infamous outlaw.

This biography cements Morton's place in the pantheon of country music. Further, it fills gaps in his career that have been undocumented previously, and shreds much of the mythology that has surrounded him for decades. Morton emerges through it as a creative, influential country artist and a showman of truly international stature.

1

NEW ZEALAND, 1916–1935

TEX MORTON ALMOST DROWNED when he was three years old. In January 1920, he was playing with other children near the Halifax Street ford, in his hometown of Nelson, New Zealand, when he "ventured too far in the stream" of the Maitai River and was swept away by a raging torrent. In desperation, he clutched an overhanging willow branch, clinging on for dear life with an ever-weakening grip, until he was rescued in thigh-deep water by a Mr. Edmondson, who had been working on the nearby Collingwood Street Bridge. "The little chap was exhausted and could not have held on much longer," a newspaper reported three days later.[1]

"Running away from home was not an unusual thing for me," Tex Morton told journalist Colin Mackay in 1967, recounting the event with embellishments. "The first time I can remember setting out to see how the world revolved was when I was three years old. I took my Jackie Coogan doll with me and had explored about half a mile when I fell into a fast-flowing river near our home. God knows how I didn't drown, but I remember grabbing at a snag jutting out from the riverbank, hanging on to it, and yelling until someone came and dragged me out. I suppose that, subconsciously, I decided even then that if you're going to be a wanderer, the chance of seeing tomorrow is diminished."[2]

This might have been Morton's first attempt at leaving home, at least as he described it. When he finally set out to explore the world, he spent most of his life rambling around Australia, New Zealand, the United States, Canada, England, and the Far East. In his later years he traveled in style and relative comfort, but early in his career, he said, he led a rough-and-tumble existence, jumping trains, sleeping in the open, singing in hotels by day, and fighting over scraps of food at night in mission homes, a life he recalled bitterly in his later years.

From the time he first left the security of his home and set out to discover the world, life was a continual journey for Tex Morton. Never content to spend more than a few years in the one location, except perhaps in his twilight years, he constantly sought new places to visit and explore. In a wider sense, too, Morton's life was a passage from one vocation to another. Commencing his professional career in the 1930s as a hillbilly singer and yodeler on radio and records, within a few years he headlined the most famous traveling Wild West shows Australia has ever seen, and had become an entrepreneurial showman. During the 1950s, he spent the better part of a decade taking a highly acclaimed hypnotism show to the United States and Canada and, he reported, had become a scholar in psychology and hypnotism. Returning to Australia in 1959, he acted in television shows and feature films.

Morton's excursion through life was characterized by a constant search for a profession that he regarded as more worthy than its predecessor—from hillbilly yodeler, to showman, to hypnotist and academic, and then to thespian—while driven the entire time to shine in his chosen profession. Perhaps this, more than anything, explains Morton's exceptionally varied career and productive life.

BIRTH AND EARLY YEARS

Tex Morton was born as Robert William Lane on Wednesday, August 30, 1916, in Milton Grove, Nelson, at the northern end of New Zealand's South Island. His parents were Bernard William Lane, 25, a postal clerk from Nelson, and Mildred Lane (nee Eastgate), 21, from Hokitika,[3] on the western coast of New Zealand's South Island. Robert—or "Bob," as he was known to the family—was Bernard and Mildred's first child. The family later included two other sons, Rex and Kim, and a daughter Barbara.[4]

Lane's father was among the fastest Morse-code operators in the telegraphy section of the Nelson post office, and he later taught young Bob his skills on the telegraph machine, as well as encouraging his son's interest in crystal-set radios and electrical technology, a fascination that continued throughout

Bob's life.[5] Bob's paternal grandmother doted on him, especially since he was her first grandchild, and avidly followed his career.[6] Lane later sang "Wee Jeanie Hunter" in memory of her,[7] dedicating the song to "Jane and Will, my grandparents."[8] His paternal grandfather, John William Lane, a religious man who sang in the church choir, was an engineer and factory foreman,[9] well respected in the local community. To an extent, Bernard was musical, too: he played the piano. Bob and sister Barbara were also captivated by music but were drawn to different genres. Whereas Barbara pursued opera and classical music, although not professionally, Bob loved the early hillbilly music that he heard from records and others around him. He had progressed to these musical styles from being a member of a church choir,[10] and was also inspired by the songs of visiting seamen. Nelson was a bustling seaport, and ships from far-flung places as well as local fishing vessels docked at its wharves. In the 1920s, sailors from distant countries frequented the docks, nearby hotels and boarding houses. Some of these travelers brought music from their home countries, perhaps a guitar or other instrument, and even records from afar. Bob mingled with them, learning new songs and guitar playing to add to his rapidly growing repertoire. Barbara especially recalled her brother telling of picking the brains of sailors on the Nelson docks.[11]

The Lanes lived in a modest family home, close to the Maitai River. In 1927, the town council built a swimming pool nearby.[12] Bob, like his siblings and friends, spent many hours in the river and the pool, and he later became an accomplished swimmer. He and his friends would regularly take musical instruments to the river or pool and play music there. Sometimes he strummed a ukulele while floating in a rubber inner tube.

From his earliest years, Bob displayed an adventurous spirit and a talent for telling tall tales. His brother Rex recalled that Bob pitched a tent in scrub near the river, and sometimes slipped away at night while his parents went out, reading comics and singing in the tent, before returning to his bedroom shortly before his parents came home. On one occasion, he arrived home late after visiting a local entertainment parlor and invented a tale of how he had assisted a young girl after an accident there. Rex recalled that Bob had a lively personality and was "more of a leader than a follower," though his stories sometimes "diversified from the truth."[13]

The Great Depression of the early 1930s was the most shattering economic experience ever recorded at the time in New Zealand: exports plummeted as unemployment soared.[14] The calamity affected the Lanes, too, but the family was financially better off than many of its neighbors because Bernard's job as a public servant offered some immunity against unemployment, even though he endured four wage cuts. During his career, he assiduously studied at home and eventually was promoted to the rank of senior supervisor of the mail room.[15] Barbara remembered him as a decent family man who was often away hunting and shooting, sometimes accompanied by Bob.[16] At one time, Bernard built a canoe for his son, and taught him to shoot with a 22-caliber rifle. Love of both the outdoors and music was a factor in Bob becoming an Eagle Scout and gaining his entertainer's badge.

Bob Lane sometimes invented a fictional account of his past. In 1939, he told a magazine that his father was an American "of more than ordinary enterprise" who had migrated to Nelson with his young Texan wife.[17] In a later version, he described being packed off to the USA to live on his aunt's tobacco plantation in Kentucky, where he was known as "the young Pommy [English person]." "Jove, but the life in Kentucky was grand!" he enthused. According to the story, he regularly ran away to join traveling circuses. "I seemed to do it twice a year," he said. Then he told the reporter of his meeting with "Montana Bill," a snake charmer and sharpshooter who taught him to shoot. According to Lane's mythical story, Montana Bill died when one of his snakes bit him. And then, just when Bob was "starting to get the meat out of it," his family told him that he had to return to New Zealand. But instead of following instructions, he ran away to Los Angeles and afterwards worked his way back to Nelson as a cabin boy on the *Lurline*.[18] From his earliest years, Bob Lane spun webs of exaggerated stories that bordered on outright deception and stretched credulity to its limits; but equally, he was a raconteur par excellence who could enthrall audiences in hotels and the like, where he would lean against the bar and regale his attentive audience for hours. "He told bullshit," said his friend, Colin Mackay, "but good bullshit, just the same."[19] Even his own mother affectionately described her eldest son as "the biggest liar unhung."[20] In later years, many people accepted Bob Lane's accounts of his life as reliable fact, but the truth often lay somewhere else.

Bob Lane's earliest formal education was initially at Bishop's School, then at Central School, a boys-only primary school until 1927,[21] within walking distance of his parents' house, so close he had lunch at home before returning for afternoon lessons.[22] In December 1929, he gained his proficiency certificate and a later reference from the school described him as "a boy of great ability in many directions having intelligence and originality above average," as "reliable," and "of excellent moral character."²³ He worked at the Nelson Post Office that January vacation.²⁴ On February 4, 1930, he was enrolled in Nelson College, the only male secondary school in Nelson at the time, and about three kilometers²⁵ from his home. Nelson College was a highly regarded educational institution that catered to boarders and day boys alike from all over the southern hemisphere,²⁶ its most famous alumnus being physicist Ernest Rutherford who had won the Nobel Prize for Chemistry in 1908. Education at the College was free.²⁷

Thirteen-year-old Lane was placed in form 3A in 1930, suggesting he was in a class of students all of whom had excellent academic results, but the following year was relegated to form 4C, which "would appear to indicate he was not academic," according to a former deputy principal of Nelson College.²⁸ His sister Barbara, however, said she still has many of his school reports, and they show he consistently scored high marks in assignments,²⁹ though it's likely these were mainly from primary-school assessments. She has an essay written by her brother, titled "A Fairy Story: In 1975," which was awarded an A-pass and was described by a teacher as "a marvelous essay."³⁰

Nelson College's curriculum was decidedly traditional and didn't appeal to Bob Lane, who recalled his school days as follows: "Various and sundry learned gentlemen were trying to fill my young head with the intricacies of Euclid—Plato—the latest writings of Lord Rutherford ... and thump, whack and cane into me such interesting trivia as French, Latin, Physics, Algebra, Geometry, Journalism, cricket, "rugger," [rugby] painting (whoops!)—basic military training—history and other such interesting subjects."³¹

Lane's performance at Nelson College was disappointing. His results for 1930 were abysmal and although his attendance was excellent (he was absent for only seven half-days all year), most teachers reported a lack of study and concentration. He was absent from school for much of 1931, even though there was some improvement in a few subjects.³² A letter from the principal to his parents in April 1931, near the end of first term, stated: "The consensus of opinion among the masters is that your boy can do better. Some say he does not learn his lessons. He will do any written work there is to be done but not the learning. There seems to be no doubt he can do well if he likes."³³

As he later recalled, serious study bored him. "At Nelson College I didn't want to be Lord Rutherford. I didn't want to split atoms or anything. I didn't want to be the finest surgeon in the world. I wanted to run away from home and be a hobo like Jimmie Rodgers which I bloody well did," he later recalled.[34] Also, reflecting earlier, in the 1960s, he mused: "When I think of all those wasted years at college—who wants to be a famous scientist—or a stupid doctor—or a raving politician? I'm going to be like Jimmie Rodgers—a world famous bum—a singing hobo!"[35] Jimmie Rodgers was, of course, the famous American singer whose songs were sometimes about hobos. His records were released in Australia from 1929 onwards, and Bob likely first heard them while he was attending Nelson College.

So, instead of studying, Bob Lane gradually drifted into the entertainment world, appearing in school plays and learning the guitar. "At school I was a pretty good student, but an A-1 extrovert," he said. "Every chance I got I aped the masters when they were out of the room and was always the first to volunteer ... for school plays and concerts."[36] As Robert Lane's passion for music flourished, his interest in academic study likewise waned.

He left school around August 1931, when he turned 15, the age limit to which education was compulsory in New Zealand, at the time. He had completed fewer than two years of secondary education, later explaining his departure as "just in the natural course of things,"[37] but the exit upset his parents who had sent him to Nelson College to give him every chance of becoming an engineer, a minister, or something else equally respectable in their eyes. According to his recollections, though, the closest he ever came to fulfilling his parents' ambitions was to apologize to the local minister for not going to church as often as he should, and once, to work as an offsider to an engineer on a road gang.[38] His sole interest became singing and playing "hillbilly" music, which was then making inroads to Australia and New Zealand. An early exposure to country music was at his grandmother's home, as brother Kim recalled: "It was at Grandma's that we used to crank up her old gramophone and play hour after hour of Will Fyfe[39] and the only three or four hillbilly records available to use—a couple of Harry Torrani and one of Goebel Reeves. It was this last mentioned that [Bob] sang along with, 'The Tramp's Mother', backed, I think, with 'Letter Edged in Black.'"[40] Harry Torrani was a British Alpine yodeler whose records were released in Australia during the 1930s.

Two of Bob's friends in the 1930s were Bill Homan and Alan Howatt.

Homan was a boarder in the Gear home. Every Sunday morning Homan and Howatt practiced their singing and playing. Soon afterwards, they were joined by Lane. "Bob [Lane] was definitely the leader and dominant character," recalled Bob Gear, who was then about 12 years old: "He was an intelligent, lively, likeable character who, given an opportunity, would be assessed as 'most likely to succeed'. He was certainly the best guitar player and singer of the three at our place."[41]

Lane also remembered playing guitar and singing with neighborhood musicians in Nelson while a teenager.[42] They formed a group that practiced at Alan Howatt's home on Sunday mornings, playing everything "from mountain music through Maori melodies to jazz and ragtime."[43] A friend was Gilbert ("Gil") Harris, an exceptionally talented performer and a knowledgeable record collector who, a decade later, waxed four songs in Sydney as "The Whispering Yodeller." The fledgling band played at local parties, dances and charities.[44] By 1929 the group consisted of Lane and Gil Harris, who were both guitarists, Alan Howatt, Benny Morgan ("a Maori chap" who could play guitar, mandolin, fiddle, banjo and ukulele), Joe Barret (a Pacific Islander steel guitarist, said to be "of world class"), Ray Bonishea (ukulele) and Leo Redshaw (accordion). Bill Homan was an occasional member and Edgar Pike sometimes played clarinet. They were especially popular performing at dances.[45]

Lane and Harris probably started playing instruments like ukuleles, later switching to guitars, which they played in Spanish style. That is, they learned to play the guitar in the style of a cowboy singer and not "flat," as with a Hawaiian steel guitar. The two were fascinated by music and collected and exchanged records with each other.[46] Harris, according to Lane, was the only person in all New Zealand, apart from himself, who could play in the hillbilly style. The two listened to records by Jimmie Rodgers, Carson Robison, Frank Luther and Goebel Reeves at Lane's grandmother's house.[47]

Lane was initially influenced by American citybilly artists like Vernon Dalhart and Carson Robison from about 1926 onward, and then from around 1930 by Goebel Reeves and especially Jimmie Rodgers. "My ambition was to sing like Jimmie Rodgers," he said.[48] Perhaps it was Rodgers's yodeling that stimulated his interest in the more complex Swiss-style yodeling of Englishman Harry Torrani whose first Australian release was in 1932, suggesting that Lane's proficiency with Alpine-style yodeling probably didn't fully develop until he was about 16 or 17.

LEAVING HOME

After dropping out of school in 1931, Lane was employed as a delivery boy for a drapery store, for about a year.[49] He then worked for a while in a variety shop, but the regimented lifestyle grated on him, so he picked strawberries and apples, worked in timber mills, and was part of a roadwork crew, he said. Occupations like these were mundane, however, so instead he tried his hand at entertaining, but the local scene was limited. If he were to seek a life in show business, he would have to range farther, so he departed Nelson for an unknown future in the entertainment world. Another reason for leaving his hometown was a sense of shame in singing hillbilly songs near his parents, for fear of embarrassing them. "I wouldn't have dared," he later said.[50]

He had made up his mind to leave home by mid-1933, arming himself with references from Central School, McKay's store, Wood and Sons and a Mr. Pinson, all of which were favorable. Mr. Pinson, for example, described him as "honest and trustworthy" and sympathetically wrote, "one cannot expect a boy with ambition to remain in a position where there is no chance for further progress."[51] Another referral said he was "truthful, clean in appearance, and of good character."[52] These references and letters of commendation were all dated around May 1933, suggesting the intrepid teenager abruptly ran away shortly afterwards. Maybe he and his long-suffering parents had argued and then fallen out over his preoccupation with a kind of music that was definitely "low-brow" in their eyes, and so he ran away from home to avert further arguments and to avoid dishonoring his family.

He headed to New Zealand's North Island, where he was employed as a kitchen hand with Wirth's Circus. He also sang with Tut Coltman and his Blue Five dance band in Napier, and afterwards with Epi Shalfoon's Dance Band, all the while learning guitar and singing hillbilly music, jazz, blues and dance tunes.[53] He and a friend busked together, insisting that they weren't dependent on welfare, but instead were honest musicians plying their trade.[54] Times were harsh, so Lane's itinerant lifestyle meant he constantly went hungry, and lived and slept "rough." His wanderlust would have worried his parents, too, and there are unverified reports of his being accosted by either his father or the local police, to force him to return home.

About this time, Robert Lane began referring to himself as Robert Morton, or Bob Morton, and then as Tex Morton. Despite his later protests at being called "Tex," he chose the sobriquet himself, perhaps as early as 1934. A

March 1934 advertisement in the *Waihi Daily Telegraph* stated: "WANTED—Pupils for Spanish Guitar and Ukelele; 1/- per lesson. Also learn Yodelling and Singing by new system.—Write Tex. Morton, P. O., Waihi."[55]

Two days later, the newspaper reported that Mr. "Tex" Morton sang several songs at a P & T [parent and teacher] dance, where he was "well deserving of the generous measure of applause accorded."[56]

Waihi is a small town on New Zealand's North Island, some 800 kilometers from Nelson,[57] about as far away from Lane's home as any other location in the country. Lane had left home permanently and was trying to make it as an entertainer, busking in the streets and teaching guitar. He later stated that he had changed his name to "Morton" to avoid embarrassing his family,[58] although conceivably, it's just as likely he chose the name for show-business reasons: "Tex Morton" sounded much more Western and authentic than "Robert Lane." Even then, he realized that public image was just as important as his music. After Waihi, he traveled to Auckland, where he boarded for nine pence a night and supported himself by giving guitar lessons for a shilling per time.[59]

Much later, he told an embellished story of the circumstances that led to this name change: he was busking in the streets of Waihi in 1931, he said, when he was questioned by a burly policeman, who asked him his name. The anxious runaway glanced nervously over the policeman's shoulder and, spotting a sign that read "Mortons Garage," blurted out "Robert Morton, sir!"[60] But like many other stories Morton told, this is probably apocryphal, although at the time there was (and still is) a Mortons Garage in Waihi.[61] Most likely he had left home for good, traveled to Waihi (in 1934, not 1931), and had changed his name to "Morton" (from the Mortons Garage sign). It's also likely he was approached by the law—his brother, Rex, said that when their son had run away, the family had contacted the police, who later located him in Waihi,[62] but Morton possibly overstated the story by simultaneously combining the encounter with the policeman and seeing the sign which inspired his new name. Journalist Colin Mackay noted that Morton never varied the details of his anecdote about the policeman and the garage sign—unlike the numerous modifications he introduced with other yarns—suggesting that there was more than a mere grain of truth to the tale.[63]

Lane spent much of 1934 in the North Island around Napier, Waihi, Auckland and Rotorua. That March, he was again using the name "Tex Morton," when he performed in Auckland with Neville Carlson's revue which was touring New Zealand hospitals,[64] though he appears to have made only one, or possibly very few, appearances with the group. He also sang and yodeled during movie matinees in Waikato, near Auckland, in September.[65] By then, he was described as being "late of The Gaieties, Melbourne,"[66] suggesting he might have toured with the revue in Australia.[67] If so, it was most likely as a stagehand because his name does not appear in newspaper advertisements for the show, from 1932 to 1934. In nearby Hamilton, his busking caused crowds to congest in the streets and he was asked by police to move on.[68] Years later, he recalled those days: "You'd spend the days roaming the streets, singing in pubs [hotels], looking for work, planning to run away to sea or whatever the hell you were going to do. You couldn't get any work. Go to one of the missions at night; say a few prayers, bow your head, get converted ... after the meetings there'd be a mad rush for the scraps—things were pretty tough in those days. Always on your mind was this ambition to get away somewhere, find a job, or see the world."[69]

Around 1934, Lane referred to himself using monikers like "The Yodelling Cowboy"[70] before he adopted the sobriquet of "The Yodelling Boundary Rider." These epithets were possibly inspired by Jimmie Rodgers's handle, "The Singing Brakeman." Both names referred to the artist and to his occupation, which in Morton's case is an employment he invents. (A boundary rider maintains the outer fences of an Australian cattle or sheep station.)

From now on, Robert Lane will be referred to as "Tex Morton."

Most likely in 1934, rather than earlier, Morton made some private recordings featuring his singing, yodeling and guitar playing. They were made using a Speak-O-Phone machine that cut an aluminum disc with a recording head. A bamboo needle was required to play the recordings.[71] Morton recollected making the records in Wellington while he was staying at an aunt's house. He occasionally performed on the local radio station, and at parties and dances, dressed as best he could in Western clothes: an army hat turned sideways, a homemade belt, and an old boy scout shirt that was "stripped of insignia." At the time, he sought out a "back-alley workshop" advertising that it could make records. Morton said he made about six recordings at two shillings each, a considerable sum that was probably given to him by his aunt.[72]

Morton scratched his new nom-de-plume, "Tex Morton," and the song titles on the back of at least one surviving disc.[73] Two discs included "At the End of the Hobo's Trail" coupled with "The Insult"; "Mexican Yodel" and "The

Last Roundup" were on the third record.[74] Goebel Reeves's "At The End of the Hobo's Trail" had been released in Australia in April 1931.[75] Morton's renditions of it were especially poignant: his singing—supported by yodeling and straightforward but effective guitar accompaniment—was well-matched to the sentimental lyrics. "The Insult"—about a rough and tough cowboy who is offended when offered a ginger ale—was an American folk song collected by John Lomax and published in *Songs of the Cattle Trail and Cow Camp* in 1919.[76] Morton emulated Harry Torrani's "Mexican Yodel"[77] with spirited Alpine-style yodeling, and Billy Hill's "The Last Roundup" was performed in a mature, authentic style that belied Morton's youth.[78]

2
"THE YODELLING BOUNDARY RIDER"

TEX MORTON SAILED to Australia as a teenager, after being persuaded to make the trip by some touring Australian showmen and singers.[1] The exact year in which he made the move is uncertain, though, and Morton added to the confusion in subsequent interviews. Years later, he said the year was 1932.[2] Yet in 1969, he recalled living in Nelson in 1933, practicing music with his friends;[3] and at other times he gave the date as April 1934,[4] or by inference, as just 1934.[5] There is good reason, however, to believe that he traveled to Australia in 1932 (or even mid-1934), returned to New Zealand, and then sailed for Australia a second time, probably in late 1934 or early 1935.

Morton might have traveled to Australia in 1932, while he was still living with his parents in Nelson. He recalled stowing away on a tramp steamer that left Bluff, on New Zealand's South Island, and sailing to Australia, where he auditioned for broadcast on Sydney radio, only to be rebuffed.[6] The next day, he said, he worked his way back to New Zealand.[7] Morton's brother Kim believed Morton accompanied Wirth's Circus to Sydney, as a horse wrangler in late 1932, and then returned.[8] A newspaper reported Morton's recollection of his time with Wirth's as follows: "The ringmaster Philip Wirth spotted [Morton] strutting up and down and entertaining the queues at the ticket office by doing imitations of himself in the circus ring. 'We want a kitchen boy, not a bloody clown,' grunted the old circus magnate as he paid Morton off."[9] Wirth's Circus was in Australia that year;[10] perhaps Morton joined it for a short time, only to be fired shortly afterwards, although the story may be apocryphal.

Morton's other brother, Rex, recalled that Morton had "jumped a ship" in Invercargill (near Bluff) when he sailed for Sydney,[11] presumably for the first time. In a 1939 interview, Morton stated that he went to a radio station when he arrived in Sydney and asked for an audition. "The answer," he said, "was flatly and uncompromisingly 'no.'" He was so dispirited that he promptly returned to New Zealand. "Then I got to thinking maybe I should have stuck it out and tried other stations," he reflected. "The Auckland Show was then in progress and that gave me a chance to earn enough money to pay for a steerage passage back to Sydney on the *Monowai*. That was about April or May 1934, and I had a friend with me by the name of Dan Howarth, who professed to know just how to bust into broadcasting."[12]

In 1939, he said he came to Australia in 1934, "hitchhiked to Newcastle, gave an audition to the biggest radio station in town, leaving the executives of [the] same regularly unimpressed and, feeling somewhat crestfallen, returned to New Zealand and started street singing all over the country." This statement, one among a host of implausible tales in a magazine article, nevertheless suggests that Morton independently made an initial but unsuccessful venture to Australia prior to leaving New Zealand for good, though the 1934 date he gave could well have been 1932.[13] Perhaps he made an initial foray to Australia in 1934 with The Gaieties, while he was in the North Island, followed by a second move later in 1934 or early 1935.

Before he left New Zealand for the second time, Morton returned to his hometown of Nelson in June 1934. The "crooner, yodeller and guitar soloist," local news said, "created a furore" by singing "The Last Roundup," "Texas Rose" and "The Shadow Waltz" during a community concert in the School of Music.[14] A report stated he had recently arrived from Melbourne where he had appeared with The Gaieties, further suggesting his first move to Australia was in 1934. Perhaps the intention of his visit was to reconcile with his parents before he sailed to Australia; on the other hand, it might have been to demonstrate the success he had achieved since leaving home. Realizing that he was irrevocably determined to be an entertainer, his parents might have wished their errant son well and perhaps gave him a keepsake to remember them by.[15]

Morton was in Waihi in March and September 1934, and at least one of his Speak-O-Phone recordings must have been recorded in 1934 or even later. Also, he was issued a driver's license at Gore (on South Island) in April 1935; his occupation was entered as "radio salesman,"[16] so he was still in New

Zealand for some time until early 1935. Taking all this into account, it seems likely that Morton left New Zealand a second time sometime after April 1935.

He later describes his transit to Australia:

> A little frightened, facing for the first time the facts of life—not ready as yet to be born into the cold, hard outside world—clutching my precious tin recordings, my small cardboard suitcase containing spare sox, toothbrush, boy scout knife, father's safety razor and all those other appurtenances generally carried by famous world adventurers—I walked on board the smelly, heaving inter-island . . . ferry at 3:30 the next day. A storm was blowing up. I sat in a men's toilet, locked the door and waited. "Sorry mate, full-up—try the next one." At 8 pm the old "Matangi" put her nose out to sea preparatory to battling again across one of the world's most notorious ocean crossings.
>
> Next morning around nine—whitefaced, shaken, trembling and still frightfully seasick, I was safe back in the comforting womb of sleepy hollow—wiser, not sadder, but more determined than ever to follow my mature decision to make a success of my chosen life's work which lay ahead.[17]

It was common for people to stow away on ships, at the time. The stowaway only needed to have a friend who was a sailor on one of the vessels; the buddy on the ship would hide the stowaway and sneak food to him or her. This practice was called "ringbolting."[18] Perhaps Morton ringbolted from New Zealand to Sydney.

It's difficult to reconstruct Morton's travels in Australia in 1935, because he gave such inconsistent accounts of his early experiences, and specific details are scarce. We have only his recollections and yarns that were prone to memory lapses combined with his legendary ability to exaggerate. Morton said he and a friend, Dan Howarth, arrived in Sydney with only three shillings between them. Given the similarities in their names, it's tempting to speculate that "Dan Howarth" and his boyhood friend, Alan Howatt, might have been one and the same person. Morton's recollection went this way:

> We spent the [first] night in some cheap dump . . . in one of those side streets at the back of the Town Hall. The next morning we went up to Central Station, changed our clothes in the washroom and left our bags in the cloakroom. After that we decided we'd better take to the road. We'd heard Queensland was the best state for a pair of hobos, so we walked across the Sydney Harbor Bridge to catch a train. . .Gee, I'll never forget the thrill of riding in our first electric train as far as Hornsby! When we got out, we asked the newsboys which was the way to Brisbane.[19]

The pair eventually reached Queensland in a disheveled and dirty state. They boarded at the Brisbane YMCA, a shelter for swaggies (vagabonds) who used Brisbane as a springboard for traveling further north. Morton recalled brawling with other itinerants. "We fellows at the YMCA were the respectable hobos," he said. "The extra rough elements used to lodge elsewhere. Every now and then there'd be a battle between the two factions and the police would have to intervene."[20]

He teamed up with a harmonica-playing bagman ("hobo"), busking and doing odd jobs. After Howarth found employment as a waiter in a Brisbane hotel, Morton earned enough money to pay for train fare further north. At Gladstone, he was attracted by George Sorlie's tent show which was playing in the area, but he was unable to convince Sorlie that his singing and yodeling would be an asset, so he found other work instead, singing outside Alfie Foster's tent. (Sorlie's Musical Revue Company was in Rockhampton in June 1935, and Bowen in July 1935.)[21] He then headed for Rockhampton and worked as a spruiker (barker). "The Russian Cossacks were in Rockhampton that year," Morton recalled,[22] adding:

> The fellow in charge of the proceedings saw me hanging around one night, so he asked me to go in the ring and give a song. Just about that time I'd completed the first song I'd ever written, called "The Yodelling Bagman." I guess there must have been two or three thousand spectators 'round the ring that night. Anyway, when I got a few little engagements out of it to sing at a guinea a time, I began to think I was a real big shot.[23]

In August 1935, Morton was issued a busking license at Rockhampton.[24] Two months earlier, he had been charged with "having used obscene language ... and having assaulted Charles Smith" at Rockhampton and was booked under his name of "Robert William Lane," with his stated age as 19, though his nineteenth birthday would have been weeks away. Smith was a local policeman who had attempted to arrest the teenaged showman; the hot-headed youth admitted he had been drinking and using obscene language and was fined two pounds for bad language and one pound for assault. Since he was broke, he was permitted to travel to Mackay to obtain the required funds from his employer and pay the fines there. It's not known whether he was able to come up with the money. If he didn't, he would have been imprisoned for ten days.[25]

Several years later, Morton gave an exaggerated version of the altercation. He was drinking in a local hotel, he said, when a policeman got into an argument with him, and the pair exchanged blows. Other policemen joined in, but Morton ran outside with his mate "Wally." The two leapt in a police car and fled—only to be arrested later and thrown into the "boob." Consistent with the newspaper report of his arrest, Morton said he jumped a train from Rockhampton to Mackay to re-join the circus.[26]

He recalled traveling to Proserpine where he was very nearly taken by a crocodile—surely another fantasy. He then reunited with "Wally," worked in the cane fields, and opened a shooting gallery at Innisfail.[27] The two jumped the rattler (train) from Townsville to Rockhampton and then traveled south to Brisbane, where Morton was arrested by a policeman, whom he entertained by singing. Fortunately, he was released from custody and met "Tex Dawson," another entertainer. In Brisbane, he said, he sang at a community conference where he impressed a Mr. McCall from the "Columbia Gramophone [Graphophone] Company". Then he tried boundary riding before returning to the big smoke of Sydney.[28] Much of this narrative, however, seems to be fiction rather than fact.

In later years, Morton listed his height as five feet nine and a half inches and described his eyes as "brown" and his hair as "dark."[29] Even as a teenager, he was regarded as cocky but game. A journalist described him as "slender and 165 pounds of wiry, rather than bulky build" when they met in Canada during the 1950s. He recalled the self-confident Australian once flattened a "six-foot-four giant" by wrapping a trench coat around his arm, throwing it over his aggressor's head and then "launched a right that couldn't have traveled more than eight inches," breaking the attacker's jaw and leaving him face down on the pavement.[30] In his youth, though, when he was eking out a living on the fringes of poverty, his appearance was different—skinny and pasty-faced—"a real young lair [brash youth]"—always supremely confident in his own abilities.[31] Morton also developed other characteristics, some of which—swearing, drinking and smoking, for example—were accentuated by living away from home. They may even have symbolized an intentional departure from his conservative parents' values. His drinking was legendary: when once challenged to a drinking contest by some locals during the 1960s, Morton was still going strong after four consecutive days of imbibing.[32] His chosen poison was whiskey.

Morton, however, also possessed affable traits. His sister, Barbara, recalled that he was "the most restless person—smoke, smoke, smoke, pacing up and down—talk, talk, talk, nonstop." At other times, "It became, 'Oh damn,' moan, moan, moan." She described him as "a real city boy" who frequently sought the company of others. "He could gather people around him because he was so interesting, and he could always tell tales and spin yarns. He would have them around like a king holding court, just mesmerized by what he was saying. Mind you, my mother always used to say he was the biggest liar unhung. He did have all these experiences, but I think he embellished them a lot."[33] His inflated tales and easygoing nature, however, made him popular with others, some of whom afterwards remembered warmly the self-assured teenager they had met in the 1930s. Norbert Batchelor, who traveled with Morton in Queensland in 1935, described him as a "cheeky bugger" who was well-liked by other entertainers. He didn't make much money and was frequently hard-up, financially, Batchelor said, but he was admired by crowds.[34]

It's not surprising that Morton journeyed to northern Queensland and then returned to Sydney more or less the same way. The circuit was popular with traveling shows, and there were railways on which wandering bagmen could hitch rides. His early days on the road and jumping trains[35] were likely the inspiration for some of his songs like "Sergeant Small," "The Yodelling Bag Man" and "Travel by Train." At times, Morton traveled in passenger compartments with other entertainers, who covered him with a blanket when ticket inspectors approached.[36]

Back in Sydney, Morton performed on radio, busked outside railway stations and sang on harbor ferries. He also worked on the newly constructed Harbor Bridge even though he was unqualified for the job.[37] Later, he said, he worked at Luna Park[38] for a neon-sign company[39] but, owing to "his complete lack of electrical knowledge," he left after a few weeks, an ex-workmate recalled, some 60 years later. Morton, who described his meals as "shit," was eating canary seed for breakfast but despite his circumstances the youngster always had a cheery, friendly personality.[40]

Morton later performed on radio, first for commercial station 2KY-Sydney, and then the prestigious national network, the Australian Broadcasting Commission (ABC)—a case of "boiled lollies to chocolates," as he described it.[41] Announcers on the national network turned a blind eye to him having performed on 2KY-Sydney, which was then regarded as decidedly "down market" and "working class".[42] With his confidence growing and more experience under his belt, he was determined to become a guitar-playing, yodeling cowboy.

RECORDING FOR COLUMBIA

Morton said his first major break occurred when he won the novelty vocalist section of the 2KY-Sydney Radio Trials talent quest, hosted by "Uncle Rus" Garling [43] and that he subsequently went on to record for Columbia Graphophone,[44] then the only recording company in Sydney. But the 2KY Radio Trials were not advertised until some six months after his initial recordings[45] though Morton was a featured performer at a community concert at Sydney's Ashfield Town Hall on February 25, 1936—the same date he made his first Columbia recordings. Perhaps he confused performing over the airwaves that evening with a belief (or yarn) of his winning the Radio Trials. The community concert that night was especially memorable because he was given prominent billing as "Tex Morton, the Yodelling Cowboy," and sang "Goin' Back To Texas," "Dan, The Yodelling Man," "When the Bloom Is on the Sage" and, curiously, the Mills Brothers' "How'm I Doing,"[46] which they had recorded as "How Am I Doin'" in 1934.[47] In fact, the young singer had been performing on ABC radio station 2BL-Sydney as early as February 21, where he was billed as "the yodelling cowboy" (or sometimes just "yodeller"). It's also possible he confused his big break with winning a talent quest, than coming more from performing over the air waves with a national radio network in early February 1936, broadcasting as far away as Broken Hill, Melbourne and Grafton.[48]

Morton himself might have approached the Columbia Graphophone Company in Sydney, on his own sometime around 1935, to make records. At the time, Columbia's sales manager was most likely Tim Tyler. Morton remembered meeting with a "Jim Taylor" (surely Tim Tyler) in 1935 and was told to come back later. After he had become better known in Sydney, Morton said he contacted Tyler again. This time, Tyler was more enthusiastic about recording the New Zealand busker and inquired if Morton knew any songs by Jimmie Rodgers. Fellow performer Smoky Dawson thought at the time that Tyler was interested in recording American hillbilly material,[49] and this is supported by a 1939 article in which Morton said Tyler told him that Columbia thought there might be a future for a local artist who sang like the recently-deceased Blue Yodeler.[50] Morton advised Tyler that he certainly knew of Rodgers—in fact, he said, he had all his records—and he also knew Australian songs like "Wrap Me Up in My Stockwhip and Blanket" that he had "picked up while kicking around Australia."[51]

Morton and Tyler seemed to get on well together. Tyler's job entailed deciding which overseas discs would be released on Columbia's labels, along with auditioning and recording local talent. Morton was his first major discovery in the hillbilly field, and from 1936 until 1939 it appears the relationship between producer and artist was harmonious. Morton's headstrong insistence on always being right was possibly tempered by his relative inexperience with recording, and Tyler appeared to give him some latitude by allowing him to be accompanied by other artists, conceivably giving him a free hand in the studio. Smoky Dawson, a contemporary, doubted that Tyler would have been autocratic with Morton, who "wasn't one to be told anything."[52] Tyler was Morton's producer until late 1939 when he took leave to join the Royal Navy.[53] He later resigned from Columbia Graphophone and was employed as an executive with a British perfume company.[54]

On Tuesday, February 25, 1936, Morton, most likely playing a Gibson guitar,[55] made his first commercial recordings at Columbia Graphophone's studios in Homebush, Sydney. The first two songs, "Texas in the Spring" and "Goin' Back to Texas," were about American cowboys, whereas the second two, "Happy Yodeler"[56] and "Swiss Sweetheart," were self-composed showcases of Alpine-style yodeling.[57] It was as though Morton and Tyler weren't sure as to which direction the aspiring new artist should take—a singer of cowboy and hillbilly songs or a fancy yodeler, instead.

"Texas in the Spring" (also known as "The Roundup in the Spring") was about a cowboy in New York reminiscing about herding cattle in Texas. Morton's youthful voice had traces of an American accent, and his rendition was enhanced with two bursts of spirited yodeling. His guitar playing was simple, but expressive and effective. Morton probably learned the song from a disc released in Australia in early 1935 by the American artists Asa Martin and James Roberts (recording as Glen Fox and Joe Wilson).[58] He most likely heard the other ersatz cowboy song "Goin' Back to Texas" on a 1929 recording released in Australia by Frank Luther and Carson Robison.[59]

Morton's yodeling clearly showed the influences of Jimmie Rodgers, Goebel Reeves and Harry Torrani (the last especially evident on Morton's two self-penned Alpine numbers), but he had developed something of a novel variation, prominent in the break on "Texas in the Spring," and in the introduction and break on "Goin' Back to Texas"—a sound that at times seemed a bit like gargling and was described as "a bizarre trilling yodel."[60] It was a modification of Goebel Reeves's trill yodel, done at the back of the throat.[61] Nolan Porterfield, Jimmie Rodgers's biographer, explained it as a sort of "fluttering growl," adding that although he didn't care much for it, on the whole, Morton was about "as good as they come."[62] Singer and yodeler George Payne recalled that Morton's trill yodeling was extremely difficult to learn, stating "Tex had a flamboyant approach to yodeling."[63] Morton had adapted (or refined) the style from some of Goebel Reeves's records, in which Reeves incorporated "Tyrolese [sic] warbling" into his yodels,[64] a sound that has been described as something like "a caffeine-drenched warbler, mixing birdcalls with speed yodeling."[65] Collector and discographer John Edwards noted that Morton "seemed to have gained quite a lot of Goebel's style," including aspects of the trill yodel.[66] Morton's ebullient yodeling was especially popular with the public.[67]

Columbia Graphophone released the records on their budget-price Regal Zonophone label and gave him the moniker, "The Yodelling Boundary Rider," which they printed on the labels of his records. Morton later distanced himself from the name "Tex" and the "yodelling boundary rider" epithet:

> So I just gave up, and finally, when it appeared on the records as "Tex" Morton ... [and] of all the bloody things "The Yodelling Boundary Rider"—that wasn't my idea either—that was some bright boy at one of the radio stations somewhere ... I didn't want to be "Tex," I wanted to be Bob Morton, Kiwi [New Zealander] Morton—I didn't want to be "Tex" ... I wanted to be Bob, but then they stuck Tex onto me and when 'The Yodelling Boundary Rider' thing came on, even I saw it was a bit of a rib [joke], but it caught on.[68]

But like the self-named moniker "Tex Morton," the "Yodelling Boundary Rider" epithet was also possibly invented by Morton himself, especially since he had billed himself as a "yodelling cowboy" only a few days earlier, although the variation could very well have been Columbia's idea.

Over the ensuing years, sales for the "cowboy" disc were 50 percent more than those for the "Swiss" record,[69] suggesting the public preferred cowboy songs to Alpine-style yodeling. The die had been cast: Morton was to become a hillbilly singer, although both "Happy Yodeler" and "Swiss Sweetheart" were by no means his least popular songs over the following years.

A week later Morton was back at Columbia's studios to lay down another four songs. Abandoning the purely Alpine style of his first session, he instead concentrated on hillbilly fare. "Wyoming Willie" was a 1932 Carson Robison song that had been released in Australia as "I Was Born in Old Wyoming."[70] "You're Going to Leave the Old Home, Jim," was a sympathetic rendition of a well-known hobo song, sometimes titled "There's a Mother Always Waiting You At Home, Sweet Home."[71] It was written in 1903 by James Thornton[72], an Irish-American Tin Pan Alley songwriter and vaudeville performer. Morton undoubtedly learned it from a 1931 Goebel Reeves recording, "The Tramp's Mother".[73] He also recorded "The Oregon Trail" and "Carry Me Back to The Lone Prairie." Curiously, neither of these songs had been released in Australia at the time.

Morton said he returned to New Zealand following these recordings and was living hand-to-mouth from busking, when he spied a huge cardboard cutout of himself in a music-shop window, "hat on, head back, mouth open and tonsils showing," as he described it. Beneath this arresting image, in large letters, was written: "TEX MORTON, THE YODELLING BOUNDARY RIDER. THE LATEST COWBOY SENSATION." He said his discs were selling like hotcakes in New Zealand and Australia, and that Columbia was frantically trying to locate him to record again.[74] Although this yarn is most likely embellished, there's some evidence that he returned to New Zealand in July 1936, Morton's efforts had hit the mark: by May of that year, all his records up to that time had been released and were being advertised in the Australian and New Zealand press.[75] Columbia had even prepared a standard advertisement, describing their new luminary as a "sensational discovery."[76] Morton later attributed his early success to being "a darn novelty."[77]

In July 1936 Morton recorded two more western-type songs, both British. "The Prairie Is a Lonesome Place at Night" and "Sing, You Cowboy"[78] were written by London-based songwriter Michael Carr and Irish composer and lyricist Jimmy Kennedy. Most likely Morton learned both songs from a disc released in Australia in 1935, by the English group The Hill Billies.[79] Not to be confused with the American group of the same name, this band was comprised of Ted Ford (guitar, banjo, group leader), Bill ("Ezra") Sirett (fiddle, harmonica, jaw harp, guitar, lead vocals), Ben ("Old Ben") Evans (banjo), and Con ("Lefty") Calnan (accordion).

About two months later, Morton cut "Ragtime Cowboy Joe," "Old Ship O' Mine (The Sailors' Hillbilly)," and two Australian compositions "Wrap Me Up in My Stockwhip and Blanket (The Dying Stockman)," and his own song "The Wandering Stockman."[80] "Wrap Me Up in My Stockwhip and Blanket (The Dying Stockman),"[81] was probably written by Horace Flower in the 1880s; the lyrics were published in the *Portland Mirror* in 1885.[82] Flower and his brother, Charles, were keen songwriters in the late nineteenth century. According to his son, Horace Flower "loved the bush ballads which his brother wrote, [and] which he set to his own music that he twanged out on his banjo." The Flower brothers were familiar with an English song, "Wrap Me Up in My Tarpaulin Jacket," about a dying soldier, composed by Charles Coote with music originally by Major Whyte Melville, and upon which their stockman version was probably based.[83] A Frank Crumit version of "Wrap Me Up in My Tarpaulin Jacket" was issued by His Master's Voice in Australia,[84] and Morton recalled he had heard his grandfather singing that song in his hometown of Nelson.[85] The Australian poet Andrew Barton ("Banjo") Paterson included "The Dying Stockman" in his 1905 book, *The Old Bush Songs*, and Morton's lyrics closely though not identically followed the version in Paterson's book. Noting the song's theme of youth cut down in its prime, folklorist Graham Seal wrote that "dying sailors, cowboys, timber-cutters and airmen litter the field of English-language folksong; 'The Dying Stockman' is one of a number of Australian variants of this widespread and popular theme."[86]

"Wrap Me Up in My Stockwhip and Blanket" was the first instance of an Australian folksong recorded in hillbilly style. References to "stockman," "dingoes," and "coolibah," firmly established the song's setting as Australia, and not American prairies. It arguably qualifies as the first Australian country music bush ballad to be recorded, particularly since its origins are in late nineteenth-century poetry. In much the same manner, verse by the likes of Henry Lawson and Banjo Paterson were afterwards set to music by Slim Dusty,[87] who was to be inextricably linked with the Australian bush ballad genre. Dusty later made recordings of "The Dying Stockman," including a version on his influential album, *Australian Bush Ballads and Old Time Songs*.[88] Morton's version is currently part of the Sounds of Australia Collection which commemorates outstanding and influential Australian recordings.[89]

"THE AUSTRALIAN HILL-BILLIES"

No less important was "The Wandering Stockman," which Morton wrote— the first self-penned song he recorded with an Australian setting (although with some minor changes to the lyrics, it could just as easily have been about a wandering cowboy in the West). In October 1936, Morton recorded again in two brief sessions, the first of which saw him cut "Just Drifting Along" and "The Yodelling Bag Man," on which he was accompanied by harmonica player Harry Thompson.[90]

Thompson, later described as "Australia's first chromatic harmonica recording artist," was born in Glasgow in 1914 and migrated with his brother to Australia in 1928, under a Salvation Army program. After working in the bush, he returned to Sydney and, inspired by recordings of Larry Adler, bought a chromatic harmonica, taught himself to play, and entered radio-station talent contests. It was at such a competition that his and Morton's paths possibly crossed,[91] probably around 1936. Morton claimed that they both appeared on the 2KY-Sydney Radio Trials. Morton said he won and Thompson was the runner-up, but this story most likely was fictional (unless Morton was referring to only one heat and not the overall final results). Perhaps they met at another talent quest, though afterwards, apparently, they both went their own ways. Thompson reunited with Morton sometime in 1937, and the two formed a double act, "The Australian Hill-Billies." They performed on the Tivoli vaudeville entertainment circuit,[92] and made more recordings for Columbia. In 1937, they toured with Jim Davidson's Australian Broadcasting Commission (ABC) Dance Band billed with popular musical-comedy artist Gladys Moncrieff.[93] The duo appeared at the Grafton Jacaranda Festival, where their show was described as follows:

> Singing the songs of the romantic prairies of Texas, Messrs. Tex Morton and Harry Thompson, known throughout the Commonwealth as the Australian Hill Billys, [sic] made themselves idols of the crowd with their first item. They were dressed as cowboys and acted as if they had been born and bred in that sage-scented country. The Hill Billys rendered several items during the evening. The efforts of Harry on the mouth organ charmed the crowd, and the yodelling of his skilful colleague proved popular with all sections of the audience. They were received with considerable enthusiasm.[94]

But both wanted to be the main star of the show; consequently, they argued frequently,[95] and their act folded soon afterwards. Thompson later joined the Australian Army, and eventually died from malignant throat cancer in 1988.[96]

Of greater interest was "The Yodelling Bag Man," a self-penned paean about the carefree life of a train-jumping hobo, aspects of which may have been autobiographical. Morton had probably written the song in 1935, and according to historian and author Eric Watson, it ranks as "the first thoroughly authentic Australian country song in the new idiom ever recorded."

Morton's lyrics clearly anchored the song in Australia with the locations "Adelaide," "Queensland," "New South Wales" and "Cairns," instead of Texas, or the prairies of North America—but he also used Americanisms like "hobo" and "on the bum." Morton's description of his instrument as a "Spanish" guitar described how he played it "cowboy style," as opposed to holding it in the then popular "flat," Hawaiian style.[97] Five days later, on October 20, 1936, Morton recorded "On the Gundagai Line," which might have been inspired by Jimmie Rodgers's "Hobo Bill's Last Ride", since both were about hobos dying in train carriages, and "All Set and Saddled," about a stockman or cowboy riding from a city to "Sleepy Valley" to reunite with his buddies.[98]

In October 1936, Morton signed a contract with Columbia. Instead of the flat fee of about five pounds per disc that he was being paid, he would now receive an advance of five pounds per record, as well as royalties of one penny[99] per double-sided record on 85 percent of gross sales.[100] From then on, a stream of royalties would be more profitable than receiving only a flat fee, although the income from record sales was still far from lucrative: based on these figures, Morton's best-selling records would only earn him something like 100 pounds each for total sales while they were in Columbia Graphophone's catalog (sometimes for as many as twenty years).[101] Presumably, the contract would have been renewed annually, as it was in 1938.[102]

Because he was the only Australian "hillbilly" performer at the time, Morton often appeared with variety and vaudeville performers and not as a part of "packaged" country music shows on tour. These only became common after more than a decade later, especially once populations shifted from the country to cities. In 1936, he was active around Sydney, busking and appearing on harbor ferries, for Sunday night "Showboat" cruises that seemed to commence around October,[103] and which combined night-time cruises with live entertainment. Newspaper advertisements of October 1936 mention Tex Morton ("The Yodelling Boundary Rider") with his "banjo" (Spanish guitar) singing on the "Showboat,"[104] at times with accordionists and classical singers, all performing on the same cruises.[105] Morton recalled that his "Showboat" engagements earned him 30 shillings a week—more than enough to pay for his rent and meals at a cafe.[106]

That month, he also performed on 2BL-Sydney with Jim Davidson's ABC Dance Band as "Tex Morton (yodeller)," and the following month appeared at the Sydney Tivoli in a revue starring the comedian Roy Rene. During one show a large sector of the audience left in disgust at Rene's offensive jokes,[107] some of which were described as "hard to swallow."[108] "I acted as straight man for George [Wallace] and Roy [Rene]," Morton recalled. "We did quite a bit of touring with ten-man shows. It was a big deal for the country people to see Sydney's top comedians—even if we did roll into town in clapped-out cars."[109] Morton appeared at Tivoli shows in Melbourne and Adelaide, and returned to Sydney in January 1937,[110] where he resumed performing on the harbor cruises.

3

THE YODELING BOUNDARY RIDER BECOMES A STAR

Morton's career was on the upswing a year or so after his first recording session, as he later remembered:

> Then it happened.... It was 1937 and things became a crazy dream. Every record I made was a big hit. I had my photograph taken with the then Prime Minister, Joe Lyons, had a long conversation with former Prime Minister Billy Hughes (I was amazed when he called me "Tex"), met show business celebrities like Larry Adler and the Mills Brothers, and caused traffic jams when I appeared in the streets. Souvenir hunters ripped the clothes off my back and stole my hats, clothing firms and music firms swamped me with offers to endorse their goods, I was asked to speak at luncheons and open fêtes, and to make guest appearances on every top radio show. I couldn't believe any of it.[1]

Actually, the Mills Brothers and Larry Adler visited Australia in 1939, and not 1937.[2]

MARJORIE

In 1936, Morton was renting a room in an apartment complex called the "Focs'l" in Sydney with several other young people. Living downstairs in the same building were Marjorie Frederica Brisbane, who was about 18 years old at the time, and her mother, Elizabeth Thornhill,[3] who was probably the proprietor or manager of the apartments.[4] Marjorie and Morton met when her mother invited him to accompany them to the beach one Sunday. She recalled Morton was kind and polite, especially to her mother—attributes that

Marjorie found attractive. That night, he was working on board the "Showboat" at the harbor, and according to Marjorie, he persuaded her to accompany him.[5]

With his customary flair for embellishing fact with fantasy, however, Morton invented a wildly different story of their meeting. He told a magazine that his future wife had sent him a fan letter after he had won a talent quest on station 2KY-Sydney. To his astonishment, he recounted, it bore the same street address as his own, and had been written by a girl who lived downstairs in the apartments where he boarded. "Filled with curiosity," he exaggerated, he knocked on her door and made her acquaintance. It was, he gushed, a case of love at first sight: "I couldn't look at any other girls after I saw Marjorie."[6]

Marjorie recalled that later in their courtship Morton would frequently take her to shooting galleries where he would practice sharpshooting. She remembered he was entering local talent quests and busking in the streets. "He was very confident . . . and he knew it," she said.[7] At the time she was working in a shoe store and as a part-time model.[8]

Following a whirlwind engagement, Morton and Marjorie were married on Wednesday November 24, 1937, at the prestigious St. Philips Church of England in Sydney. Marjorie recorded her age as 19 and her occupation as a salesgirl; and Morton (using his birth name of Robert William Lane) gave his occupation as "singer" and his age as 21. Marjorie's mother signed the consent form for her daughter.[9] As evidence of Morton's popularity, the marriage even warranted an article in the *Sydney Morning Herald* which announced the newlyweds would spend their honeymoon on horseback, camping out, and Morton would make personal appearances—a yarn to be taken with a grain of salt, since the same piece improbably stated that Morton's father had been a cowboy in Texas.[10] In May the following year, an entertainment magazine ran another article on Morton and his new wife.[11]

The couple sailed by steamship to New Zealand, where Morton introduced Marjorie to his family in Nelson.[12] Morton's parents, Marjorie suspected, were not impressed that their son was a hillbilly singer. This accords with Morton's own memories: although he always spoke of his parents with warmth and affection, he acknowledged that their way of life was never for him.[13] "My parents were . . . wonderful people who tried their damnedest to make me a 'respectable' citizen," he later reflected, adding that "My two brothers, Rex and Kim, and my sister, Barbara, are solid citizens. I was the one out."[14] Barbara, however, recalled that although her parents initially disapproved of their eldest son's lifestyle, their attitude towards him changed over the years, and they were proud of his achievements, although some aspects of his later life still irked them.[15]

The honeymoon was most likely the first time the Lane family had laid eyes on their nomadic son since his last visit to Nelson in 1934. For youngest sibling Barbara, who was seven at the time, it was a special event, celebrated by Morton giving her a doll.[16] To brother Kim, he brought "the very latest in BB guns," but in demonstrating the weapon's firepower Morton blasted a hole in the family home's front bedroom window and chipped a mirror.[17] Although Marjorie was welcomed by the family, she felt they were rather disapproving and sensed she was on the "outer": she was young and happy-go-lucky, whereas her husband's family were very stern people. "They had their own idea of how things should be done," she said, "and you didn't have the son that ran away and brought the bride home to meet the parents." The couple spent Christmas 1937 with Morton's family, and then went to Wellington, where Morton performed on radio and in a nightclub.

Back in Australia, Marjorie accompanied Morton on his touring shows. Late in 1938, she joined her husband in a revue called "Why Be Serious" that showed in Sydney and then toured New Zealand the following year. The showbiz lifestyle attracted Marjorie, but her marriage would be on the rocks a few years later. On that tour, she met Dorothy Carroll who was to figure so prominently in her husband's life. Throughout much of her marriage, Marjorie assisted her husband by selling tickets, and sometimes was a sounding board for his songs and guitar runs—in the early years, he would regularly ask her opinion on his latest compositions.[18] Later, often poor, she single-handedly raised their twin sons while her husband pursued his career at home and abroad, but she stood by him when he was in difficulties. In a 1994 interview, she ruefully quipped that, in retrospect, she "shuddered to think" of her marriage,[19] which lasted some 42 years, in theory anyway, until it was dissolved in August 1979.[20] She died in 2001.[21]

LIONEL BIBBY, SHARPSHOOTER

Early in his career, Morton became an expert sharpshooter. He said that Lionel Bibby, a crack rifleman, had coached him into polishing his precision shooting.[22] "Tex was the best shot of all the singing cowboys," said compatriot Smoky Dawson. "He could put a bullet down the barrel of the other person's gun if ever he'd have a mind to."[23] Bibby undoubtedly refined the shooting skills Morton had acquired as a youth.[24] Sharpshooting became one of Morton's trademark acts, and well into his career he continued to demonstrate astonishing feats with a rifle, often with his traveling companion "Sister" Dorrie (Dorothy Carroll) who toured with him during the 1940s. According to Dick Carr, Morton's steel guitarist, Morton used to shoot pieces of chalk from her hand, "between fingers, close to the flesh."[25] Sometimes, he would cut a cigarette, clenched between the teeth of a subject, in two with a 22-caliber bullet. It's likely that Morton learned some of these tricks directly from Bibby.[26] Producer Hal Saunders recalled he was still able to perform these feats, "with live bullets going within two inches of his assistant's head," after imbibing numerous double Scotches (with "no ice," as he ordered them) for about an hour beforehand.[27] This fact was confirmed by Dorrie, who said that one time, in Broken Hill, Morton was "as blind as a bat" (drunk) in the local hotel, and riding a small motorcycle on the bar, when the town's police sergeant hurried to tell her not to participate in any trick-shooting acts that night, because of Morton's insobriety. Dorrie told him that Morton would be okay, and when the time came, the act went off without a hitch. "If I saw him open that gun case, I knew he was all right," she said. There were only two occasions when he didn't perform his marksman's act in the years she spent with him. Newspaper reports tell of Morton shooting small coins tossed in the air, and of him also firing pistols and a 303 rifle. One spectator who attended a show in 1940 recalled Morton placing a cardboard disc over the rifle's barrel to obscure his aim, holding the rifle upside-down with the butt against his forehead, and hitting a small disc swinging on a piece of string held by an assistant some 20 meters distant.[28]

With his renowned flair for mixing with celebrities, Morton sought locations where he knew entertainment people hung out. He claimed to have met the swashbuckler and fellow raconteur, Errol Flynn, at the Australia Hotel. "Flynn was a mad sexpot. Every party he went to he tried to turn it into a sex orgy," he said. "When I met him years later he was doing the same thing—only a bit more successfully."[29] However, Flynn was in Sydney in 1932, Port Moresby in 1933 and departed for London in November 1934.[30] He later flew from Britain to Hollywood, and was in Los Angeles by 1935,[31] so when Morton was in Australia, Flynn was in the United States filming *Captain*

Blood, and he remained in Hollywood afterwards, although the two might have met on a possible 1932 visit to Australia by Morton. Even so, it's unlikely that the much older Flynn would have fraternized with a brash Morton at the time.

RECORDING AGAIN

On February 23, 1937, Morton cut two more songs: "Lonesome Valley Sally" and "Take Me Back to Dream by the Old Mill Stream."[32] "Lonesome Valley Sally" had been recorded by several American artists, including The Girls of the Golden West, but their 1934 disc was not released in Australia until September 1941, on Regal Zonophone—much later than Morton's recording.[33] The American big-band vocalist Dick Robertson also waxed a version that was issued in Australia in October 1935,[34] from which Morton's adaptation was possibly based. The nostalgic "Take Me Back to Dream by the Old Mill Stream," written by Silvester Long Cross, Mat Howard and Leona Tracey in 1934, was noted in the October 17, 1942 issue of *Billboard* magazine, as part of an advertisement, prominently headlined "America's Greatest Catalog of Cowboy, Hillbilly and Native Popular Ballads," showing a page from the *American Music Catalog*, published by American Music, Inc.[35] The Cantrell Brothers' New Palais Royal Dance Band recorded an orchestral version of the song in April 1937.[36] Dudley Cantrell was known to Morton, so perhaps the band leader had been influenced by the boundary rider.

Morton made two more recordings ten days later. "The Black Sheep," a song written in 1897 by American William Gould (as "The Black Sheep Loves You Best of All"), told of a son who had been unfairly labeled the black sheep of the family by his father, who later faced eviction to a poorhouse by his other sons and a conniving daughter-in-law, only to be saved at the last minute by the loyal son, who was immediately forgiven and finally accepted by his father.[37] Morton described the lugubrious composition as "a morbid bloody thing"[38] but over time the song, coupled with "You Only Have One Mother,"[39] was his biggest seller, with total sales of some 36,000, an impressive statistic given that in 1937 the Australian population only numbered slightly less than seven million.[40] Morton possibly learned it from a 1935 Shelton Brothers disc which, though not having an Australian issue, might have been a U.S. shipment rejected as unsuitable for an Australian release by Columbia and then given to Morton, who would be free to record it.[41] Alternatively, Morton innuendo, with Morton boasting that his yodel is "longer and stronger" than his rival's, and that he yodels better than the Swiss Mountaineer to whom his sweetheart is attracted. "The Big Rock Candy Mountains" (sometimes titled "The Big Rock Candy Mountain")[57] was a well-known hobo song from the United States, where it had been recorded by several artists; Morton might have learned the song from either Harry McClintock's or Goebel Reeves's versions,[58] and Australian popular singer Art Leonard had also recorded it in 1929.[59] Singer Athol McCoy regarded Morton's trick yodeling on this number as among the best of all his recorded performances.[60]

"Rockin' Alone in an Old Rocking Chair,"[61] a sentimental favorite in the pantheon of songs about aging mothers, was written in 1932 by Bob Miller who also composed "My Mother's Tears" and "Story of a Dear Old Lady."[62] The song had been recorded in the United States by several artists, including Miller himself, but none of these had Australian releases, although the American announcer and pitchman, Jack Savage, recorded a version in London in August 1936,[63] and this was issued in Australia on Decca, in May 1937, titled as "Rockin' Alone (in an old rockin' chair)" by Jack Savage and His Cowboys. Savage's disc, which was almost certainly the inspiration for Morton's version, sold slightly over 1200 copies, until it was deleted from the catalog in 1946.[64] Arch Kerr, who produced Morton later in his career, recalled that "artistically, [Savage's] record was much ahead of Tex's, yet the Tex Morton version sold ten to one against it, which showed Australian people preferred the local artist."[65] According to discographer David Crisp, however, the series of Decca recordings on which Savage's release was issued generally sold poorly anyway, though he contended that Morton's version was superior to that of the smooth-sounding Savage.[66] Columbia paired it with Morton's composition "There Are Tear Stains on Your Letter Mother Dear." The coupling of the two numbers on the one disc was a marketing triumph: it was second in retail sales for all Morton's early recordings, with total figures exceeding 30,500 records, yet again demonstrating the popularity of sentimental songs with Australian audiences and record buyers of the time.

The "famous" Morton performed at the Blackheath Theatre in a variety show with vaudevillians Whacko Shand (Ron Shand)[67] and Letty Craydon in October 1937,[68] and later in the year with Jim Davidson's ABC Dance Band. In 1937 and 1938, Morton, sometimes with Harry Thompson, performed with Davidson and the internationally renowned Gladys Moncrieff, "Australia's

Queen of Song." Morton and Thompson had previously made radio broadcasts with Davidson and his band, without Moncrieff,[69] and joined him on tour about October 1937, when the show was announced, initially performing at Newcastle Town Hall[70] and other places like Grafton.[71] Morton recalled Moncrieff had been selected because of her popularity with musical comedy fans, whereas he had been chosen as a more low-brow performer, appealing to blue-collar audiences. Despite their different backgrounds, the two got along famously.[72] One advertisement displayed a picture of the young boundary rider seemingly upstaging the more conventional acts.[73] His performance was described as "a pleasant variation with tuneful yodelling to guitar accompaniment."[74] That he was now performing with recognized classical and popular artists and musicians was testimony to the young hillbilly's emergent reputation with, and acceptance by, the general-public audience.

Moncrieff's career was temporarily halted by a car accident in March 1938. That month and the next, Morton and Thompson were broadcasting on 2FC-Sydney on the same program as bandleader Dudley Cantrell.[75] Prime Minister Joseph Lyons was in the audience when the boundary rider performed at a banjo club revue,[76] and a newspaper reported that he was selling one hundred thousand records a month and earning 150 pounds a week from royalties[77]—likely exaggerations by Morton, who also fed reporters fictitious accounts of his early life.[78] Morton's return to the stage was described as "welcome tidings."[79] He performed at the Embassy Theatre throughout most of 1938.[80] In October, Morton signed with the esteemed Australian Broadcasting Commission for a ten-week period, split between Sydney with Davidson, and Melbourne where he was to appear with Harry Bloom's band.[81] By December 1939, Moncrieff was again touring with Morton,[82] whom she described as "without a doubt, the greatest, most lovable character in the world since dear old Will Rogers was in his prime. His love of the outdoors, horses, music, shooting, singing, all go into the makeup of a 'real guy.'"[83] At the outbreak of war in Europe in 1939, Morton, Moncrieff, Peter Finch and Jim Davidson's dance band performed at a rally in Martin Place (Sydney) to raise money for the war effort.[84]

In mid-1938, the boundary rider told *Tempo* magazine that he intended to go to London. "I'm going to start all over again," he gushed. "When I arrive, I'll drag out the old gitter [guitar] and go busking in the streets. Not ordinary busking though, first class street singing—Yipp-eeee!" This was yet another of Morton's fanciful plans to pursue fame and fortune overseas, none of which eventuated during the next decade. On another occasion, he related to the press about having been offered a three-year contract with London's BBC.[85] A year later, he again announced that he was leaving soon to join Jack Hylton in London.[86] Hylton was a jazz-inspired pianist and major band leader, in some ways the British equivalent of Jim Davidson,[87] suggesting that the Australian aspired to touring with popular English acts, as he had done in Australia.

In March 1938, Morton recorded another four songs. James Nelson's "The Greatest Mistake of My Life" had been recorded in the United States in 1937 by Jimmie Davis, but there had been no local release of Davis's recording. The British actress and singer Gracie Fields recorded it in November 1937, and Jim Davidson waxed it in January 1938,[88] from which Morton might have recorded it as a cover version, in hillbilly style. The self-composed "I'm Dreaming Tonight of the Old Folks" was a sentimental composition yearning for old times of the singer's youth, and for his parents who also miss him. In September the following year, the American artist Dickie McBride recorded it for U.S. Decca[89]—the first Australian hillbilly song to be recorded by an American country singer. McBride's more polished version was enhanced by a sympathetic accompaniment of bass, guitar, fiddle and electric steel guitar. "The Letter Edged in Black," a staple of old-time country music written by Hattie Nevada in 1897, was probably influenced by Australian releases by Vernon Dalhart and Bradley Kincaid, and "The Yellow Rose of Texas" was likely inspired by a Gene Autry recording released in Australia in December 1934.[90]

In April 1938, Morton and Harry Thompson made four more recordings for Columbia Graphophone, with Morton yodeling and singing and Thompson playing harmonica on American songs, including "My Blue Ridge Mountain Home" (probably learned from a Vernon Dalhart and Carson Robison releases),[91] and "When It's Night Time in Nevada" (almost certainly from a Carson Robison and Frank Luther disc issued locally in 1931).[92] The Singing Stockmen (Arthur and Norm Scott) subsequently reprised the song, with Hawaiian-style backing, as "Night Time in Nevada," in 1939 for Columbia.[93] It was the first Australian "cover" of a recording by Morton. Although "Weeping Willow Tree" was one of the Carter Family's best-known songs (as "Bury Me Under the Weeping Willow"), it was probably Lester McFarland's and Robert Gardner's somewhat different 1927 recording (as "Weeping Willow Tree"), or Art Leonard's 1932 version, that was Morton's and Thompson's inspiration.[94]

The nineteenth-century song "Red River Valley" was already a cowboy classic when the duo cut it. A version by the English group The Hill Billies had been released locally in August 1935, coupled with their version of "Old Shep." In Australia both "The Red River Valley" and "Weeping Willow Tree" had also been recorded by Art Leonard in 1932, so his influence on Morton's and Thompson's recording of these two songs cannot be discounted. [95]

SERGEANT SMALL

Some three months after the session with Thompson, Morton returned to Columbia's studios to record more songs, including one that very soon afterwards became controversial. "The Martins and the Coys," loosely based on the famous Hatfield and McCoy dispute from 1881 to 1891—but more of a burlesque send-up of the rube, hillbilly stereotype—was later waxed by the American entertainer Bob Dyer (in England, and later released in Australia in 1940), and by the U.S.-based group the Hoosier Hot Shots in 1939.[96] It had been written by Al Cameron and Ted Weems in 1936, and recorded by popular entertainers of the day. Gene Autry sang it in the 1936 movie, *The Big Show*. [97]

Morton's own "I Left My Heart in Red River Valley" might have been inspired by the American traditional tune "Red River Valley." It was standard hillbilly fare, with lyrics conveying the singer's desire to return to Red River Valley and to a "gal waiting there." On the other hand, the 1900 popular song, "Bird in a Gilded Cage," was an unusual choice for a hillbilly singer. Written by Arthur Lamb and Harry Von Tilzer, it described the predicament of a despondent woman who married for wealth and not for love.[98] More than likely Morton heard it from an Australian-released disc by Frank and James McCravy, who recorded it in 1928,[99] or possibly from Elzie Floyd's and Leo Boswell's version, also released in Australia (in 1930).[100]

"Sergeant Small," Morton's most controversial song, was about a railway policeman who, the song claimed, used deception to trick train jumpers. Morton's lyrics, which were highly critical of the sergeant, whom he later described as "a bad copper,"[101] expressed an aggressive wish to even the score with the policeman:

> "I wish that I was fourteen stone and I was six feet tall,
> I'd take a special trip up north to beat up Sergeant Small."

Sergeant William James Small was a railway policeman stationed in Quirindi, New South Wales, during the Great Depression. His granddaughter told a journalist in 1982 that the sergeant was a strict but fair man. Initially, she said, the railways turned a blind eye to hobos, but their tolerance soon waned when train jumpers defecated in rail cars and pilfered goods. Railway authorities eventually complained to police, who were ordered to arrest the hobos. Ironically while Sergeant Small apprehended train jumpers, his wife prepared hearty meals for the unfortunates incarcerated in her husband's cells.

Morton's wife, Marjorie, said her husband had once been arrested by Small. Morton, she said, was busking wearing an expensive watch given to him by his family. Upon seeing the timepiece, Small assumed it was stolen and promptly arrested the entertainer. She recalled her husband harboring a long-term loathing of Small, whom he had described as an animal, and that he wanted to make the song even more critical of the sergeant.[102] In a 1938 magazine interview that appeared three months before he recorded the song, Morton spoke of a notorious policeman who "gets dressed up as a hobo himself and sneaks along by the sides of the trucks," tricking trainjumpers into identifying themselves when the imposter inquired if there was any room in the rail car. "As a matter of fact, Tex Morton has just completed a song, not yet published, about that same policeman," the report asserted, and said that "Tex is confident that it is the best he has yet written."[103]

In a 1960s radio program Morton recalled Small's nickname was "leather legs"; he had a reputation among bagmen, said Morton, who asserted he'd encountered the policeman shortly after arriving in Australia, because he foolishly rode a train through Quirindi instead of avoiding it, only to be arrested by the sergeant.[104] At the time, Morton was penniless: just after he had been released from the lock-up, a local resident supposedly gave him two shillings out of pity.[105]

Shortly after Morton's disc was released, an aggrieved Small complained to Columbia about the song which, he argued, had defamed him. For his part, Morton claimed to the press that Small had threatened to sue him[106] but had died before the case went to court—a dubious story, since the sergeant lived until 1944.[107] In fact, Morton later contradicted himself by telling journalist Colin Mackay that he and Small ultimately became good friends.[108] A September 1938 report in *Tempo* magazine stated that Small initiated an injunction against Columbia, and the recording was withdrawn from Columbia's catalog. Radio stations were prevented from playing it, and Morton was not allowed to sing it in public. Marjorie said Columbia agreed to break the master of the song.[109] The report also stated that the disc had sold two thousand copies in two days,[110] conceivably an exaggeration. Columbia then had Morton record "Move Along Baldy" so it could be coupled with "The Martins and the Coys," instead of the controversial "Sergeant Small." Morton said he wrote "Move Along Baldy" in Kings Cross, Sydney, while leaning against a hotdog stand.[111] The new release was given a different catalog number, accounting for the fact that Morton recorded an odd number of songs (93) for Regal Zonophone.[112]

In November 1938, Morton recorded six more songs. He probably learned the mildly risible "Old Man Duff" from recordings by Frankie Marvin when he was a teenager.[113] Contrasting with the lighthearted "Old Man Duff" was the overt sentimentality of "Dreaming With Tears in My Eyes," forever associated with Jimmie Rodgers, who had recorded it in New York, in May 1933, only eight days before he died. Strangely, there was no Australian release of Rodgers's recording and, at the time, no other American artist had recorded it by that title. In 2008, the prestigious German Bear Family label reissued Morton's version on a compact-disc set of Rodgers's recordings by other artists. The liner notes stated that Morton "sounds amazingly like the young Ernest Tubb, another Rodgers disciple who was then also beginning his career."[114]

Particularly noteworthy among the six songs of this recording session were the three Morton compositions: "Young Pat Maloney," "Dying Duffer's Prayer," and "Crime Does Not Pay." The first was unusual because its subject, Pat Maloney, was neither a stockman nor a cowboy, but instead a sailor; it told of Maloney's sweetheart's callous disregard for her beau's death. "Dying Duffer's Prayer" was about a fading young cattle duffer (rustler) who had been shot by the law, requesting that his mother not be told of his disgrace. Apart from the lyrics referencing Australia, the song could have been typical of American compositions about Wild West cowboys. "Crime Does Not Pay" recounted the tale of a petty criminal and his mate "Bluey," both of whom had been jailed for robbing chocolate-vending machines.[115] On their release they were warned by a warden that crime does not pay. Bluey failed to heed the admonition and eventually was killed, dying in a gutter, but the singer, who followed the straight and narrow, reflected on the warden's sage lecture. "My Old Crippled Daddy" was possibly inspired by a Frank Luther disc, "That Silver Haired Daddy of Mine," released in Australia in November, 1934.[116]

THE COVERED WAGON SHOWS

In early 1938, Morton and Harry Thompson recorded a series of 15-minute radio programs, called the "Covered Wagon" shows, for the Macquarie Broadcasting Network. The sessions, at Pagewood studios in eastern Sydney, were supervised by recording engineer Eric Cleburne. They were recorded on 16-inch discs,[117] played from the inside groove outwards, and were pressed in limited numbers for radio, bogusly touted as live, on-air programs. Each disc was double-laminated and contained one fifteen-minute show on each side. There were thirteen shows in all.[118] When author Ray Grieve interviewed Thompson in 1986, he discovered that Thompson had two episodes of the shows—the others having been lost to the ages.[119]

In 1990, Cleburne recalled he could still picture Morton with his guitar, seemingly lost in the spacious, heavily-draped Pagewood B-studio. Mistakes were fatal: they couldn't be edited out, so a new recording would have to be made every time someone made a blunder. Some shows had to be recorded repeatedly. At times, the lacquer discs would generate an unsatisfactory hiss at "hard patches," and the recording would have to be abandoned.[120] Recalling making other transcriptions of this type, producer Hal Saunders said, "It was tension, tension all the way, especially when you were getting to the last minute."[121]

Morton and Thompson were skilled at using the newly-developed RCA model 44B single ribbon microphone. They were expert at speaking off-mike and fading-out when the script called for it. Sound effects were generated by a specially-designed machine in the studio, but sometimes they were played from records on turntables in the control room. The Telefunken recording apparatus, driven by a synchronous motor, brought the technical qualities to an acceptable level.[122]

The two surviving "Covered Wagon" shows reveal the enormous influence of the American ethos: speaking and singing with phony but convincing, nonetheless, American accents, "Tex" (Morton) and "Slim" (Thompson) serenaded about the Blue Ridge Mountains, Wyoming, Texas and the Western prairies. So closely did these shows mirror some of the popular United States programs of the time, they were even identified in a catalog of transcription discs as an American production.[123] The Macquarie Network deliberately attempted to create an American-style Western atmosphere by adding sound effects of horses' hooves and canned laughter, because it was felt that previous Morton concerts had lacked such authenticity.[124] The American setting, too, was incongruous with Morton's prior attempts to localize his music by singing Australian songs, and dressing in stockman's clothing instead of Western outfits. The two extant shows were also comprised of banter between Tex and Slim, often involving clichéd jokes, like:

> SLIM: By the way, I've got a letter here for you...
> TEX: That's mighty fine Slim. Thank you very much. Say, this here's from one of my fans. "Dear Mr. Morton. I like your singing so much I have decided to write you this letter and send you something for your throat..."
> SLIM: Go on, go on, read the rest of it.
> TEX: "So please find enclosed two razor blades."

These interludes were punctuated by canned studio laughter. Musically, Morton's repertoire on the two surviving shows was drawn from his previous recordings: "My Blue Ridge Mountain Home," "Wyoming Willie," "Weeping Willow Tree," "Texas in the Spring" and "Ragtime Cowboy Joe." Thompson played popular instrumentals such as "Liebestraum" and "South American Joe" on his chromatic harmonica. Overall, the "Covered Wagon" programs were lightweight, entertaining snapshots of a mythical American West, skillfully created by Morton and Thompson, and received enthusiastically by listeners in "radioland." They had a long shelf life and were featured on the Macquarie Network for several years after they had been made. In 1942 a magazine reported that the "Covered Wagon" programs were still being broadcast on station 2GB- Sydney, where they were described as "grand" and "bringing listeners Hill Billy songs and Hill Billy gags with just a little of the philosophy of men who have lived long in the wide open spaces."[125]

In 1939 Morton met guitarist Dick Carr in Sydney.[126] Carr was to play a significant role in Morton's career, and much later in forming the Buckaroos, a seminal country music backup band used on studio recordings from the 1950s through the 1960s. Carr's musical career began in 1926, when he played Hawaiian steel guitar. He switched to the Spanish guitar two years later and played with small groups during the early 1930s. In 1935, he joined a modest band playing in a Tasmanian night club. "Four brass, four saxes and rhythm—all top men—I could hardly believe my fortune," he recalled.[127] He stayed in Tasmania for three years, and sang and yodeled on a local radio station. In

February 1939, he packed his bags and moved to Sydney, where he met Buddy Wikara, who managed the Hawaiian Club. Along with Norm Scott, Carr was employed as a steel-guitar teacher.[128]

While in Sydney he met Morton at a Kings Cross coffee lounge. Carr recalled Morton busking around the Cross, often earning as much as 50 pounds a week. "This was big money in those days," he mused.[129] One day, over a cup of coffee, Morton asked Carr if he'd tour with him. At first, he turned down the offer: "I said 'No . . . you'd have me sleeping in one of the trucks in no time," he recalled. But Morton persisted and promised to buy him a new Ford van, adding that he could recruit two more accompanists as well. Thinking he was kidding, Carr said, "Yes." Morton took him to the nearest Ford agent, "pulled out a wad of notes that would choke a horse," and bought a new van on the spot.[130] Carr thought Morton had been touring for a year or so when he joined; "where he got the finance from I don't know," he wondered.[131]

By early 1940, Morton was touring with traveling rodeos, featuring buckjumping horses, circus-style acts, and his singing and trick shooting, performed in his circus tent. He continued touring in this manner for the better part of a decade. Carr remembered that Morton's tent was able to seat some two thousand people. Morton's vehicles included a pole truck, a tent truck, a seat truck, and a kitchen truck. Morton traveled in a Buick with extra speakers mounted in two added headlights on the front bumper. "We'd go slowly through the town, announcing the show and the location and the starting time," he wrote. Carr was astounded at the crowds, "packed in every night, six nights a week, people sitting on tarps [tarpaulins] around the ring, about 2,500 every night," he recalled. But Carr found touring with Morton to be nerve-wracking, so he left about eighteen months later[132] and returned to Sydney, where he played in nightclubs, all the while retaining an interest in country music. He died in 1995,[133] after having both his legs amputated because of passive smoking caused by performing in hotels and nightclubs.[134]

4

ARCH KERR AND
NEW HILLBILLY ACTS

IN LATE 1938 and early 1939, Morton and Marjorie were touring in New Zealand with the Tivoli's revue "Why Be Serious." The cast included the American singing and dancing comedian Will Mahoney, with his partners Bob Geraghty and Evie Hayes, described by the press as a "distinguished American radio, stage and screen artist", comedienne Violet Carlson, dancing juggler Whitey Robert, whistler Johnny Bryant, American tenor Lawrence Brooks, various other vaudeville acts, and Dorothy Carroll ("a vivacious soubrette") who was also the wife of the revue's stage manager Bruce Carroll.[1] Morton was also scheduled to perform a series of broadcasts for the New Zealand Broadcasting Commission while he was with the show.[2]

The troupe departed Sydney on December 16[3] for a tour that was to last from December 24, 1938 to March 3, 1939. Whereas Mahoney, Hayes and Geraghty were to be paid a total of 300 pounds per week, Morton's pay was only twelve pounds,[4] highlighting the relative insignificance of then comparatively-unknown Morton—although, Mahoney would earn substantially less than the reputed 5,500 dollars per week he had been paid in the United States[5] where he had been a major name on the American stage.[6] Dorothy Carroll was paid the same amount as Morton.[7] In his home country, however, Morton, who was described as "the renowned cowboy yodeller, whose records are well known throughout New Zealand," was a crowd favorite.[8] Barbara recalled meeting up with her brother during the tour and seeing him perform, though she was embarrassed by his music because she preferred opera or Frank Sinatra.[9]

RECORDING IN 1939

Following the New Zealand venture, Morton's first recording session for 1939 was in May, when he recorded four songs, three of which were his own compositions. "Bonny Blue Eyes" was standard hillbilly fare, whereas the superior "My Old Bunkhouse Buddies" told of a city dweller who set out to reunite with friends in the American countryside, judging by the words "range," "Stetson," "corral" and "ranch house", only to find their dwelling deserted and some of his pals dead. It was an unusual lyric for Morton at the time—an Australian composition set in North America—especially given Morton's penchant for writing about local themes. "Travel by Train" was probably written during, or inspired by, Morton's earlier traveling days. In the appealing "Murrumbidgee Jack," written by band leader Frank Coughlan,[10] Morton sang of his girlfriend who had run off with a rival, Murrumbidgee Jack, "six or seven years ago," while Morton (personifying his record-label moniker) sang of boundary riding, all the while living a life of delusional optimism, believing or hoping that she would eventually return to him. Writer and historian Max Ellis described "Murrumbidgee Jack" as "heart rending in its naivety" because "it is not sung as a sad song" but, instead, with a jaunty and hopeful air. Ellis described the singer's persona as either extremely optimistic or even "dumb" because he still believed—after "six or seven years"—that his girl will eventually return to him, even though she most likely would have married Murrumbidgee Jack and had children with him. Ellis considered the song one of the saddest he had heard.[11]

In what might have been Morton's final session with Tim Tyler producing, he recorded four more songs in September 1939, against rumblings of war in faraway Europe. Both the sentimental "Dreams of Silver (and Memories of Gold)" and the humorous "I'll Be Hanged If They're Gonna Hang Me" had been recorded by American artists but were previously unreleased in Australia. "I'm Gonna Yodel My Way to Heaven" was based on either Frankie Marvin's 1931 recording,[12] or the 1932 version by his brother Johnny.[13] Alternatively, Morton might have acquired it from the English group the Hill Billies, who also had an Australian release of this song in February 1936.[14]

"Rocky Ned (The Outlaw),"[15] the first of his paeans to buckjumping horses, was about Rocky Ned, known as "The Four-Legged Fury," who was a highlight of Thorpe McConville's rodeo shows from 1934 to 1940, and no one successfully rode him during that time.[16] Morton's exuberant rendition guaranteed the song as a future classic of Australian country music. The horse was originally part of the Lennon Brothers's Wild West Show and was later bought by the Gill family, who then sold him to Thorpe McConville.[17] Morton never toured with McConville, who regularly introduced his prized buckjumper as "the horse that made Tex Morton famous."[18] It was said the animal could twist and curl 30 times in ten seconds. Gordon Attwater was the only person confirmed to have ridden him to a standstill, in 1929—it took him 74 seconds—and afterwards he had to have his neck in a plaster cast for six weeks.[19] Rocky Ned might also have been ridden by Jack Reilly and Lynn Smith. In 1935 a team of American cowboys using their own large "western" saddles were unable to tame the mount.[20] Somewhat fancifully, Morton stated on radio in the 1960s that he had attempted to ride Rocky Ned during the 1930s but had only lasted a few seconds.[21] The buckjumper had to be put down when a truck carrying him and other horses careened downhill and overturned near Kilmore, Victoria, on April 2, 1941,[22] breaking his legs.[23]

Two songs from Morton's penultimate recording session of 1939 featured the Irish-American wrestler and singer Pat Fraley, who claimed to have started out as a rough rider in a traveling American rodeo outfit, operated by silent-movie star Tom Mix in the late 1920s. When touring America, he had often sung on radio; his wrestling career had commenced around 1931. Arriving in Australia in early June 1939,[24] Fraley later sang over 3AW–Melbourne. Morton might have met Fraley in 1939 when he became acquainted with visiting American wrestlers who were boarding in an apartment in Sydney. One of them was "Brother Jonathan" (Jonathan Delaun Heaton), known as the "Salt Lake Rattlesnake."[25] Morton said Fraley was an amateur folk singer who could impersonate Burl Ives.[26] As a wrestler, he was described as a "wild Irishman" who was "no gentle mauler, and [was] well-versed in the rougher maneuvres of the industry."[27] He was "short and stocky, and always brought a whole sack of beer with him,"[28] a characteristic that would have endeared him to Morton. Even in his later years, Morton "used to talk about Fraley a lot," recalled journalist Colin Mackay.[29] Fraley was acquainted with Morton from 1939, for about two or three months.[30] He returned to the United States in 1940, where he remained until 1946, when he rejoined Morton in Australia until 1949 or 1950.[31]

In 1939, the duo recorded "Hand Me Down My Walking Cane" and "Let The Rest of the World Go By," two popular songs that had been embraced by a plethora of hillbilly artists in the United States. The Australian Edison Company had released "Hand Me Down My Walking Cane" by Marion Evelyn Cox and Harvey Hindermyer on cylinder and disc in 1920.[32] "Let The Rest of the World Go By" had been issued locally by McFarland and Gardner,[33] and also by Bob Nichols (Clayton McMichen) and Riley Puckett with Bert Layne, in 1930.[34] The two songs might also have been well known to Fraley.

Both "The Original Ned Kelly Song"[35] (later titled "The Ned Kelly Song") and "The Day I Left Daddy Alone" were Morton compositions.[36] The first was a narrative of the infamous Australian outlaw's violent life (which ended on the gallows in 1880) and was noteworthy for its tongue-in-cheek ending about modern-day price gouging. Morton might have modeled it on a folksong. He later hinted that he had performed it on radio before recording it.[37] About a month prior to Morton's session, Smilin' Billy Blinkhorn, a Canadian artist who had migrated to Australia, had waxed his own composition, "Poor Ned Kelly," with an ending similar to Morton's song, but Morton's recording outsold it by about two-to-one over the next decade.[38] The use of "Original" in Morton's first title might have been to downgrade Blinkhorn's version, since Morton saw Blinkhorn as a rival at the time.

Ten days later, Morton recorded "Billy Brink the Shearer." Morton credited it to Brother Jonathan, the American wrestler, but it's more than likely the song was only arranged by Morton from an old bush song "Bluey Brink,"[39] about a hard-drinking shearer who was conned into drinking sulfuric acid by Jimmy, the bartender. The simple narrative about an Australian outback character imbued the song with definite bush-ballad qualities as well as encapsulating Australians' ability to spin far-fetched yarns. In contrast, "Little Sweetheart of Days Gone By," Morton's own composition, had a lyric typical of some Jimmie Rodgers's songs (perhaps Rodgers's 1928 "My Old Pal," released in Australia in August 1929).[40] "When The Bloom Is on the Sage," with its opening line "When it's roundup time in Texas," was written in 1930 by Fred Howard and Nat Vincent (in the group The Happy Chappies) and recorded by them that year.[41] Their version was released in Australia in June 1931, and Morton possibly heard it as a teenager.[42] The reflective "Sleepy Hollow", yet another song evoking a long-lost sweetheart and a home of days gone by, was written by Carson Robison, who recorded it several times between 1930 and 1931; two of his versions were released in Australia. [43]

By 1939, Morton was on his way to becoming a star of radio and records.

In November, station 2KY-Sydney took out a full-page advertisement boasting that Morton's "Radio Round-Up" program had attracted 1,300 letters in four days and it displayed a map of Australia with dots showing places from where letters had been received. The major areas were in the eastern states of New South Wales, southern Queensland and Victoria, but the emergent star had also been heard in remote Western Australia, parts of the Northern Territory, and regions of South Australia and Tasmania as well, suggesting he was already a nationally known celebrity.[44]

BILL SCOTT

A key factor in Morton's fame was the American promoter, William ("Scotty") Scott, who had arrived in Australia with the 1937 Marcus Show, as its business manager. Scott had previously been associated with talent campaigns by the Western Association of Motion Picture Advertisers (WAMPAS), which identified starlets who displayed future promise in the movie business.[45] Marjorie Morton said American comedian Bob Dyer, also with the Marcus Show, had argued with Scott who then left the show while it was still in Australia.[46] After quitting, Scott stayed in Sydney and was supervising the construction of the Minerva Theatre in 1939[47] when Pat Fraley persuaded him to take on the role of Morton's manager. Although initially reluctant, Scott relented and took the position after hearing Morton sing.[48]

In 1940, Scott accompanied Morton on tour in the island state of Tasmania, to gauge his popularity.[49] The venture was a resounding success, with packed houses everywhere, and cemented Scott's faith in the rising star. "The Tasmanians had never seen me before, but they had been listening to my Saturday night shows on the ABC," Morton reflected. "People flocked from all over Tasmania to our show, and many of them followed us from town to town. I was mobbed every time I showed my face and eventually had to go hiding to get a bit of rest."[50] A 1940 magazine reported "things are certainly looking up for this young boundary rider. He is now the proud possessor of two very fine Pontiac cars, one of them being used by his newly acquired manager, Bill Scott (of Marcus Show fame), and the other, Tex uses himself. We don't know how you do it, Tex."[51]

Future recording artist Athol McCoy especially remembered the visit.[52] Unable to get seats at a movie theatre where Morton attracted huge crowds by singing at intermission between films, McCoy's brother approached Morton and told him the group had traveled some 100 kilometers[53] and were upset they couldn't see the show. To McCoy's astonishment, the affable Morton escorted them to the hotel where he was staying, borrowed two cane chairs, and gave them to the party so they could watch him perform. Morton, McCoy recalled, sang "I'm Gonna Yodel My Way to Heaven," "Rockin' Alone in an Old Rocking Chair" and "Rocky Ned." "You could have heard a pin drop when he sang "Rockin' Alone in an Old Rocking Chair," McCoy said.[54] At the time, Morton was regularly supplementing his income by singing in movie theatres at intermission. Early in 1940, Scott had advertised that he was "making exclusive arrangements with picture [movie] theatres for this great box-office attraction, Tex Morton" to appear at movie showings.[55] Another magazine advertisement in 1940 reiterated the text: "Bill Scott, late of the Marcus Show, will be in Tasmania making exclusive arrangements with Picture Theatres for the great box-office attraction, Tex Morton. Give your customers a real treat at very little additional cost—if any—to you. Tasmanian Theatre Owners write or wire, and Bill Scott will drop in to see you."[56]

Folklorist John Meredith recollected selling movie tickets at a mainland cinema in 1938 or 1939 when Morton was also entertaining there, and said the singer not only pestered him to learn how many tickets had been sold—he was given twenty-five percent of the show's takings—but when it was his time to perform, much of his act consisted of telling smutty stories. "He only sang three numbers," Meredith rued.[57] A 1939 magazine report confirmed the arrangement: "Tex Morton is playing country dates on a percentage with the picture houses [theatres]," it read. "The business has been bigger than the best drawing [for] pictures they have played." And, another piece asserted the singer had "arrived back in Sydney with a bagful of references from country picture [theater] managers."[58]

Scott remained with Morton until 1942 or 1943, after which George Melrose was appointed Morton's manager. So successful was Scott that his 1950 *Billboard* obituary stated, "one of his outstanding stunts was his publicity campaign which started Tex Morton."[59] Smoky Dawson described Scott as "the great organizer and the first from overseas with American know how."[60] Dawson said, "We were so naive in those days, but he knew exactly how to promote our music. He knew the effect that it would have on the ordinary bloke in the bush. He'd smoke on his big fat cigar, and say, 'Aah got the big

American know how. I'll show you how to do it!'"[61] A Morton fan described the silver-haired Scott as "a short, fat, cigar-smoking man," whom Morton introduced as "his only friend."[62] Scott was contemptuous of Australian managers, believing they didn't do enough for their clients. "Australian managers seem to make a dead set against local talent, and offer them the same miserable pittance everywhere," he said, boasting that "Tex Morton today is making one-thousand percent more than the best offer any manager in Australia would give him. I can't understand their attitude. I know twenty acts in Australia I could sell on American radio in half an hour, but it is just a waste of time trying to get local managers to see that."[63]

ARCH KERR

One of the leading forces influencing the development of country music in Australia was a man who regarded country music as decidedly low brow, and preferred big-band music to hillbilly songs: Archibald ("Arch") Kerr. Born in 1907 in the north Queensland town of Charters Towers, Kerr's lifelong interest in music and recording was sparked upon hearing an Edison phonograph when he was four years old. In 1913, his parents bought him a piano and he commenced a serious study of music that persisted throughout his life. His family moved first to Ipswich in 1914 and then, in 1917, to Brisbane. He completed his schooling in 1921 and successfully applied for a position as an office boy with Harrold's Music Warehouse, all the while also studying at a technical college. After passing his examinations, he was promoted to manager of the warehouse's record section, a responsible position because of the imperative to restock following the Great War. Although record sales dived during the Great Depression, for Kerr, the era was one of great opportunity. Kerr was a professionally-trained musician, could play piano, clarinet and saxophone,[64] and was an early pioneer of using amplified guitar in danceband groups. Dissatisfied with the casual attitude of freelance dance bands in Brisbane, he formed the group "Arch Kerr's Nitelites" in 1930. The band's first engagement was at Addie Cantwell's Dancing Academy; this was followed by appearances at venues such as the Australian Hotel, the Trocadero and Blue Moon Palais, all in Brisbane.[65]

After he married in February 1938, Kerr abandoned playing music professionally in favor of a "regular" job[66] and, while on his honeymoon in Sydney, applied for a position at Columbia Graphophone. On July 4, 1938, he was appointed assistant sales manager, under Tim Tyler. In 1939, Tyler, on leave, departed for England and when he didn't return, Kerr was promoted to record sales manager,[67] a position that combined the roles of sales manager, artists and repertoire manager, musical director, producer, and production supervisor, for a company that maintained a catalog of some 30,000 titles performed by approximately 1,600 artists or groups. Later, Ron Wills successfully applied for Kerr's old position of assistant record sales manager, with a weekly salary of six pounds.[68]

During the 1930s and 1940s, Columbia Graphophone had a monopoly on local issue of recordings and releases from other countries until late 1949, when the rival Australian Record Company commenced recording local hillbilly artists on its Rodeo label. This domination had a significant effect on the growth of Australian country music. Columbia not only decided which artists to record, but also those overseas recordings it would release locally, as well as the number of discs to be pressed, thereby effectively defining what constituted country music in Australia. Throughout the 1940s, these decisions were left almost solely to Kerr and his assistant.[69]

Kerr disliked hillbilly music, and his narrow, fixed view of it shaped Australian country music for a decade. Because of his rigidly imposed directives, local hillbilly music was almost always restricted to a singer/yodeler with simple guitar accompaniment, and songs that were either sentimental or centered on rural themes—white-faced cattle, stockmen in uniform, and horses, for example. Generally, he was opposed to backing bands (although he relented for some sessions) and believed that solo singers who sang and yodeled with just guitar accompaniment were more likely to be successful. In 1978, he stated:

> A good guitar accompaniment is much better than a mediocre band accompaniment ... it's been my experience that many, many fans around the country buy ... records so that they can copy them. They can hear ... guitar chords, and they can sing the songs themselves and play the guitar chords ... they appreciate your recording much better than if it's got some involved accompaniment which they can't emulate.[70]

Kerr also believed that backing bands added an unnecessary layer of sophistication to the music: "The whole basis of country ... recording [was] that it should be unsophisticated [with] no attempt to boost it up too much, because immediately you start to boost it up you get beyond some people and they just can't understand it."[71]

Because sales in country music effectively subsidized the recording of other types of music released on Columbia's more expensive labels, even Kerr had reason to thank Morton and his ilk. "We reckoned that the income derived from our country recordings made it possible to record a great deal of the music for the full-priced labels," observed former Columbia executive Ron Wills in 1989.[72]

Wills, who was Kerr's assistant from 1940 to 1942 and from 1946 until 1947, observed that Kerr "was a very hard man to get along with and was always supremely confident that he was the person who was right."[73] Bush balladeer Slim Dusty said Kerr ("the supreme commander")[74] had complete control over what country music was to be recorded and released on Columbia in Australia, describing him as arrogant, dogmatic and treating country music only as a means of making money instead of an art form in its own right. "He didn't like us," Dusty said, meaning Kerr didn't appreciate hillbilly music. Dusty recalled Kerr was "a tough bloke" and "if he said 'no', it was no."[75] Smoky Dawson stated, "Arch Kerr was the one who made the final decision" about what songs would be recorded, adding that he was intolerant of people who argued with him.[76] And it wasn't necessarily a matter of disagreeing with Kerr that might anger him; merely questioning his judgment could set him off. But, he said, Kerr's judgments were objective even if he did not permit some prospective artists to record.[77]

Kerr and Morton clashed, especially when Kerr signed two new Australian country music performers in 1939, Buddy Williams and ex-Canadian Smilin' Billy Blinkhorn, not only for their talents but also, especially in Williams's case, to foil what Kerr perceived as Morton's increasing arrogance and rudeness towards him. Williams, who had experienced an abusive and loveless life first at an orphanage and then at the hands of exploitative, cruel foster parents, had been musically influenced by Jimmie Rodgers, Goebel Reeves, Wilf Carter and Morton himself. Williams made his first commercial recordings on September 7, 1939, and Blinkhorn on October 27, 1939. Like Morton, both were yodelers and accompanied themselves on guitar, and both were more than capable as songwriters in the emerging Australian hillbilly genre. Arch Kerr recalled a heated exchange in his office with Bill Scott over Blinkhorn's Columbia recordings; afterwards, Morton reduced his appearances in city cinemas, possibly in order to counter his rivals' new-found popularity.[78]

5

SISTER DORRIE

MORTON DIDN'T ENLIST in the armed forces during World War II. Perhaps he was a pacifist, in view of the fact that he later recorded two anti-Vietnam War songs: "21st Birthday" and "The Widow Next Door."[1] Realistically, as Slim Dusty suggested, he was more useful for the war effort through raising funds and entertaining troops, than serving in uniform.

Morton recorded his own compositions, "Freight Train Yodel" and "Aristocrat" in March 1940.[2] The horse Aristocrat belonged to the Skuthorpes, buckjumping circus owners who, along with "Lance" (Skuthorpe), are mentioned in the song. A 1939 newspaper reported that Aristocrat "will buck to throw any man out of any saddle," and declared that the horse had never been ridden, despite having been shown in all of Australia's major cities. Spectators were promised ten pounds to anyone who could ride him.[3] Nearly a decade later, the Skuthorpes were still promoting the buckjumper: a poster from the late 1940s promised 20 pounds to anyone who could stay in his saddle for 15 seconds.[4] Morton wrote "Aristocrat" following the success of the earlier "Rocky Ned," though cumulative sales of "Aristocrat" surpassed those of "Rocky Ned" by some 10,000, and just eclipsed those of a later classic buckjumping song, "Mandrake," making "Aristocrat" Morton's most popular roughriding composition, although it was paired with the successful "Freight Train Yodel" which boosted sales considerably.

Early in 1940, Morton had toured with Lance Skuthorpe Sr. and his children, Lance Jr. and Violet. Skuthorpe Sr. had a hearing problem and couldn't understand discs played on gramophones, so Morton arranged for the two of them to listen to his recording of "Aristocrat" at Columbia's studios. The terrified old man was fitted with headphones and had dire thoughts of being electrocuted, but on hearing the playback he was ecstatic, and insisted on having the song played again and again. "As we were leaving," Morton recalled, "old Lance blew his nose loudly and repeatedly. His eyes glistened and he was obviously very impressed. He strode down the steps with his shoulders back and the jaunty air of a sixteen-year-old. 'By George!' he kept muttering, 'What do you think of that now? By George! How can I ever thank you?'"[5]

"Freight Train Yodel" was a spirited anthem in celebration of train jumping. In a 1942 interview, Morton recalled sitting in a Sydney cafe, feeling depressed when he heard the distant whistle of a train. "Instantly, I visualized it gathering speed as it commenced its long trek to the bush. I became completely oblivious to the people around me, and there flashed across my mind, a title—'The Freight Train Yodel,'" he said. "Instinctively, my hand grasped a serviette [napkin], and I started to write the words."[6] It was, he said, an attempt to write an Australian hobo-type song.[7]

It's likely that Arch Kerr would have supervised this and all future sessions for Columbia. Perhaps the stage was already set for future differences of opinion between these two headstrong personalities, and Morton also had to contend with the added threat of rivals like Buddy Williams and Smilin' Billy Blinkhorn. Consequently, there would have been smoldering tension in the air.

In May 1940, Morton cut six more tracks,[8] including "She Came Rolling Down the Mountain," considered by some to be mildly risqué. "If You Please Miss Give Me Heaven," written in 1901 by Charles Harris ("the king of the tearjerkers"), was about a young child using modern (for 1901) technology by "telephoning" her dead mother in Heaven.[9] It was similar to the Carter Family's "Hello Central ! Give Me Heaven" and later numbers about phoning Paradise, but Morton was probably influenced by a McFarland and Gardner disc released in Australia in 1930.[10] It's possible that Morton learnt "Just Plain Folks" from a Bradley Kincaid disc about a youth who, after leaving home, had become both wealthy and snobbish, much to the dismay of his aged parents.[11] "Beautiful Queensland," among Morton's better sellers over the years, was a minimalist lyrical rewriting of W. Lee O'Daniel's song "Beautiful Texas."[12] O'Daniel was a Texan politician, songwriter and singer, famous for giving Western Swing pioneers Bob Wills and Milton Brown their starts in the music business.

"The Stockman's Last Bed" was an attempt to capitalize on "Wrap Me Up in My Stockwhip and Blanket," though judging by sales figures, the public preferred the earlier song. Morton possibly learned it from a 1938 version by Louis Isidor Lavater, an Australian composer and poet who gave up a career in medicine for one in music.[13] It had been previously published as sheet music in 1846, then in the *Queensland Native Companion Songster* in 1865, and in Banjo Paterson's 1905 book, *The Old Bush Songs*."[14] Morton and Lance Skuthorpe Jr. wrote "Old Boko and Me," although the composer credits on the record have sometimes been credited to "Stewthorpe/Morton". The song described the unregulated, carefree life of an outback rider.[15] In November 1940, Morton cut two more self-compositions: "Old Rover" and the narration "You'll Never Be Missed (Monologue With Guitar)," a genre he persevered with in future years.[16]

"SISTER" DORRIE

In late 1938 Morton met his longtime traveling and recording companion, Dorothy Carroll, who was born as Dorothy May Ricketts on January 8, 1910, in Gippsland, Victoria.[17] Dorothy recalled that when she was a child, her family frequently entertained themselves with musical evenings.[18] "My dad used to play all these instruments when we were out in the bush," she remembered. She learned the piano-accordion at the age of four, and later mastered other instruments, including autoharp. She and her father once entertained about 2,000 people at Brisbane's Trocadero dance hall, with Jim Davidson's ABC Dance Band. "The people wouldn't let us stop," she recalled.[19] As a teenager, Dorothy worked with Rex Payne at Brisbane's Theatre Royal, where she learned to tap dance.[20] From then on, she remembered, she was determined to break into show business.[21] In the 1930s she appeared as a soubrette in Tivoli Circuit shows touring Melbourne and Sydney. In February 1933, she married Bruce Carroll, then the manager of a Tivoli theatre, and the two had a son, Roger, born in April the following year.

Morton's wife Marjorie recalled that Morton, who knew Bruce Carroll, appeared in a Tivoli show when Dorrie was in the chorus. Against her husband's wishes, Dorrie toured New Zealand in the "Why Be Serious" Tivoli revue with Morton that year.[22] Bruce Carroll was stage manager.[23] Although Dorrie's background was in vaudeville, she had no difficulty performing country music.

"We used to sing together and mess about ... Tex started to yodel ... well, I just sort of got into it," she remembered. "You know how you ease into these things without knowing it." Another time, she recalled she would play a tin whistle while Morton performed on guitar, and both would harmonize on songs like "Hand Me Down My Walking Cane."[24] Marjorie suggested the sobriquet "Sister Dorrie"[25] because American sister acts like the Andrews Sisters were famous. "It wasn't Tex Morton and *his* sister," Dorrie said. "It was Tex Morton *and* Sister Dorrie," leaving it unclear as to whether she might have been a cast member's sibling or a nursing sister (senior nurse) or even belonged to a religious order.[26]

In 1941, Dorrie ran into Morton again in Sydney. Morton was driving a red Buick with "Tex Morton Number Two Car" painted on it. He told her he was putting a band together and invited her to join his show. The next day the two recorded "(Honey, I've Got) Everything but You."[27] Dorothy said she joined the touring rodeo with her husband's blessing (although Bruce Carroll later denied this) and traveled to Forbes the following day—more likely it was about a fortnight later[28]—commencing an association that continued for the better part of a decade. Dorothy was amazed at the crowds that Morton's shows drew. "I'll never forget the number of autographs they signed.... They had to have the police come and direct the traffic ... thousands and thousands," she recalled, speaking of fans that flocked to the touring rodeo, night after night, echoing Dick Carr's estimates of Morton's enormous popularity.[29]

Dorrie was an integral part of Morton's trick shooting—Morton once described her as "a victim of my sharpshooting act."[30] Their performance would commence with her holding a lighted candle. First, Morton would shoot through the flame, and then with a second shot extinguish it by blasting the candle's wick. Then, she'd throw a disc upwards, and Morton would shoot it in mid-air. Next, she'd hold a playing card, with its edge facing Morton, and he would split it in two. "The last one was the cigarette in my mouth," she recalled. After the burning ash had been shot from the cigarette's tip, Morton would extinguish the cigarette with another bullet. Sometimes, she'd place four pieces of chalk between her fingers, each of which were blasted apart by shots from his rifle. But the act was not without peril: once, a bullet sheared off the top from one of her fingers. Fortunately, two paramedics rushed her to hospital to have the wound stitched. Dorothy was given penicillin, and the finger placed in a splint. The local doctor was flabbergasted that she hadn't fainted; he might have been even more shocked to learn that Morton had her assisting him in his sharpshooting act the following night, this time using her other hand. Once, he could have blinded her when he took longer than expected to aim and she turned her head just as he fired. The bullet whistled perilously close to her head and blasted the brim of her cowgirl hat. "I could have got it right in my eye," she said.[31]

Dorothy described Morton as "a funny, erratic man," who was sometimes full of optimistic but unfulfilled promises. Once, she said, when he was in Canada in the 1950s, he told her to join him immediately. She was all prepared to go—only to next hear from him eighteen months later when he was in London. "Are you ready yet? Prepare. Leave for England immediately," his telegram read. She ignored it. She fondly remembered the "unbelievable" rapport between them that sometimes bordered on the telepathic, with each seeming to know the other's thinking. "He thought the world of me, and I thought the world of him as a partner," she said. But they fought at times over music. "Stubborn ... a mule wasn't in it," she described his desire to dominate arguments. "But overall, he was a good person. Poor old Tex." She even wrote a poem about Morton, praising him and his accomplishments in pioneering Australian country music. "There was only one of him," she thought.[32]

Dorrie said Morton loved old people and would frequently give money to elderly folks he met on his travels, and would talk for ages with them. "He loved animals, and he loved old people," she said, although he "didn't have any time for children, because they couldn't think for themselves."[33] Morton's future partner, Kath, confirmed that the entertainer liked the elderly, and sometimes handed them cash.[34] But Morton's behavior and actions occasionally were illogical, Dorrie recalled. He would buy things on the spur of the moment, often when he didn't need them. She also said he loved stopping at hotels and imbibing with the locals, regaling them with entertaining tales. Once, Dorrie refused to join Morton while he was drinking at a hotel, so she walked the horses instead, pushing ahead to the next town while Morton continued drinking. She had gone some distance when Morton drove past her and, deliberately ignoring her, left her to continue riding alone in fly-infested, barren country that she described as "a desert." It was evening when she reached the next town, where her partner had been holding up the bar at the local hotel for most of the afternoon. Morton made light of her distress by driving through town and mocking her arrival through the loudspeakers on his car. She described such behavior as "irrational." He never inconvenienced himself, she said.[35]

Morton's brother Kim, who traveled with the couple during the 1940s, wrote that Dorrie would afterwards harshly criticize her partner if his marksmanship was too close to her fingers. He also recalled the arguments Tex and Dorrie used to have as they were composing songs. He especially remembered one particular night when Morton was speeding in his Buick and spied a "huge ginger tarantula" clinging to the windscreen, close to his face. Morton, who loathed spiders, dived into the back seat, but Dorrie calmly took the wheel, stopped the car, and coolly removed the arachnid. "The rifle shooting took a bit longer that night," Kim wrote.[36]

Overall, Dorrie recalled her experiences with Morton as memorable and pleasant;[37] but her hardscrabble years in vaudeville, as well as having grown up with guns and horses, had prepared her well for touring with Morton and his immoderate lifestyle. The two sometimes argued in public: one fan recalled attending a show where Dorrie, who was selling tickets, and Morton were quarrelling. In exasperation, Dorrie hurled the takings into the crowd.[38] Colin Mackay, Morton's friend in later life, also said every so often the pair openly clashed with each other.[39] Dorrie's son, Roger, described her as strong willed, independent, hard, and shrewish at times—characteristics that no doubt put her in good stead for a turbulent life on the road with the headstrong "yodelling boundary rider."[40] The couple split in 1950 when Morton headed for greener pastures in North America. During the 1960s, she worked for a kitchen-appliance firm,[41] but during the 1970s she and Morton were reunited.[42]

Colin Mackay thought that the two were deeply in love with each other during the 1940s, saying, "she was the love of his life." Yet, Dorrie didn't trust Morton because of the abundance of willing females at his concerts, and possibly because he made no effort to marry her, though both were wed to others at the time. Morton was a "man's man," always one of the blokes, Mackay believed, thus he didn't publicly express his affection for his stage partner but was always defensive when speaking of her. Mackay believed that Dorrie terminated their relationship when Morton departed for North America in 1950, but she retained deep feelings for him afterwards.[43]

6

THE EARLY WAR YEARS AND THE TWINS

IN MARCH 1941, Morton recorded four songs for Columbia.[1] The atmosphere in the studio would have been noticeably cooler than in the 1930s, with friction escalating between Morton and Arch Kerr. "The Drover's Wife" was derived from an earlier English song that he learned from a friend he'd met on the Tivoli circuit, Fred Bluett,[2] a London-born vaudevillian who migrated to Australia in 1891. It was about the wife of a drover, begging her errant, unfaithful husband to return to her.

"In The Luggage Van Ahead" was the well-known American composition titled "In The Baggage Coach Ahead," written in 1896 by African-American songwriter Gussie L. Davis. It was probably based on one or more poems that might have described a true incident about a baby crying on a train while its mother was "dead, in the coach ahead."[3] Morton almost certainly learned the tearjerker from Vince Courtney's more formal 1928 version, "In the Luggage Van Ahead."[4] Courtney, in turn, probably learned the song from a 1925 Vernon Dalhart record, "In The Baggage Coach Ahead," released in Australia on the Lincoln label.[5] Dorrie's duet on the Bob Miller number "(Honey, I've Got) Everything but You" was the first instance of a country music recording with an Australian female—the first solo female artist was Shirley Thoms, who made her initial recordings some two months later in May of that year. Dorrie recalled Morton had especially asked her to sing this song, which she described as "a beautiful little number."[6] Come Back to the Valley" was almost certainly taken from Frankie Marvin's 1931 recording of "Come Back To The Hills," released in Australia on Panachord, and on Regal Zonophone.[7]

For his penultimate recording session for Columbia, in May 1941, Morton was accompanied by Sister Dorrie (Dorothy Carroll) and his Roughriders band, which probably consisted of Dick Carr (steel guitar), Tom Wallis (bass), Al Kinloch (fiddle) and Herbie Marks (accordion). At least, they are the members listed in a 1957 Tex Morton discography compiled by the noted authority, John Edwards.[8] Dick Carr, however, listed the Roughriders as comprising Reg Robinson (bass), Herbie Marks (accordion and piano) and himself ("plectrum and steel guitars").[9] Morton recalled their personnel as Carr, George Reed (also known as George Raymond) on fiddle, and either Dorrie or Tommy Sharp on accordion.[10] These varying recollections, however, aren't necessarily contradictory, as band personnel almost certainly changed over time, and Carr may have evoked a later incarnation of the band members. Certainly, a violinist/fiddler not mentioned by Carr was present on these recordings. Dorrie described the Roughriders as "excellent" and "a beautiful band."[11] According to Ron Wills, Arch Kerr's assistant at the time, Morton and Kerr argued at the recording session about the band and its name. Wills suggested the name "The Roughriders" and it was accepted.[12] The band's name could be spelled either as "Rough Riders" or "Roughriders." For consistency, the latter spelling has been used in this book, because that is how it appeared on record labels.

It's doubtful that Arch Kerr, who produced the session, concurred with Morton over using full-band accompaniment, so emotions would likely have been tense at the time. Six songs—more than the usual number—were cut at the May, 1941, session. On the other hand, the Roughriders significantly enhanced the recordings, with Morton's distinctive guitar style coming through strongly. Dick Carr's steel guitar playing was effective, both behind Morton's singing and during the occasional solo; the fiddle varied, from sedately pleasant on "Through the Sin of a Son," to mildly "hot" on "When the Cactus Is in Bloom" which also featured an impressive solo by the accordionist. Dorrie contributed significantly, particularly on "Through The Sin of a Son," in which she took a lead-vocal singing part, as well as yodeling in duet with Morton on "When the Cactus Is in Bloom."[13]

Red Foley's "Old Shep" would turn out to be one of Morton's best sellers and, he said, his most requested song.[14] Over time, the number (paired with "Through The Sin of a Son")[15] sold over 26,000 copies, making it his fourth most-popular record. Morton probably learned it from Foley's version and not from the British group the Hill Billies,[16] whose somewhat different recording of it had been released in Australia in November 1935 (paired with "Red River Valley").[17] "Through the Sin of a Son" had been originally written and recorded by the Australian Vince Courtney. Morton might have learned the song from Courtney's disc, or even from sheet music. Dorrie sang the first verse, relating feelings of a mother whose errant son had "left his parents in disgrace," after which Morton narrated a spoken piece over Kinloch's sympathetic violin playing.[18]

Morton, Dorrie and the Roughriders reprised Jimmie Rodgers's "When the Cactus Is in Bloom," but with more verve than Rodgers's 1931 version.[19] Morton and Dorrie harmonized and yodeled ensemble, the instrumental break featured Kinloch's somewhat bluesy fiddle, and Carr's steel guitar was "hotter" than Cliff Carlisle's accompaniment on the Rodgers disc; Marks then completed the break with some spirited accordion. Arguably, "When the Cactus is in Bloom" best demonstrated the Roughriders's versatility.

According to the songwriter credits, "Don't Say Goodbye" was written by Morton and Dorrie, but Dorrie claimed she wrote it herself (Morton possibly added his name as co-writer later). In a 1942 article, Morton said he and Dorrie were having supper one night in Sydney's California Cafe, when they heard a young couple arguing. When the man got up to leave and said "goodbye," his partner said, "Don't Say goodbye if you love me." Morton thought the line would make a fine title, and the two penned the words straight away.[20] "Rover No More" was a folksong extending back to the late-sixteenth century. Morton likely learned it during his youth in New Zealand—he recalled he had "dug it up at the waterfront."[21] On the other hand, folklorist John Meredith stated that the song had been collected from "old timers" in Australia, so Morton might have acquired it on his outback travels instead.[22]

"Mandrake," like "Aristocrat," described a buckjumping horse in Morton's traveling rodeo. Mandrake has been variously described as a yellow-bay trotter-buckjumper[23] and a big-grey[24] whom Morton had purchased for 30 shillings,[25] when the horse was called "Slippery." Colin Mackay, on the other hand, said Mandrake was a large black mount with a white streak near his nose.[26] He had proved to be hazardous to ride, having thrown Queensland roughriding champion Arthur Winters who is referenced but not named in the song. Morton said that Mandrake was "the best buckjumper I ever had."[27] Larry Dulhunty, a showman, said Mandrake was initially known as "Charters

Towers."[28] Dulhunty asserted that Indigenous roughrider and singer Billy Bargo "and a couple of other riders" left Morton's show because they had difficulty riding Mandrake, as the horse would sometimes roll back on his rider.[29] (Bargo was an excellent singer and, some said, sounded like Morton.)[30] In later years, Morton boasted that he had once ridden Mandrake to a standstill, a claim his friend Colin Mackay confidently dismissed as "bullshit."[31]

According to a familiar story, Mandrake and eleven other horses in Morton's show had to be shot when a semi-trailer transporting them overturned while negotiating a storm-damaged, crumbling road,[32] in an attempt to let an ambulance pass.[33] A 1949 newspaper report, however, stated that Mandrake and Aristocrat had escaped uninjured, but three other show horses and a mule[34] had to be put down. Such accidents were constant hazards to traveling circuses. In 1945, Morton's rodeo suffered a comparable mishap when a truck attempted to pass another vehicle while careening downhill, but the edge of the roadside gave way and the truck slid six meters down an embankment at the foot of a steep hill. No animals were hurt, but five members of Morton's crew were injured and had to be hospitalized.[35]

By the end of 1941, Morton had recorded eighty-nine songs for Columbia Graphophone, many of which were self-compositions. "Mandrake" and "Old Shep," both recorded that year, would ultimately be among his best sellers, but it seems the rift between Morton and Arch Kerr had widened, because Morton didn't record at all the following year, unlike other Australian country singers: in 1942 Morton's rival, Buddy Williams, waxed six songs, as did Smoky Dawson, the Sundowners, and June Holm; Shirley Thoms made eight titles.

THE TWINS

On Monday, September 8, 1941, in Brisbane, Marjorie gave birth to twins, Bernard John and Robert ("Bob") William, named, respectively, after Morton's father and Morton himself. Morton, who was touring at the time, proudly announced their arrival to a wildly cheering audience.[36] The twins met their father about a fortnight afterwards, when Marjorie drove from Brisbane to Goondiwindi to introduce them to her husband.[37] Bernard and Bob were photographed in their father's arms, which appeared in a magazine published shortly afterwards; the article reported that they had journeyed some 3,000 miles with their parents on Morton's traveling shows,[38] and hinted that Marjorie was having difficulties simultaneously touring and caring for two infants: there was a description of an untidy hotel room littered with stage paraphernalia and diapers, and a drawer in which the infants had slept the previous night.[39] A 1942 newspaper reported that the twins had toured extensively with their parents in the eastern states, sleeping in suitcases, and in chests of drawers in hotels. Once, in attempting to avoid some emus while driving, Morton rolled his car with the twins inside, much to Marjorie's alarm. She threatened to take the children home with her unless Morton drove slower than thirty miles an hour. The boys were frequently guarded by a dingo, who watched over them while their parents were performing.[40] Their condition so alarmed a nurse treating them at a Brisbane hospital that she afterwards described them as being "covered in [a] measles rash" and "filthy." They were still awake at one o'clock in the morning on a chilly August night, she remembered.[41]

The birth of one baby to a young couple would have been difficult enough, let alone traveling with Morton's show at the same time. Some months after the children were born, Marjorie either had them cared for by others while she toured with her husband, or she remained at home to mind them herself.[42] This enforced absence would have done little to cement their marriage. By that time, she and her husband were drifting apart, and a few years later they would become estranged. Singer Joan Martin recalled meeting Morton and "his young wife," whom Morton seemed to ignore. "I had the impression that Tex was totally involved with his career," she wrote.[43]

By 1942, there was a new woman, Dorothy Carroll, in Morton's life. Dorothy's husband Bruce recalled seeing a former employee of Morton's in a Melbourne hotel in 1942: the man was lying on a bed with his tunic and boots off, and Dorothy was in the bed.[44] Later, he said, he walked in on his wife and Morton in a Sydney apartment. Morton's boots "were lying on the one bed in the flat," and Morton was still there the next day.[45] By then, Marjorie was absent from touring for lengthy periods of time, caring for the couple's children, so it wasn't coincidental that Morton and Dorrie forged a personal as well as professional bond at the time. In fact, Smoky Dawson believed that Dorrie had "set out to get" Morton.[46] The relationship between the two would certainly have been regarded as scandalous at the time, though it seemed to be well known.[47] From then on, Marjorie seemed to be stoic in accepting that Morton was living his own life apart from her. Surprisingly, she didn't divorce him; instead, she toured with him in later years, and stayed at his dude ranch in 1949 and early 1950. Around 1947, she and the twins lived in Nelson with Morton's parents for about 18 months. Barbara, Morton's sister, recalled her father helped to raise the children "with firm discipline."[48]

In August 1942, Morton, Dorrie and the Roughriders played at the Majestic Theatre in Adelaide in the production "Sons of Fun." A review declared: "Tex, Sister Dorrie and two members of the Rough Riders figure in only one number, but it is the highlight of the show." Morton was described as "a good-looking yodeller . . . who [received] the most applause."[49] In January 1943, Morton formally amended his name from Robert William Lane to "Tex Morton" by deed poll.[50] The change became official about January 19 and was re-ratified on January 25, 1950,[51] yet again calling into question later assertions that he had always disliked the name "Tex," especially since he had been using that moniker as early as 1934, almost certainly of his own choosing. Marjorie and the twins also changed their name to "Morton."[52] It's not known if Morton ever applied for Australian citizenship,[53] although his sister thought he would have.[54]

THE BIG BUST UP

Morton's final recording session in April 1943 was likely a tense affair, with the clash of two egos—his and Arch Kerr's—and the added complication of having the Roughriders with him. Morton and his band—without Sister Dorrie—cut four songs at the session, including the memorable numbers "The Story of Parson Joe" and "The Good Old Droving Days."[55] Kinloch's complementary fiddling enhanced "The Story of Parson Joe," about a reformed alcoholic warning a young man about the evils of drink, only to discover that the man was his own son. "The Good Old Droving Days," an energetic, rollicking anthem of droving on the Australian plains, has been described as "immortal."[56] The somewhat derivative "The Flowers Never Bloom in Lonesome Valley" and "'Neath the Silver Willow Tree" rounded out the session.

And then, it ended. When the freewheeling, intransigent Morton and Arch Kerr, Columbia's equally opinionated and inflexible record sales manager, came to an impasse, Morton walked out on Columbia. For his part, Kerr was blasé about Morton's absence from the recording scene. When Ron Wills returned to Columbia in 1946, he suggested to Kerr that they should record more sessions with Morton. "Arch was the complete egotistical person, and his reply was, 'Tex knows where we are, let him come and ask,'" Wills wrote. Morton didn't record for Regal Zonophone again, although some 40 years later all 93 of his songs would be reissued on the familiar red-and-green label, in sets of vinyl albums, cassettes and compact discs, accentuating their enormous importance not only to Morton's career, but as the bedrock of Australian country music as well. In time, they justified Morton's title of "the father of Australasian [Australian and New Zealand] country music."[57] But in late 1943, Morton's recording career was quiescent, and it would be several years before he recorded commercially again—and not for Columbia.[58]

Over the years, speculative reasons for the breakup between the hillbilly star and his producer have circulated. Prominent among these was that the two fell out because of the Roughriders and their payment. Ron Wills recalled Morton and Kerr arguing about the band at the 1941 session in May, but acknowledged that "when it came time to have a backing group, then the company accepted the cost,"[59] although it's possible Kerr might have been more than happy to pay for backing groups for more sophisticated types of music, but not for Morton's hillbilly offerings, or for professional musicians, but not for what he would have considered amateurs like the Roughriders. Morton acknowledged that Kerr was "quite happy" for him to record with a band, provided he paid for it himself, which Morton said he did.[60] With his experience as a professional musician, Kerr wouldn't have regarded the group to be up to scratch, although they most certainly were for a hillbilly band. Morton later explained his side of the story:

> I had formed the Roughriders band—this was when I had the big rodeo and circus going. They were all good; they were all the best available at the time. I had formed these boys, but they [Columbia] couldn't see. They said, "They're too expensive for your sessions." So, I said, "Right—I'll pay for it." I used to bring these people all the way down from Queensland, to cut a recording session, in my own car. There was Dorrie, Dick Carr and other odd bods. I'd bring them all down, pay their wages, put them on the session, and I wouldn't get any reimbursement for it. I used to predict then that people would get tired of just guitar and voice.... Anyway, that's why I finally broke with [Columbia].[61]

Most likely, the dispute arose because of conflicting, strong-willed personalities. Morton and Kerr clashed frequently. Morton informed Kerr that he'd record when he was ready; and when he did turn up, Kerr recalled, "We had fun and games. We had all sorts of difficulties. One time I remember we had him sitting up on a platform, so we didn't pick up the stamping of his feet. He got a bit independent at times."[62] Smoky Dawson thought that Kerr found sessions with Morton to be "distasteful," and recalled Kerr bristled at Morton's arrogance and lack of respect for him—Morton referred to him not as "Mr. Kerr" but as just "Kerr"—so Kerr signed Buddy Williams (who not surprisingly had a similar style and sound, since he had been influenced by Morton) in order to keep the recalcitrant boundary rider in line.[63] Dawson said Morton was "one of the few exceptions [who] didn't bow [to Kerr] and didn't audition. He was more or less, in a way, so much a showman that he was able to just push himself in, and he always had a good manager in Bill Scott."[64] Scott, in fact, most likely bolstered his star's reputation, as Dawson remembered: "[Morton] was . . . young. He was pasty faced. You'd never think this kid—he looked like warmed up putty—not a bit of color in his face, skinny . . . showing great strength. He'd want to take on the biggest fighter in the world—as game as Ned Kelly. He was a real young lair [show-off] . . . he was influenced by the fact that Scott had got hold of him and had told him he was better than what he was."[65]

On the other hand, Morton claimed that Kerr dissuaded him from recording his own songs and tried to tell him how to sing and yodel.[66] Morton was especially irked by Kerr signing Buddy Williams, whom he saw as a rival with a repertoire and style largely copied from his own. Bernie Burnett, who was once married to Williams, thought that Kerr signed Williams as a deliberate foil to the headstrong Morton. Kerr, she said, wanted to have "some opposition to Tex Morton, as Tex was so good, he outsold everyone with anything he recorded. Also, Tex was beginning to get a bit too demanding."[67] Kerr phrased it more diplomatically: "At this time, of course, we only had Tex Morton, and the field was bigger than Tex could cover because he couldn't produce enough songs to take care of it," he said. "We wanted a bit of variety and of course, in a case like that, you always have a backstop—you don't rely on one artist to cater for the demand. You want a backstop, and that's just what I was looking for at the time, and Buddy fitted the bill excellently."[68]

Broadcaster John Minson thought that Morton resented being treated as a mere product by Columbia. Morton recalled that "Kerr . . . was being a star maker. He had Buddy Williams up his sleeve, and he had a dozen other young fellows, all up and coming. . . ."[69] But Ron Wills wrote: "Tex Morton was not worried. He had left us in April 1943 and never came back. Mainly, I must add, because he was never invited to make more records."[70]

About this time, either Morton or Bill Scott sent Buddy Williams a tersely-worded telegram, purportedly with this message: "Just to let you know I'm here with my solicitor. You've had a fair go and have been warned, so now just try to walk, talk, sing, dress or even look like me, once, and I'll go to the limit of the law."[71]

Williams's daughter Karen had the telegram but later lost it. Her father laughed when he received it, because he hadn't copied Morton at all, she said.[72] According to Bernie Burnett, Williams received the missive but Morton didn't follow up with further legal action.[73] Nevertheless, there was long-standing hostility between the two for decades afterwards, with Williams once describing Morton as "the biggest bastard on two legs"[74] and Morton equally vehement in his attitude toward someone whom he deemed as an upstart. In 1967, Morton recorded "Tex Morton's Protest Song (Burn Another Folkie)" with a pointed reference to Williams (who wasn't specifically named in the song) having "no ideas," once Morton had left Australia in 1950. "I've always tried to come up with new ideas," Morton wrote. "And it's only to be expected that others will copy any successful trend or sound. Some blokes do it quite blatantly and unashamedly," he continued. "Quite flattering, actually!" [75]

7
TEX MORTON'S REGAL ZONOPHONE LEGACY

THE 93 SONGS THAT Tex Morton recorded for Columbia Graphophone's Regal Zonophone label between February 1936 and April 1943 were the bedrock of his repertoire, and although his career stretched well into the 1970s and he recorded other unforgettable songs, by and large it is the earlier material for which he is mainly remembered. Morton's Regal Zonophone recordings were epochal in the development of early Australian country music, spawning artists who were influenced by Morton and his style, like Buddy Williams and Slim Dusty, both of whom freely acknowledged his immense influence. Williams and Dusty later became major artists themselves and, in turn, influenced others, but the seminal local icon in early Australian country music was indisputably Tex Morton. Almost single-handedly, he created an Australian country music style by copying, adapting and modifying the sounds he had heard, mainly from the United States, into a dynamic form that increasingly referenced Australia. Historian and writer Eric Watson asserted: "Tex Morton's great contribution to Australian country music lies firstly in the interest he stimulated in the form originally, and in the quality of his work; and secondly in the fact that he set a very original style for a country music of our own."[1]

Country singer Trevor Day thought that, although 50 percent of Morton's Regal Zonophone output was "disposable," the others were "pages from our history book" that would never be forgotten.[2]

The origins of Morton's Regal Zonophone recordings can be grouped into several categories, the most easily identifiable comprising songs he wrote, co-wrote or arranged himself, even though some of his own compositions might have been influenced by others. For example, "On the Gundagai Line" was similar to Jimmie Rodgers's' "Hobo Bill's Last Ride." Of the ninety-three songs he recorded for Regal Zonophone, thirty-eight (41 percent) were his own compositions, some of which— "Rocky Ned," "Aristocrat," "Mandrake," "Freight Train Yodel" and "The Good Old Droving Days," for instance—became Australian country music standards.

The second category comprises Australian songs that were not written by Morton, including the traditional "Wrap Me Up in My Stockwhip and Blanket" and "The Stockman's Last Bed." Despite Morton's unwavering assertion that "Billy Brink The Shearer" was an original composition, it fits this category because most likely it was an old bush verse.[3] Altogether, six numbers can be included in this group, bringing the total number of Australian compositions to forty-four (47 percent of all Morton's songs)—an impressive figure, given the fledgling state of the nascent Australian country music industry at the time. Morton composed the bulk of Australian works himself, progressively shifting the focus to local settings and characters.

The largest category of Morton's Regal Zonophone legacy comprised his versions of other artists' recordings, mainly from the United States but also perhaps a few songs from British group the Hill Billies. Some forty-eight songs (52 percent of his total output) fit this category. Of these, thirty-three songs (35 percent overall) were most likely influenced by overseas records that were issued in Australia prior to Morton's recording them, leaving a further fifteen (16 percent) for which there were no known local releases.[4] Several possibilities could account for this latter category.

One explanation is that Columbia may have given Morton discs that had been sent to them for potential Australian release. The company had arrangements with overseas labels to issue country music locally. Overseas companies would send Columbia Graphophone copies of their latest 78-rpm discs. Columbia would then audition these discs and decide which songs they would release through their own labels. The foreign companies would then send recording "mothers" (similar to "masters") so that Australian Columbia could issue versions locally. It's possible some records that had been rejected for Australian release could have been given to Morton, who would then be free to record his own covers of them. Morton may also have heard discs that had been imported into Australia prior to 1927, after which the government imposed a tariff on such discs.[5] Certainly, imported discs have turned up in private collections, suggesting some individuals acquired the music directly from the United States.[6] Likewise, 2KY-Sydney maintained an extensive library of 78s, many possibly bought directly from the USA.[7] Morton himself stated in a 1969 interview that "sometimes [I'd] have a rare record that had not been released in Australia."[8] Finally, "Old Ship O' Mine" does not appear to fit into any of the above categories.

When the sales data is analyzed, however, a somewhat different picture emerges. Taking the overall sales for Morton's Regal Zonophone output (omitting "Sergeant Small," for which there is no information) and, most likely assuming incorrectly, since there is no suitable alternative, that customers were equally likely to buy a disc for either one side or the other, Morton's own compositions accounted for some 43 percent of total sales; other Australian compositions accounted for about a further 7 percent. In other words, nearly 50 percent of sales were for Australian compositions (Morton's own or others). Sales of songs for which Morton's inspirations were most likely from overseas sources also accounted for nearly 50 percent of all sales broken down into 32 percent for songs that had an Australian release and a further 17 percent for songs that had no Australian release. The percentages are almost identical if sales figures, adjusted for the number of months the discs were in the Regal Zonophone catalog, are used instead: sales for Australian compositions accounted for about half of all sales. These numbers should be regarded with caution, however, since it's improbable that customers were equally likely to buy a record for one side or the other. Doubtless, they bought a record for a particular song. In this respect, sales of Regal Zonophone G23064 are instructive, since one side was "The Black Sheep" and the other was Morton's own "You Only Have One Mother." Sales of the latter were no doubt enhanced by customers presumably buying the record for "The Black Sheep"—a case, perhaps, of Morton's sales riding on the sheep's back. (Because Columbia frequently kept discs in their catalog until the 1950s, sales figures used here refer to these extended periods.)

Table 1 shows the number of songs recorded by likely source, as well as the total long-term sales for records in each category, and the percentage of sales for each category. ("Sergeant Small" has been eliminated from the analysis because there are no sales figures for it.)

Many of the artists who influenced Morton were citybillies like Vernon Dalhart, Carson Robison, Frank Luther and Frankie Marvin, likely because they were significant, early inspirations for his music. Perhaps seventeen songs (18 percent) of the total ninety-three songs he recorded between 1936 and 1943 stemmed from citybilly sources and formal versions recorded by American artists. Morton also seemed especially drawn to Goebel Reeves and recorded three songs associated with him despite only five records by "The Texas Drifter" having been released in Australia at the time.[9] "He always intrigued me," Morton said.[10]

Table 1: Number of Songs and Sales By Category for Morton's Regal Zonophone Releases (excludes sales data for "Sergeant Small")

SOURCE OF SONG	SONGS		SALES	
	Number	*Percentage**	*Total*	*Percentage**
composed by Morton	38	40.9	277 638	42.8
other Australian songs	6	6.5	42 431	6.5
total Australian compositions	44	47.3	320 069	49.3
foreign, local release	33	35.5	209 310	32.2
foreign, no local release	15	16.1	113 217	17.4
total foreign	48	51.6	322 527	49.7
other	1	1.1	6584	1.0
total all issues	93	100.0	649 180	100.0

*This table shows that Australian songs—either composed by Morton or folksongs—were popular with the record-buying public as the percentage of sales (column 5) exceeded the percentage of recorded songs in those genres (column 3).

None of Morton's songs about the American West was traditional. All were either the creation of commercial, Tin Pan Alley–type songwriters, or of artists like Carson Robison who wrote about a romanticized conception of the West. Since the composers of many of these "western" songs didn't live in the West, but in New York or Oswego, Kansas, where Robison was born, it mattered little even if they resided in faraway Britain. Michael Carr and Jimmy Kennedy, who penned "South Of The Border" for Gene Autry, prompted him to remark: "How two Englishmen could write a song about a country they had never seen for a movie cowboy they had never met is a question I wish I could answer."[11]

Morton's repertoire paved the way for the Australian bush ballad, a genre integral to later Australian country music (although it certainly does not represent the total range of modern-day Australian country music). "Wrap Me Up in My Stockwhip and Blanket" was the first recorded country music bush ballad, and many of Morton's compositions were exemplars for others to follow. Morton's sales of his own and other Australian compositions proved there was a ready market for Australian songs, even if the majority were not bush ballads. Morton later asserted that Arch Kerr was opposed to him recording Australian folksongs or bush ballads, though Kerr himself stated that "we had the material, the background to build an Australian type of music."[12] With Kerr's blessing, Morton's protégées, like Buddy Williams, Smoky Dawson (whose Australian-based songs Kerr especially liked),[13] Shirley Thoms, Gordon Parsons, and others, continued writing and singing about local themes until a recognizable bush ballad style emerged. Slim Dusty, the artist most closely associated with Australian bush ballads, was especially influenced by Morton.

Much of Morton's Regal Zonophone repertoire consisted of sentimental songs. During the Great Depression, American singers like Jimmie Rodgers and Goebel Reeves sang of tramps, train-riding hobos and hard times. Their songs occasionally told of the tough lifestyles of those who had to ramble, to seek work. Reeves especially accentuated the travails of the vagabond: according to Veronica Mratinich, most of his hobo songs "emphasize the depressing and lonely elements of a hobo's life. Laments abound about his lack of a wife, children and home, and how often his thoughts and dreams are his only consolations."[14] Morton most likely identified with these songs too, given his experiences of the early 1930s when, unemployed, he lived in abject poverty and often had to beg for food.

This fondness for sentimentality was shared by other Australian performers, too. Tony Russell, commenting on early Australian hillbilly records, stated "the preference of public and performers alike—and it seems to have been a natural one—was for the cowboy idiom, in which could be included sentimental balladry, yodel songs and story or event songs."[15] Smoky Dawson recalled "the further out [from the cities] you got, the more they liked the yodeling songs, and 'Old Shep' and 'Rockin' Alone in an Old Rocking Chair'. The biggest sellers were the sad ones."[16] Buddy Williams accounted for the popularity of sentimental songs in the 1930s and 1940s: "Things were more sincere. People are much more light-hearted today, but things meant something in the early days. I think it was the lifestyle of the people, too, because times were pretty tough and I think that's why people felt the sorrow; and it wasn't hard to bring a tear to a person's eye when you sang a song that had some meaning to it ... those were the types of songs that I used to sing."[17] Similarly, Dusty Rankin, recalling country music of the late 1940s said, "Back in those days it was all sad songs."[18]

One estimate from Morton's Regal Zonophone output is that about 55 percent of his recordings could broadly be described as sentimental. Assuming, as before, and potentially incorrectly, that the public was equally likely to buy a record for its A or B side, sales of Morton's sentimental songs similarly accounted for about 54 percent of the total sales of his Regal Zonophone discs. Even though Morton's best sellers were undoubtedly sentimental, the average sales for sentimental songs were only about the same as for non-sentimental recordings.

Table 2 shows the percentage of titles Morton recorded for Regal Zonophone by their dominant themes and attributes (excluding "Sergeant Small"). Thus, from the second column, of the ninety-two songs considered, about 17 percent were about mothers and 11 percent about fathers.[19] The third column shows the sales of discs with the attribute as a percentage of all sales of Morton's records. The totals of the second and third columns exceed one hundred because there were frequently several attributes present in the one song. The fourth column displays a "likeability" index that has been simplistically computed from the average sales-per-disc of songs with and without the attribute, as follows:

Likeability Index = $\log_e$ ((average sales of songs with the attribute) / (average sales of songs without the attribute))[20]

A positive index suggests that songs with the attribute were more popular, based on long-term sales, than songs where the attribute was absent. A negative result indicates the opposite: songs with the attribute present were less popular than those where it wasn't. This relatively crude likeability index should be treated with caution, however, since it assumes that people bought Morton's records with no preference for one side or the other, and because it sometimes has been based on a small number of titles.[21]

Results suggest that, on average, sentimental songs were preferred about the same as non-sentimental songs (because the likeability index was close to zero), and that the record-buying public tended to prefer songs about mothers, fathers, horses, trains and dogs, but only slightly, except for mothers and horses. In contrast, songs about cowboys, stockmen, and sweethearts and girlfriends appeared to be favored slightly less, but the differences were small. There did not appear to be any decided preference for songs about the sea, hobos, and Swiss mountaineers featuring Alpine-style yodeling. The "jail/crime/hanging" theme is somewhat muddied because it comprises comedic songs (such as "I'll Be Hanged If They're Gonna Hang Me") and serious songs (like "Crime Does Not Pay"), so its likeability index should be regarded with caution.

Generally, it seems that people bought Morton's discs without an overall preference for any category, although his biggest sellers were sentimental songs, closely followed by "Aristocrat," "Mandrake" and "Freight Train Yodel," none of which could be classed as sentimental. Morton's Regal Zonophone recordings had eclectic themes, reflecting his strategy of intentionally varying the types of songs he sang, in trying to please as many as possible. He advised other performers to "find out what the people like, and sing it."[22] The public requested different types of songs, he recalled, and he did his best to accommodate them, both on record and at live performances.[23] This need for diversity extended to the use of the Roughriders, too. "I used to predict [at the time] that people would get tired of just guitar and voice," he said in 1969. It wasn't a matter, either, of recording solely with the band, he thought, but the variety of his material would be enhanced by using the Roughriders every now and then.[24] Results in Table 2 suggest he was most likely correct, as the likeability index for songs with the Roughriders was 0.26. His duets with Dorrie also appear to have been especially popular, even though the sales for "Old Shep" most likely boosted their likeability index of 0.37. As a "counterbalance," however, there appeared to be a slight preference for discs without Harry Thompson and Pat Fraley, although the public was probably influenced more by song choice rather than accompanying musicians. Overall, there was a slight preference for Australian compositions (likeability index of 0.10).

In later years, Morton bristled at being described as a hillbilly singer. "I'm a folk singer," he snapped. "That hillbilly tag has always annoyed me. Sure, I sing cowboy songs, but I sing sea chanties and other folksongs, too."[25] He saw himself as a collector and interpreter of folk music, but nearly all his recorded output on Regal Zonophone was clearly in the hillbilly genre.

Table 2: Dominant Attributes In Morton's Regal Zonophone Recordings (excludes data for "Sergeant Small").

ATTRIBUTE	RECORDINGS %	SALES %	LIKEABILITY INDEX
Song Theme			
sentimental	55.43	54.32	-0.05
mother	17.39	21.00	0.23
father	10.87	11.21	0.03
girlfriend	32.61	29.80	-0.13
train	6.52	7.13	0.10
horse	7.61	10.04	0.30
dog	2.17	2.61	0.19
sea	3.26	3.31	0.02
hobo	9.78	10.43	0.07
cowboy	16.30	13.15	-0.25
stockman	10.87	10.09	-0.08
comedy	9.78	11.23	0.15
Alpine/Swiss	3.26	3.23	-0.01
jail/crime/hanging	7.60	5.31	-0.38
Accompaniment			
Roughriders	10.87	13.62	0.26
Sister Dorrie	5.43	7.69	0.37
Pat Fraley	2.17	1.04	-0.75
Harry Thompson	6.52	5.35	-0.21
Source [26]			
composed by Morton	40.22	42.77	0.11
all Australian songs	47.83	49.30	0.10
foreign, local release	35.87	32.24	-0.16
foreign, no local release	16.30	17.44	0.08
all foreign	52.17	49.68	-0.10

Table 3 highlights some descriptive statistics for Morton's Regal Zonophone recordings. It shows that Morton's most productive years, based on the number of songs he recorded, were from 1936 to 1939—before World War II, prior to Arch Kerr's promotion to record-sales manager, and competition from other hillbilly artists like Billy Blinkhorn and Buddy Williams. Based on average sales-per-disc, Morton's later recordings were generally as popular as his earlier discs, though there were fewer of them. The spike for 1941 was doubtless influenced by some of his best sellers, including "Old Shep" and "Mandrake," and possibly by his popular Wild West Rodeo shows, too, which were then touring.

In all, Morton's Regal Zonophone output was prodigious. Some 649,180 records by him were sold in Australia from the time they were released until the time they were deleted from the catalog (often as late as the 1950s). This total does not include the unknown sales for "Sergeant Small." Morton's lowest seller sold a respectable 6,774 copies, and his best seller 36,117, a figure that's remarkably high, when all other discs in the Regal Zonophone catalog are considered. His average long-term sales-per-disc was about 14,000. Since Australia's population in 1940 was only about seven million,[27] this is a staggering figure and demonstrates the colossal impact of local country music, and Morton in particular, in the late 1930s and early 1940s Australia. Contemporary newspapers often stated Morton's sales were of the order of 10,000 per month. The computed average of his long-term sales over seven years suggests that while this figure was probably true for 1936 and 1937, it was somewhat less in later years. Counting Regal Zonophone sales only, Buddy Williams, in comparison, sold some 518,000 discs and Slim Dusty over 335,000 (boosted by "A Pub With No Beer," which sold over 75,000 copies on 78s), though both these artists continued recording long after Morton.

Some authors have implausibly over-inflated Morton's Regal Zonophone sales, however. Commenting on some of the more outrageous claims that have been made, discographer David Crisp wrote: "That grandiose uninformed statement that Tex sold more than everyone else put together needs to be shot down in flames, but it would be pretty safe to say he sold more than any other 'Australian' hillbilly of that 1930-1940s era. And he kept selling with no new releases."[28] Morton's sales compared favorably with some of Bing Crosby's best sellers, although Crosby had many more Australian releases than Morton in the same period, and his discs were more expensive—hence more profitable—than Morton's. But Morton's sales were usually on a par with many other popular acts, with figures continuing to impress long after their initial release.

Table 3: Some Descriptive Statistics For Morton's Regal Zonophone Recordings

YEAR	NUMBER OF SONGS	NUMBER OF SESSIONS	AVERAGE SONGS RECORDED PER SESSION	TOTAL RECORD SALES	AVERAGE SALES PER DISC
1936	18	6	3.0	127 968	14 219
1937	16	5	3.2	141 876	17 735
1938	19	5	3.8	104 714	11 635*
1939	16	4	4.0	87 722	10 965
1940	10	3	3.3	74 504	14 901
1941	10	2	5.0	89 216	17 843
1942	0	0	-	-	-
1943	4	1	4.0	23 180	11 590
Total	93	26	3.6	649 180	14 113*

*excludes "Sergeant Small"

Using release dates of records issued in Australia, it's possible to discern a general trend in Morton's musical development. As a teenager in New Zealand, Morton was unquestionably influenced by the recordings of "citybillies" like Vernon Dalhart, Carson Robison, Frank Luther and Frankie Marvin, as many of his later commercial recordings suggest. "I think Carson Robison would be the one—'Peg-Leg Jack', numbers like that, 'Barnacle Bill' started us off," he recalled;[29] but in the early 1930s he was drawn to the harder-edged music of Jimmie Rodgers and modeled his style on that of the Blue Yodeler. He was most likely influenced by the British Alpine-style yodeler Harry Torrani from about 1932, onward. He recalled that even in 1933 the public regarded him as a "darned novelty," playing his guitar, wearing a cowboy hat and singing Jimmie Rodgers songs. Sometimes, he said, he would "get up and sing one of my Jimmie Rodgers numbers—I'd sing it as much as I could like Jimmie Rodgers—and people would just say 'ho hum', because I was singing songs that were unknown to them. 'Dear Old Sunny South By The Sea,' 'Waiting for a Train', that type of thing."[30]

Barry Mazor, an expert on Rodgers, wrote: "Morton was one of the most adept Rodgers interpreters anywhere, expert in phrasing, guitar accompaniment, and the integration of the two. A saddle-weary, wistful sense of experience permeates his singing, an inherent suggestion of the blues mentality akin somewhat to Ernest Tubb's, which comes through even though he does not sing blues."[31]

Morton recalled that it was Rodgers who had profoundly influenced him and his singing style. He even invented stories of having lived in the United States, and of meeting Rodgers and his friends. Although these tales were undoubtedly fictitious, Morton was probably attempting to accentuate the link between his music and Rodgers's recordings, and to reinforce his authenticity in performing early country music outside North America. Morton recorded only two of the Singing Brakeman's songs ("Dreaming with Tears in My Eyes" and "When the Cactus Is in Bloom") for Regal Zonophone; perhaps Columbia dissuaded him from covering Rodgers's material, since many of the original versions were already in their catalog. In later years, Morton recorded other songs by Rodgers, and two of these were issued internationally on compact disc by Germany's prestigious Bear Family Records.[32] When Morton became popular and was given credit for kick-starting Australian country music he asserted that, because he had modeled much of his style on that of Rodgers, "the real credit [for the development of Australian country music] should go to Jimmie Rodgers and people like him."[33] This contention was supported by Mike Paris and Chris Comber, two British country music authorities who described the influence Rodgers had not only on Morton but also on early Australian country music in general: "From the beginning of his career . . . Morton's guitar style, vocals and repertoire were all heavily influenced by Rodgers, though his yodeling owes more to the unusual style of Goebel Reeves. As [folklorist] John Greenway has suggested, the Rodgers influence is common in modern Australian styles."[34]

"When this 'father of Australian country music' wrote songs, they would be squarely in the Rodgers mode in sound and theme," wrote Rodgers scholar Barry Mazor, of Morton. "His celebrated 'On the Gundagai Line' is a Rodgers-like but specifically Australian hobo number, and he also performed nostalgic songs about his mother and his dear old pals that featured Rodgers guitar runs."[35]

Although Morton's usual accompaniment was just his own guitar, Rodgers's backings ranged from solo guitar to small hillbilly bands and Hawaiian and jazz groups, to Louis Armstrong and his then-wife, Lillian. Morton borrowed much from Rodgers's singing, yodeling, and guitar style, but some of Rodgers's music veered away from pure hillbilly—Tony Russell noted that Rodgers saw himself as a gardener in the local parkland of popular music, rather than in the backyard plot of hillbilly.[36] Morton's music was unambiguously in the hillbilly fold, with increasingly Australian influences.

Dr. Damien Kingston, a lecturer at the University of Tasmania's Conservatorium of Music, analyzed Morton's singing and guitar playing, and the performance of the Roughriders. His evaluation is as follows, with figures in parentheses referring to the time, in minutes and seconds, after the recording commenced:

> Morton sang with a light vibrato, often in a conversational manner, drenched in country and blues melodic inflection. At the extremes of his register, Morton's vocal range was considerable, covering at least four octaves in select performances; Morton combined this impressive range with a variety of expressive techniques and approaches. Morton's melodic pitching is impeccable throughout his recorded output, a fact that may not seem obvious at first listen, due to his extreme use of slurs and grace notes when rendering a melodic line—commonly Morton will approach the original melody from a tone away, either above or below, and slur into the melody note. Other expressive devices include the deliberate use of vocal cracks; this approach commonly utilizes a grace note in the falsetto register falling rapidly to the desired melody note.
>
> In addition to these materials, Morton employed a range of "novelty" vocal techniques in many of his performances, including the mimicking of trains, vocal trills, semispoken passages and affected accents, and most prominently the yodel. Yodeling passages were used for a variety of purposes throughout Morton's recorded output; commonly however the yodel appears in introductory passages or between verses as a 'fill' or vocal ornamentation. When used in this manner a common melodic line often recurs. Below is a simplified version of the phrase written in the key of C major:

> The above phrase appears in many pieces recorded by Morton, most commonly employed over a I Major chord, the introduction to "Young Pat Maloney" (0.05) being an obvious example. The phrase is also often altered or adapted to

suit differing harmonic situations such as in "Dreaming With Tears in My Eyes" (1.24), where a variation of the phrase occurs over a I-V-I chord progression. Morton also utilises yodeling in different melodic contexts, veering from the prominent phrase discussed above, "Bonny Blue Eyes" being a wonderful example of differing melodic content yodeled. Tracks such as "The Railroad Bum" exemplify yodeling utilised in conjunction with trills in a "novelty" fashion.

Morton's guitar style utilises a mix of open chord voicings, alternating bass notes and scalar runs between different chords to create a highly effective accompaniment for his vocal delivery. The voicings used on the majority of Morton's recorded tracks are "open" voicings; seldom can barre chords be heard in use—these voicings are supported by an alternating bass note establishing a "two feel" bass line throughout. These bass lines typically alternate between the root note and the fifth of the chord. When changing from one chord to another, the bass notes are often connected by brief diatonic scalar passages; "Old Man Duff" provides a good example of this guitar style in action.

In creating differentiation between sections of a piece, Morton often varies the duration with which he sustains chords or bass notes. A common means of differentiation involves shortening the length for which chords are sustained, achieved through articulating a chord with a staccato attack by either muting with the palm or quickly releasing the chord grip with the fretting hand, Morton also arpeggiates voicings occasionally to vary his accompaniment and punctuate vocal melodies.

In an ensemble context, Morton can be heard in performance with his "Roughriders" band consisting of guitar, bass, fiddle, slide [steel] guitar and accordion. The members of the ensemble all perform on their instruments in a conventional manner, fulfilling the role common to their instrument in music of the idiom. Firstly, due to the expanded ensemble and the presence of a bass player, Morton utilises less of the two-feel bass line in his guitar playing, leaving this to the bass player. Additionally, as there are now two more melodic instruments in the ensemble, there is less need for Morton to include the brief scalar passages so common to his solo performances. "When the Cactus Is in Bloom" provides a good example of the how the ensemble functions. Both the fiddle and slide [steel] guitar play what are presumably improvised counter melodies during Morton's singing whilst the bass plays a typical "two-feel" bass line outlining the 1st and 5th degree of each chord. This continues until there are short instrumental solos from each instrument. Whilst these solos are rarely virtuosic in their content, they are entirely appropriate and effective in the context of the song.[37]

Technical excellence alone, however, does not an artist make. Morton's heartfelt singing, yodeling and simple guitar style transcended his limitations and appealed to large numbers of the public in a manner unlike many other, more musically accomplished, artists. Author Eric Watson wrote:

> The sheer drive and vitality that he could breathe into a number, the superb control of his voice, the intensity of feeling for his subject, the effect and sympathy he could achieve with half a dozen first position chords and three or four elementary runs. Listen to "Freight Train Yodel" on the old Regal Zonophone disc. There are three chords, plus the tonic 7th, and one first-lesson run, yet though I've played that disc and heard it on radio several thousand times, the guitar playing still fascinates me, and I believe it to be one of the most effective pieces of accompaniment I've ever heard.[38]

Morton's singing and guitar playing were models for future Australian country music artists who were inspired by him, like his one-time rival Buddy Williams, and Slim Dusty, the future "king of Australian country music." But there were scores—if not hundreds—of amateurs who bought a Tex Morton guitar, one or more of his Nicholson's songbooks and some of his records, and tried to sing and yodel like the boundary rider. Indigenous Australians were influenced by Morton, too. Aboriginal country artist Herb Laughton remembered Morton traveling through Central Australia, and recalled his performances were an inspiration for him. "I used to mimic Tex Morton all the time," he said.[39] Also, Lionel Rose, boxing champion-turned-entertainer, was inspired by Syd Santo who sang and yodeled in Tex Morton style.[40] Similarly, Indigenous artists Harry Williams[41] and Kevin Gunn[42] first learned to play Tex Morton songs on guitar.

The general absence of backing groups on Morton's records prior to 1941 no doubt was a stimulus for him to render his guitar playing more expressive and effective. When he was busking, his only accompaniment was his own guitar, so he would habitually stay up at nights practicing guitar runs and devising new ones—key factors once rivals like Buddy Williams and Billy Blinkhorn appeared on the scene. Thus performers differentiated themselves by trademark yodeling and guitar playing.

Morton clearly identified with working-class people, explaining that his music was more likely to appeal to the blue-collar classes rather than to musical sophisticates who sometimes looked down their noses at his music. When he toured with Jim Davidson and the formally trained Gladys Moncrieff, for example, he proudly acknowledged that his and Moncrieff's audiences were likely to be poles apart: she appealed to the more cultivated crowd, whereas his followers were more often working-class folk.[43] His songs reflected this, with recurrent references to hobos, stockmen, cowboys, and prisoners; further, in "Just Plain Folks" he was critical of the snobbishness of some upper-class people. In addition to his romanticized escapist songs about the West and the Outback, Morton's identification with the down-and-out surely resonated with Depression-era listeners during the 1930s and afterwards.

Folklorist Graham Seal noted that while Morton's motives were mixed between commercial popularity and a deep interest in everyday life, he helped ensure the continuity of the Australian bush-song tradition into and through the era of electronic, early radio and sound recording.[44] Morton's connection to rural Australia was strengthened by his friendship with Banjo Paterson and his poetry, and through his touring Wild West circus and rodeo. While he recorded only a few traditional Australian compositions for Regal Zonophone—paving the way for the Australian bush ballads of the likes of Slim Dusty—he most likely sang and recited more of them on his radio shows. Clippings from his personal memorabilia reveal a close affiliation with the bush and riders such as the Skuthorpes.

Seal summarized how Morton's Regal Zonophone recordings fused local themes and motifs with American-style hillbilly music:

> Morton's own compositions also link with important themes and issues of Australian folksong tradition.... The free and easy, if hard, itinerant lives of the overlanders, swagmen and other bush laborers of the nineteenth century is the basis of songs about the bagmen of the 1930s who travelled by train (illegally) rather than by horse, but whose ethos and experiences were very similar. Morton used terms derived from American country music, such as "hobo" and "bum" and "durn." But he early perceived an interest in his audiences for recognizably Australian story songs that used Australian terms and told Australian stories.[45]

Seen through the lens of the twenty-first century and the continual evolution of country music—to the extent that a great deal of contemporary country music bears little resemblance to its earliest incarnation on discs—Morton is regarded by many as an authentic, hardcore country artist, though others have dismissed him as something of a "dead hillbilly," a far-flung reminder of the music's past. Throughout his career, however, Morton went to great lengths to prove himself as a bona fide country music performer. A barrier at the time might have been that he was not an American and so he attempted to create fictitious links to performers like Jimmie Rodgers and an imaginary upbringing, and later, claims of performing alongside Hank Williams.

Simultaneously, he created an image of both a truly Australian hillbilly and Western performer by writing songs with Australian settings and characters, and modifying his stage dress from cowboy clothing to that of an Australian stockman or boundary rider, all the while maintaining American connections by promoting his touring shows as "Wild West" entertainment and, at times, using American enunciations in his speech and songs.

Arch Kerr conceded that there was a conscious attempt on Columbia's part to incorporate local themes and settings in Australian country music to establish "Australian country ... songs as Australian, and not merely copies of American stuff." He argued that "we had the background to build up an Australian style of musical recording."[46] Kerr thus instructed his artists to sing with Australian accents, and was especially critical of Morton because, he contended, Morton sang with American inflections. But Kerr emphasized that Australian country music was much more than singing with an Australian tone, and involved lyrics centered on local motifs as well. Tony Russell wrote that characteristics of early Australian country music included "distinct regional accents, modifications of the borrowed style, and, gradually, a development of an Australian country consciousness."[47]

In its simplest form, localizing Australian country music apart from its American progenitor involved simple substitutions that rendered songs "Australian": "Beautiful Queensland" is an obvious example. Further along the continuum, Morton's "On the Gundagai Line" was an original composition clearly set in Australia; so too with "Murrumbidgee Jack" and "Aristocrat." At the extreme end of the continuum might be wholly developed bush ballads with robust links to an Australian heritage—"Wrap Me Up in My Stockwhip and Blanket," for example—leading to fully evolved compositions by the likes of Slim Dusty. Clearly, there was much more to creating an Australian country music form than merely adopting a local tone of voice, though some latter-day performers do sing with strong, arguably exaggerated, Australian accents.[48]

8

TEX MORTON'S FABULOUS WILD WEST RODEO

A SIGNIFICANT FACET of Morton's legacy during the 1940s was his traveling Wild-West rodeo, in which he toured with buckjumpers and roughriders, circus acts, whip-crackers and others, as well as performing himself as a sharpshooter, singer and yodeler. Two major roughriding families who toured with him during those heady years were the Skuthorpes and the Gills. The tours commenced in 1940 and involved, along with an eclectic range of acts, an extensive train of vehicles to haul the horses, circus acts and equipment. Touring lasted until 1949, except during 1942 and 1943, when wartime fuel rationing forced Morton off the road. The combination of rodeo, circus and hillbilly singing was novel in Australia at the time, and other artists like Buddy Williams and Smoky Dawson later followed Morton's lead, blending singing with other circus-style acts while on tour.

The concept of merging hillbilly music with roughriding shows was not new, however. In the United States, musicians like Otto Gray and his band had toured with comparable rodeo-type acts, though historian Kevin Coffey said such combinations "were not at the upper echelon" and they gradually faded out over time.[1] Nevertheless, the pairing of hillbilly music with roughriding and circus shows was no mere imitation of the American concept, since Morton, and those who followed his example, personified Australian rural workers and not gunslinging cowboys from the American West. The concept was built on a long-established tradition of roughriding and buckjumping shows that had been part of the local entertainment scene since the 1850s. Lance Skuthorpe Sr., Thorpe McConville and the Gills all had their own touring shows well before Morton came onto the scene, but incorporating hillbilly stars of radio and records yielded an especially lucrative combination.[2]

From the outset, manager Bill Scott encouraged his protégé to embark on Wild West shows. Initially, the two settled on a strategy of combining Morton's singing and sharpshooting with a team of roughriders, and touring country areas with them, even though on paper it seemed to be like selling ice to Eskimos. Similar approaches had failed before but, blended with the Skuthorpes' buckjumping show, an inaugural four-month trial early in 1940 was a huge success with country folk queuing up to attend.[3] One appearance was in April 1940,[4] only a few months after the successful Tasmanian tour. By about May 1940, however, Morton was touring with the Gills—Stan, Jack and Kitty.[5]

Scott, who optimistically contemplated international exposure for his young star, even wrote to Prime Minister John Curtin in 1941, seeking financial support for Morton's roughriding show to tour the United States, and suggesting that American audiences would be mightily impressed with the Australian riders.[6] That year, Scott was telling reporters that he had secured a Hollywood contract for his young star, and confidently believed that the entire Wild West Rodeo show would travel around the United States.[7] International travel seemed to be something of a pipe dream with Morton, though: he habitually stated his intention of touring overseas, something he only achieved in 1950. In 1938, for example, he told a magazine that he was leaving Sydney for England and America.[8] Two years later, with characteristic entrepreneurial flair, Scott boasted that Morton would be a motion-picture star in the United States.[9] The same year, Queensland's *Cairns Post* announced: "It is therefore with a pang of regret that we read now of Tex's forthcoming departure for overseas. For very shortly, he says farewell to the sunny shores of Australia and sets sail for the golden streets, the bright lights of Hollywood."[10] The same paper, however, later stated that "owing to war conditions ... Tex Morton's trip to the United States has been held over for the time being."[11]

THE SKUTHORPES AND THE GILLS

Morton initially teamed with the Skuthorpe family of roughriders when Scott suggested the two acts combine, although it's possible that he had previously met one or more of the family in Sydney. The patriarch of the

Skuthorpe Family was Lance Skuthorpe Sr., generally acknowledged to have been the first Australian to run buckjumping as the main act in Wild West shows.[12] The older Skuthorpe is still remembered for his publicity stunt of 1896, in which he jumped a horse, virtually sideways, over a fence six feet high onto a narrow, six-foot-wide ledge, one side of which was bounded by a perilous, yawning 300-foot chasm above Blue Lake, near Mount Gambier,[13] repeating Adam Lindsay Gordon's feat of 1864.[14] He also wrote short stories—the *Bulletin* had published one of his works, "The Champion Bullock Driver," in 1921.[15] Following a successful career as a showman and roughrider, Skuthorpe, his wife Violet (also a roughrider), and their three children settled near Sydney, after an arduous life on the road.[16] Author Jenny Hicks wrote that Lance Sr. and his son Lance Jr. "carried themselves with an air of authority,"[17] and described Lance Jr. as "a bit of a Renaissance man" who was a formidable horseman, an amazing athlete, and a fearsome fighter, and that "among the tough, gnarled-skinned traveling showmen, he was rated the best bare-knuckle fighter of his generation." As a youngster, he had ridden horses in his father's touring shows and had buckjumped bareback in challenges against people his own age in the towns they passed through, always staying on long enough to win despite being thrown occasionally.[18] His father described him as "easily the best buckjump rider I have ever seen."[19] Yakima Canutt, the Hollywood stuntman who had coached young Lance, claimed he would make a superb rodeo performer in America.[20]

In 1938, Lance Jr. and his sister Violet toured with Western star Colonel Tim McCoy's show in North America. Chaperoned by their mother, the Skuthorpes performed alongside three other Australian roughriders,[21] impressing American audiences with their expertise and daring; Violet was described in a newspaper as "a regular Boadicea for courage."[22] They dressed in Australian costume: white moleskin trousers, concertina leggings, elastic-side boots, red shirts, cowhide waistcoats, and hats turned up at the side. The Skuthorpes, however, had to leave after six months, when their visas expired,[23] but before McCoy's show folded in 1938, losing some 300,000 dollars.[24]

Morton was a mate of Lance, the senior Skuthorpe. "I loved the old fellow like a father," he said. "Hour after hour we'd sit by the campfire after the horses were fed—while the boys were dismantling our 'rodeo-circus' tent and gear 'til the early hours of the morning, when the old man recounted tale after tale of the 'old days.'" He was, said Morton, "one of the quickest thinking, shrewdest old timers" he had ever met. Skuthorpe Sr. even took Morton into the bush to introduce him to his mates from earlier days to demonstrate his horse-training skills. Morton had a copy of the old bushman's story "The Giant Of Brady's Gap" in his personal files.[25] Journalist and friend Colin Mackay said the elder Skuthorpe was one of only two people Morton idolized and always referred to him with the salutation "Mr.," the other person so highly esteemed being Lionel Bibby.[26]

Morton also toured with the Gills, who accompanied him in the early 1940s. Stan Gill had married Violet Denner, and the couple had seven children. Stan was described as "a true salt-of-the-earth man who would back you to the hilt as a friend, and packed a punch like a kick from a mule for anyone trying to do you down."[27] In 1940, Stan Gill Jr. married Kitty West, one of the finest female roughriders of the time. She was Australia's world-champion female buckjump rider in 1945, 1947 and 1951. Known as the "Queen of the Cowgirls," she occasionally appeared in the ring wearing a black outfit intended to arouse men in the audience into a frenzy.[28] A 1940 newspaper report lauded her for her feat, "unheard [sic] of in riding, from Cairns to Perth and back, across the Nullabor Plain, all on the same horse." Stan and Jack, a paper said, "have carried off every Australian all-round championship against all comers, for the past five years."[29]

Jack Gill was a superb whip-cracker and could strike a match with a lash from four meters and crack a huge whip some 50 feet long.[30] Author Jenny Hicks thought there was rivalry between Jack Gill and Lance Skuthorpe Jr. It was said that Jack was the superior roughrider, as he could stay on very spirited horses, but Lance had a prettier style. All three—Jack, Stan and Lance—were hard, tough and wild. They were first-rate fighters and Lance, it was said, was the finest all-round athlete of the three.[31]

Morton's Wild West rodeo shows were a massive success from the outset. Since the income from his recordings was insignificant in the main, the earnings from traveling rodeos enabled him to become moderately wealthy. Additionally, it allowed him to make personal contact with fans who lived in the country. Dressed in khaki, Morton typically presented himself as a smooth-talking stockman, although he nearly always used the term "Wild West" in naming his traveling shows, doubtless attempting to cash in on Hollywood imagery, which was especially popular at the time.

Morton was a showman par-excellence. He had it all: from spruiking crowds and fabricating a fictitious, colorful past, to performing himself and guaranteeing the public came away begging for more. "Tex Morton was legendary for 'sucking them in,'" wrote Jenny Hicks.[32] He could put a positive spin on just about anything, like the time his show was in an enclosure with tiered seating and a hessian[33] (fabric) wall, but no roof, and it was raining, and he exhorted people to come in and see the show "to get out of the rain."[34] It was as if showmanship had been infused into his DNA. He might even have been the most effective showman Australia has produced. Morton didn't just act the part of a showman when it was required of him, he lived and breathed the life as well. "He was a showman 24 hours a day," recalled Slim Dusty in an interview,[35] and from another account, described Morton as "the greatest showman of his time that we've ever had in this country. He's never been surpassed, and I doubt if he ever will be."[36] Morton relished the roving lifestyle demanded of his occupation, too. His 1970 song "The Travelling Showman"[37] extolled the carefree wanderlust of touring days—packing up at daybreak, driving through unfamiliar countryside far from oppressive cities, hunting and fishing, giving his wife jewels, and educating his children and grandchildren in the ways of the world, alternately earning and then losing small fortunes. Years of peripatetic touring embedded the details of bucolic roads and towns on Morton's psyche, too. Journalists who drank with him during the 1970s, for example, remembered his encyclopedic knowledge of rural locations. They recalled that he seemed to know every small town, and the names of all the hotels and their barmaids, too. In contrast to his younger days, according to some of the journalists' accounts, he was friendly with the local police.[38]

Much of the credit for the triumphs of the early Wild West Rodeo shows belonged to Bill Scott, who had conceived the idea in the first place. Most likely Scott would travel ahead of the main entourage and publicize his protégé's imminent arrival by placing advertisements in newspapers, days in advance of Morton's appearance—necessary, given the distances fans would often travel to see their star—as well as planting prewritten, romanticized, largely fictional accounts in local papers probably eager to fill column space with such "exclusives" of Morton's rise to fame. Typically, an advertising blurb consisted of a concocted, embellished rags-to-riches narrative of Morton's early life, then expounding on the sheer size of the show, and forecasts that the singing sharpshooter would soon be on his way to Hollywood. Scott would have made bookings with town officials, organized local show grounds or similar venues, and was probably in charge of supervising financial dealings, paying rental for hire of grounds and organizing the payroll for Morton's crew.

Morton's popularity at the time was legendary. "The country people worshipped Tex and traveled hundreds of miles to see and hear him," Dick Carr remembered.[39] Morton regularly drew two thousand to three thousand people a night, six nights a week.[40] When the seats were filled, fans would sit on tarpaulins that covered the ground around the ring, to view the show, and children would now and then sneak into the tent by crawling underneath the canvas, away from the big top's entrance. Morton was aware that some of his audience had not paid to see the performances, and his crew would keep interlopers out by pushing on the tent walls, from the inside.[41]

THE FIRST TOURS OF MORTON'S WILD WEST SHOW

Morton toured with the Skuthorpes in his first full-fledged circus and rodeo in 1940. Later that year, his show had expanded, and he was with the Gill Brothers instead. There were buckjumping horses, ridden by some of Australia's best roughriders, including Queensland champion Arthur Winters, Johnny McCormack, Tom Curran, "Bushman" Bill Francis, along with the celebrated Gill family. There were Indigenous riders, too, like Billy Bargo ("the finest Aboriginal rider Australia has produced") and Sam Kelly ("probably the oldest roughrider in the world today"). Among the drawcards were female equestrians— "the society-girl roughrider," Gwen Duncan, and Kitty Gill—even Morton's wife, Marjorie, appeared as a "lady trick rider."[42] Circus acts showcased Kid McCleod ("the world's greatest rope spinner") and escape artist Leon Fredini. Morton sang towards the end of the show and performed as a sharpshooter and a whip-cracker—it was said he could part a man's hair with a stockwhip from a distance of twenty feet.[43] Morton's brother Kim accompanied the circus during the 1940s[44] and Morton named his favorite horse after him.[45] Kim said Morton was a respected boss, tough but fair. "Anyone up to any nonsense was out," he declared. "It was a fantastic life. You were out in the open; you worked hard; you played hard."[46]

At Townsville in 1940, in a show compèred by Philip Wirth (of Wirth's Circus), crowds marveled at Jack Gill's whip-cracking skills, striking a match fifteen feet away with a stockwhip, and Morton's sharpshooting—he demolished a cigarette clasped in an assistant's mouth and then split a playing card held sideways at forty feet,[47] before entertaining the crowd with his singing. Morton told a reporter that he proposed to take the show to Hollywood, boasting that Australian riders were equal to or better than any in the world.[48] In Mackay, the governor of Queensland was so impressed with Morton's rodeo that he brought some of his imperial friends to view it, declaring it to be "the type of entertainment that Australian people want."[49] The 1940 tour—recurrently advertised as "Tex Morton's Wild West Rodeo and Circus," or sometimes as "Tex Morton and his Australian Wild West Rodeo Circus"—trekked through northern New South Wales and as far north as Townsville in Queensland, and back again, ending with prolonged sojourns in Newcastle and Sydney in November. A magazine review read:

> Splendid entertainment from beginning to end, Tex's show is deserving of the highest praise. Thrilling displays of rough-riding by leading Australian exponents of the art (both male and female), trick riding by clowns, demonstrations by strong men, and numerous other attractions keep the audience on the qui vive for a full two and a half hours. And Tex himself. What an artist! That careless drawl, that odd mixture of sophistication and naiveté in his speech. From the moment he takes the microphone, Tex has his listeners right in the hollow of his hand. You may not like yodelling, but you've got to admit that Tex is a past master at it.[50]

In 1941, again with the Gills, the rodeo headed south from Sydney before winding north to Queensland as far as Cairns, then inland to the Atherton Tableland. The rodeo spotlighted the roughriding of Billy Bargo and lone female rider Gwen Duncan. Contortionist and escape artist Leon Fredini again wowed the crowd with feats of strength, Ernie Harrison showcased rope-spinning tricks, there was a roughriding competition, and Morton ("the star of the show") sang with his Roughriders band and shot a card, held edgeways, in half.[51] But when he endeavored to travel to Queensland, he had to take his outfit off the road due to wartime fuel rationing. Instead, he transported his rodeo by train.[52]

In June, the attraction again drew massive crowds, showcasing Morton singing with his "cowboy band," roughriding by Bargo, the Gills and Bushman Bill Francis, plus Morton's and Dorrie's sharpshooting act.[53] The circus then headed south to Melbourne, variously named as "Tex Morton's Wild West Show," "Tex Morton's Wild West Rodeo" or "Tex Morton's Wild West Rodeo and Circus." The associated equipment was worth 6,000 pounds, and the transport fleet included the world's largest horse trailer, some forty feet in length, capable of accommodating thirty horses.[54] The years 1940 and 1941 were, it seems, the golden age of Morton's traveling rodeo—it must truly have been a magnet to country folk with its roughriding, circus acts, novelty events for children, and Morton's peerless sharpshooting and singing with Dorrie.

Roughrider Joe Ellul was with Morton and the Gills in the early 1940s and recalled that the showman was especially easy to get on with and was "one of the boys." He was generous with money, too. Ellul said Morton typically had seven to ten buckjumpers and was an outstanding shot with a rifle.[55] Buckjumping exhibitions could be unnerving for audiences at times, according to one spectator, who remembered Morton at one show repeatedly advising patrons to sit well away from the ring, to no avail. "As the mare bucked around the ring, urine flew out of her like a busted hose and the remaining people at the ringside caused a great deal of amusement as they responded, scrambling over each other trying to get out of range!" he wrote.[56]

On tour, Morton slept in his caravan, "The Queen of the Road," and was always ready to prepare a barbecue. Morton used a specific ironbark wood as fuel, and could cook potatoes, sausages, steak and the like. He loved cuisine and in later years had a special recipe for chili con carne. He'd habitually be up until the early morning, conversing on his ham radio to others all over the world.[57] For some reason, he encouraged fans and fellow entertainers alike to scratch their names on his car.[58] A 1940 magazine article comically stated: "Have you seen Tex Morton's car? ... For some strange reason Tex persuaded every inhabitant in Queensland to scratch their name on the body, or maybe he didn't. Anyway, there's approximately ten million of them indented on the paint (what's left of it)."[59]

Morton would routinely appear on radio, singing and promoting that night's show. An announcer on 2KM-Kempsey, recalled one visit:

> The rumor was that Tex Morton and his mobile rodeo were coming to Kempsey any minute. There's a knock on the door at the studio, and a smiling gentleman, his hat on the back of his head, and an entourage of Sister Dorrie and three other musos, whose names I can't recall. He said who they were. "I'm Tex Morton and I have come to tell you about the show that is coming to town for the next few days." So Tex came in with Sister Dorrie and his musos with their instruments and he said, "What program have you got running at the minute?" ... and he said, "Oh well, what about a live show free and I'll tell the folks about

the Tex Morton Show." So, in a quarter of an hour he set everything up in our tiny studio, the microphone was ready to switch on, and I crossed from the normal record show to Tex Morton live. And he came on like gang busters. He was just wonderful. He sang half a dozen songs. He, of course, plugged loudly and successfully the fact that his show was starting tomorrow and how much it would cost, and the kids were especially welcome. He would be here three days and then, "I move to wherever" and introduced his Sister Dorrie.[60]

Another announcer with radio station 2TM-Tamworth during the 1940s remembered when Morton and Dorrie occasionally visited to promote their rodeo-circus, they "always impressed everyone at the station ... as they could do something we had not experienced before," then continuing, he wrote: "You set the level before they went on to air, and you could read a book from there on. They were so experienced that you didn't have to chase levels with these two; they moved in and out of the mike so well that levels were perfect all the time."[61]

Early in 1942 Morton and some of his crew were drinking during off-hours at a Melbourne hotel when the premises were raided by the police, who charged the licensee with illegally disposing of liquor and having persons unlawfully on the premises. Morton and his mates, however, failed to appear in court in March, and he was fined one pound[62] for not attending, when he had been a subpoenaed witness. The law followed up by contacting Morton's manager, Scotty, whose address was listed as South Yarra, an affluent Melbourne suburb that suggested he was earning big-time while promoting Morton.[63] In hindsight, one wonders if paying Morton's fine might have been the straw that finally broke the camel's back for Scott, who seems to have vanished from the scene shortly afterwards. Perchance Morton's freewheeling lifestyle had proven too much even for his American manager.

By 1942, Morton had separated from Wirth's Circus, but advertisements promised the same two-hour shows that Wirth's had boasted.[64] By then, he had incorporated boxing into his program which then consisted of thirty-two acts compèred by Stan Gill.[65] Sharpshooting and whip-cracking performances could be especially stressful for the sometimes-hapless accomplices. An assistant to whip-cracker Brian Gill recalled the tension involved: he had to hold a cigarette in his mouth while Gill flicked it off with his whip, or place a small coin on his tongue for Gill to remove it with his lash. "Every time he did that, I would shut my eyes and hope for the best," he said. "Sometimes he turned up half cut [inebriated] and then I would really pray."[66]

ENTERTAINING THE AMERICANS

In 1942 Morton had an initial two-week engagement to entertain American troops at their base in Rockhampton, Queensland. Camp Rockhampton was home to the US 41st Infantry Division, part of the US Army Corps, between July 1942 and early 1944.[67] Accompanied by Dorrie, Morton stayed some twenty months instead of the contracted fortnight. It's possible that the United States Army commandeered the circus and underwrote it.[68] The show was sometimes advertised as "Tex Morton's Frontline Carnival."[69] It was stationary, and attended by Australians and American servicemen alike. Soldiers from the United States could pit their skills against locals in boxing and roughriding competitions, allowing Australians to let off steam by challenging the visiting GIs who, it was said, were "overpaid, over-sexed and over here," a grievance felt by some Australians who resented the better-paid Americans forming relationships with Aussie females.[70] Morton recalled altercations between inebriated Australian and American troops at his shows: "Often drunken free-for-alls would flare up in the stands and the troops would set about each other with anything handy—bottles, seats, boots—the lot. When this happened, we would turn out the lights and leave them to it while we went back to my caravan to play stud poker."[71] Morton recalled that "some of our poker games ran for days. We played with ... American generals, Aussie privates, curious civilians, anyone with a few quid [money] to chance. We swore a lot, drank a lot and complained bitterly about lack of sleep, but the game still raged on."[72]

Early in 1944, Morton resumed touring on a reduced scale, showing at Queensland and northern New South Wales as "Tex Morton's Rodeo" or "Tex Morton's Rodeo and Circus," promising "two and a half hours of thrills, spills and red-blooded action" with twenty outlaw horses, bucking steers and comedy mules for children to ride.[73] Admission prices were three or four shillings for adults and one shilling and sixpence for children.[74] Given these prices, and assuming a nightly crowd of some 2,500 people, consisting of families each comprising two adults and two children, the nightly takings (with his bigger tents) would have been some 280 pounds. Since the average annual wage for male managers and clerks in 1940 was about 376 pounds[75] this is an extraordinary figure, although Morton's overhead costs at the time are unknown. Assuming he showed an average of only three performances a week, with these attendances, the figures extrapolate to takings of over

40,000 pounds per annum—comparable to over 2 million Australian dollars in today's currency.[76]

In 1945, Morton again toured with the Skuthorpes, passing through New South Wales and western Victoria and then to South Australia. The tour was interrupted by Morton and Lance Jr being charged with rape in July, resulting in Dorrie leaving for a few months after a tiff with Morton; but in the meantime, Marjorie accompanied her estranged husband and assisted with his sharpshooting act. Dorrie didn't return until around November that year.[77]

"Tex Morton's 1946 Rodeo and Circus," again with Lance Skuthorpe Jr, commenced in South Australia before embarking north to New South Wales, and then further north to Queensland, returning to Melbourne through New South Wales and Victoria. While passing through Canberra, the national capital, Morton visited Parliament House, where his vivid tie was complimented by politicians.[78] By then he owned a larger tent capable of seating almost 3,000 people; it had dimensions of 90 by 150 feet and was worth some 1,000 pounds.[79] The entourage was likened to a miniature city, with its own lighting system, army-type cookhouse, caravans and trucks. Morton told a reporter that locals were invited to try their skills on buckers like "Mandrake," "The Villain," "Blackout" and "The Snake."[80] In January, at Gawler, South Australia, however, some in the audience complained bitterly about the four shillings and eleven-pence admission cost and the incorrectly advertised location of the circus.[81]

In 1947, Morton pooled his rodeo with Ashton's Circus. The larger show featured country singers and yodelers, acrobats, gymnasts, high-wire acts, clowns, comedians, trick riding, bicycle acts, performing dogs and ponies, buckjumping, whip-cracking, sharpshooting, knife throwing, and bull riding.[82] According to Doug and Phyllis Ashton, Morton and Ashton's each had a fifty percent share in the enterprise, and a typical night's entertainment was comprised of alternating buckjumping and circus acts. Doug Ashton later said Morton had the best horses in Australia and the cream of Australian roughriders. He recalled Morton as very professional, easy going, extremely amiable and unproblematic to work with. "With Tex Morton we got stacks of money," he said. "As a matter of fact, he got too much money too quick. Everywhere we went we had packed houses. He had a very good following." Morton, he confirmed, was an extraordinary showman: "These days, he would have made a million dollars."[83]

By 1943 Morton's manager was George Melrose, later described as the advance representative and touring manager for the traveling rodeo on the 1947 tour of South Australia and Western Australia.[84] Previously, Melrose had been an actor in stage plays and at one time had managed a Shakespearean company.[85] A 1947 article declared that he had been with Morton for five years, making 1942 the date he had joined the show. Melrose already had long-term experience with traveling rodeos. Like Scott, he predicted that Morton would soon be leaving for Hollywood to make pictures, this time with the James Cagney Company, adding the novel twist that a kangaroo would also be cast in Morton's movies.[86]

CROSSING THE ARID NULLARBOR

In 1947, as "Tex Morton's Circus and 1947 Wild West Rodeo" or "Tex Morton's 1947 Circus and Rodeo," the show headed westward from Melbourne, through Victoria to outback New South Wales and then to South Australia, before heading farther west, traversing some 1,000 kilometers of the arid Nullarbor Plain by train, on eight flatbeds, and two passenger cars for its thirty-eight performers.[87] Morton was still with Ashton's during this tour, and the show included "the cream of the circus world," including boxing ponies and high-jumping greyhounds, along with "daredevil riders and famous outlaws," as well as Morton and Dorrie, all performing in a tent capable of seating 2,700 people.[88] After a stopover in Perth, Morton then returned eastward across the Nullarbor by road, since coal was in short supply,[89] to South Australia and then Victoria. While crossing the Nullarbor, two trucks that broke down had to be towed for 200 miles.[90] Brother Kim vividly remembered the incident: "How many people know that we set a world record as we drove back over the Nullarbor from the West (due to the rail strikes in Victoria)? My truck sheared a horseshoe clip on the front universal and dropped the drive shaft into the dirt a couple of hours after we left Norseman. From there I was towed for four days and three nights until we finally found someone near Adelaide who could effect repairs."[91]

Later that year, Morton and his entourage were at the Brisbane Exhibition in Queensland,[92] and while in Brisbane he also sang at intermissions in movie theatres.[93] An advertisement described his show as "circus and zoo"[94] and "thrill circus,"[95] or simply as "Tex Morton's 1947 Circus."[96]

In 1948, Morton again teamed with Ashton's Circus, commencing with a tour of the island state of Tasmania, most likely with a stripped-down version of his full show. After covering the length and breadth of the island, he was back in Victoria, with his full rodeo and circus, which again was described as resembling a miniature township, with its mobile army cooker, power plants and camping tents.[97] From there, the intrepid showman ventured northward through New South Wales and to Brisbane before returning to Sydney, where he was interviewed by the British-born singer and broadcaster, Wilfrid Thomas.[98]

In 1949, probably to raise much-needed funds for his forthcoming North American venture, Morton and the Skuthorpes toured northern New South Wales and then headed to Brisbane before returning to Sydney. The show was advertised as "Tex Morton's Rodeo and Circus" and, optimistically, also as a 1950 show and circus. This was Morton's final Wild West tour before he departed Australia for North America. A 1950 *Billboard* article reported that his show consisted of seventy-three people, a 105-foot round-top tent with 42-foot centers, pulled by twenty trailer-trucks, or a combination of twenty-five flatbed trucks and five cars of baggage.[99]

THE THRILL OF IT ALL

In the 1940s, the spectacle of a seemingly-endless procession of trucks, caravans, trailers, horses and colorful characters passing through a rural town, with its star loudly spruiking the show through the speakers on his fancy Buick, almost always generated sufficient excitement for schools and businesses to declare half-day holidays, in order to witness the parade. Morton's rodeo had taken the country by storm, blazing a trail for others to follow in ensuing years. "Thrills, spills and red-blooded action" was an advertising catch cry.[100] Morton habitually heightened the drama by promoting bogus claims on radio, such as declaring that one of his horses was missing and offering a reward for its return. [101]

The shows were inspirational as well. As a boy, country singer Reg Lindsay attended the Tex Morton Show and remembered that it was Morton's lifestyle that attracted him to music. Lindsay was especially moved by the sense of autonomy in Morton's touring and his ability to support himself solely by entertaining.[102] Likewise, Slim Dusty wrote: "As a kid I had envied Tex Morton's star position in show business—his tailored suits, the big car, the crowds clamoring for his songs and for his autograph,"[103] and Smoky Dawson recalled the enormous impact Morton had in his heyday, with his persona of an outback singer and yodeler living a carefree existence.[104]

When the rodeo hit town, locals were invited to try their luck on the buckjumpers to win prize money, if they could stay on their mount for the allotted time. Every roughriding circus, it seemed, had a horse that had never been ridden in a challenge, and Morton's was no exception. "One thing I always noticed about traveling shows was that they had no hesitancy in allowing some of the locals to ride their buckjumpers or compete in some feat or other," recalled a spectator. "It always filled in the program at no extra cost to the outfit."[105] Ordinarily, circuses didn't have a chute to restrain the horses while the rider mounted the beast—those were American inventions (although this doesn't appear to have always been the case).[106] Instead, the horse was often blindfolded and tethered to a snubbing post. When the rider mounted the animal, a snaphook released the horse which was then free to buck.[107] Sometimes the audience rider would be harnessed by a belt to a pulley system that could lift him into the air when he was dismounted. Riders who looked like they were being successful were occasionally hoisted prematurely from their mount to ensure they wouldn't win the prize money on-offer. When one disgruntled participant complained about this, Morton smiled and replied, "It's all in the game, son."[108] Although he was sometimes photographed astride horses in his shows, Morton was no more than a passable rider. "The popular belief at the time," wrote Jim Bennett, who knew him from his early days in Sydney, "was that he couldn't ride a rocking horse."[109]

Morton sometimes had an abrupt, if humorous, manner with crowds. At a 1944 show, he asked the audience if they had any requests they wanted him to sing. A chorus of boys sitting at the front of the crowd called out for "Mandrake." "Shut up you little buggers," Morton snapped. "You probably never paid in the first place!" Then he pointed to an elderly lady, who asked for "Old Shep." Another time, a performer who specialized in fancy rope tricks had imbibed too much before his act. With characteristic flair, Morton introduced him as "Australia's greatest performer with a lasso." When the intoxicated man stumbled onto the stage and repeatedly fell over attempting to spin his ropes, the audience at first chuckled and then burst out laughing. Seizing the moment, in a clever save, Morton strode on stage and announced, "Ladies and gentlemen, the reason I previously introduced this artist as 'Australia's greatest performer with a rope' was to gain your attention.

He is, in fact, Australia's greatest comedian."[110] In 1945, three audience members had to be taken to a hospital after a row of seats inside the tent collapsed, throwing 200 people to the ground.[111] One lady even suffered broken ribs. Though he gave a Meccano (erector) set to a boy who had broken a leg in the accident, Morton was reluctant to pay the hospital bills of injured spectators. When they threatened to take legal action, he remarked at his next show that "some people will complain about anything."[112] Seats also collapsed at another show in 1948, generating great excitement in the crowd. Morton stepped forward, declared the show must go on, and chastised sections of the audience for complaining.[113]

Eschewing over-the-top Western dress, Morton adopted the local equivalent of a singing cowboy—a singing stockman, if you like, or in Morton's case a yodeling boundary rider. Morton and his compatriots regularly appeared in "outback" apparel—hat, boots, and a fancy shirt, for example. A 1949 magazine article described his outfit:

> He put on a pair of high-heeled laceless Australian stockman's boots—"I never wear anything else now. Low-heeled shoes make my leg muscles ache." On top of the wardrobe was a wide-brimmed stockman's hat, and his shirt and trousers were of the same open-air style. He wore a silver belt with a magnificent silver buckle.... He lives the part of the singing cowboy every minute of the day, just as completely and intensively as most of us live our own fantasy lives for a few moments in our dreams.[114]

Barbara Lane said her brother "was always dressed very smartly, to the point of conceit. The best of everything, silk ties and always the Stetson hat. He always had nice shirts . . . he was mad keen on shirts. He always had to have two pockets and always liked a gold pen in one of them."[115]

Morton's Wild West imagery, so evident in his rodeo shows, strengthened the links between hillbilly music and rural areas, without doubt, an innovative and effective marketing strategy. In his radio shows, as well, he highlighted the persona of a singing stockman (and even though he was often referred to as a cowboy, it was clearly in an Australian context); but when he sang of the West in his Columbia recordings, it was a mythical, romanticized visualization, largely the product of songwriters influenced by Hollywood's portrayal of the Wild West, and certainly not that of authentic cowboy songs. Much later, bush balladeers like Slim Dusty sang realistically of ringers, horses, cattle roundups and the like, in an era when much American country music had largely forsaken Western themes for those of drinking, cheating and divorce, among others.

One enthusiastic Morton fan was Slim Dusty, the future "king of Australian country music." In 1990, he recalled seeing shows at Kempsey three times, and gratefully acknowledged the advice that Morton gave him the third time he saw him:

> I fronted up with my process [privately recorded] record and he gave me a good reception. He played it on the speaker system before the show and said, "This is your own local boy, Slim Dusty." I traveled with the show for about two weeks around Macksville and Coffs Harbour. I even did a few songs in the tent, in his show. He was very cooperative, gave me a lot of tips in his own professional way, and said you've got to be with the people, with your fans, but always be that little bit aloof—something which I've never ever forgotten.[116]

Constant touring, however, had its downside. Smoky Dawson recalled that, though the life of a traveling showman conjures up the spirit of adventure, the lifestyle was "nine parts blood sweat and tears, and one part the intoxication of being the centre of the universe to a packed audience for a few brief moments. You have to really need its special rewards to stand the rugged existence."[117] He recollected frequent brawls on the touring circuit, with locals sometimes trying to burn down the tent.[118] There was rivalry between competing shows, too, resulting from time to time in incidents of even outright deception when advertising posters were torn down or plastered over.[119] A persistent problem was drunken troublemakers wanting to enter the ring and ride. Because it was too dangerous to mount a buckjumper when drunk, circus hands would sometimes manhandle the intoxicated offenders out of the tent and pummel them.[120] Perhaps this was the cause of a nasty, even dangerous, situation in 1946 at Morton's show in Tumut, when several locals and Morton's rodeo hands exchanged punches.[121]

An even more serious confrontation occurred at Morton's show in Wonthaggi in 1947, when an argument erupted between one of his hands and irate members of the public. The dispute escalated into a brawl after one of Morton's "cowboys" broke the jaw of local coal miner Gordon Dell.[122] A riot ensued, with enraged townsfolk breaking into Morton's caravan, demanding that he hand over the offending employee for summary justice, and threatening to set fire to the big tent in reprisal. Fortunately for Morton, the police intervened and stopped the melee, but that didn't stop others from smashing

Morton's vehicles, slashing tires and destroying car radiators. Morton afterward claimed the incident had been sparked by one of his crew beating up a local boxing champion in a pub brawl, and the local champ's friends continuing drinking and whipping themselves into a frenzy before wreaking revenge on his rodeo.[123] But, he said, when he confronted the angry mob, they backed down, and left teary-eyed after he sang "Old Shep" to them,[124] a preposterous account, wildly at odds with existing coverage of the riot.

The incident was extensively reported in newspapers throughout Australia, but broadcaster Neville Pellitt later provided a different scenario after he had tracked down Gordon Dell, who was in his seventies when Pellitt interviewed him.[125] Dell said that he and a comrade were walking home from the Wonthaggi Workman's Club when he saw one of Morton's stagehands molesting a young girl. He confronted the offender, a scuffle broke out, and a pack of Morton's employees attacked him, breaking his jaw.[126] When the police arrived and learned what had caused the fight, they insisted the night's proceeds be donated to local charities and escorted the circus out of Wonthaggi the next day, with the instruction never to return. Morton paid twelve pounds to Dell to cover his hospital expenses.[127] A neighboring town's council heard of the incident and politely requested Morton to stay away from their community, too. "It was all a matter of a couple of roughnecks in his road crew who caused it all," Pellitt wrote. "All the bums and hangers on were a constant headache for Tex, who . . . had plenty of problems of his own."[128] Cec O'Leary, who attended some of Morton's shows in the 1940s, recalled that several of his circus hands were particularly unfriendly, excessively aggressive, and prone to picking fights.[129]

It was incidents like these, combined with the reputations of traveling showmen, which fanned the notion that their rodeos were unsavory: Peter Colman, a teenager at the time, remembered his mother expressly warning him not to go to the Tex Morton show. "Those were very conservative times," he recalled.[130] Tex Croft, another young local resident of a town where Morton's show had toured, said his mother, too, had stopped him from attending Morton's rodeo because there was a rumor that someone had threatened to shoot Morton.[131] Of more concern to parents was the notoriety hillbilly singers and roughriders had acquired, for being immoral. When the Morton show hit town, "it was time to lock up your daughters," said historian Jenny Hicks.[132] Women were frequently attracted to the fancily-dressed rodeo riders, sometimes provoking jealousy from their boyfriends who occasionally tried to bash their "pretty boy" competition. Consequently, most riders were tough and effective with their fists.

Morton was a heavy drinker and regularly imbibed before and even during shows. Sometimes sessions at the local hotel meant he would only perform when he was ready, conferring a degree of unpredictability to the night's proceedings.[133] Slim Dusty remembered Morton appearing at odd intervals during his shows, too.[134] "Tex liked a drink. Always, backstage, was a bottle of whiskey," recalled fellow showman Tommy ("The Amazing") Orchante, a member of the audience at one of Morton's 1967 shows in New Zealand. After inviting him on stage, Morton whispered in his ear, "Good on ya mate—I'm off for a drink," returning sometime later to resume his act.[135] Morton was so inebriated in Tasmania in 1940 that he had to be carried to the show in a chair.[136] "Tex was fairly tanked" during another show, according to an audience member.[137] One time at Port Macquarie, Morton had been drinking backstage for about 40 minutes, when he abruptly exclaimed, "[expletive], it's only interval. I thought the show was over!"[138] It was well known that if Morton was drinking then the crowd was told he had been detained in a local garage, having his vehicles fixed. His Australian friend, Jimmy Dean, who said he toured with Morton during the 1940s, recalled that Morton would "smoke and drink like a fish," but though "he was a bit of an outlaw" he "knew the right side of life."[139]

Mike Burraston, Morton's friend, related a comical tale of the showman's drinking:

> Tex's traveling show had arrived in an outback country town and all day the workers had been erecting the tent and seating for an evening performance. When all was completed, the local crowd started streaming in. Finally, the tent was full, and everyone was waiting for the show to commence. Unbeknown [sic] to Morton's manager, Tex was half a mile away holding court in the bar of the local pub [hotel], entertaining the locals with tales of his exploits. The waiting audience in his tent, however, [was] becoming restless, so the manager instructed a lad to get down to the pub and get [Tex] back to the show "pronto." The lad raced to the pub and tried in vain to get Tex moving. "I'll just finish me drink, lad, and tell one more yarn," Tex chortled.
>
> By the time Tex made his way back to the big top the crowd's booing and jeering was heard all over town. Tex strode to the center of the arena, took the

microphone and announced, "Ladies and gentlemen, my apologies for the delay. However, many of you would have noted the little frail grey-haired grandmother who collapsed at the entrance a little earlier. I am pleased to report that using my medical skills I managed to keep her alive until the ambulance arrived, and you'll be thrilled to learn that she made a full recovery!" The crowd erupted with cheering and applause and Tex started to sing.[140]

Although Dorrie recalled her partner disliking children,[141] Morton's shows attracted people of all ages, and there were special rides and competitions for youngsters such as "best blindfolded boy boxer," "best girl skipper," and "best boy glutton ice cream eater."[142] Morton always seemed to have time for children, as in Inverloch, when he stepped out of a hotel to be greeted by a throng of enthusiastic youngsters. He immediately took out his guitar and sang 'Old Shep' for them.[143] As a child, Mary Schlue especially remembered excitedly anticipating Morton's rodeo: "The arrival would be closely followed by the kids . . . even those whose parents couldn't afford the admission fee would talk to the performers, watch the big tent go up and look at the animals. . . . His show in the eyes of a child was wonderful . . . I think every kid in Henty knew 'Rocky Ned,'" she reminisced.[144] A teenaged Kevin King especially remembered meeting his idol on tour in the mid-1940s and being invited backstage by the hospitable showman.[145] In Mackay in 1946, Morton gave a youngster five shillings after encouraging him to yodel "I'll Be Hanged If They're Gonna Hang Me" and lending the boy his guitar to practice on.[146] His friendly, easygoing rapport with children was nowhere better-demonstrated than in a performance he gave for "all the boys and girls" in 1966, singing "The Cat Came Back," hobo songs, and yodeling tour-de-forces, with the children laughing and joining in enthusiastically.[147]

Morton's lifestyle, however, sometimes had unintended consequences. In a classic case of "don't try this at home," an impressionable teenager accidentally shot himself in the chest when he attempted "the Tex Morton trick" by spinning a 22-calibre rifle on his finger with the safety catch off. Fortunately, he survived.[148] In 1941, several youths staged an impromptu rodeo by rounding up cattle in a paddock and attempting to ride them "cowboy style."[149] Larry Dulhunty recalled that he and his teenaged friends, encouraged by Morton's train songs, held competitions to see who was the best at jumping onto moving trains.[150]

9

MARKETING TEX MORTON

MELBOURNE, VICTORIA, was home of the 3AW Hawaiian Club during the early 1940s. The club was managed by Morton's friend, Buddy Wikara, who was also associated with Tex Banes. Banes, then freshly discharged from the army, was running Hawaiian Club socials and dances, where he had established a rapport with audiences. He was also an aspiring hillbilly singer who could yodel and play guitar. When Morton visited the club in 1943, Wikara introduced him to Banes because, as Banes recalled, he was the best-known hillbilly performer in Melbourne at the time.[1]

Morton was aware of the potential rewards of combining his recording career with retailing merchandise. In a 1937 article, he had hinted at the business opportunities that arose when country music was pooled with selling guitars. "I find the more simple and easy the song, the better it sells," he wrote. "I think this is because the majority of hill billy fans own a guitar, ukulele or mouth organ themselves, and readily pick up a new melody to play at Bill Smith's wedding party, or the local charity concert."[2] That year, he had endorsed "Tex Morton Guitars" sold by J. Stanley Johnston in Sydney.[3] A 1937 advertisement reassured potential buyers that "every instrument is thoroughly tested by Tex Morton, look for his signature,"[4] suggesting that he endorsed particular brands and models by signing them, an attractive incentive to buyers, given his popularity at the time. In 1940, Allans Music ran an advertisement in which a youthful Morton proudly endorsed Gibson guitars. "Only a Gibson is good enough," the boundary rider sagely stated. Morton eventually realized the profits that could be made by manufacturing and selling his own trademark guitars and promoting them directly to aspiring entertainers through the Australian Hillbilly Club that he helped to form in 1944.[5]

Tex Morton guitars were sold by mail order for fourteen pounds and ten shillings each,[6] including instructions for learning to play. Manufactured by Harry West in a small factory in Ferntree Gully, Victoria, they were made of plywood—and were known by some as butter-box guitars, a reference to plywood boxes that were used to transport butter at the time. The instruments were painted white, perhaps as a marketing ploy to render them instantly identifiable. With an eye on continuing radio play, the promotional copy with "Tex Morton's Home Study Course For Hill-Billy, Spanish Guitar," also available through mail order, advised aspiring hillbillies that "should you strike any difficulty with any of the songs in my album, write to ... radio announcers and ask them to play the tune you want. They like getting letters and will be only too happy to oblige you."[7] Beginners who struggled through all fourteen pages of the typewritten course were assured thusly: "Well, Pal, by the time you've got through all this, you'll know a lot more about a guitar than I did when I first started to hit the headlines, and that goes for Wilf Carter and some of the best-known cowboy stars today."[8]

A 1948 advertisement for the "genuine" Tex Morton guitar reassured readers that "no matter where you live, you or your child can learn to play a Tex Morton Guitar and bring into your home the charm of music—have a chance to widen the circle of friends—or achieve a musical career. You don't require a teacher or need to have any knowledge of music."[9] Some months later, a subsequent promotion trumpeted, "Learn more in two weeks than in six months with an ordinary music warehouse!" and included a remark from a happy customer attesting to the claim.[10] Two models, a standard and a jumbo, were distributed. Later, a deluxe model was produced.[11] The guitars continued to be sold by mail order until at least 1951.[12]

Whenever he was in Melbourne, Morton would invite Banes to his touring shows, and afterwards the two would talk together in Morton's tent. In 1944, after hearing him sing Jimmie Rodgers's "Daddy and Home,"[13] Morton sensed that Banes had the ability to relate to an audience and suggested that he and Wikara form a hillbilly club in Melbourne, which later was known as the Australian Hill Billy Club. The club would hold monthly meetings, and members would be taught to play the guitar.[14] Undoubtedly, Morton also sensed a business opportunity: one of the aims of the association would be to sell the white Tex Morton guitars—each featuring a lariat-wielding cowboy on a horse—that were being pitched by mail order to wannabe cowboy and cowgirl singers. Banes assured Morton that he could teach pupils a two-chord song on the guitar within a week. Hence, a pupil was more likely to purchase one of Morton's guitars within a few days of commencing to learn the instrument. Subsequently, The Australian Hillbilly Club was formed in 1944 essentially from a merger of Melbourne's Banjo and Hawaiian clubs.[15]

Throughout Morton's early career, Nicholson's Music published a series of Tex Morton songbooks, the first of which was *Album of 21 Original Hill Billy Songs*, containing three songs written by the boundary rider. More were to follow, including *Tex Morton's Wild West and Rodeo Songbook*, advertised in 1940. Allans Music cashed in on the market, too, by publishing *Tex Morton's Australian Bush Ballads And Old Time Songs*. Songbooks were useful adjuncts to the sales of records and guitars, as they helped aspiring hillbilly stars to sing and play country music. Dudley ("Dud") Cantrell, a popular band leader of the day, transcribed some of Morton's recordings to musical notation for a songbook.[16]

Another sideline was Tex Morton comic books. The National Library of Australia, which holds an incomplete set, stated on its website that the series ran from 1947 until 1950. The comics, published by Sydney Allied Authors and Artists and printed by the Sydney *Truth* and *Allied Sportsman*, were titled *Tex Morton's Wild West Comics*.[17] They contained news of Morton's travels, words and music to some of his songs, illustrated comic strips lauding Morton as the hero in fictionalized accounts of his exploits, and a pen pal column. Readers were encouraged to submit their photographs for publication. "Action! Stories! Club News" and "Fun!" was how one issue extolled its contents. Membership was free unless a child wanted to be a full member, in which case the youngster would receive a club lapel badge, a "handsome certificate of membership" and an autographed picture of Morton, for the cost of a shilling.[18]

Although it was never expressly stated, it seems that marketing country music in 1940s Australia hinged on selling records to inspire some listeners to buy mail-order guitars, instruction manuals and songbooks, all without the need for backup bands.

10

LEGAL TROUBLES

THE RAPE CASE

In July 1945, Morton and Lance Skuthorpe were charged at Sydney's Central Court with having raped twenty-two-year-old Dorothy Ellen Doyle.[1] Both Morton and Skuthorpe pleaded not guilty, and each was released on bail.[2] The initial hearing in mid-July was adjourned until July 31. Smoky Dawson recalled many of Morton's friends rallying to support him during the crisis, including Buddy Wikara who traveled from Melbourne to Sydney and engaged "the best barrister he could find" for his friend. Dawson described Morton as a "shaking, wheezing nothing" when the charges were laid.[3] Morton's wife, Marjorie, remembered that at the time she was living in a flat in Kings Cross, Sydney, while her husband and Skuthorpe were staying at the Commodore Hotel. She said she first learned about the case when she read about it in the morning newspaper and recalled that Morton and Skuthorpe arrived at her apartment later that day, whereupon Morton asked her to be present in court for the hearing. Skuthorpe told her that his wife, Gloria, would also be at the hearing. Marjorie described the showmen's mood as "sorrow and tears."[4]

It was commonly believed at the time that the sentence for rape was death by hanging. Wikara said "they were going to hang" Morton,[5] and Marjorie recalled a prisoner in a cell, during a court hearing, calling out that Morton would be hanged the next morning.[6] But according to Professor Lisa Featherstone, of the University of Queensland and an expert on the history of sexual crimes in Australia, although the death penalty was on the books until

1955 in the state of New South Wales, it was not applied in rape cases—the penalty was usually commuted to life imprisonment—hence it was unlikely Morton would have been facing execution.[7] Nevertheless, there was robust public debate at the time about harsh penalties for young men and, at the very least, Morton and Skuthorpe had every reason to fear a lengthy prison term if they were found guilty.

During intensive cross-examination,[8] Doyle alleged that she and her friend, "Betty," and the two accused men had driven to Hornsby where Morton had his show, "to catch some horses,"[9] on Sunday, July 15.[10] The following Monday night, she and Betty had met with Morton and Skuthorpe, who had taken them to a Chinese restaurant and the four had then gone to a private house on Dillon Street. Doyle said they drank beer, and afterwards Betty left the house after arguing with Morton. She testified that Skuthorpe had tried to kiss her in a bedroom, but she had pushed him away.[11] Then, she said, Morton entered the room[12] and they all sat on the bed and "had a drink." She stated that Morton had used "bad language" and the two showmen then described what they were going to do with her. She asserted that a short time later, during a ten-minute struggle,[13] Skuthorpe pushed her on the bed, Morton removed her clothes[14], and while Skuthorpe held her down by the shoulders,[15] Morton raped her.[16] She stated that Skuthorpe did not rape her,[17] by which she most likely meant Skuthorpe did not have sex with her.

The owner of the Dillon Street dwelling, John Bickerton, testified that he had returned to his house at about 11:45 pm on the Monday night. On entering his bedroom, he found Morton and Skuthorpe sitting on the bed and Doyle standing up.[18] Empty beer bottles and glasses were scattered on a table.[19] Doyle, he claimed, appeared to have been "perfectly happy," though he also noted she was hysterical and intoxicated; she made no complaint that either Morton or Skuthorpe had assaulted her, but asked Bickerton to help her. One of the showmen told him, "We have had a little party and are leaving now."[20]

Afterwards, Doyle left the house and met with her husband, John, who stated his wife was crying and told him "something terrible had happened" to her.[21] John Doyle phoned the police at one o'clock in the morning on that Tuesday. Detective-Sergeant Oswald Milgate interviewed Doyle who made a statement at five am, and Milgate followed this up by questioning Morton and Skuthorpe in their room at the Commodore Flats, where he found the two asleep in bed. When confronted by the police, Skuthorpe proclaimed, "Everything that happened at Dillon Street was okay by her. What a thing to say about me! I would not do a thing like that."[22] Morton also denied he had committed rape and said sex with Doyle was consensual.[23] "[Expletive], that's awful. I'm a man of the world, and women aren't that hard to get," he exclaimed with expressive candor.[24] The government medical officer, Dr Percy, confirmed that he had examined the plaintiff and found nothing that would indicate rape had been committed.[25]

Marjorie recalled that Doyle presented herself as "a picture of innocence" at the hearing and was dressed like a schoolgirl with her hair in pigtails.[26] The barrister representing Morton and Skuthorpe implied that Doyle was an unreliable witness who had worked as a prostitute, and furthermore, he suggested that she had lied in an attempt to blackmail the accused. Under extensive questioning, Doyle implied that she may have been a "bad girl," and that she had "at times occupied rooms at a private hotel with servicemen." But she denied offering to "work it hot" if she were given a job selling tickets at Morton's shows, and stated that this meant acting outside the law. She also refuted having taken off her clothes one time when she was drunk, or of having "rolled a Yank" for thirty pounds.[27] She stated that she had not lived as a prostitute for the previous five years[28] and disclaimed suggestions that her first husband had forced her onto the streets to earn a living.[29] Marjorie recollected that Skuthorpe's wife, however, recognized a pimp in the courtroom crowd, and drew the court's attention to him. He was subsequently removed.[30]

John Doyle denied his wife was a prostitute or that she had occupied rooms at the Menzies Hotel "with various men," although his wife stated she had stayed with about three or four men at that hotel.[31] He also repudiated having a conversation with another person in which it was suggested they try to trap Morton and blackmail him.[32] If Morton and Skuthorpe had been set up, however, it would seem the motive wasn't blackmail, because there was no hard evidence that anyone had tried to extort money from them. The intention of the rape accusations might simply have been to ruin their reputations.

Although the showmen were committed to trial, the proceedings came to an abrupt halt in mid-August when the Crown filed a "no true bill" of the accusations of rape,[33] suggesting there was insufficient evidence to convict the defendants. "The case fizzled out," recalled Marjorie.[34] While Dorothy Doyle might have withdrawn the charges because she didn't want to be grilled again in a full trial, it's just as likely her evidence was wanting: the magistrate, for example, expressed dissatisfaction with some of her testimony.[35] According to Smoky Dawson, the charges were dropped because Doyle admitted out of court that, under pressure from others, she had "copped" the two showmen in an attempt to compromise them. "It was a setup," Dawson said. He suggested Morton's flamboyant lifestyle of flashing his money around and drinking in bars attracted undesirables and even criminals. "Tex was a target," he recalled. "He was one of those characters who would always drink.... When you're drinking, you're meeting everybody. You're always in a pub."[36] Journalist Colin Mackay who wrote a series of articles about Morton in 1967, said Morton had expressly requested him to write about the case to clear his name, but the editor deleted references to it. Mackay believed it was a setup, too. "She didn't have a leg to stand on," he mused. "She thought she'd get a quid [money] out of it."[37]

The case might also have been dropped because it was thought that Doyle was a prostitute[38] and, according to Professor Featherstone, it was culturally not seen as possible to rape a prostitute, because she was consenting, and rape cases involving sex workers would probably be "weeded out" by the police and prosecutors before they went to trial.[39] So, if Doyle were a prostitute, the Crown would have automatically revoked all charges.

Morton's ever-tolerant wife, Marjorie, stood by him during the case. Contrary to some assertions, she did not leave him shortly after the trial since the two were already separated. In fact, she accompanied her husband on tours until later that year. Furthermore, she believed her husband's story that sex with Doyle was consensual, since Doyle had been drawn to Morton and Skuthorpe because of their lifestyle and reputations.[40] Marjorie was insistent about Morton's innocence, stating, "I knew that he wasn't capable of what they were [alleging]—it wasn't him. Girls came too easy for him—he didn't have to do anything like that," she said.[41] She recalled that, immediately after the hearing, she and Skuthorpe's wife visited their husbands in a police cell, where Morton told her, "I didn't do it.... She was a prostitute," and she believed him. The court case, however, was the catalyst for Sister Dorrie's temporary separation from Morton: although he might not have been guilty of rape, he had betrayed her trust in him.[42]

Still, there still lingered some doubt over Morton's and Skuthorpe's actions that night: the two had not been found conclusively innocent of the charges, which had merely been dropped after the committal hearing. But, had the case proceeded, even without any solid evidence of a setup, testimony most likely would have simply boiled down to their word against Doyle's, with a resultant verdict of not guilty. Furthermore, the absence of medical evidence suggesting rape, and possibly some inconsistencies in Doyle's testimony, also would have been in the defendants' favor. Nevertheless, the case generated Morton's first negative newspaper coverage since he had arrived in Australia a decade earlier. Marjorie recalled the sensational publicity didn't do her husband any good in the short term,[43] and his sister Barbara said her father was especially distressed by the lurid reports that appeared in newspapers, the details of which he kept to himself.[44] The case had even longer term implications that persisted throughout the ensuing decades: rumors and half-truths about the rape case persisted well after the court hearing and, according to journalist Colin Mackay, they were the reason that the much later television series *This Is Your Life* did not feature an episode on Morton, even though Mackay had already written a draft of a script for the proposed show.[45]

Following the case, Morton returned to touring with his rodeo. He was with the Skuthorpes and in October that year was in Gippsland, without Dorrie, who had left Morton's circus and rodeo, probably because of Morton's admitted infidelity during the rape-case hearing. At Morton's request, Marjorie toured with the show and assisted her husband in his sharpshooting act.[46] In an advertisement at the time, she was given the exotic stage-name "La Belle."[47]

MARJORIE SUES FOR SUPPORT

The forbearance Marjorie exhibited during the rape case had its limits, though. In September 1946, she took her husband to court over child-support payments which, she claimed, he had failed to honor. Marjorie said she had toured with Morton's shows as a ticket seller, but about June 1941 had ceased working, owing to her pregnancy and the birth of their twin sons in September that year.[48] She had been forced to borrow money to pay for her costs of living during confinement at home while providing childcare for two newborns[49] but, even afterward when she resumed touring with Morton, the twins were being boarded out at a cost of three pounds per week.[50] Eventually, she quit touring altogether and cared for the children at home. During that time, the couple were separated for long periods of time, without Marjorie always knowing her husband's whereabouts, despite her contacting the Showmen's

Guild "many times." Throughout those separations, it appeared that Morton had occasionally and irregularly sent his wife money in lump sums. Sometimes the payments were as much as twenty or twenty-five pounds, but they "were so few and far between" that they didn't cover all her expenses and she had still been out of pocket.[51]

Morton denied his wife's claims of default and testified that he had an arrangement with Buddy Wikara for Marjorie to be paid ten pounds weekly from the sale of Tex Morton Guitars and his music-tuition courses. He also provided a wad of receipts for money telegraphed to his wife while he had been touring. He had only a little over a pound in his bank account, he said, having recently drawn seventy pounds from it.[52] On one occasion, he stated, he had waited at his wife's house for five and a half hours before she came home drunk; he also denied being known on the show-business circuit as "a most extravagant spender on liquor."[53] He testified that he was "providing for her and the kiddies," but he would not allow his sons to "grow up around the circus." Furthermore, he had given her two pounds to buy the twins a pet dog. Finally, he said, he believed that Marjorie was pursuing him maliciously.[54]

Marjorie testified that Morton would generally hold three to six shows per week. She estimated the takings from each show to be about 150 pounds, with weekly expenses of about 250 pounds, yielding total annual earnings of about 5,000 pounds (a figure Morton argued was exaggerated threefold), plus, she believed he had capital assets of another 5,000 pounds.[55] In June 1945, she had taken out a summons against her husband in Sydney for child-support, and Morton had agreed to return to her—but he failed to turn up on the due date, and the next day hung up on her when she telephoned him at the Commodore Apartments. She also contended that she was unaware of her husband's arrangements with Wikara to pay her child-support and could not be held liable for her separation from her husband.[56]

When she became aware of the charges of rape brought against her husband, she agreed to stand by him. But, she said, "He did not come home to me and the children, as promised." She supported her husband during the court case and afterwards toured with him, but in December 1945, while the couple were on tour, he was drinking heavily and threw fifty pounds in her lap, ordering her to go home—but then later took forty pounds from her bag and told her to get home the best way she could on the remaining ten pounds. On returning to Sydney, she was forced to board with Lance Skuthorpe's wife.[57]

Dorrie had temporarily split from Morton after the rape case but re-joined his show towards the end of 1945.[58] It was probably at that time that Morton brusquely insisted that Marjorie leave.

Following more unfulfilled promises of child-support, and still in debt, Marjorie confronted Morton in July 1946 at the Brisbane Exhibition where, she said, her husband had made some 3,000 pounds in profit.[59] She admitted that she had sold Morton's saddle and guitar to pay for travel costs to Brisbane. At that meeting, Morton gave her a total of seventeen pounds, partly to pay for medicine for one of their sons, and also offered her a house at either Nelson, New Zealand, or in Brisbane, Sydney or Melbourne on the condition that she would not pursue maintenance costs against him in court. She refused.[60]

Morton declared that the guitar and saddle Marjorie had sold were priceless. The guitar, he said, was from his early street singing hobo days. "I wouldn't have parted from it for anything," he told the court. He also revealed that he had legally changed his name to "Morton" three years earlier, at about the time he was estranged from his wife. Marjorie, he said, accompanied his touring show for a time after the separation, handling the advance bookings while the twins were boarded, but afterwards she had returned to Sydney. "I had my own reasons for not staying with my wife," he said. "We did not agree."[61]

In October 1946, the court ruled there had been failings by both parties: Morton had provided enough money to his spouse, but at irregular intervals, and Marjorie had not made the most of the funds she had received. The court decreed that Morton pay his wife eight pounds per week,[62] but Morton successfully appealed the verdict. In that case, the judge simply instructed him to make regular, "adequate" payments.[63]

Some fifty years later Marjorie recalled: "I only wanted enough money to look after my children. I was really desperate . . . I had been working, but it got a bit much for me."[64] She was particularly worried about her boys. At the conclusion of the case, she recalled she obtained some child-support from her husband, but it soon dried up.[65] Then, almost excusing her husband's erratic payments, she said he only "forgot" to send her money. Long afterwards, she didn't condemn Morton for his at-times extravagant, hard-drinking lifestyle, or for his attitude towards her which, on the surface, appeared to be callous and uncaring, but she did say that her husband was a very strange man. "There was only one person, and that was Tex Morton," she recalled.[66]

Both the rape and the maintenance cases offer insights into Morton's relationships with women at the time. Although he was married with children, Morton was not only having an affair with Dorrie, but had opportunistic sexual relationships with other women as well. In the twenty-first century, in hindsight, it's easy to regard Morton and his hillbilly music as passé, but for the times his unconstrained, hard-drinking lifestyle and music, regarded by many as on the fringes of respectability, would likely have earned him a reputation akin to heavy-metal rock stars of later generations. Author Jenny Hicks described the impact Morton and Skuthorpe had on young women during the 1940s:

> Both men were intelligent, talented, good-looking and trouble. Tex drank too much, Lance gambled, and both had a weakness for women. When "Sex" Morton and "Pants" Skuthorpe were in town, it was time to lock up your daughters. Teenage girls used to follow the buckjump shows from town to town, "groupies" they'd be called now or "buckle bunnies." Dickie Skinner, who rode for the Skuthorpes throughout the forties, remembers the "Charlie Wheelers" (Sheilas) as they used to call them: "We used to have to climb trees to get away from them."[67]

DRUNK AT THE WHEEL

A less serious charge occurred in Tasmania in January 1948. Morton had been waiting for Dorrie in his car in Launceston. He was inebriated and, according to the arresting constable, "slumped over the [steering] wheel," with his breath smelling strongly of liquor. He admitted to having downed about six beers that afternoon and was subsequently charged for having been in control of a motor vehicle while intoxicated.[68]

Morton subsequently posted this notice in the Launceston *Examiner*:

APOLOGY

I, Tex Morton, would like the residents of Campbell Town (and especially the kids), who attended my show on Wednesday night, to accept my apologies for my non-attendance at the Circus.

I was waiting for Sister Dorrie, to drive her to your town, to meet you all, when I fell asleep. I was "pinched" and charged with being drunk in charge of a car. (Stationary, mind you, NOT driving it.)

I was fined £5 and had my license cancelled for twelve months—for the horrible crime of taking "40 winks in charge of a vehicle." —I intend to appeal and hope to bring my show to your town sometime soon, if we can arrange it.

Meanwhile, all the solicitors are on holidays, so, see you later. By the way, as I was unable to obtain the services of a lawyer, I defended my own case. Wouldn't I make a terrible lawyer?

Very Soberly Yours,

TEX MORTON

P.S.—Have you ever wondered how tired Circus people become, what hours they sleep, and when? About three or four hours nightly is the average. (That's why they all look wrinkled and tired.) [69]

After losing his license to drive in Tasmania, Morton placed this humorous advertisement in the same newspaper: [70]

WANTED
CHAUFFEUR
MUST NOT DRINK
UNIFORM SUPPLIED

Must be able to work 7 days per week, 24 hours per day, without sleep.

SEE TASMANIA
ON GOOD WAGES
EX-SOLDIER
PREFERRED

WRITE
TEX MORTON
CIRCUS
HOBART

TEENAGER BOB LANE PRACTICING IN NELSON.
COURTESY OF BARBARA LANE AND GORDON SPITTLE.

THE LANE FAMILY, LATE 1930S. BOB FOURTH FROM LEFT AT REAR, BETWEEN HIS MOTHER AND GRANDFATHER. THE OTHERS ARE LANE'S FATHER, SIBLINGS, AND GRANDMOTHER. COURTESY OF KATH MORTON.

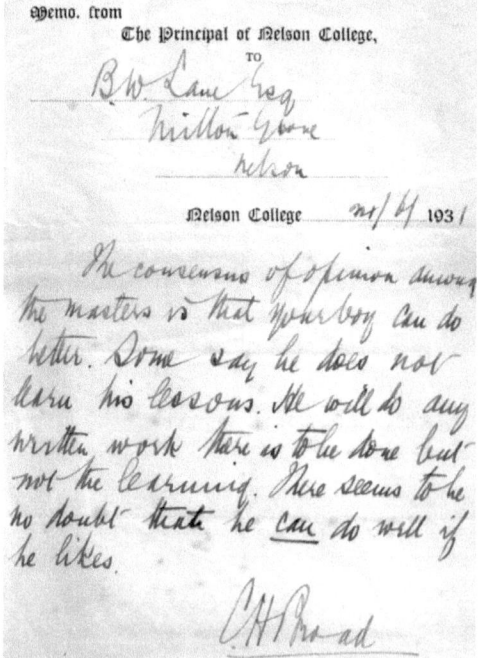

LETTER SENT TO BOB LANE'S PARENTS FROM NELSON COLLEGE, 1931. COURTESY OF KATH MORTON.

MORTON'S FLEDGLING BAND, EARLY 1930S. *LEFT TO RIGHT*: MORTON, POSSIBLY GIL HARRIS, POSSIBLY JOE BARRETT, POSSIBLY LEO REDSHAW. COURTESY OF BARBARA LANE AND AUDIOCULTURE (NZ).

THE YOUNG BOUNDARY RIDER.

MORTON'S FIRST COMMERCIAL RECORDING, FEBRUARY 25, 1936. COURTESY OF DAVID HARDY.

MORTON, CA. 1938.

MORTON, 1940S. COURTESY OF TEX BANES.

BUCKJUMPING IN AUSTRALIA, 1940S.

LANCE (THIRD FROM LEFT) AND VIOLET SKUTHORPE
AND THEIR CREW, 1940S. COURTESY OF KATH MORTON.

TEX MORTON COMIC BOOK.

GOOD NEWS FOR YODELLING FANS!

TEX MORTON, the world-famed Yodelling Boundary Rider, will be in attendance at WILLS & COY.'s warehouse from...

4 TILL 5 ON MONDAY AFTERNOON, JANUARY 22

Full stocks of Tex Morton's records are available from Wills & Coy. at 2/6

BUY YOUR FAVOURITE FROM HIS REPERTOIRE AND HAVE TEX MORTON PERSONALLY AUTOGRAPH IT FOR YOU.

ON STAGE AT THE PRINCESS THEATRE TO-NIGHT THIS FAMOUS ARTIST WILL ANNOUNCE THE WINNER OF THE NEW 1940 H.M.V. PORTABLE OFFERED IN

WILLS & COY.'s
HOLIDAY COMPETITION

ON TOUR IN TASMANIA, 1940.

CROWD THREATENS TEX MORTON'S RODEO

MELBOURNE.—Tex Morton's rodeo circus outfit was threatened by an angry crowd at Wonthaggi before the show began on Saturday night.

Tactful reasoning by two constables saved the tent, performing animals, motor transports, and sleeping quarters. Some damage was done.

Early in the evening some men from North Wonthaggi were walking along at the rear of where the rodeo was pitched when an argument arose with some of Morton's hands.

In the brawl that followed the rodeo company outnumbered the local men, and Gordon Dell, of Wonthaggi, had his jaw broken in two places. It was alleged that he was kicked.

Half an hour before the show was to begin, enraged friends of

UNWANTED PUBLICITY.

NEWSPAPER PHOTOGRAPH OF MORTON AND HIS TWIN SONS.

MORTON'S WILD WEST RODEO, 1940S. COURTESY OF KATH MORTON.

DUNEDIN, NEW ZEALAND, LATE 1949 OR EARLY 1950. *LEFT TO RIGHT:* BILL DITCHFIELD, COLE WILSON, MORTON, DORRIE, NOLA HEWITT, COLIN MCCRORIE. COURTESY OF BARRY SKINNER.

MORTON WITH DIXIE BILL HILTON. COURTESY OF KEITH TITTERINGTON.

PERFORMING HIS ACT OF WALKING ON THE PARAPET OF A BUILDING, BLINDFOLDED. NEW ZEALAND, 1960S. COURTESY OF KATH MORTON.

WITH BUDDY WIKARA AT THE HAWAIIAN CLUB, 1940S.
COURTESY OF KATH MORTON.

THE GREAT MORTON, 1950S.

ENTERTAINING INDIGENOUS FANS IN THE AUSTRALIAN OUTBACK.
COURTESY OF KATH MORTON.

WITH THE HAMILTON COUNTY BLUEGRASS BAND. *LEFT TO RIGHT*: GRAHAM LOVEJOY, MILES REAY, PAUL TRENWITH, ALAN RHODES, MORTON, COLLEEN TRENWITH. COURTESY OF KATH MORTON.

ENTERTAINING CHILDREN, 1960S. COURTESY OF KATH MORTON.

MARJORIE MORTON, EARLY 1960S. COURTESY OF BOB MORTON.

THE GREAT MORTON IN THE USA, 1950S. COURTESY OF KATH MORTON.

THE GREAT MORTON AT THE SEVILLE THEATRE, MONTREAL, 1950S.
COURTESY OF KATH MORTON.

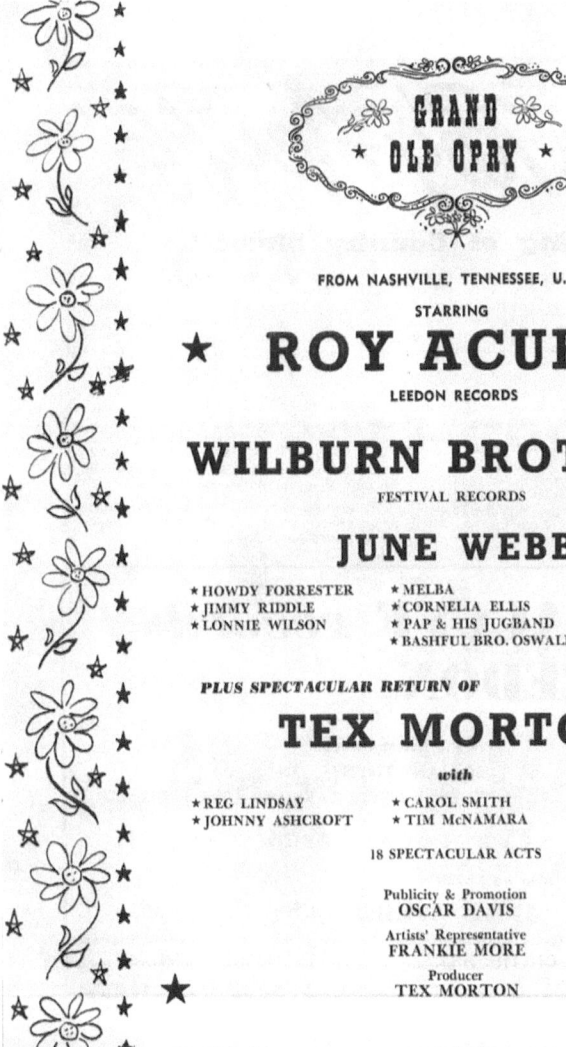

PROGRAM FOR THE GRAND OLE OPRY TOUR, 1959.
COURTESY OF KATH MORTON.

KATH MORTON IN TEX'S SHOOTING ACT, CANBERRA, 1964.
COURTESY OF KATH MORTON.

WITH GUNSYND, THE CHAMPION RACEHORSE, 1970S.
COURTESY OF KATH MORTON.

KATH MORTON NEXT TO THE BUST OF TEX, JULY 23, 1991.
COURTESY OF KATH MORTON.

LANCE SKUTHORPE JR. AT THE 1938 CALGARY STAMPEDE.
COURTESY OF KATH MORTON.

ON THE SET OF *WE OF THE NEVER NEVER* WITH ANGELA PUNCH MCGREGOR. COURTESY OF KATH MORTON.

11

TEX MORTON'S DUDE RANCH

"ALL SET AND SADDLED"

From early to mid-1942, Morton recorded a series of thirty radio shows called *All Set and Saddled*, possibly at Columbia's Homebush studios, sponsored by Persil's Guardian Soap. They were cut on 16-inch double-sided laminated discs.[1] The programs comprised music, drama, storytelling, and comedy; they were not recorded before a live audience, but some applause was overdubbed. The series went to air in late 1942 and copies of the shows were circulated from one radio station to the next. (There were about a hundred commercial radio stations in Australia at the time.) As many as twelve copies of each show were produced, but only one set has survived. Initially the programs were a half-hour in length—hence they would fit on the two sides of a single transcription disc. Later, they might have been expanded to forty-five minutes. By and large, music in *All Set And Saddled* was comprised of familiar songs associated with Morton, often with outback or Western themes, like "Freight Train Yodel," "The Stockman's Last Bed," "Red River Valley," "When the Bloom Is on the Sage" and "When the Cactus Is in Bloom," or sentimental favorites like "Rockin' Alone in an Old Rocking Chair." An advertisement described the series as a "half-hour weekly session present[ing] an Australian version of the American cowboy tradition with Tex Morton and his friends 'Shorty' and Sister Dorrie in yodeling and straight songs of the outback."[2]

A 1943 magazine reported that *All Set and Saddled* brought listeners "Australia's favorite cowboy in the songs you like to hear him sing—cowboy tunes, sung to the strumming guitar, plaintive melodies from the lonely plains and the real scent of the bush in the lusty outback ballads that lives [sic] forever in Australia's heart." A photograph showed a pensive Morton with "Shorty" (Dan Agar, an English comedian and character actor) and a brunette Dorrie clutching a stockwhip. All were dressed in outback-style clothes with hats.[3] Another report from 1943 advised:

> Laughs and exciting cowboy adventures to the tune of the famous Rough Riders Band swinging out those sentimental old Aussie ballads—this is the new type of entertainment in "All Set and Saddled." And your favorite boundary rider sings and yodels in harmony with Sister Dorrie, with this well-known cowboy band to complete the outback setting. What Shorty, Tex Morton's offsider, lacks in height he certainly makes up in humor! Shorty thrives on excitement . . . Join Tex Morton—the fast riding guitar strumming hero of the outback—each Monday night at 8 from Station 2UW [Sydney], with his cowboy pals and rough-riders in the wide open spaces. "All Set and Saddled" is bound to blow your cares away.[4]

The same year, Morton recorded more shows, with Dorrie, the Roughriders and "Shorty". Introduced alliteratively as "that melody minstrel of the mulga" and "your yodeling cowboy friend," Morton sang familiar songs from his repertoire interspersed with Jimmie Rodgers standards, his empathetic love for the Singing Brakeman shining through on the transcriptions. On some shows, Dorrie sang popular-style numbers like "Sail Along Silvery Moon," or Gene Autry's "There's a Gold Mine in the Sky," but nothing detracted from the overall sense of down-home, informal hillbilly festivity, with the affable host proffering sage advice like: "You know Shorty, it doesn't pay to go anything but straight" before launching into "The Ned Kelly Song," or opining on the origins of songs and of the pleasures of the outback lifestyle. The setting was a fantasy location, far removed from city life, and celebrated with folksongs "perhaps first sung to clashing shears" with hillbilly fare like "The Tramp's Mother" or "Everything but You." But the perceptible air of relaxed informality masked a dedicated professionalism that ensured performers and musicians spoke and sang on cue, without fluffing their lines or the music, and all within the constraint of a tight timeline.

In 1948, Morton recorded more radio broadcasts with Dorrie and the Roughriders. The opening theme was enhanced by galloping horses' hooves and ringing gunshots, but otherwise the mythical setting was outback Australia. A song by Morton's mentor, Jimmie Rodgers, "My Little Lady," with Dorrie duetting, was another standard Morton hadn't previously recorded.

He recited a monologue, "The Soldier's Sweetheart" (not to be confused with the entirely different song of the same title, by Jimmie Rodgers), which he said was written by two Australian ex-diggers (soldiers), one of whom he knew personally; he had been a prisoner of war, Morton believed, and died after the war ended.[5]

Nolan Porterfield, Jimmie Rodgers's biographer, commented: "I especially enjoyed the radio shows, which offer more of the 'flavor' of the time, as well as a fuller sense of Morton's personality. His singing and showmanship are quite good. Occasionally there's a certain element in his yodel that I don't much care for (I can only describe it as a sort of 'fluttering growl'), but on the whole he's about as good as they come."[6] Morton later described the radio programs as "good off-the-cuff sessions I used to think to myself as world class."[7] By and large, Morton's radio-show repertoire was anchored on tried-and-tested chestnuts, familiar American songs, Jimmie Rodgers standards, and the odd Australian folksong or verse that he hadn't recorded previously. About the only innovative recordings were the narrations of "Soldier's Sweetheart" and "Along the Stock Route." It was as though Morton was looking backwards to familiar songs from earlier times instead of composing new titles. And although the Roughriders enhanced his performances beyond much of the miserly backings Columbia Graphophone provided for their artists, he seemed oblivious to changing trends in the United States where hillbilly music was becoming country music and transitioning from rural and western themes to songs with which city slickers could identify. This is not to deny the quality of his radio performances, however. His voice was still strong, his yodeling as good as ever, and the radio programs, with full-band accompaniment, matched or even exceeded his Columbia efforts. But his musical transmission was stuck in neutral, whereas in years gone by it had been in overdrive.

TEX MORTON'S DUDE RANCH

In September 1948, Morton was in Wisemans Ferry, New South Wales, where he spent a night in the local hotel and voiced an interest in log cabins, a riding school, trail rides and musical nights.[8] About a month afterwards, he converted this vision into reality by buying a ranch in Penrith, about 60 kilometers west of Sydney.[9] By October 1948 he had taken over the J. F. Dude Ranch at Castlereagh naming it "The Tex Morton Dude Ranch," where he intended to use the property to rest his horses and buckjumpers.[10] The same month, "Tex Morton restaurant proprietor" successfully applied for a liquor permit at the ranch;[11] and by November that year the ranch offered a special weekend rate and patrons could enjoy riding, dancing, tennis, billiards and swimming. The cuisine was excellent, an announcement boasted, and the eatery was licensed.[12] This advertisement was used repeatedly until 1949.[13]

Major buildings, some of which had been built in the 1890s, consisted of a house, several bunkhouses, and a shower and toilet block. Nearby was a large concrete sullage pit, a dam and horse yards. Lance Skuthorpe Jr. lived close by. Morton lived in the house, flanked by colored paving stones, which was also used as a guest home, and was later advertised as capable of accommodating one hundred people.[14] The Do Drop Inn was nearby, close to Castlereagh Hall.[15] The overall area of the property was about thirty-five acres.[16] A lengthy unpaved road ran alongside the ranch. "Chief Little Wolf" (real name, Ventura Tenario), an American wrestler who had migrated to Australia in 1937, would run up and down it for training—Morton seemed to enjoy the company of wrestlers.

Marjorie and the twins lived at the ranch[17] and, in what must have been a fascinating social dynamic, Dorrie also stayed there and sometimes managed the estate.[18] Bob Morton, one of the twins, fondly recalled living on the property, though he said he had few memories of the place and time: "I was like a young boy who couldn't soak in enough of what dad had there. I was supposed to be in bed of a night-time, but me and my brother and other friends . . . it would fascinate us to go out and see . . . every night was a party there . . . every night all the lights would come on—red, green, blue."

Bob recalled his father had a billiards room and a fully-licensed dance hall[19] with a storeroom full of decorations. The twins traveled to and from the nearby Agnes Banks Primary School on a horse and cart.[20] There were sometimes fancy-dress parties and dances on weekends with live bands. On Sundays, guests were entertained by horse races, Shetland pony rides and Wild-West-style covered wagons, and children could swim in the nearby Nepean River. The Dude Ranch assisted the nearby community by supporting local charities. In October 1948, for example, Morton staged a large rodeo, barbecue, rodeo ball and gymkhana at the ranch to aid the Nepean District Hospital.[21] The following month Morton and Dorrie performed at a concert for patients in a military hospital,[22] and the couple raised seventy-five pounds by staging a barbecue, talent quest and dance at the ranch, to aid a Christmas charity.[23] Similarly, the local Country Women's Association (CWA) expressed grateful thanks to Morton, Dorrie and some ranch hands for letting 138 "deaf and dumb" [sic] children ride on Shetland ponies generously provided by Morton.[24]

Australian comedian and actor George Wallace and Morton were great friends, according to Kim Lane, who said Wallace ensconced himself at Morton's property where he was free to imbibe alcohol during the beer strikes of the mid-1940s, only occasionally traveling to the city to make radio programs. In 1960, Morton was in New Zealand when his friend was close to death and had begged to see him before he died. Wallace clung to life, just long enough for his mate to fly to Sydney and bid him farewell for about twenty or thirty minutes, before he would allow himself to pass on.[25]

The ranch might have helped with accommodation for some of the locals, too. A 1959 article stated that the guest house had offered affordable accommodation for elderly citizens. "These old people couldn't manage on their pensions and pay what they were called upon to pay in Sydney. They went to the Dude Ranch on their own account," it said, possibly in response to criticism of "certain water connections" (probably regarding sewage) by Penrith's health department.[26] But the ranch had a mixed reception among locals. "Tex was very friendly and likeable," said one neighbor. "He would sit on the veranda of the hotel and begin to sing until everyone joined in. He had several spots in Penrith where he performed. . . . he was a big hit with the Penrith population. One lady told me she took all the family to the barbecues there, but other people said the police had to keep an eye on the rough parties."[27]

MEETING RALPH PEER

In January 1949, Ralph Peer and his wife, Monique, arrived in Sydney after a nerve-wracking flight from Auckland. Later that month, the Peers were entertained by Morton and Buddy Wikara. Monique's diary entry described the meeting:

> We had a most interesting visit today in our cramped quarters, with Tex Morton, the Australian singing star, who can best be described as the Gene Autry of Australasia. He does not call himself a cowboy, but "Australia's Singing Stockman." He has a most engaging personality, and we got along very well. His friend and

"pardner," Johnny Waikura [Buddy Wikara], came in later to play the guitar, and we had an oldfashioned hill-billy singfest. We certainly missed our old friends Bob Gilmore and Nat Vincent, because I am sure they would have appreciated this show as much as we did.[28]

Ralph Peer had organized the legendary Bristol recording sessions in 1927, at which Jimmie Rodgers and the Carter Family were "discovered," although other talented hillbilly recording artists like Ernest Stoneman were also present. Peer had made most of his wealth by owning song copyrights. His Southern Music Publishing Company, established in 1928, owned a veritable mother-lode of hillbilly and other songs, many of which had been hits.[29] Morton was almost certainly aware of Peer's links to Rodgers, and it's likely he actively sought him out when he heard of his coming.

The Peers arrived in Australia on December 21, 1948, and spent Christmas Eve with Dudley Fegan, head of the Australian Record Company (ARC). Peer confirmed that he was on a world tour, aiming to find a hit record which, he said, could originate from anywhere.[30] After a brief trip to New Zealand, Peer met with the board of Southern Music Publishing, Australasia, which he'd established in 1946,[31] and formally constituted Peer-Southern Australasia.[32] Peer also contracted Morton as a songwriter and made connections for the Australian's intended career in North America.[33] Alan Crawford, previously managing director of Peer's London office, was signed by Peer to run his Sydney operation.[34]

In Australia, Peer-Southern became allied to the newly-formed Rodeo label in Sydney, intending to break Columbia's market monopoly. Dudley Fegan was persuaded by Crawford to make gramophone records at ARC under the "Rodeo" label.[35] Crawford and George Aitken of ARC conceived the initiative of running talent quests to identify new artists who might then record for the label. Popular identity John Dunne, an announcer and producer for radio station 2SM-Sydney, approved their idea and allowed hillbilly singer Tim McNamara to run a talent quest in the station's auditorium. Reg Lindsay won the inaugural event in January 1951, narrowly beating George Payne and Shorty Ranger, and went on to record with Rodeo,[36] eventually waxing over 40 numbers for the label.[37]

Peer's visit motivated Morton to finally move to the United States. Early in February 1949, only a month after meeting the Peers, Morton advertised sales of assets at his dude ranch. Included were five cars, an elephant, two caravans, two large semi-trailers, two Ford three-ton trucks, two mobile cookhouses, trailers, lighting equipment and even a Gypsy Moth airplane.[38] The ranch was advertised as for sale in August 1949, with Morton cited as a defendant in a case involving a public auction of the rights and title to part of the estate, in the form of a lease extending for three years from the first of August 1948, suggesting he had problems with finances.[39] The ranch and its assets were finally disposed of in 1950. In April that year, the entire property ("a going concern if desired") was advertised as for sale[40] and two months later assets were removed from the estate.[41] The ranch was finally sold in June 1950.[42]

After the ranch had folded, Morton said that he looked on it with unhappy memories—it was one enterprise that was unsuccessful[43] because, he said, it was twenty years ahead of its time.[44] Smoky Dawson said Morton was virtually bankrupt when he sold the ranch. "He was so foolish with his money," he recalled. "He was never one for banking or saving money. He'd spend it as fast as he got it."[45]

12

THE TASMAN AND RODEO RECORDINGS

LEAVING AUSTRALIA

In late 1949, Morton and Dorrie embarked on a "farewell" tour of New Zealand's South Island. They probably spent Christmas with Morton's family in Nelson,[1] then journeyed to the North Island where Morton performed at concerts, before traveling to Australia, probably around March 1950.[2] For five or seven shillings, an adult could see the "star of radio, records, stage and screen ... the greatest and most versatile entertainer of our time ... , [with an] amazing and sensational sharpshooting act."[3] Dorrie's presence, however, was not welcomed by some in Morton's family: sister Barbara recalled her brother and mother arguing over Dorrie who, she said, was "a floozy in Mum's eyes."[4] The tour also showcased Morton's return to the recording studio after a six-year absence.

In 1949 and early 1950, Morton, with various combinations of Sister Dorrie and his Roughriders, recorded 25 sides, 24 of which were issued on New Zealand's Tasman label.[5] Simultaneously, 22 were released in Australia on Rodeo—the first recordings for the label.[6] It's been frequently stated that Morton recorded all 25 sides in a marathon recording session at Noel Peach's Astor studios in Auckland, New Zealand, with Dorrie and a group that most likely was comprised of a pick-up band of New Zealand musicians organized by drummer Wally Ransom (Ralph Peer's New Zealand representative for Southern Music),[7] including Johnny Bradfield on rhythm guitar, George Campbell on bass and electric steel guitarist Will Jeffs.[8] Morton recalled that he and Ransom "dug up" a scratch band ... it wasn't a bad little band—just scratch boys around Auckland."[9] Jeffs's playing approach was Hawaiian, but he adapted it to country style on the recordings. "I wasn't at home with Morton," he reflected. "I liked the music, but I wasn't on the same side of the street."[10] Nevertheless, the steel guitar accompaniment on several recordings was particularly effective and sympathetic to the genre. Jeffs said that Pat Fraley, Morton's wrestler friend, was also traveling with Morton who, Jeffs remembered, would wear his hat when he was recording—Morton thought his voice bounced off its brim—but would drink coffee hatless during breaks.[11] Researcher Chris Bourke, however, cited both Tommy Kahi and Bill Sevesi on steel guitar, suggesting there might have been at least three sessions in Auckland.[12]

There have also been lingering doubts as to whether some recordings were made in Australia. The noted discographer and researcher John Edwards believed some titles were recorded in Sydney in late 1949.[13] Certainly, Eric Cleburne, Rodeo's engineer at the time, recalled Morton recording a few numbers in Sydney,[14] supporting Edwards's idea that there were two recording locations: Sydney (most likely around October 1949) and Auckland[15] (probably January, February or March 1950). Discographer David Hardy believes that ten sides were recorded in Sydney, based on his examination of the run-out grooves of pressings.[16] Additional aural evidence supports this view.[17]

Twenty-three of the releases were licensed to Peer's Southern Music publishing company.[18] They represented a mix of old-style hillbilly numbers and more contemporary performances (where blue yodeling and overt hillbilly mannerisms were becoming passé). "Frankie and Johnny," "You and My Old Guitar" (in duet with Dorrie), "My Little Lady," "Treasure[s] Untold," and "Waiting for a Train"[19] were all songs from Morton's progenitor, Jimmie Rodgers. Morton sang these with just his guitar, showcasing his sensitive renditions of some of the Singing Brakeman's enduring classics. "Frankie and Johnny," with its flashy guitar introduction, was especially spirited, with Morton adapting and exaggerating his voice for different parts. Morton recalled that he had originally learned the song from a 1927 recording by Frank Crumit and not from Rodgers.[20] It seems to have been a favorite of his, as he also sang it at live performances. "Treasure Untold" (its correct title on the Rodgers recording was "Treasures Untold") was even reissued on the German Bear Family label in 2003 in a compact-disc compilation of Rodgers's recordings by other artists, testimony to Morton's international standing as a Rodgers-style entertainer.[21]

Morton and Dorrie duetted on "Rock My Cradle (Once Again)," composed by Billy Folger (whose real name was Cecil Smith) and one-time Gene Autry sidekick Johnny Bond. Folger wrote the song about his brother who had been killed by a Japanese sniper at Guadalcanal, calling out for his mother while dying.[22] Coincidentally, Hank Williams also recorded the song, on a transcription disc in Shreveport, Louisiana, in early 1949.[23] Two years earlier, Johnny Bond had waxed the original version in Hollywood[24] but Morton's and Dorrie's rendition was described in an American magazine as "one of its most successful recordings."[25]

Several numbers mirrored trends in contemporary American country music, as it increasingly became urbanized and focused on themes of marital infidelity. Jimmy Wakely had recorded Eddie Dean's "One Has My Name (The Other Has My Heart)" in 1948,[26] and "Slipping Around" with pop singer Margaret Whiting in July 1949, followed by "I'll Never Slip Around Again" in September 1949 (suggesting that the Tasman/Rodeo version of this number was probably recorded in 1950 at the earliest). "Slippin' Around" and its respective follow-up were written and recorded by Floyd Tillman. His recording was issued in Australia on Columbia, about August or September 1950, with a Gene Autry song on the reverse side, and sold over 32,000 copies. Tillman also wrote "This Cold War with You" and recorded it in August 1949.[27] Morton and Dorrie sang it as a duet in the style of Wakely and Whiting.[28]

By comparison, "When My Blue Moon Turns to Gold" was from an earlier era. The Sons of The Pioneers had sung the equally sentimental "Teardrops in My Heart" in 1947. "Wabash Cannon Ball" went back even further to the Carter Family, Roy Acuff and others.[29] "When You Have No One to Love You (Linda Darlin')," later recorded by Australia's Hawking Brothers, had been first recorded in 1940 by the Pine Ridge Boys whose disc had been issued locally.[30] Eddy Arnold had cut the lachrymose "My Daddy Is Only a Picture" in 1947, a song that hearkened to an earlier era of country music despite Arnold's contemporary country crooning style that was especially admired at the time. The comparably sentimental "One Golden Curl" had been recorded by Wilf Carter in 1947 with some electric backup; old-timers like Carter and Morton, it seemed, were moving with the times, even if some of their songs resurrected a prior phase of hillbilly music from the past.[31] "Don't Make Me Go to Bed and I'll Be Good," a doleful composition about a dying child, had been recorded by Roy Acuff in 1942. Songwriter Fred Rose once commented that he never really understood country music until he saw Acuff mournfully sing the song with tear-drenched eyes.[32]

Of special interest were four of Morton's own compositions, "The Soldier's Sweetheart Part 1," "The Soldier's Sweetheart Part 2," "A Stockman's Prayer," and the unissued "A Rolling Stone." Previously he had stated "The Soldier's Sweetheart" had been written by two other Australians, both ex-diggers (soldiers), one of whom was an ex-prisoner of war that he had known personally. On December 15, 1950, when he was in the United States, Morton signed all four of these songs to Peer's newly-formed publishing company in Sydney.[33] Fundamentally, they consisted of spoken narrations, a genre which Morton would later develop and extend. He had, in fact, pioneered monologues in his 1940 recording of "You'll Never Be Missed," but as he grew older his voice deepened and the recitations were more effective. Live performances showed him to be an excellent actor, too, with changing facial expressions and often different accents that enhanced the narrations. At times, he would pause, nonchalantly inhale on a cigarette, and then continue. In later years, he would record albums entirely of narrations, and producer Hal Saunders would regard him as a supreme master of the art.[34] Show-person Dolores Balaam said Morton occasionally recited Shakespeare from memory, too.[35]

Although there are no official sales figures, it's likely the public's interest in Morton had not waned during his six-year recording drought, and the discs sold well. Collector and discographer David Crisp said Morton's and Dorrie's Rodeo releases occurred frequently in collections of 78s, suggesting they were well-liked at the time: they might even have been among the most popular discs Rodeo released.[36] Dorrie recalled that "Slippin' Around" was a big seller, with sales "exceeding those of Crosby and Sinatra."[37] Given that Morton and Dorrie were both married yet together in a relationship, perhaps the song was an example of art as a mirror of life.

HYPNOTISM

At some point during the New Zealand tour, Morton became adept at stage hypnotism, doubtless cashing in on the public's enthrallment with the art. There are Australian newspaper reports from March in 1950 of him having practiced hypnosis in Australia, in which he stated he was also including hypnotism in his current New Zealand shows. He had been hypnotized while a boy scout, he recalled, and realized then that he possessed an authoritative voice, essential for hypnotizing others. "The boys were more responsive to me than anyone else," he reflected.[38] In reality, however, he most likely only became involved in stage hypnosis when he learned that hypnotist Franquin (Frank Quinn) had pocketed some 50,000 pounds while on a New Zealand tour,[39] though in 1950 he claimed he had become engrossed in the subject as early as 1936 after studying "a course in psychology" in Sydney.[40] Morton learned hypnotism from Walter Braemar,[41] an old-time hypnotist who also had mentored fellow New Zealand hypnotists Franquin and Leon Van Loewe.[42]

In late November 1949, advertisements in New Zealand newspapers claimed that "the famous overseas hypnotist Mr. Van Loewe" was appearing at Hokitika with the Tex Morton show. Van Loewe had performed on Morton's shows at least from October,[43] but the two fell out: Morton recalled they had argued (possibly over Morton's drinking) and Van Loewe had abruptly left, leaving Morton to perform the hypnosis act himself during the second part of the show.[44] In February 1950, newspapers announced that Morton would be performing at Waitara by himself as singer, sharpshooter, and hypnotist, described as: "the man with the master mind." There was no mention of Van Loewe,[45] supporting Morton's story of arguing with him and then performing hypnotism by himself. Another press report stated that "Leon Van Loewe had to leave for Auckland under unforeseen circumstances."[46] In March 1950, an article further declared that "Tex Morton has forsaken his old love, Hill Billy, and is now packing NZ houses a La Franquin as a hypnotist!"[47]

By early 1950, Morton was promoting himself as a singer, sharpshooter and stage hypnotist, describing himself as "mystic," "amazing" and "different" while demonstrating "psychometry," "mind reading," "mesmerism" and "hypnotism," while Dorrie was condescendingly reported as "the bomb-shell of 1949."[48] Joyce Stephens especially recalled attending one of Morton's shows and participating as an audience member in a display of hypnotism in February 1950. A beardless Morton had hypnotized her in a storefront window, after which she was taken to his show by an ambulance crew where he "revived" her. While she was "asleep," he extinguished a lighted cigarette on her arm and tongue.[49] "When Tex hypnotized me, he put me to sleep by singing a song he had never recorded," she later wrote, adding, "Otherwise, I could have been hypnotized accidentally if he had used something he'd recorded."[50]

LEAVING AUSTRALIA

After the New Zealand tour, in 1950 Morton and Dorrie returned to Australia, probably in March, before Morton flew to the United States.[51] The precise date of his departure is currently unknown but was sometime around midyear, probably in May or June.[52] En route, he stopped in Hawaii and soon after he landed in the United States he was worried because he woke up with an exceptionally troublesome sore throat.[53]

Dorrie moved to Perth in July 1950 to seek alimony from her husband, Bruce Carroll. Without Morton, she would have had no income, so she attempted to milk funds from her cuckolded husband instead, arguing she had assisted earlier in providing for their son, Roger (born in 1934),[54] throughout his childhood. When she first informed Roger of her intentions, he in turn told his father, who telegrammed her with: "Roger informed me of intended visit. In case you may think otherwise, most unwelcome as far as I am concerned. Bruce."[55] Described as "slim," "fair haired" and a "popular stage and radio star," Dorrie said she required a weekly income of fifteen pounds which was what Morton had paid her,[56] but almost twice as much as he was required to shell out to Marjorie for the support of their twins. She refuted the allegation that members of Morton's entourage had referred to her as "the missus" (wife)[57] but, to her dismay, the court ruled that Bruce Carroll had never deserted her. The litigation took its toll on her, too: reportedly she was "now aging and tired and seemed to be in a highly strung and nervous condition."[58] Finally, the judge granted the warring couple a divorce and Bruce Carroll consented to pay his ex-wife a lump-sum of 1,000 pounds.[59] Although Morton's move to North America had abruptly left her in the lurch, she didn't harbor any resentment toward him. In fact, they were reunited in the 1970s and she was affectionate towards her old partner even in his dying days. "Poor old Tex," she would muse.[60] Not much is known of her life between 1950 and 1972, but in her later years she was cared for by Roger, and in 1985 she was inducted into the Hands of Fame in Tamworth.[61] She died in 1992. Bruce Carroll died about 18 months after the divorce settlement.[62]

As for Marjorie, she was left in the dark about the move. "I didn't know he had left the country," she said—but, then again, her husband's unannounced absences were nothing new to her: she recalled unexpectedly having to cook all weekend at the ranch one Easter, for a newly arrived party of guests, but Morton and Dorrie were nowhere to be seen.[63] Raising two young sons while their father was in North America was a daunting task, too. Morton initially had enrolled Bernard and Bob in a Sydney boarding school, but they were constantly lonely and regularly ran away, to be with their mother. Eventually, Marjorie withdrew them from the school, and they lived with her, but with little or no financial support coming from Morton, life was harsh and thus Marjorie had to work at two and sometimes three jobs—in stores by day and hotels at night.

For his part, Morton corresponded infrequently with his sons, posting the family an occasional Christmas card or sometimes money. Bob recalled his father once sent them 400 pounds[64] and Marjorie was so ecstatic, she tossed the money up and down on her bed. "It was like winning the lottery," he remembered. Morton's absence—putting his career ahead of his family—generated resentment in his sons, even though he kept a photograph of the two in his wallet. Bob felt their father kept them as "baggage." All the while, the twins lived with the knowledge that their father was a famous, though absent, recording star and showman, but that often got them into fights when schoolmates disbelieved them. In speaking to some of Morton's contemporaries, the author found their major criticism of him was his seemingly callous neglect of his children. [65]

Some ten years later, when Morton returned from touring overseas, he made no effort to contact his family. Bob only met his father by chance when their paths crossed on a Sydney street. Bernard, especially, harbored antipathy towards his father, although the two seemed to get on better in later years. Bernard, a well-heeled abalone diver, once drove some 1200 kilometers from Portland in Victoria to Morton's house in Sydney,[66] and dumped 50,000 dollars on his father's kitchen table, telling him the family didn't want what little help he'd given them. "We didn't need you," he sneered. And, although Morton tried to help with Bob's career, Bob recalled the two were more like friends and less like father and son. He was proud of his father as an entertainer, but resented the way he had treated his family, although when the two reunited, he said, much of the bitterness evaporated. But Morton continued paying scant regard for his family. Once, when he had no money, he stayed at Marjorie's unit for three days, only to do a runner [leave abruptly] and head for Queensland on the fourth day.[67]

Bernard died in March 1983, and was buried at Portland, Victoria. His funeral was attended by Marjorie, brother Bob and his wife Kaye, and Morton himself.[68] Morton was distraught over his son's death. Perhaps a latent regret about not having connected more with his sons had haunted him; or perhaps he had tried to establish father-son relationships in his later life, when the pursuit of fame had lost its glow, but a certain reserve in his character had left that hope unfulfilled and incomplete. Whatever his motives or intentions, however, it seemed that years of being an absent father had left an indelible scar, only partly healed, on the psyches of his sons.[69]

13

THE GREAT MORTON IN NORTH AMERICA

MORTON WAS GREETED by Gene Autry when he arrived in Los Angeles. Well-known photographs show the pair together in Hollywood, one with Ann Blyth, the acclaimed actress and singer. Conceivably, Ralph Peer arranged the photo opportunity, although the two singers previously might have written to each other.[1] A search of the Gene Autry archives in California, however, failed to locate any correspondence between the two, though the archiving of Autry's files was incomplete at the time of writing.[2] Morton also said Pat Fraley met him at Los Angeles airport, but it's just possible that Fraley had accompanied him in the first place, since the two had recently been together in New Zealand.[3]

Smoky Dawson thought Morton had initially arranged to interview Autry at a Los Angeles hotel but overslept and stood up America's Singing Cowboy. When the pair did meet, however, they became drinking buddies. Morton described Autry as "a very brilliant bastard to make all that money. I have often stood with him full of brandy. He and I used to drink, and he can go back a long way. He knows a lot about folk music and early country and western. . . . Nat Vincent, who ran the Hollywood office [for Ralph Peer], and wrote 'Strawberry Roan' and 'I'm Forever Blowing Bubbles,' and I were good friends and he said you ought to talk to Autry when he's sober. Well, I could never get Autry sober."[4]

Dawson believed the newly arrived Australian and America's singing cowboy had acted up while drinking. "He was a wonderful performer, one of the greatest showmen we've ever had and gloriously rude at times, but poor old Tex had outlived his welcome," Dawson recalled, adding that "Tex and Gene were great mates and great drinkers."[5] Dawson thought that an inebriated Morton once shot out the entry lights to the Drake Hotel on Hollywood Boulevard,[6] earning Australians a bad name.[7] Although Morton and America's screen cowboy were probably friends, and might have been drunk together at times,[8] Morton's involvement with Autry most likely did not include appearing with him on his radio and television shows or his big-screen movies, as he later declared. In 1980, for example, he told a reporter that he had been watching an old Gene Autry movie on television—*Blood On The Rio Grande* or *Massacre On The River*—when he noticed a cowboy galloping on a horse. "[expletive], that's me," Morton exclaimed.[9] Autry, however, never appeared in a movie of either title.

Morton said he lived for a while in Ralph Peer's mansion in Hollywood. Smoky Dawson believed that Peer intended to assist Morton in the United States, but Morton failed to fulfill his commitments.[10] Morton was certainly well acquainted with Peer, however: his sister Barbara recalled meeting the American with her brother at Peer's estate in California around 1958.[11] Later, Morton said, he lodged at the Hollywood Plaza Hotel for some 300 dollars a month, but struggled to pay debts owing to foreign-currency restrictions. Although he received money sent to him from Australia from record sales, he was only able to access a limited amount each time.[12] He said the manager asked him to organize the entertainment for one of the bars, which he renamed "The Western Room." Morton met the expatriate Australian costume designer Orry-Kelly (Orry George Kelly), who introduced him to well-known Hollywood identities, including Charles Laughton and mobster Mickey Cohen.[13] Ron Wills remembered that Morton telephoned him regularly from Los Angeles. When Wills took Arch Kerr's position after Kerr retired in October 1949, Morton congratulated "old Ron" for replacing his nemesis and asked if Wills could arrange a recording session for him in Los Angeles. This wasn't possible, though Wills promised to organize sessions for him with Hugh Joseph, who managed RCA's Canadian operation in Montreal.[14] That appointment was never kept, though.

"DIXIE" BILL HILTON AND PEE WEE KING

Because of visa restrictions, Morton was forced to leave the United States six months after arriving, probably around January or February 1951, so he headed for Canada with a Scots Canadian and a part-Native American girl from the Hollywood Plaza. At Bonners Ferry, Idaho, the trio passed police removing the bodies of three African Americans who had died of carbon monoxide poisoning the night before, after they had left their car's motor running to heat the vehicle at the US border patrol station. Morton and his companions eventually stopped in Nelson, British Columbia, some 600 kilometers from both Calgary and Vancouver.[15]

Morton recalled that "it was in Nelson, Canada, that we first staged my hypnotism and memory act that was later to make me one of the biggest show-business names in the country."[16] Although he persisted with his singing, yodeling and marksmanship during his decade-long stay in North America, hypnotism would be his most lucrative act.

Morton was in Lethbridge[17] and Calgary (both in Alberta) in June 1951, and appeared at a local Civic Sports Center, self-promoting by boasting of an eight-and-a-half-month engagement in Hollywood as well as tours of Australia, New Zealand and South America.[18] Quite likely, he had gone to Calgary to attend the world-famous Calgary Stampede. It was then and there he crossed paths with Dixie Bill Hilton.[19]

Early in his North American career, probably from 1951 onwards, Morton teamed with Canadian country music artist Dixie Bill Hilton, who had been influenced by Jimmie Rodgers and by Canada's own Wilf Carter. By 1938 Hilton was broadcasting over radio station CKIB in Prince Albert, Saskatchewan; two years later he moved to station CJVI in Victoria, British Columbia. He served as an air gunner in the Royal Canadian Air Force during World War II. Afterwards, he lived in Calgary, and formed his first band, the Calgary Range Riders, in 1947. For the next few years, he appeared regularly at the annual Calgary Stampede celebrations, toured extensively in northern Alberta and British Columbia, and sang on radio stations in Vancouver and New Westminster in British Columbia, where he met American country music stars Spade Cooley, Tex Ritter and Merle Travis. In 1949, Hilton and the Calgary Range Riders signed with Aragon Records. They toured throughout Canada in 1951 and performed weekly on station CFOR in Orvillia, Ontario. About 1952, Dixie Bill and his group opened shows in Canada for Hawkshaw Hawkins and Grandpa Jones.[20]

Hilton said he was closely associated with Morton around 1954 and 1955, when he was the opening act and announcer for Morton's hypnotism shows, performing in Canada, the eastern seaboard of the United States, and as far south as the Caribbean, in Jamaica.[21] But the pair had first met at the 1951 Calgary Stampede, and then went their separate ways until 1952, when they worked together.[22] In 1952, the Calgary Range Riders purportedly opened shows in Barrie, Toronto, and Hamilton, Ontario, for country music legend-to-be Hank Williams, and it's possible that by then Morton was performing with Hilton on those occasions, although the precise date Morton re-joined Hilton is currently not known.[23]

In 1983, Dixie Bill fondly recalled his years with the Australian. Morton, he thought, was a "great guy" who performed hypnotism and sharpshooting, and sang and yodeled. Such was his drawing power, Hilton recalled, that their shows attracted massive attendance, and on a regular basis they would remain in the same place for a week or more. Morton usually closed his part of the entertainment with "Barnacle Bill, the Sailor," a rollicking performance punctuated by his over-the-top "old maid's voice" that audiences especially loved—occasionally he would have to do an encore. The song was a hit on the eastern seaboard of the United States, said Hilton, who thought Morton was easy to get on with and good company.[24]

But Morton wanted to record again. By 1952, Dixie Bill had a radio show in Orillia, Ontario (some 100 kilometers north of Toronto) but there were no recording studios there, so Morton and the band went to radio station CFOS in nearby Owen Sound.[25] The discs—none of which has survived—were demo records for Morton's use, almost certainly to showcase his musical and performance abilities for potential future commercial ventures. Canadian historian Rod Olstad wrote that "Tex wanted to cut a demo tape."[26] Had Morton intended to record commercially, he could easily have achieved this with Hugh Joseph in Montreal (which Ron Wills in Australia had organized), only 600 kilometers away.[27] Morton, however, had grander notions—after making the demo recordings, he "wanted to go to New York to get a record deal," Olstad noted. "He wanted to take Fred [Lang, Hilton's fiddler] along and either/or the Calgary Range Riders, but there were financial and/or immigration problems that prevented this from happening."[28] Lang left the Calgary Range Riders in 1952, but his and Morton's paths intersected again in 1956 when Morton was touring with his partner, "Wolf Girl." In their twilight years, Hilton and Morton planned to reunite, with either Hilton traveling to Australia or Morton flying to Canada, but that didn't eventuate, and Hilton was stunned when Morton died in 1983.[29] The veteran Canadian quit show business in 1956 and lived in Calgary until his death in 1991.[30]

Shirley Field, Canada's yodeling champion of 1950, recalled meeting Morton whom she described as "a very talented man." He was performing as a hypnotist and a country music artist, she said, and encouraged her to persevere with yodeling; sometimes they yodeled together.[31] She worked with Morton during some of his tours, including Caribbean performances with Dixie Bill.[32]

Morton made a move to the United States during the early 1950s. He toured with Pee Wee King,[33] probably in 1952, on theatre dates in towns like Harrisburg, Pennsylvania, Springfield and Decatur in Illinois, and the Erie Peninsula. King recalled the tour was managed by Joseph Lee ("J. L.") Frank, his father-in-law.[34] He wrote that Morton was a "personal friend," describing him as a "great performer" who featured his sharp-shooting act as well as singing.[35] Since King was the "best country and western artist" for "Cash Box" in 1952,[36] Morton was touring with a high-profile musician and certainly not a second-string performer. Frank died in May 1952,[37] suggesting that the Australian was touring with King sometime prior to then, but precise dates are unknown. One means of establishing them would be to examine the Hatch Collection of show posters printed in Nashville and used by country artists to advertise their tour appearances and dates, but country music authority and researcher Bob Pinson was unable to locate any posters from King's tours that mentioned Morton.[38] This was most likely because King had relocated to Louisville, Kentucky, and no longer used Hatch to advertise.[39]

A HANK WILLIAMS CONNECTION?

In 1987, historian Eric Watson asserted that, for some six months Morton acted as a crowd warmer and compère for Hank Williams, on tours of Canada and the United States, repeating a similar claim he had made in 1975.[40] "Tex told me personally on more than one occasion that he toured with Hank Williams for six months," he wrote. "As well as crowd warmer ... he was also Hank's minder: his job [was] to keep [Hank] off the grog.... He told some very interesting tales of the way in which Williams sometimes managed to get drunk and escape detection.... Whilst I am well aware of Tex's habit of never letting the facts spoil a good story, his Hank Williams stories did smack of truth to me."[41]

This yarn was subsequently, and uncritically, repeated by Watson and others. But there is no evidence that this was the case. Pee Wee King recalled that he himself also toured for a time with Hank Williams in Pennsylvania, but wrote that it was highly unlikely that Morton ever met Williams then, let alone toured with him,[42] although Smoky Dawson declared that King told him Morton *had* toured with Williams.[43] For much of the time, Williams had his own warm-up act, Weldon ("Big Bill") Lister, already a recording artist for Capitol in 1951 and 1952;[44] Morton's name or variations of it don't appear on any of Williams' publicity material; and those who were associated with Williams didn't recall the New Zealander at all. For example, Williams's steel guitarist from 1950 to mid-1952, Don Helms, said he had never heard of a Tex Morton, or Bob Morton, or Doc Morton, or Bob Lane.[45] In any case, it's highly unlikely that Williams, who was a big-name act from 1950 to mid-1952, would have appeared with a relatively unknown Australian performer with no American record releases to his name. In fact, those who saw Williams in his heyday remember him touring with major American country music acts.[46]

The connection between Morton and Williams, if there ever was one, is predicated to an extent on both being managed by Oscar Davis. Morton said he had first encountered Davis at the Hollywood Plaza Hotel in 1950. Davis was certainly his manager in 1953, and he was associated with Roy Acuff's show that briefly toured Australia in 1959, of which Morton was a part, so it's likely that the Morton-Davis partnership was relatively constant throughout the 1950s, even though it seems that Morton also occasionally and briefly used other managers. "During those years [the 1950s] I was in constant contact with Oscar Davis ... and a few years later sat with [him] while he told me that he had sold Elvis Presley's contract to Colonel Tom Parker for 30,000 dollars," Morton recalled.[47]

One possibility of a Morton-Williams meeting is that in late 1952 Morton might have been in Shreveport, Louisiana, home of the "Louisiana Hayride," a live radio show that had been broadcast over radio station KWKH-Shreveport from 1948. But speculating that Morton might have moved to Louisiana is purely premised on an isolated comment that Smoky Dawson made during an interview: Dawson, who was in Nashville in 1952, recalled Jim Denny, who was then house manager of the Grand Ole Opry,[48] telling him that Morton had headed south to Louisiana. Now, whether Denny even knew Morton, or even knew of him, is unlikely, so Denny's assertion that he had sought greener pastures in the Deep South is pure conjecture. In early August 1952, Denny fired Williams from the Opry. The dejected star left Nashville and headed south, first to Montgomery, Alabama, and in September returned to

Shreveport's "Louisiana Hayride," which took him in despite his persistent troubling behavior.[49] It's just possible that Morton might have followed or was already there. Williams didn't bring his Drifting Cowboys band with him, so Don Helms would not have been in Shreveport for any length of time, and hence would have had no recollection of Morton, which might explain why he had never heard of him in the first place. Williams then again hired Oscar Davis to be his manager, and it's likely that Davis was also Morton's manager at the time, too—certainly, he was by early 1953[50].

In subsequent years, Morton told stories of how he had hypnotized Williams, in efforts to cure him of his alcoholism. Some overblown tales went as far as having the despairing Williams calling Morton "a head shrinking bastard."[51] There is no evidence, however, to support most of Morton's claims of being connected with Williams. In fact, after two years of extensive research in the United States, historian Bob Pinson wrote: "Beyond the discographical data for his 1953 session with OKeh records, we have nothing to send."[52] Williams's biographer Colin Escott, who meticulously researched his subject's career, stated categorically that Morton never toured with Williams.[53] On being told of Morton's later stories about hypnotizing Williams to stop Williams' drinking, Escott once speculated that Davis, who was in Canada when Williams engaged him, might have brought Morton with him to hypnotize the ailing Williams in Shreveport[54]—bizarre as it sounds, Williams at the time was being treated by a quack doctor, so it isn't totally improbable that Davis may have taken Morton with him. By 2005, one of the few living country artists associated with Williams in his final days of 1952 was singer Billy Walker. When he was contacted, his wife, Bettie, replied, "Billy don't remember that Morton feller, but he sure does remember Oscar 'take the money and run' Davis."[55] In all likelihood, then, Morton almost certainly was not associated with Hank Williams on any long-term basis; it's unlikely he was with Williams in Shreveport in late 1952; and, according to Escott, there is no evidence that he performed on the Louisiana Hayride show, either.[56]

Nevertheless, Morton might have appeared with Dixie Bill Hilton and the Calgary Range Riders as an opening act for a Williams show in Canada. Viable occasions include Williams's concerts in Peterborough (May 1951), Toronto (May 5, 1952) and Dundas (May 6, 1952), but so far the author has not found any evidence linking Bill Hilton and Morton as support acts for any of these shows; even so, this does not preclude such appearances.[57] Certainly, there is no evidence to support many of Morton's anecdotes he related about touring with Williams and, even then, he would not have been part of Williams's entourage, but a minor, local warm-up act instead.

RECORDING IN NASHVILLE

On Friday, March 6, 1953, Morton recorded seven sides for Columbia Records at Castle Recording Studios, located in the Tulane Hotel on 8th Avenue North, in downtown Nashville.[58] The session was most likely produced by England-born Don Law who had assumed responsibility for all Columbia's country music recordings from 1952 onward, when Art Satherley, another Englishman, had retired from the business. Although Law later had the reputation for being a "hands-off" producer and supposedly was absent for some sessions with Johnny Horton, the country music authority Ronnie Pugh, also Ernest Tubb's biographer, believed Law would most likely have personally supervised Morton's recordings.[59] In keeping with standard practice in Nashville at the time, the session probably lasted three hours.[60]

The session recording sheet[61] does not name the backing group but, based on aural evidence, the late Bob Moore, premier Nashville A-team bass player, easily identified the musicians as Ernie Newton (bass), Tommy Jackson (fiddle), Jerry Byrd (steel guitar), Owen Bradley (piano and organ) and Walter ("Hank") Garland (electric guitar). Morton almost certainly played his own rhythm guitar. Moore recorded in thousands of Nashville sessions during the 1950s, 1960s and 1970s, including nearly all of Patsy Cline's recordings, many with Jim Reeves, some with Elvis Presley and others too numerous to mention, and he was acquainted with the styles of different musicians. He was certain who they were on Morton's session after listening to only two songs that were sent to him.[62]

The session might have been stressful, especially since the musicians would have been unfamiliar with Morton's personality and style. Guitarist Paul Yandell described recording in Nashville in the early 1950s: "Recording in ... the fifties, was very different. No effects, no reverb, nothing.... Back then there wasn't anything like punching it in to fix an error. If someone made a mistake you stopped and started over. If anyone thinks it's easy doing a live session, they should try it some time.... Back then, you would rehearse the day before the session then go in and do it."[63]

The first numbers recorded, "I've Known the Truth," "The Neighbor's Wife" (a rewrite of his 1941 "The Drover's Wife") and "I've Got You (Right Out of My Mind),"[64] were relatively hard-core country music numbers. "Circus Boy" and "Kiwi Song" followed—both written by Morton, and decidedly unusual for contemporary American country music. Finally, two aging chestnuts from his Regal Zonophone days, "Railroad Boomer" and "I Was Born in Old Wyoming," concluded the session. In hindsight, it appears that Morton might have run out of original, hard-core country compositions after the first three cuts, then fell back on novelties that were only peripherally country, and finally resorted to old tried-and-true favorites. "The Neighbor's Wife" was marred, however, by Morton forgetting his modified lyrics ("Bill, Bill I loved you before you got rich like you did") and lapsing into Australian vernacular ("Bill, Bill I loved you before you came into your quids [money])." Probably because of this, there's a terse note on the session sheet: "Out." The song had been rejected almost immediately, which was a pity because the backing—especially Jackson's fiddling behind Morton's deep-voice vocal—appreciably enhanced the song, bringing it up to date compared with its earlier incarnation. Moore's wife, Kittra, noted that "Tex Morton had a ton of charm" on these discs and likened him to later star Roger Miller. "You can hear similarities in their funny, zippy little vocal turns," she wrote.[65]

That there were only seven songs recorded of a contracted eight is something of a mystery, however, especially since a Columbia advertisement from the time stated that Morton (described as "the man from Down Under" possessing an "Australian style yodel") had also recorded "The Black Sheep."[66] Historian John Rumble, of the Country Music Hall of Fame and Museum in Nashville, checked the files that were kept by Don Law and could not find a second session,[67] so there is no possibility that "The Black Sheep" was recorded separately—an unlikely event in any case given the costs involved in recording, especially for a comparatively unknown Australian artist in the United States. More than likely, the session was running close to its allocated time, and because "The Neighbor's Wife" had been rejected, there was no need for an eighth song. Three discs, at most—six sides—were all that could be issued anyway. The newer compositions, all by Morton, "Circus Boy," "The Kiwi Song," "The Neighbor's Wife," "I've Got You (Right Out Of My Mind)" and "I've Known the Truth," had all been copyrighted to Peer International either some days before the session or on the day of the session itself.[68]

News of the Nashville recordings, however, did not sit well with Ron Wills, who was then the Australian sales manager for Columbia. The expatriate eagerly phoned Wills to inform him that "he had put down a session for us which he was sure that we would like," adding "it was great to be back with the old firm."[69] Wills recalled the situation:

> When [Morton] was in Canada I arranged for him to record in the RCA Victor studios in Montreal, but even though he was in that city for thirteen weeks, Hugh Joseph, the studio manager, could not get him into the studio to record. Hugh finally rang me up in despair. Tex later rang from Nashville to tell me he had made six sides for release on Columbia. When he told me that they had been made for OKeh I almost burst into tears. We had just lost the American Columbia franchise to Philips and they got the records instead of us.[70]

If Wills's recall was perfect, then Morton had told him that only six sides were viable, supporting the earlier contention that the flub on "the Neighbor's Wife" precluded recording an eighth track. Four songs were released in the United States on Columbia's new OKeh 18000 series: "I've Known the Truth" / "I Was Born in Old Wyoming" and "I've Got You (Right Out Of My Mind)" / "Railroad Boomer" were released on OKeh in July and October 1953, respectively,[71] and in 1954 on Philips in Australia,[72] New Zealand and South Africa.[73] The remaining three sides remained unissued until Sony Australia released all seven sides, unannounced, on a compact disc set in 2008.[74] Morton's Nashville recordings were the first to be made by a recognized Australian country artist in the United States.

In Australia, reviews of Morton's newest releases in the popular press were lukewarm. "I Was Born in Old Wyoming" was mistakenly described as his own composition, though it was reported that his latest efforts "reflect the confidence and success he is enjoying in [the] US."[75] Gil Wahlquist, commenting on "Railroad Boomer," dismissively declared that "Morton simply uses the material as a vehicle for a few superficial vocal tricks."[76] His song books and records from earlier days, however, continued to be advertised in the press; in particular, the Tasman-Rodeo discs appeared to have been especially strong sellers.[77]

Morton's burgeoning career in North America was also the subject of a 1953 newspaper report in Sydney's *Daily Telegraph* ("Tex Morton Has 'Em Swooning In The Aisles"), in which his feats of hypnotism were enthusiastically described, although much of the piece seems to have been written from publicity spiel. "He believes that hypnotism was his real hidden talent all along ... A carpenter must work with wood, an engineer with steel; I must work with human beings from every walk of life before I can hope to understand them," the article declared.[78]

Another newspaper report—curiously, in February, 1953, before he had recorded in Nashville—stated that Morton had already recorded in the USA and listed "The Cards Are on the Table"[79] as another song he'd written. Morton also informed the paper that he had been a friend of the late Hank Williams, had been a national champion in swimming, rifle and pistol shooting, and roughriding, and furthermore had overseen U.S. entertainment shows in the South Pacific during the War, had entertained American troops at Guadalcanal, and finally, had been a professor at the University of California in Los Angeles (UCLA).[80] A curriculum vitae extraordinaire!

A search of UCLA's archives failed to locate a reference to Morton as a lecturer or a professor,[81] although that doesn't necessarily or wholly disprove his assertion—perhaps he had given a demonstration of hypnotism to students at the university, and then inflated the performance to the realm of being a full-time educator. Nevertheless, it's inconceivable that he could have become an employed academic instructor without having the degrees required, especially given the early date of 1951, at most only two years after leaving Australia. By all accounts, he was only in Los Angeles for a matter of months—far too brief a time to have acquired a formal degree, let alone be an instructor at a university. Asserting that he had lectured as a professor at UCLA was almost certainly another tall story fabricated by the persuasive raconteur.

Morton claimed to have fraternized with prominent country artists while in Nashville, including Red Foley and Hank Snow. He seemed to especially recall associating with Snow, but he he isn't mentioned in Snow's biography, which doesn't necessarily disprove his stories.[82] Attempts by this book's author to contact Snow directly during the 1990s went unanswered. Morton, however, recalled in a radio interview:

> Hank Snow and I used to run around ... Printer's Alley in Nashville. Get down and drink all night and all day for weeks on end. Many's the time I have seen Hank ruin ... things. We used to have some lovely tapes there of all the Carter Family and Hank. And Hank would be playing them for me at three o'clock in the morning and he would tear the tapes and ... I never forgot it. Beautiful stuff. I spoke to him recently and he said, "I haven't had a drink for years now.

How are you doing, Doc?" I said, "The same as you, I'm off it now." And he said, "[expletive], I think of how we lived this long, the things we did." One night we sat down with a fellow that had a big, loaded gun looking right at us for hours. He didn't like Limeys [British people], especially Limeys with black beards. That was me. And how we got out of that.[83]

There might be some truth in this: Snow's wife, Minnie, was friendly with Mother Maybelle of the Original Carter Family and Snow had duetted on recordings in 1951 with Maybelle's youngest daughter, Anita.[84] Morton's friend, Mike Burraston, asserted that Snow once recognized a photograph of Morton as "Doc Morton."[85] At various times, Morton also mentioned meeting Carson Robison and Goebel Reeves whom he described as being senile in his later years, but a recording of an interview Reeves had with American researcher Fred Hoeptner, just before he died, in January 1959, doesn't support the notion that he had lost his mental faculties. Hoeptner, in fact, stated: "Goebel was definitely not senile when I last visited him, which was a year and a half before his death. Like Morton, Reeves never let facts stand in the way of a good yarn, and his storytelling facility was fully functional during my interview. It took me many years of periodic effort to disentangle facts from fiction."[86]

STAGE HYPNOTISM

From 1951 onwards, Morton was touring as a stage hypnotist, singer and sharpshooter. After the 1953 recordings had failed to take off, he might have assumed there was little future in pursuing a career in country music, especially given the changing face of the industry which, commercially at least, was veering away from the styles and themes of his own kind of hillbilly music, grounded as that was in the 1930s and 1940s. Morton's Nashville recordings were good, but don't stand out from a plethora of other country music recordings of the era. In addition, he hadn't had much of an opportunity to build a loyal fan following in the United States, especially as his movements to and from his Canadian home-base were hampered by harsh U.S. immigration restrictions. In any case, had he chosen to pursue a career in country music he would have to spend years establishing his credentials by touring as a support act for big-name singers, as he had done with Pee Wee King. Better to be a master of his own destiny, he might have reasoned, owning and running the show himself as he had done with his Australian Wild West rodeos.

By 1951, promoted in publicity materials as a "world famed, international" showman, Morton was performing in Canada as a stage hypnotist. Numerous newspaper reviews extolled his show,[87] and a poster advertisement declared he had been acclaimed by the press in Australia, New Zealand and South Africa. Still beardless but dressed in a conventional suit instead of Western clothing, he was sporting a small goatee beard, pencil-thin moustache and slicked-back hair.[88] The showman was especially successful at the Gesu Theatre in downtown Montreal that year. One evening, the full-capacity audience kept him on stage until midnight, and it wasn't until the lights were turned off that the performance ended. A reporter described it as "the most amazing show ever to hit the old town."[89] Another article, written decades later, stated that some thirty gendarmes had been required to control the surging crowds, which stretched for more than a block. Morton, it was reported, had grossed 247,000 dollars in four months, enabling him to live high off the hog, and to buy two Cadillacs because "it's always nice to have two."[90] Morton continued performing at the Gesu Theatre from September 8 to October 6.[91] He was photographed with French Canadian actor Fridolin (real name Gratien Galenas)[92] and a group of celebrities, including world-famous organist Ethel Smith.[93] His show was so popular that he was forced to extend his stay to at least three weeks, a fortnight longer than originally planned.[94]

Morton occasionally publicized his shows by walking blindfolded along the ledges of high-rise buildings.[95] Broadcaster John Minson, in a later article, recalled seeing a photograph of him performing the feat.[96] Canadian Gerry Taylor, who toured with him in 1956, said Morton walked blindfolded around the roof edge of Manchester Robertson Alison Ltd.'s building, the tallest in St. Johns, Newfoundland, and also drove blindfolded through a quagmire of traffic in the city. (Perhaps the blindfold might not have been completely opaque.)[97] Taylor also recalled that Morton was performing a whip-cracking act, snapping objects out of the hands of volunteers. He toured with Morton for a time, and said the showman underpaid him to the tune of thirty dollars, although he had carefully watched him count out the money. When Taylor met Morton in Brisbane many years later, Morton again conned him out of thirty dollars.[98]

High-rise walking while blindfolded complemented Morton's exhibitions of store-front hypnotism involving young women seemingly being put to sleep and then being "revived" hours or even days later. Morton also entertained at Montreal's press club,[99] where he was likely to win over newspaper reporters. He boasted to one that he had been the official kangaroo shooter for the Australian government,[100] and claimed that he had previously toured western Canada for six months and had appeared on Los Angeles television for about a year.[101]

Despite being thousands of kilometers from his hometown, Morton still remembered his mother on Mother's Day, in 1951. He mailed her a card, informing her he was "lost in the wilds of Canada," describing his new country as similar to New Zealand and Tasmania.[102] Barbara Lane recalled that he tended to post the family snippets of information during the early 1950s, but later wrote "newsy" letters home. Generally, he phoned, she said.[103]

In April that year, Morton hypnotized reporter Les Wedman in a Vancouver hotel room, having Wedman clasp his hands together, and then suggesting he would be unable to separate them. "The veins stood out on Les' head as he struggled vainly to free his hands," a newspaper stated. Morton told his subject that when he emerged from the hypnotic trance, it would be as if he had been smoking a cigarette, causing the reporter to cough and sputter after being "woken" [sic] by Morton. Then he persuaded Wedman to believe he was on a beach in hot weather and had him wash his hair with mythical sand. After singing a few songs, Morton told the reporter that he would telephone him at work and sing "Rock a Bye My Baby" which would immediately put Wedman under again, which he did, successfully. The Australian also claimed to have been the Wilf Carter or Gene Autry of Australia, and described how he had formerly hypnotized others, even curing some of stuttering.[104]

Venturing south, Morton entertained audiences in Boston, Massachusetts, in May 1952, hypnotizing volunteers onstage and convincing them they were riding in a bus, rowing a boat, perspiring, shivering, or were drunk. Morton also performed memory tricks, blindfolded. Owing to immigration officials in the United States "screwing up," however, he was forced to cut short the Boston shows and return to Canada.[105] The same year (probably in June),[106] at the Royal Alexandra Theatre in Toronto, his one-man show took a total of 25,800 dollars over three weeks in a hall that could seat some 1,500 people, each of whom paid no more than two dollars to attend. "The Aussie has been again penciled into the Royal Alexandra for four weeks, from August 18 to September 13," a newspaper reported.[107]

In June 1952, The hypnotist showed for fourteen weeks in Montreal.[108] There are photographs of long queues of people, extending over at least two city blocks, lining up to attend performances by "The Great Morton World's Greatest Hypnotist" in Montreal;[109] Morton showed again in Toronto, under a similar contract, making some 59,100 dollars in eight weeks.[110] His aggregate takings for five weeks in Montreal amounted to 135,000 dollars, and those in Toronto to 137,600 dollars for five weeks, too,[111] an astonishing amount for a one-man show, with over a quarter of a million Canadian dollars total for ten weeks' work—far in excess of what he would have made as a country music artist. A contract in October 1952, between Morton and Montreal's Seville Theatre, specified the showman would receive fifty percent of the gross receipts (excluding amusement tax) with a guarantee of 5,000 dollars a week—but if gross receipts for the week exceeded 11,000 dollars, then orchestra costs had to be deducted.[112] Morton agreed to perform four shows daily on weekdays and five shows daily on weekends, with each performance lasting a minimum one hour duration, and to print 500 window cards which the Seville would distribute.[113] A handwritten comment in 1952 stated: "Have taken $480 000 in this area,"[114] though it isn't clear whether this sum was for the entire takings or for Morton's share—which in any case would have been about 50 percent. Most probably it referred to the overall takings, but even then, Morton would have earned the best part of a quarter million in Canadian dollars; additionally, unlike his Wild West Rodeos, his expenses were minimal because he was essentially a one-man show with virtually no overheads.

There are numerous (mostly undated) photographs of Morton hypnotizing subjects in Canada.[115] His favorite feat appears to have been hypnotizing a young female in a department-store window, or similar business, and then "waking" her some time afterwards, as he had done with Joyce Stephens in New Zealand. Acts like these were often used as advance publicity for his evening performances. In Yellowknife, Northwest Territory, only some 400 kilometers south of the Arctic Circle, for example, he hypnotized a Miss Valeta Bevan and had her "sleep" in a department-store shop front by singing to her. She was driven to his show that evening in a taxi, and he revived her on stage.[116] A photograph, probably from 1952, shows another young lady seemingly dozing in a bed, with hypnotist Morton and a radio announcer standing over her. At the back of the photograph was written "thirty two hours sleep."[117] He could even hypnotize people over the radio: in 1952, in London, Ontario, a newspaper reported a subject who had been mesmerized "via air waves" by Morton. He had hypnotized her in the Grand Hotel lobby by singing on the radio broadcast, then awakened her nine hours later.[118]

Morton (described as an "internationally famous lecturer, author, psychologist and hypnotist")[119] dressed his part convincingly: the outback gear and hat had been supplanted by a conventional suit, complemented with a small, neatly-trimmed moustache and goatee-type beard, dyed black. Sometimes, his hair was parted in the middle. At the time, the master hypnotist would only have been in his late thirties or early forties, but he had visibly reached middle age, when compared with his youthful looks from the halcyon days of the early 1940s, though several newspaper reviews still described him as handsome.[120]

Various photographs of his stage performances show Morton's subjects ostensibly asleep, at times lying on the stage floor, while Morton speaks into a hand-held microphone, controlling their actions through his hypnotic powers. One photograph depicted about a dozen subjects slumbering in chairs or sprawled on the stage. In another photograph, participants were asleep while others were dancing.[121] A familiar trick was to convince a participant that he or she had caught a fish and have them hold up their prized catch. Sometimes Morton would give audience members post-hypnotic suggestions, causing them to act strangely after they had been hypnotized and then "awakened," like calling out, "Hiya Doc," after resuming their seat in the audience or, on cue, returning to the stage to ask for a cigarette. This part of Morton's act was original and was subsequently termed, in books on hypnosis, as "The Tex Morton posthypnotic climax."[122]

Morton's shows were enthusiastically acclaimed in Canadian papers, with headlines such as the following:

THE GREAT MORTON IS MASTER SHOWMAN

ANOTHER BIG AUDIENCE ACCLAIMS MORTON SHOW

GREAT MORTON ASTONISHES BIG CROWD WITH ALL ROUND SHOW

HUNDREDS TURNED AWAY: GREAT MORTON SHOW HELD OVER
BY POPULAR REQUEST

MIRTHFUL DEMONSTRATION: DR MORTON SHOW IS BIG HIT
WITH CITY AUDIENCE

GREAT MORTON THRILLS LARGE AUDIENCE HERE

CAPACITY AUDIENCE HELD ENTRANCED BY MASTER HYPNOTIST

'BEST SHOW HERE IN YEARS' IS VERDICT HERE
ON GREAT MORTON[123]

Photographs of the era show an elegantly dressed Morton clutching a microphone stand at an angle, like Elvis Presley later did, while participants were acting out his hypnotic suggestions. He augmented his hypnotism act with displays of sharpshooting, and feats of memory—such as having audience members seal small items in envelopes, then he would shuffle the envelopes and correctly return the items to the participants—and of course singing, with "the Australian version" of yodeling.[124]

In 1952, "the man with the million-dollar mind" performed his "greatest one-man show in the world" in Clifton, Minnesota, in the neighboring United States.[125] Morton also journeyed to Arctic Canada and even to far north Alaska, sometimes by hiring and traveling in light aircraft,[126] (though he was not a pilot.)[127]

Accolades for his shows continued in a seemingly never-ending parade of glowing plaudits. In late January 1953,[128] only about a month before the recording session in Nashville, The Great Morton ("The World's Greatest Hypnotist") was in Toronto, performing in a show advertised as "fantastic, fascinating and funny."[129] A report in the January 1953, edition of *Variety* magazine stated that "the handsome, black-bearded" Morton was about to break the Toronto Casino Theatre house record that had been set by pop-singer Johnnie Ray.[130] An undated review described the master hypnotist as "resembling a husky David Niven" and reported the antics he had audience members perform, like sweating on a hot beach, wrapping themselves in imaginary rugs when he informed them the temperature had plummeted, fishing in a rowboat, and reviving memories of "Sir Thomas Tightpants," an English aristocrat.[131] *Billboard* magazine asserted that "the Montreal press had tossed repeated raves over the unusual Morton performance."[132] The Toronto Casino Theatre hosted performers such as Johnnie Ray, Gene Nelson, Phil Silvers, Abbott and Costello, Sammy Davis Jr. and Frankie Lane, as well as strippers and bawdy acts. Artists who appeared there frequently also performed at the Seville Theatre in Montreal.[133]

A 1953 advertising poster for "The Great Morton - The World's Greatest Hypnotist" declared that he had performed for 16 weeks in Chicago, 114 consecutive shows in Los Angeles, and "fourteen weeks of fun in Montreal."[134] Chicago theatre critic Elliott Norton proclaimed that "not since Houdini" had there been such a show.[135] The long-hoped-for American recording career was fading, it seemed, and unquestionably was less profitable than the stage hypnotism which increasingly dominated his performances throughout the 1950s. "He was making millions," his sister Barbara recalled;[136] it seemed that he spent millions, too, in what must have been a free and easy lifestyle with no thought of investing his earnings for the future. That outlook toward spending, instead of planning for financial security, had been a trait from his earliest days in Sydney.

Morton showed in Evansville, Indiana, in March 1953, only a few days after the recording session in Nashville, suggesting that even then his focus was on hypnotism.[137] A critic, however, complained that the show was "slow in spots and overlong, running forty minutes past the allotted time," and not "entertainment in the usual sense."[138] In an advertisement, Morton's routine of hypnotizing a young female was featured as promotion for mattresses in a Sears Roebuck catalog. "You don't have to be hypnotized to enjoy sound sleep on Sears Harmony house bedding," it announced.[139] The showman was so famous at the time, it seems, that he could sell merchandise for large retailers.

In June 1953, The Great Morton was performing as a headline act, along with an all-star variety revue, for a week-long engagement, at New York's Apollo Theater in Harlem.[140] "Morton has created quite a sensation all over Canada and the United States," a commentary gushed. He "guarantees to convince the most skeptical patron that hypnotism is not a phony, but a science." Morton's seventy-five-minute act dominated the evening, leaving a critic for *Variety* magazine clearly unimpressed. "It wasn't until around the midway mark that he began to stir any real interest," the reviewer complained, although he noted that Morton's hypnotism and memory recall were extraordinary, despite the showman "impairing his act" by referring to the antics that subjects performed as "silly."[141]

In July that year, "the hypnotist par excellence" was back in Canada, showing in Ontario at Hamilton and Toronto.[142] Morton informed the audience during one of his shows that he had recorded eight "Australian folk songs," referring to the March Nashville session some months earlier, although all sources point to his recording only seven songs at that session.[143] In August, "the man with the million dollar mind," Robert (Tex) Morton B.A., Ph.D., was in Sydney, Nova Scotia, where he again played to enthusiastic reviews. He informed a reporter that it had been his mathematics teacher at Nelson College—"Severne" was his name, he said—who had taught him memory training.[144]

In late 1953 or early 1954, Morton's parents joined him in Canada; Barbara, fresh from having qualified as a nurse, reunited with them soon afterwards (possibly in 1954). Her brother paid for her air fare as a reward for graduating. The four then traveled to England, arriving in Liverpool sometime after the coronation of Elizabeth II in June 1953. Barbara especially remembered touring with her parents and illustrious brother, leisurely driving in his impressive Cadillac to places like Stratford-on-Avon and London. Barbara and her parents were away for about four months and she said they returned home "about July or August." She continued her career in New Zealand, studying maternity nursing and midwifery,[145] while her brother journeyed on to France, before returning to Canada. There are photographs taken in England, possibly from a later tour, with "Lew and Leslie Grade" printed under them, showing Morton's hypnotized subjects, with one audience participant kissing a sleeping female.[146] Perhaps it was especially feasible to perform in the United Kingdom because his New Zealand or Australian citizenship was recognized there, whereas his references in the United States didn't guarantee long-term employment. At some time in the 1950s, Morton visited Hawaii—there is a photograph of him there with the American actor and entertainer Joe E. Brown.[147]

Morton was in Portage la Prairie, central Manitoba, in December 1954; the local newspaper described his performance as "the best show here in years." He hypnotized three young men, convincing them they were taking a two-hour bus tour, impressed the crowd with his sharpshooting, and sang about four songs.[148] Five days later, he appeared in nearby Brandon, Manitoba, where his show was lauded as "good, clean fun";[149] its star extolling himself as "the most versatile and entertaining showman of our time."[150] In the ensuing years, Morton continued with his act throughout Canada, venturing as far south as parts of the United States and the Caribbean with Dixie Bill Hilton, who acted as master of ceremonies for him in 1954 and 1955, so Hilton said, but the author couldn't locate online newspaper reports or other evidence, apart from his assertion, of the two performing together during that time. At Fort William, Canada, in 1954, crowds had to be turned away from his first three shows, so another performance was scheduled. His act was described as "the high point of merriment" by a "peerless and versatile performer."[151] Morton was in Jamaica in January 1957;[152] whether this was with Hilton or was a different trip is uncertain, although Hilton retired in 1956.[153] A 1957 Jamaican newspaper advertisement called for a "young lady volunteer" to be "hypnotized before the public" by Morton over radio Jamaica. The volunteer would then be taken to the State Theatre in Kingston where, that night, she would be awakened by a well-known local identity believing him to be Prince Charming—a repeat of his "hypnotism by radio" act that he had earlier performed in Canada. "No one else listening to the broadcast of course will be affected," the advertisement astutely reassured.[154]

Recalling two of Morton's hypnotism shows, one correspondent wrote: "We thoroughly enjoyed [his] performances, and we still laugh about some of the things that happened on stage." He was later "flabbergasted" to learn that the hypnotist had been a "cowboy singer [who] had recorded extensively."[155]

14

THE GREAT MORTON, HYPNOTIST

DURING HIS NORTH American sojourn, Morton attempted to shred much of the mystique of hypnotism that surrounded the subject, ostensibly to distinguish himself among other stage hypnotists. "Demonstrating the great potentialities of the human mind, The Great Morton is a far cry from the stage hypnotist of years ago," declared magazines in 1953 and 1955. "He draws aside the veil of secrecy and mysticism which has for so long [been] hypnotism."[1] Morton explained hypnotism as a valid, scientifically defensible extension of the power of suggestion, a view accepted at the time by psychologists and the medical profession. This approach was complementary to his other claims of having pursued and lectured on hypnotism in academic and medical circles, seemingly elevating him above that of a stage performer to a scholar.

Morton, who listed his occupation on a 1958 insurance policy as "Doctor of Hypnosis,"[2] claimed to have been awarded a Bachelor of Arts degree in psychometric hypnosis from Palo Alto University in Los Angeles,[3] but this is questionable since he had only rudimentary educational qualifications from New Zealand, having left school at fifteen with a less-than-impressive academic record. A bachelor's degree requires satisfactory entrance examination results and afterwards some three years of full-time undergraduate study. Perhaps the degree was an honorary one or maybe the university was awarding "mail order" degrees at the time. Another scenario more-or-less accords with a statement by his brother Kim: "He walked into McGill [University, Montreal] and asked what the chances were of getting a diploma. They said, 'If you've got the money, we've got the time,'"[4] although it scarcely seems likely that the respectable McGill University would market degrees for cash. Another institution, though, might have awarded Morton qualifications for payment. Nelson-based historian Alan Turley wrote that the alleged Palo Alto degree "was probably bought."[5] While asserting that Morton purchased an Arts degree conveniently overcomes issues with actually studying for it, the proposition still results in him gaining a bogus, worthless qualification—and one unlikely to have been accepted by a reputable university as a prerequisite for a doctorate.

By 1953, Morton was insisting that he had a doctorate in hypnotism.[6] During the 1950s, he was frequently described as "Dr. Robert Morton, B.A., Ph.D." Afterwards, when he was in Australia, Morton stated that he'd lectured at McGill University and Sir George Williams College (another university in Montreal), and that his doctoral thesis focused on the history of hypnosis,[7] with particular emphasis on its use by Indigenous Australians.[8] It also purportedly described hypnotic types of practices used by the Arctic Eskimos, American Indians, New Zealand Maoris and Hindu priests.[9] At various times, it was claimed that Morton gained his doctorate at McGill University,[10] but this is untrue: a search of McGill's archives revealed no record of a Robert Morton or a Robert Lane being awarded a Ph. D. at McGill between 1950 and 1957.[11] It's just possible, though, that Morton was awarded an honorary doctorate (or purchased a worthless one) from another university and later embellished the story by announcing it had been gained from prestigious McGill University. At other times, he said the doctorate had been awarded by a conveniently vague, un-named Canadian university; and frequently he only mentioned lecturing at McGill.

On other occasions he claimed that his doctorate had been awarded by the University of California[12] but this is also incorrect: an archivist at the university's Los Angeles (UCLA) campus stated categorically that "no Ph.D. was issued to either a Robert Morton or a Robert Lane by UCLA in any year."[13] As for his conjecture to have lectured there in the early 1950s, no mention of him could be found in the university's online archives for 1950 and 1951. At the time the university's requirements for an undergraduate degree were four years of study and fifteen units of academic work.[14] In 1980, he told a reporter that he took his doctorate at Western University, California, in the early 1950s,[15] but an online search mainly located the Western University of Health Sciences, which was founded in 1977.[16] In any case, apart from the implausibility of acquiring a genuine doctorate in what amounted to only a few years, Morton's constant changing of (or omitting) the name of the university that purportedly awarded him the degree lends little support for any truth in his claims.

On the other hand, Barbara Lane, certainly not one to accept at face value everything her brother told her and who was skeptical of some of his claims, confirmed that the family always believed Morton had a doctorate of some sort, though not from McGill. She thought the only connection Morton had with the university was that his apartment on McTavish Street in Montreal was across the road from McGill.[17] (McTavish Street presently runs through the university.)[18]

Morton's recurring claims of having academic credentials were doubtless to enhance his reputation as a highly regarded hypnotist—necessary to convince audiences at his shows that he was indeed a professional and not an amateur performer. And also, because subjects who believed his claims were more likely to follow his suggestions, than if they considered him to be a mere pretender or just a showman.

Morton lectured at the Toronto Institute of Hypnotherapy with Stephen Steiner, a Canadian hypnotherapist.[19] The Toronto Institute, however, was almost certainly not a high-level academic organization. Steiner said he had met the Australian around 1953, when Steiner was also performing as a stage hypnotist at the Top Hat night club in Montreal. Afterwards, he stated, Morton toured northern Canada and then later looked him up in Toronto, where he had founded the Toronto Institute of Hypnotherapy some three months previously. "I invited Robert to participate in some lectures with the groups I was teaching," Steiner recalled. "He enjoyed working with the groups for a short period of time, but his desire was to perform on stage."[20]

Morton said he had lectured to doctors and dentists in Montreal and at the Los Angeles Institute of Hypnotherapy and Hypnoanalysis, describing the use of hypnosis to cure afflictions such as stuttering and paralysis, and at the prestigious McGill University "before the finest assembled neurosurgeons and psychologists."[21] This might well have been yet another overblown embellishment, however, because it's likely that his lecture at McGill University was only to students of the university's Psychology Club, and consisted largely of hypnosis as entertainment. In December 1952, Morton's lecture and performance were enthusiastically reviewed in *The McGill Daily*, a magazine produced by the university:

McGILL MUMMIES MESMERISED AS MORTON MOLDS MASSES
BY BARBARA NATHAN

Every chair, bench, table, airduct and window sill was occupied last night when Dr. Robert (The Great) Morton gave a lecture and demonstration on hypnotism and hypnotherapy under the auspices of the Psychology Club. People were piled three deep against the walls inside and outside the Union Ball-room in order to secure a glimpse of the famous entertainer. An estimated 800 students were present. Dr. Morton began his "lecturette" by explaining that he possesses no supernatural powers and cannot invoke evil spirits. "The human mind can be likened to a wagon and a workhorse—the driver of the wagon is the conscious mind and the subconscious the workhorse. The driver may be replaced, but the horse remains to pull the load." This according to Dr. Morton is the principle of hypnosis. The Aborigines of Australia appear to be the first people to have made use of this art; they "willed" their victims to death.

A different form of hypnotism is Mesmerism, practiced in Paris and Vienna by M. Mesmer. This man cured many forms of functional nervous disorders (such as stuttering) by hypnotherapy. "A form of hypnotherapy very popular at present in California is diet control. A hypnotist can make a person stick to their diet by hypnotizing them; telling them to stop eating sweets, and awakening them with the instructions still imprinted on their subconscious mind."

VOLUNTEERS

Then Dr. Morton asked for ten or twelve volunteers. Twenty avid prospective subjects barged their way to the creakingly makeshift platform and offered their services. These people were asked to stand up in single file while Dr. Morton selected those which he considered would make good subjects. The number was finally whittled down to nine "who turned in a superb performance." Dr. Morton ably caught one of his subjects whom he had convinced would fall backward into his arms. Another strange sight was that of a young gentleman seated in a corner and cheerfully rotating his arms. The subjects next found themselves on a fishing trip, rowing clumsy row boats, baiting hooks with slimy green frogs, and catching hoppers. They were then requested to smile prettily for one photographer, who in this case happened to be Peter Hall. Immediately after the fishing trip, a severe heat wave enveloped the nine victims when, much to the amusement of the audience, [they] began removing certain articles of clothing. Suddenly the mood changed and the subjects were witnessing a very sad movie. They very obligingly provided tears in large quantities.

Dr. Morton closed the performance by thanking Hilliard Jason for planning the evening, and left amid thundering applause.[22]

Morton might have maintained his association with the university on into 1953: the *McGill Daily* published another article on him ("The Great Morton—Adventurer ... Poet") in February that year.[23] Perhaps, too, Morton's lecture at Sir George Williams University was also to students: in an undated newspaper report, he stated he was an honorary member of the Students's Executive Committee there.[24]

Although Morton was first and foremost a stage hypnotist, he also thought deeply about aspects of the subject. In an undated typewritten essay found amongst other memorabilia, he wrote about "Hypnotism and Reincarnation" under the name "Dr Robert Morton," and discussed hypnotic regression in which subjects recall their past and, sometimes, so-called previous lives. He described an experiment he conducted in which he gave a subject dates and facts about a famous historical figure, before hypnotizing him or her. The subject then recalled a past life as that historical person. Morton's intention was to demonstrate that hypnotic regression might not always be what it seemed. He also declared that there is often a fine line between fact and fantasy, especially with children but also with some hypnotized people; and in a revealing statement, he wrote: "It is not my intention to attempt to debunk another person's religious beliefs, but ... according to my beliefs I can not feel that our God intends us to 'look beyond the veil'. As I say, I like to think of myself as a Christian—although I admit, on occasion, a quite puzzled Christian."[25] It's not known what Morton's religious views were, as he kept them to himself. Neither his sister Barbara nor his later partner Kath could say categorically what they were,[26] although based on the statement above he might have been an agnostic. Aspects of his attitude towards others, such as his generosity to those less fortunate, were clearly Christian attributes, however.

Fortuitously for Morton and other stage hypnotists, the public at large was intrigued by hypnotism during the 1950s, particularly with the claimed retrieval of past lives. Whereas hypnosis had been used by some American psychologists after the Second World War to treat post-traumatic stress disorders, more sensationally, amateur hypnotist Morey Bernstein professed to have discovered multiple personalities of Colorado housewife Virginia Tighe. One of her personalities was said to have been a long-deceased Irish woman from Cork, "Bridey Murphy."[27] Reports like these added to the fascination with hypnosis.

From the outset, there were two branches of hypnosis: an academic (or medical) branch and a division which comprised lay hypnotists, including stage hypnotists like Morton. Academic hypnotists were represented by the American Society for Clinical and Experimental Hypnosis (SCEH), established in 1949 and the American Society of Clinical Hypnosis (ASCH), founded by Milton Erickson in 1957. Membership of the SCEH or the ASCH required a doctorate in medicine, dentistry or psychology. Hypnotism was finally accepted as academically valid in the United Kingdom when the British Medical Association formally recognized it as a scientifically legitimate technique in 1955. Lay hypnotism, on the other hand, did not require official medical qualifications, and frequently treated the art as a form of entertainment, though not exclusively, since some lay hypnotists attempted to cure smoking addiction, excessive weight gain and the like. Frequent use by stage hypnotists, including Morton, of the title "Doctor" further confused the public and gave the misleading impression that practitioners were fully-accredited academic hypnotherapists. On the other hand, some critics of Erickson, like British stage hypnotist Derren Brown, have since been deprecatory of his anecdotal style of reporting results.[28]

In later years, professional bodies such as the SCEH and ASCH regarded lay and stage hypnosis as unethical, but it was championed by Boston-based Dr. Rexford L. North, who was associated with the 1950s *Journal of Hypnotism* and the National Guild of Hypnotists (NGH), both of which were intended to further the profession's integrity. North, a dentist who became deaf during his career as a result of meningitis, was intriguingly reported by *Billboard* magazine as a "pre-war astrology pitchman of New York."[29] As of 2017, the NGH was still operational, had published books including *Inside Secrets of Stage Hypnotism* and *The Crash Course in Selling Hypnosis*, had conducted training programs in hypnosis, and held annual conventions.[30] It was recently described as "a professional organization comprised of dedicated individuals committed to advancing the field of hypnotism" and as "a resource for members and a vehicle for legal and legislative action."[31] In the early 1950s, stage hypnotists occasionally felt the need to protect their occupation against criticism from academics, and North's journal was an outlet for their views. In his article "The Case For Stage Hypnotism," for example, North wrote "every once in a while a howl is heard about the horrors of presenting hypnotism upon a theatre stage," but he defended the practice because, he said, he enjoyed performing, especially since he liked making money, and also because he saw it as a means of introducing hypnotism to the thousands of people who attended his shows. Besides, he asserted, stage hypnotists were sometimes successful where academic hypnotists were not, although he conceded that a handful performers gave the occupation a bad name.[32]

Morton had undoubtedly read of hypnotism and was able to describe its history accurately, from the time of Franz Mesmer through practitioners like James Braid to his present day, creating the impression that he was a highly qualified academic who had studied the subject in depth. Certainly, Morton was very intelligent and appears to have presented a view of hypnotism broadly in accordance with modern theories, so he cannot be entirely dismissed as merely an opportunistic showman. He made the cover of the *Journal of Hypnotism* in 1953, and was described as having a doctorate.[33] The journal, however, was not a high-quality, professionally monitored publication but instead a somewhat well-intentioned but lesser magazine, if one can judge by its cover with theatrical, stylized text, commercial advertising within, and articles like "How to Make Money With Hypnotism," "Anyone Can Develop Hypnotic Ability" (implying that hypnotists do not necessarily need medical qualifications),[34] and "Man Loses Savings— Hypnotism to Blame?,"[35] and what appears to have been blatant promotion for Morton:

> Bob is well known throughout Canada for his tremendously successful and popular demonstrations in the field of hypnotism. Originally from Australia, where he is renowned not only as a hypnotist but also his native land's leading balladeer, Dr Morton is today unquestionably the leading international exponent. A smooth and polished technician, his demonstrations attract not only huge turnouts of the general public but it is well known that professional hypnotists return again and again to study the perfected ease with which he holds his audience from start to finish. We urge our readers to watch for Dr Morton's appearance in their localities.[6]

Apart from this, there was nothing else about Morton in the journal, nor do future issues in surviving collections mention him—which is not to say that he wasn't featured in the publication, since the collections might be incomplete. The magazine, however, was described as "a trade journal for practicing hypnotists," suggesting it wasn't an academic publication at all.[37]

By the early 1950s, Morton sported a trimmed beard and moustache, the latter of which he retained in later life even after dispensing with the beard, bestowing the facade of a highly qualified academic, seemingly emulating the fictional Svengali's mystique, far removed from his yodeling boundary-rider image of days gone by. It almost certainly confirmed in Morton's eyes, at least, that he had ascended several rungs up the ladder of success, although he still sang hillbilly songs at his performances and blasted cigarettes, sandwiched between the lips of courageous, if sometimes nervous, assistants, with a 22-caliber rifle.

On balance, Morton would be considered a lay practitioner by today's standards, and although that wouldn't disqualify him from practicing and even attempting medical hypnosis techniques, he wouldn't have been accredited at an academic level. In the 1950s, however, the distinction between fully qualified and lay hypnotists was blurred in the minds of the public; even stage hypnotists often put their craft to well-intentioned therapeutic use, although in Morton's case, he was first and foremost an entertainer. In 1951, for example, he was at pains to inform the *Montreal Herald* that he was "not available at all for professional consultation,"[38] and in 1965 he stated, in the language of the day: "There are always some . . . who want me to help them personally by hypnosis. People with homosexual tendencies. Nail biters. Bed wetters. I could spend the rest of my life helping them. I'm not in that business. I just tell them to go and see a good doctor."[39]

Morton had to look the part for his stage act. His appearance and aura, his introductory patter and his stated claims of academic credentials would have had the effect of convincing many in his audiences that he was the real deal, and not merely an enthusiastic amateur. "Stage hypnosis is not a con," wrote stage hypnosis practitioner and author Terence Watts, "but it is showmanship." It contrasts with medical hypnosis, Watts asserted, because the stage hypnotist uses theatrics and relies heavily on confidence in his approach, showmanship, belief in the technique, and the willingness of his subjects to perform simple tasks.[40]

To begin with, Morton would have stated that subjects cannot be hypnotized against their will, thereby providing an "escape clause" in case participants did not respond positively to his instructions—insurance against potentially embarrassing events, such as attempts by some to deliberately ruin the show through proving they couldn't be hypnotized. Sometimes the hypnotist informs the audience that only intelligent and open-minded people can be hypnotized, perhaps as a form of inducement. An advertisement of Morton calling for volunteers in an Australian newspaper, probably in 1970, declared that "seriously minded" participants were being sought, but definitely not "pranksters or jokers." "Such levity will not be tolerated," the ad curtly warned.[41]

Morton then looked for enthusiastic volunteers—subjects more likely to go along with his suggestions—and prefaced his performance by assuring them they would not be in a deep trance, or unable to control their movements, conceivably to increase the likelihood that they would respond to his suggestions once they realized they were not in a trance. "Perhaps ten to fifteen percent of [the population] are highly hypnotizable," claimed Professor Amanda Barnier of Macquarie University.[42] Clearly, Morton was seeking to identify these subjects, apart from other volunteers. Deliberate selection of audience members was described in the report of his presentation to McGill University students.[43] In 1955, a reviewer in Evansville, Illinois, complained that he took "far too long" to select three volunteers, only one of whom appeared to be hypnotized.[44] In a later Far East show, a Hong Kong newspaper reported, he took an unusually long time to select volunteers who were likely to be hypnotized. "My experiments cannot be a complete success unless subjects are completely willing," The Great Morton declared.[45] Having selected likely candidates and then relaxed them, Morton would have participants imagine familiar situations, like being cold or thirsty, and then convinced the most impressionable subjects to act out alien and out-of-character situations, such as clucking like a chicken, usually with the anticipated humorous results.

Some of Morton's subjects did fall into fully mesmerized states, though. Canadian Gerry Taylor recalled being hypnotized by Morton in 1956, at both St. Johns in Newfoundland, and in Labrador when he was at university. "I fell into the deepest hypnotic trance he'd ever seen," Taylor said. "Took him a half hour to bring me out of it, and I'm not sure he completely accomplished that." In 2014, Taylor described Morton as "the most fantastic, multitalented entertainer I had ever met and seen on stage."[46]

Morton also mastered feats of memory, probably at the time he initially learned hypnotism in New Zealand in late 1949 and early 1950. While blindfolded, he was able to correctly recall the names of twenty-five objects that an audience had announced, with the items written on a blackboard.[47] He could also remember up to 100 articles called to him by audience members.[48] Sometimes, for humorous effect, he would pretend to forget an item, only to recall it later. Memorization of large numbers of objects can be assisted by using several techniques, including: associating objects with hypothetical spatial locations, imagining links between situations and the objects to be memorized, and associating an object mentally with an activity, such as "stacking" items.[49] According to some sources, these strategies are more effective when matched with the preferred learning style of the person memorizing objects, whether through visual, auditory or kinesthetic (tactile) cues.[50]

Nevertheless, the apparent speed with which Morton learned and perfected memory techniques is difficult to explain without crediting him with exceptional cognitive powers in the first place. Irrespective of the strategies he used, Morton's feats of memory required extensive mental processing, skill and concentration. Unlike singing, where a flubbed line could easily be overlooked, or hypnotism where difficult subjects could be excused because of their resistance to suggestions, memory feats could easily fail, and spectacularly, on a single mistake. Sometimes Morton resorted to outright deceit to achieve an effect. Morton acolyte Mike Burraston told Peter Burgis how the showman used a hidden microphone to astonish audiences with his "mind reading" act:

> I remember Mike Burraston telling me about Tex's mind reading act, which was based on his ham radio skill. With Tex blindfolded on stage an interviewer roamed the audience asking members various questions ("where did you meet your wife?") in whispered tones ("In Scotland, how wonderful").
>
> "Tex, can you tell us where this couple met." Tex would appear to concentrate and then announce, "That lucky couple met overseas, and romance started in Scotland." Following confirmation by the stunned couple an explosion of applause [came] from the amazed audience. Tex's gift was assisted by the concealed microphone carried by his interviewer and the receiver in his own hat. Mike had the gear in his garage.[51]

15

THE GREAT MORTON IN HOLLYWOOD

MORTON'S FINAL YEARS IN CANADA

In 1955, Morton appeared at the Orchid Lounge in Springfield, Illinois, with the Pat Sheridan Quintet, where again his performance was lauded by the local press. "A good two and a half hours entertainment which we thoroughly recommend," a report stated in an advertisement.[1] Morton was based in Montreal until 1956; sometime in that year, it seems, he moved to Ontario, where he remained until 1958,[2] although in August 1957 an insurance policy still listed his address as 1231 Catherine Street, West Montreal, and his occupation as "Dr. of Hypnosis."[3]

Barbara returned to North America in 1956 or 1957 to be with her brother again and worked for about eighteen months there, touring with him as far north as the Arctic Circle. He was still making big money, she said, but he was a soft touch and gave thousands of dollars away. "He made fortunes and lost them," she thought. She recalled her brother would typically open the show with his singing, yodeling, sharpshooting and whip cracking, then perform his hypnotism act after intermission—this time dressed more formally in black-tie and tails. Barbara remembered touring scores of tiny towns and hamlets, performing in all manner of venues. "It was quite an experience," she reminisced.[4] She couldn't recollect whether he was drinking excessively during her time with him, but said he nearly always had a bottle of whisky at hand.[5] Ken Brumley, editor of the local weekly newspaper in Kitimat, British Columbia, also described The Great Morton's performances there, which were most likely in 1956:

Tex arrived... by vintage Cadillac complete with secretary, and we soon agreed to his welcome as a show-world "doctor." His performance as a hypnotist doctor went with a brilliant success, with his secretary acting as featured "Wolf Girl," often serving Tex with plastic cups of "water" aimed at keeping his throat moist. At a party later, I was astounded at his acceptance by the local medical fraternity.

Tex's show was not musical those two nights, but his hypnotist performance was professional, accompanied, strangely, with shooting lit cigarettes from the mouth of "Wolf Girl," also on stage. Tex could not have been better received by his audience at Kitimat, even if he had included a couple of his "Aussie" songs. He obviously didn't want to be known as an "Aussie singer."[6]

But in faraway Australia, where interest in him lingered in some quarters, Morton's whereabouts and activities were a mystery. A 1953 Sydney newspaper reported he was breaking attendance records at theatres and auditoriums in Canada and the United States,[7] but as the years rolled on, details of his career in North America were unknown to most Australians, as this reply to a reader's inquiry in 1957 showed: "Little has been heard of Tex Morton since the OKeh recordings which were recorded by him in the USA two or three years ago. To my knowledge, he has not recorded since and when last heard of, he was practicing as a hypnotist, under the title of Doctor Robert Morton."[8] Some months afterwards, Australian readers were assured that Morton was intending to close his show to establish a clinic for the study of hypnosis in medicine, and that Morton had gained a BA and PhD at a Canadian university, largely supplanting his singing career.[9]

Although Morton had previously been managed by Oscar Davis, there were others who oversaw business on his Canadian tours, but their names are currently unknown, except that in January 1957, in Toronto, he either signed or renewed a six-month contract with a J. Ian Reid who was to act as his manager and, according to the agreement, would receive 20 percent of the take on the first 2,000 dollars, and ten percent of the money thereafter.[10] By then, Morton had carved a reputation as a showman of international standing. *Globe* magazine in August that year included his photograph (as "The Great Morton") in a special tribute to the Royal Alexandra Theatre in Toronto, alongside shots of celebrities Al Jolson, Harry Lauder, Lillian Gish, John Gielgud, Margot Fonteyn, Mae West and Orson Welles, among a pantheon of other stars.[11] Another review described his explanation of hypnosis as "singularly original, fresh and convincing" and called him "a supreme master of mental concentration."[12]

Canadians, it seemed, were awestruck by the Australian performer, and newspaper reviews referred to him in glowing terms as "the Charles Laughton of the southern hemisphere," for example, with a "versatility as unique as Danny Kaye's," enhanced by his "salty Australian charm and dry humor."[13] Hypnotism was definitely the most popular act in his shows, and though audiences also thrilled to his sharpshooting and feats of memory recall, some were mildly critical of his singing: "Morton's balladry was the weakest part of his performance," one review candidly confirmed, though conceding, "but this is to be forgiven in a man who does so many other things well." The review continued: "Last night's audience kept the performer until nearly midnight with its calls for more of his jack-of-all-trades entertainment."[14] In later years, Morton asserted that his singing was, by and large, popular with Canadian audiences because they especially appreciated the old songs he routinely sang.[15] He also narrated poetry, often by the likes of Banjo Paterson and British-born Canadian poet Robert Service,[16] whose verse, like that of Paterson's, was sometimes derisively sneered at as doggerel by some literati, though both writers were especially well-liked by the public. Morton recorded recitations of Service's "The Cremation of Sam McGee" and "The Shooting of Dan McGrew" purportedly in North America and they were later released in Australia.[17]

In March 1958 Morton appeared in Russell, Manitoba, where he provided "two and a half hours of first-class entertainment" showcasing hypnotism, memory tricks, and singing, also convincing five audience members they were on a bus ride.[18] The same month, he showed in nearby Flin Flon, a mining town close to the Saskatchewan border, where his act was yet again judged to be "a big hit." The local newspaper especially lauded the second part of his show—"a demonstration of mass hypnotism extraordinary," as the paper described it—and judged it to be worth double the admission price alone.[19]

Morton didn't lack female companionship in Canada. "He had another lady friend ... Marilyn," Barbara Lane said. "A real good looker with a figure to go with it. I don't think she liked me," she recalled. A newspaper appraisal of the times described Morton's assistant as a "very beautiful" woman who held a cigarette in her mouth and cards for Morton to shoot.[20] Perhaps Marilyn was the "Wolf Girl" that fiddler Fred Lang had mentioned to Rod Olstad. Barbara also said her brother had a relationship with French-Canadian actress Marjolaine Hébert, who was active in radio and television during the 1950s.[21] The strikingly attractive Hébert might have met the hypnotist while he was in Quebec.[22] Barbara has numerous photographs of the couple and affirmed that they were together for about two years.[23]

At the time, Morton was a one-man show, regularly on stage for three hours at a time: memorizing objects, singing and yodeling, sharpshooting, reciting poetry and, for most in the audience, it seemed, the star attraction, hypnotizing. The North American shows were unquestionably more demanding than his performances in his Australian Wild West Circus days, when usually he only had to shoot, sing and announce, and where circus acts and roughriding would provide him with a temporary respite from performing. But since he was now the sole performer, he didn't have to split the takings among others in the show (except for "Wolf Girl" and his manager), as in Australia, plus he was relieved of having to transport the equipment and animals that were part of his Australian circuses, thus his overheads would have been minimal, and his takings correspondingly lucrative. Given his inclination for wild exaggeration, it's surprising he didn't make more of his Canadian success after he returned to Australia, because there was no need to embellish stories of his achievements and income as a stage hypnotist during the 1950s.

THE CARNEGIE HALL "CONCERT"

Morton claimed to have performed at a concert in New York's prestigious Carnegie Hall sometime during the 1950s, but the exact date is unknown, although he told journalist Colin Mackay the year was 1954 and, he recounted, he'd been invited to recite the poetry of Banjo Paterson, Henry Lawson, Rudyard Kipling and Robert Service.[24] He once claimed the concert was broadcast on radio to an audience of twenty million people.[25] Another time, he said he was invited by the American Institute of Hypnotherapy. He told a magazine in 1959 that he "staged his one-man show at New York's Carnegie Hall"—but by this he might have meant just performing stage hypnosis.[26] Canadian Robert Platt, who compiled an online Tex Morton discography, however, was unable to confirm with Carnegie Hall staff that Morton had ever performed there. Certainly, Platt could find no reference to such a concert (or concerts) in the *New York Times*. If Morton did record at Carnegie Hall, rather than in the grand hall, it was almost certainly in one of the smaller recital halls that accommodated about 260 people, and possibly he was at a private function.[27] Alternatively, Morton might have simply invented or embroidered the story, and the tapes he thought had been recorded at Carnegie Hall might have been of other recitals instead.

On his return to Australia in 1959, Morton gave producer Hal Saunders a "motley collection of tapes" of variable quality that he had brought back from North America. Saunders and recording engineer Robert Iredale, described as "a young electronics genius,"[28] spent many days re-engineering them to release standard. Saunders recalled there was audience applause on the tracks Morton claimed were from Carnegie Hall, suggesting Morton was performing before an audience of some sort, but on other recitations Iredale dubbed in fake clapping from Festival's sound effects library.[29] The tracks formed the basis for the 1959 album, *The Tex Morton Story*[30] with liner notes stating that organ accompaniment was by Ian Barrie who, Morton said, was a famous Wurlitzer organist.[31]

Morton's version of "The Cowboy's Prayer" perhaps hearkened to his early years: the composition had been recorded by Goebel Reeves in 1934 and released in Australia in July 1935.[32] Likewise, "Home On The Range" was perhaps based on a 1932 Carson Robison Trio recording issued in Australia early in 1934.[33] "Rio Grande," "Clancy of the Overflow" and "Waltzing Matilda" mirrored his long-term interest in Banjo Paterson's poetry, and "The Cremation of Sam McGee" and "The Shooting of Dan McGrew," both from the pen of Robert Service, were likely learned while he was touring North America. "You'll Never Be Missed" was a reincarnation of his 1940 narration; and Rudyard Kipling had written the poem "Chant Pagan." Morton's expanding interest in spoken verse was nowhere better captured than in these selections.

Amongst memorabilia from Morton's Canadian tours are amateur ("ham") radio licenses, with the call-signs VE2AHZ and VK2AHZ. Morton was an enthusiastic wireless operator and regularly stayed up late at night, conversing with other operators. He was a member of the Amateur Radio Emergency Corps, enabling him to transmit vital information during crises such as floods, storms and other calamities. Morton raised funds to establish a central radio station for communicating with the outside world in the event of such catastrophes. His license was renewed in the United States in January 1959, and later on, in New Zealand and Australia at regular intervals. A 1970 renewal in New Zealand stated his call sign was ZL2AVM.[34]

HOLLYWOOD

In late 1958 or early 1959, Marilyn (who might have been "Wolf Girl") journeyed with Morton and Barbara to Hollywood and, shortly afterwards, she left while Morton and Barbara stayed there.[35] Morton returned to Australia in 1959, but his sister remained in the United States for about four years, at times working as a nurse in a Los Angeles hospital, and also as an on-set nurse for television series and movies—*Dragnet*, *Lassie* and *The Untouchables*, were several of those. Her bosses were Lucille Ball and Desi Arnaz. "It was fun—very interesting," she remembered. After about four years in the United States, she too returned to New Zealand.[36]

In 1958, researcher and collector John Edwards wrote that American Fred Hoeptner had advised him that Morton was living in Hollywood permanently at the time, working in artist promotion and the music publishing business, though when contacted in 2017, Hoeptner said he couldn't remember meeting the Australian—but this was some 60 years afterwards.[37] In July 1958, Edwards noted that Morton and Hoeptner had met at a folk-music lecture by Dr. John Greenway at the University of California, in Los Angeles.[38] In April 1958, Morton was photographed after having performed for a Boys Town charity concert.[39] His stationery letterhead declared that Robert "Tex" Morton was involved in publishing, management, promotions, films, television, radio and performing, and gave his office address as 6331 Hollywood Boulevard,[40] a few blocks from Grauman's Chinese Theatre and the Hollywood Roosevelt Hotel.

Morton's claims of being Gene Autry's friend in Hollywood evidently didn't extend to his appearing on Autry's *Melody Ranch* radio show, the last series of which ran from 1945 to 1956.[41] Autry authority Dick Hill indicated he had never heard Morton on any *Melody Ranch* episode, and thought it highly unlikely that he appeared at all.[42] Similarly, an online search of all cast members of *The Gene Autry Show* television series (aired 1950–1956) and Autry's *Melody Ranch* shows failed to retrieve any entries of "Morton" or "Lane."[43] In any case, Morton's time in Hollywood, probably during 1958 and 1959, was well after Autry's radio and television shows had folded. Morton also claimed to have acted in some Autry westerns like the non-existent *Blood On The Rio Grande*,[44] but again this appears implausible because Autry's last motion picture was in 1953,[45] five years before Morton returned to Hollywood.

One possibility, however, is that Morton might have appeared in minor roles as a bit part in his earlier days in Hollywood, in 1950 or 1951, when Autry was active in movies and television, and his *Melody Ranch* radio shows were being broadcast, but Morton's roles were too insignificant to mention (perhaps he might have been in a crowd scene or the like). Efforts to contact Autry during the 1990s were unsuccessful, and the extent to which the two were friends is unconfirmed by searches of the Autry archives. Similarly, the Gene Autry Museum also stated that they had nothing of Morton in their collection, but that alone does not necessarily disprove Morton's claims.[46]

Morton repeatedly said he acted in movies and television programs in Hollywood.[47] For example, country music historian Eric Watson referred to a photograph of him, dressed in a fringed coat, curiously worn over a shirt and tie, as "in a TV character role in Hollywood,"[48] and described him as "one of Hollywood's most sought after TV character actors."[49] Similarly, another image of Morton attired in a sailor's hat and leather jacket was captioned "Tex Morton as a character actor [in] Hollywood."[50] Both images, however, were probably nothing more than publicity shots (some are clearly marked "John E Reed Hollywood." Reed was a well-known Hollywood glamour photographer).[51] More than once, it would seem, Morton had portraits taken of himself in various costumes and poses, probably for publicity and promotional purposes, and later asserted they had originated from actual movies or television shows. He also claimed to have appeared in the television series *Gunsmoke*,[52] but his name as either "Morton" or "Lane" is not listed in an online database of all actors who were in the series which ran on television between 1955 and 1975.[53] Again, it's just possible that Morton's role, if any, was too minor to mention. In 1959, Morton said he had appeared as a French-Canadian mounted policeman in the popular American television show, *Sergeant Preston of The Yukon*. The assertion, printed beneath a snap of Morton with a fur hat, was in a Tasmanian newspaper in late 1959.[54] *Sergeant Preston of The Yukon*, starring Richard Simmons, ran from 1955 to 1958[55] but an internet search of cast and crew yet again revealed no mention of an actor named "Morton" or "Lane."[56]

Morton also told of meeting Hollywood stars like Bing Crosby, Bob Hope, Dean Martin, Jerry Lewis, Robert Mitchum, Robert Newton, Herbert Marshall and Charles Boyer, and said he appeared on programs hosted by Tex Ritter and Steve Allen,[57] but his name is absent from a complete listing of the

Steve Allen television shows.[58] He is not listed in a complete online compilation of guest artists on the Ed Sullivan Show, either.[59] Some commentators have claimed that Morton might have worked for Walt Disney studios, as a bit-part actor or voice-over narrator,[60] but when queried Disney replied they had no record of his working for them.[61]

In an Australian resume, Morton wrote that he had appeared for three weeks at the Pasadena Playhouse in Los Angeles, had been a member of the Montreal Studio and Drama Club for five years, and had played Teddy Roosevelt in *Arsenic and Old Lace* and a missionary in *Strange Cargo*[62]—but the character cast of *Arsenic and Old Lace* does not include Teddy Roosevelt; perhaps Morton had confused him with "Teddy Brewster," a character in the play.[63] *Strange Cargo* was a 1940 film starring Clark Gable and Joan Crawford, predating Morton's arrival in the United States by a decade,[64] though Morton might have acted in a stage adaptation of the movie.

Morton asserted he had taken over from Peter Finch and Wilfrid Thomas on BBC radio programs when he was in England, although almost certainly he would have been a guest on Thomas' program, and had narrated poetry and prose from the likes of Paterson, Lawson, Kipling, Dickens and Shakespeare. He stated that he had played various roles in other American television shows like *Annie Oakley* and *Circus Boy* in the United States.[65] But Morton's name does not show in a listing of actors who appeared in the *Annie Oakley* television series which ran from 1954 to 1957 and starred Gail Davis as Annie Oakley. Furthermore, it's unlikely that he would have acted in movies with Davis, anyway, since it doesn't appear that she made any in Hollywood after 1957;[66] He's also absent in a complete online register of cast members in the television series *Circus Boy*, which ran from 1956 to 1958.[67]

In addition, the Academy Foundation of Hollywood was unable to locate any information of Morton (or Lane) in their records, except for his later appearances in Australian movies and his 1983 obituary in *Variety* magazine.[68] While this doesn't disprove his assertions that he was a Hollywood actor, at most it suggests that if he did appear in television and movies there, it didn't accord with claims in his resume.

But there are elements of Morton's resume that are closer to the truth. It claimed he acted for the Montreal Studio and Drama Club, and had appeared in the Lux TV Playhouse television programs in Los Angeles,[69] a series that often starred renowned actors.[70] It's entirely feasible that Morton worked in some of these programs, perhaps in minor roles. He certainly appeared (credited as Robert Lane) in the Lux Playhouse television drama *A Game of Hate* starring the beautiful classical singer and actress Kathryn Grayson.[71] The program script, dated September 19, 1958, was subsequently televised that November.[72]

According to Barbara Lane, her brother was friendly with expatriate Australian actors, including Ronnie Randell who had a successful career in radio, stage and film, both in Australia and America. He organized the necessary paperwork for Morton to remain in the United States.[73] Morton also fraternized with Peter Finch and the ex-Australian actor and lothario, Errol Flynn, Barbara recalled, although she thought her brother didn't stay long with the movie stars. "He was always his own man," she said.[74] Finch, though primarily based in the United Kingdom during the 1950s, was in Hollywood about 1959.[75] Flynn similarly made a comeback in 1957 following a five-year break,[76] so the Australian stars were in Hollywood when Morton was there.

16

BACK IN AUSTRALIA

MORTON RETURNED TO Australia in 1959. His partner in later years, Kath Morton, said he was tired of living in Hollywood,[1] but there might have been other reasons. Perhaps his Hollywood business wasn't making money because, when he did return, he was not financially well heeled. On the other hand, he might simply have yearned to return to his antipodean homeland. If he needed money, he could have revived his hypnotism act, though the advent of television in the 1950s was associated with a corresponding decline in live entertainment: Morton stated in a newspaper article that hypnotists had become two pence a dozen by the late 1950s—hence his escalating involvement in acting and management in Hollywood.[2]

THE GRAND OLE OPRY TOUR

In true Morton fashion, he returned with fanfare: there was no quietly slipping unnoticed through the Sydney airport. Instead, he brought with him a *Grand Ole Opry* show, headed by "the king of country music," Roy Acuff, and his band, the Smoky Mountain Boys, with other celebrated acts like the Wilburn Brothers, a young Melba Montgomery and June Webb, "the prettiest Smoky Mountain Boy".[3] The tour was managed by Morton's old manager, Oscar Davis, and Frankie Moore,[4] and might have been Morton's idea in the first place, although Acuff's biographer, Elizabeth Schlappi, said Davis and Moore conceived the idea and persuaded Acuff to accept a percentage deal instead of a flat fee—which would prove to be a disastrous move for

Acuff, as events unfolded. Possibly, Davis had initially persuaded Acuff to tour Australia and afterwards invited Morton, whom he knew well. In February 1959, *Billboard* magazine announced the impending tour, adding that the troupe might also appear in Hawaii.[5] They departed America in February 1959,[6] stopping in Honolulu, most likely without Morton, who probably flew alone to Sydney to promote the forthcoming tour and bolster his own reputation, telling a magazine that he "was in association with a movie company and intend[ed] producing a film in Northern Queensland" that would be internationally released.[7]

Although the credentials of the Americans were impressive on paper, none of them was well known in Australia. Critic Ray Brown concluded: "There were no known names amongst the group and the music was new to many."[8] A better choice might have been *Opry* performer Hank Snow, a Jimmie Rodgers acolyte whose style would be more appreciated in Australia, since Rodgers's recordings already had been popular from the 1930s onwards.

By that March, the Americans had arrived in Sydney, where a magazine announced that Morton had previously performed on the *Grand Ole Opry*—another fabrication, since there is no evidence of Morton ever appearing on the show.[9] The first performance of *The Grand Ole Opry Tour* was at the Sydney Stadium, an old barn-like structure that was mostly used for boxing and wrestling matches. Morton, listed in the official program as "producer,"[10] compèred the show and sang the occasional song. Some tickets for the first shows were bought by Fleming's Food Stores, who gave them to customers as an incentive for buying groceries. Around 10,000 people attended the show on the first night, Thursday, March 5; there were two shows on Friday, and these attracted a total of about 4,500; plus, there were three shows on Saturday which also drew a total attendance of close to 10,000. Correspondent Ray Brown was favorably impressed by the program, enthusiastic about Acuff's group, and spoke highly of the Australian performers who also appeared.[11]

Newspaper reviews, however, were scathing. Alexander Macdonald, of the Sydney paper *Weekend*, mocked Morton and said he and others attending nearly dozed off when Morton sang "Rocking Alone in an Old Rocking Chair." Then he lambasted the Americans using descriptions such as "a clear-cut case of strangulation of the tonsils," "He of the split larynx" and Acuff as "a martyr to arthritis who screeched with agony at every hop." He concluded his postmortem critique with "it was more than I could bear."[12] Macdonald was later described as an "old-style bohemian" who was "constantly embroiled in conflicts with creditors, editors, bank managers and women." It was said that he reveled in language that was at times gifted and even absurd, although it lacked the common touch.[13] Undoubtedly the hillbilly music on display was beneath him, so he snobbishly used it as a vehicle for demonstrating his expertise with wordplay, though some in the crowd apparently agreed with him. There were reports of audience members booing performers and hurling objects at them while they were on stage.[14] Acuff was especially upset because audiences jeered at him for talking too much.[15]

Following the Sydney performances, the tour was next scheduled for Melbourne, and then Adelaide, where it was called off by Acuff, owing to poor attendance. "Our music is not known here," he told reporters. "The audiences are not acquainted with our country and western music and our stay in Adelaide is too short to educate them. Tex Morton, the Aussie, is the only one known to Australia and it was a disaster when we lost him with an attack of laryngitis."[16] Given that he might have been aware of scheduled bookings in advance of the shows, it's tempting to speculate that Morton was ultimately glad to distance himself from what was rapidly turning out to be a flop of major proportions,[17] though another report acknowledged "Tex Morton went down with an attack of laryngitis after the first night and was only able to sing one song at the other shows ... he was really sick."[18] Elizabeth Schlappi wrote that "attendances were good, but not good enough to meet expenses" and believed that if the shows had been held in Brisbane instead of Adelaide, the results might have been better. The tour was rumored to have made a loss of some 10,000 pounds,[19] and Morton later dismissed it as a "grand old floppery."[20]

According to Johnny Ashcroft, one of the Australian warm-up artists, the Americans lacked enthusiasm and went through their routines mechanically as if it were "just another job," whereas the local performers gave their best and received a rousing reception; so, when Acuff's group performed after the interval, up to half the audience dwindled away. Ashcroft recalled witnessing Acuff in the dressing room after the show with his head in his hands, bemoaning "What went wrong? What happened?"[21] Acuff's at-times pompous lectures about country music in the United States were not appreciated either.[22]

Afterwards, there were rumors of a falling-out between the Americans and the Australians on the tour,[23] but these were almost certainly false. Morton instigated them when he was interviewed on the ABC station 5AN-Adelaide, in about 1981. He described the ill-fated tour as "a bloody disgrace" and the Americans as "bloody awful people to handle" and "real hillbillies," who "got on the booze" and "let us down badly." Acuff, he said, "treated Australians like hicks."[24] He also claimed to have fired Acuff,[25] though this was stretching the truth, as he had no such powers. Furthermore, his depiction of the Americans was clearly unwarranted: Pete "Brother Oswald" Kirby and June Webb[26] both stated that the two groups had mixed well, and the overall mood was one of friendliness. Local artist Athol McCoy, who met the touring artists, confirmed this, too.[27] In fact, when McCoy was specifically questioned about drinking on the tour, he stated that alcohol consumption was mild and involved, in the main, social drinking. "No one got drunk," he said.[28]

ROY ACUFF'S OPEN HOUSE

Acuff was singularly unimpressed with his reception in Australia, complaining that he had "lost his shirt" on the tour.[29] Country music expert Max Ellis recalled he and broadcaster John Minson meeting Acuff in Nashville in 1977. When discussion turned to the 1959 Australian venture, Ellis remarked that "he was rather negative about [it] to say the least."[30] Acuff, he remembered, was particularly critical of Morton,[31] implying the two had a falling out. Some good was salvaged, however, when Acuff and his troupe recorded thirty-nine Roy Acuff *Open House* television shows at TCN Nine Studios in Sydney—but because some songs the group recorded were neither public domain nor in the Acuff-Rose catalog, the series proved to be dreadfully expensive in the end.[32] For his part, Morton declared, he wanted no role in the production and ensured that his name was not on the credits—though he wasn't involved in producing the series to begin with.[33] Acuff's troupe finally departed Australia on April 25 the same year,[34] after a two-month stay.

Exactly why Acuff chose to make the television shows in Australia is a moot point, especially given that the number of American artists who could be featured was limited, compared with a much larger pool in the United States. The programs were reportedly produced and owned by an American company, possibly one associated with Acuff.[35] But in October 1959, John Bryden-Brown, described as "managing director of Marketing Services (Australia)," was reported to have recently returned from the United States, where he had negotiated deals, on the one hand between Channel Nine (TCN Nine) and Marketing Services of Australia, and on the other, between companies in America, raising the issue of who owned the series in the first place—Acuff or TCN Nine. This suggests that Channel Nine originally owned the series and sold it in the United States. Bryden-Brown said that there was a market in the United States for Australian television shows, but not with "kangaroos jumping out of every scene". Furthermore, he asserted, television shows could be produced in Australia much cheaper than in the United States. "All the Americans—from performers to technicians—are such expensive workers if they're any good that they can really be used only in big money shows," he reported. "The talent available lower on the scale is much inferior to that available in Australia. Because of this we can produce good TV at a price which makes it an attractive proposition in America."[36]

ON TOUR AGAIN

Morton commenced touring almost as soon as he returned to Australia. He was in Launceston, Tasmania in late 1959, billed in a local newspaper as "The Great Morton—the finest one-man show in the world today." The advertising spiel included "Guitarist and folk singer! Unusually clever comedian! Memory expert! Ace sharp-shooter! Terrific show-man! Fascinating lecturer!"[37] Tex Croft and Nola Hirst were with him, and the show was promoted as "Tex Morton Grand Ole Opry" (resurrecting memories of the catastrophic Acuff tour). One advertisement listed his fundraising for charities, including the Police Boys' Clubs, Lions International, Rotary, and others including the Mine and Millworkers Union funds.[38] His performance for youngsters at St. Giles' special school was especially praised, and his interest in the welfare of children with disabilities was commended by the Chairman of the then Society for the Care of Crippled Children. Morton sang on radio, too, on Jack Munting's *Down the Hillbilly Trail* program, and *The Country and Western Club*, both on 7EX-Launceston[39] At the time, he also had a half-hour show on ABC network-stations 2CY and 2CN (both in Canberra).[40]

In 1960, Morton was again in New Zealand, performing his three-hour, one-man show for organizations like the Jaycees and Lions, featuring his marksmanship and memory feats, and recounting his previous exploits for journalists, most of whom reviewed his acts favorably.[41] He donated half the proceeds to grateful charities. One report stated he had returned to New Zealand for a brief holiday but had been persuaded to assist local charities instead.[42] Judging from the takings—an estimated 1,400 pounds for one show[43] and 800 pounds for another[44]—he was still popular with local audiences.[45] "I find people in the bigger centers appreciate the one-man aspect more readily than in the smaller centers," he informed a reporter.[46] In a bizarre incident in New Plymouth, Morton hypnotized a Maori, Ossi Kohi, and asked him about two pig hunters who were then missing near East Taranaki. Kohi gave a description of where he thought the men were, and subsequently the New Zealand Army discovered the two, in circumstances remarkably similar to Kohi's description. The hypnotist mused that he was puzzled, while not discounting the fact that the incident might have been a genuine case of clairvoyance.[47]

By March 1961, Morton had reunited with Ashton's Circus.[48] Later that year he appeared in Canberra, this time with a much larger show promoted as a "Wild West Rodeo Circus," featuring circus acts and mule-riding entertainment for youngsters. Children under the age of eight were admitted free if they brought along a hand-drawn picture of the feline in Morton's song, "The Cat Came Back,"[49] which he'd recorded about a year earlier for the long-play album, *Tex Morton Looks Back*, on the Festival label.[50] Morton probably learned it from a 1931 Otto Gray disc.[51]

RECORDING AGAIN

The 42-year-old Morton was not a wealthy man when he returned to Australia. Hal Saunders, who was then artists and repertoire coordinator for Festival Records, recalled he was living in a caravan park in North Ryde, Sydney, and down on his luck. "He had lost all the millions he had made," thought Saunders, who was anxious to sign him with Festival:

> He agreed to come to Pyrmont [in Sydney] and discuss a recording contract with Festival. At that time no record company paid advances to their artists, who often had to wait six or twelve months for royalty statements, so you can imagine the horror of our secretary, Ron Chatto, when Tex demanded an advance payment of one hundred pounds . . . against each album before he would begin recording! I managed to persuade the committee that we would get our

money back and so the ... album *Tex Morton Looks Back* was recorded, released and sold more than enough to cover the advance.⁵²

Another of Festival's efforts by their new star was *The Tex Morton Story*,⁵³ a long-play album released in 1959, comprising of an eclectic selection of performances purportedly made while Morton was in North America, including "The Cremation of Sam McGee," "I Belong to Glasgow" and "Clancy of the Overflow." Most likely Saunders saw an opportunity to capitalize on Morton's homecoming without having to organize recording sessions, and Morton was in dire need of cash, anyway. American folklorist Archie Green, particularly impressed with Morton's "Don't Go Down The Mine Dad," also known as "The Dream Of The Miner's Child," wrote that "Morton, an Australian country-western performer influenced by Jimmie Rodgers and Goebel Reeves, sings only the first verse and chorus but adds to it a recited version of the boy's dream," remarking that Morton invoked mining tragedies from around the world and used terms such as "draegerman" (a rescue miner), to extend the theme from one disaster into generalizing on the perils of mining.⁵⁴

Festival released *The Versatile Tex Morton* in 1959, apparently banking on Morton's fans buying re-worked versions of music, for which their star was renowned in his glorious Regal Zonophone years. Although his renditions were criticized for lacking the spirit of his earlier classics, nonetheless they sold well,⁵⁵ and *The Versatile Tex Morton* was reviewed favorably as "a valuable asset" to his fans and "well worth a listen" to those who weren't.⁵⁶

In 1960, Festival released *Tex Morton Looks Back*,⁵⁷ again comprising re-workings of his earlier hits and mainly older-style songs. Morton and the backing musicians were so professional that recordings were usually completed after only one take,⁵⁸ but they lacked the vital spark of much of Morton's previous efforts. Reviewer Eric Watson was singularly unimpressed, complaining, "To begin with, his singing style, with which we are chiefly concerned, has slipped badly. Festival are currently releasing newly recorded 45s which for the most part are from his old [Regal Zonophone] repertoire, and whilst they are still done in the same style, still obviously Tex Morton, this time they just don't 'come off.'"⁵⁹

Morton altered direction again by recording two spoken-verse albums: *The Sentimental Bloke By CJ Dennis* in 1961, and *Tex Morton Reads Banjo Paterson*⁶⁰ the following year. "In order to retain some sanity during the crazy cacophony of the rock 'n' roll era, I looked around for quieter and more soul-soothing items to record," Saunders wrote. "Having always been interested in literature, I persuaded my committee to let me try an album of verse." Despite warnings that the initiative would turn out to be a dud, he persisted. Morton's recordings were extraordinarily successful, and "every actor in Sydney bombarded us with suggestions for spoken word albums, most of which we rejected," he recalled.[61] The Paterson album was favorably reviewed: Morton brought the poems to life, one critic declared, and "treats [the poems] with respect,"[62] though an assessment of *The Sentimental Bloke* somewhat dismissively recommended that "teenagers might buy the album for their parents."[63] Saunders, in fact, was mightily impressed with Morton's talents; at one night-time recording session, he told Kath Morton that her partner was a genius,[64] and later wrote: "The greatest larrikin [rowdy person] of all our artists was, in my opinion, our finest verse reader—Tex Morton. It was not only his mastery as a mimic in many languages but from having worked with him over a number of years I would say he had the ability to get right inside a verse and become whoever was the subject of it . . . Obviously the cigarettes and whisky and wild, wild women didn't affect that talent."[65]

But Morton was unpredictable which was exacerbated by his loathing of recording,[66] and failed to appear for a scheduled session with Saunders one Monday. With all three studio musicians eager to commence, the news came through that the singer had flown to Hong Kong the previous Saturday—after he had been paid an advance of 100 pounds and was only part-way through recording an album.[67] Eighteen months passed, and then Saunders received a telegram from Morton in Hong Kong, and according to Saunders, along the lines of: "Seriously ill in hospital—send two hundred and fifty pounds for hospital and air ticket home."

"Only Tex Morton could have done that and got away with it. We sent the money," recalled Saunders.[68]

And waited . . . and waited. The exasperated Saunders was finally informed that the singer had landed in Melbourne but had immediately set out on an Australia-wide tour. Then, at about five-o'clock one Friday afternoon, Morton phoned Saunders to instruct him to organize a recording session that night. Morton was in Sydney, but was due to fly to Brisbane on the following Monday. In desperation, Saunders contacted three musicians and engineer Robert Iredale and arranged the session, which commenced at nine-o'-clock that night and lasted most of the weekend. Saunders wrote that Morton, who was steadily imbibing whisky, finished the album and then suggested they carry on recording another. "You can send me the cheque later," he quipped. And so, they continued, Saunders recollects: "We would work until one of us was exhausted and then flake out on one of the couches in the studio.... More coffee, sandwich, whisky—and on—and on. Tex remembered and performed material that he'd picked up in America, and that I'd never even heard of. Wonderful stuff."[69]

The marathon finally ended, some forty-eight hours later, at eight-o-clock on Sunday night. An exhausted Saunders turned up to work on Monday at morning-tea time, only to be bawled out by his boss for arriving late. Saunders reviewed the master tapes and described the recordings as "priceless material" featuring an impressive mastery of dialects, and an eclectic mix of songs, varying from comedy to tragedy. "These would be real winners," he thought. Saunders retired in 1965[70] and nothing happened with the recordings between then and 1983, when Morton died and Saunders phoned Festival to inform them of the precious performances on the master tapes. By then, Festival had moved to a new building. To help, Saunders traveled to the new premises, went to the strongroom, and asked for the tapes. The engineers looked "rather shame faced" he wrote. Then they replied, "Oh those—we heard he had died and as we were short of tape, we didn't think they'd be any use to anyone." They had erased the tapes. Saunders nearly cried.[71]

While he was recording for Festival, Morton was also performing live, at times in a circus some "thirty or forty" miles[72] from Sydney. Saunders said the star was "living it up" at Sydney's fancy Chevron Hotel where he would phone room service about every ten minutes to order a double Scotch—"no ice." On one occasion, Morton was running late and casually ordered a rental car, inviting Saunders to accompany him. "That man performed his sharpshooting act, with live bullets going within two inches of his assistant's head, as though he had never heard the words 'double Scotch,'" Saunders wrote. "What a man."[73]

An interesting recording from 1962 was "Kevin Barrie."[74] Eighteen-year-old Kevin Barry was an Irish republican who was hanged by the British in 1920 for participating in an ambush in which three British soldiers died. The song "Kevin Barry" was composed in his honor; it was possibly an antecedent of the immensely-popular Bluegrass number, "The Legend Of The Rebel Soldier." Morton might have heard "Kevin Barry" (which he recorded as "Kevin Barrie") when he was in Great Britain during the 1950s.[75]

During the early 1960s, Morton appeared in Shepparton, Victoria, for five nights. Broadcaster Neville Pellitt recalled he was then touring as a one-man show—hypnotist, memory expert and "a little comedy"—and expressly stated he wasn't performing as a singer. One memory act was comprised of Morton listing twenty objects, called out from the audience, on a blackboard and recalling them—forwards or backwards—in perfect order with his back turned towards the list. In one performance, however, he mistakenly attributed "PA" (for "public address") to "Prince Albert," a well-known brand of American tobacco. This bothered him for the entire week, Pellitt said. On another occasion, Morton and Pellitt were in a store, being served by a sales assistant who'd been in the audience of Morton's show the previous night. "Tex just snapped his fingers and the young fellow was immediately asleep," recalled an astonished Pellitt. "Auto-suggestion," declared Morton, as he brought him around again.[76]

17

THE GREAT MORTON IN THE FAR EAST

IN 1962, Morton "went walkabout" (took off) and abruptly left Australia for the Far East—Hong Kong in particular and then United States military bases in the region.[1] In June of that year, he performed at Hong Kong's Imperial Hotel in a show that mirrored the format he'd used in North America.[2] He also appeared at the City Hall in Hong Kong, where he was described as living up to his international fame.[3] Yet again, he had volunteers from the audience act out improbable situations, sometimes with post-hypnotic suggestions.[4] On one occasion, a throat condition prevented him from singing; on another, he didn't perform his shooting act. "No two shows are exactly the same," he nonchalantly informed a newspaper reporter. When he did sing, however, "the affable New Zealander" was called on to encore several times.[5]

In 1978, journalist Frank Crook recalled he had saved Morton's life twice: once, in Hong Kong, when the singer had nearly suffocated from falling, head down, in a bowl of steaming rice, and another time when he had set himself alight after falling asleep while smoking at the King Kong nightclub in Hong Kong. Crook sprayed him with water from a soda siphon some five meters away.[6] Crook also remembered that Morton was a contestant in an oyster-eating competition at the restaurant, but took so long eating and enjoying the meal that he fell way behind the eventual winner—much to the annoyance of some spectators, who threatened violent retribution afterwards.[7]

As well as performing in Hong Kong, Morton toured Tokyo, Singapore, and the Philippines (probably at United States army bases).[8] It seems, though, he wasn't well: there are reports of American doctors treating him in the

Philippines (possibly with the side-effect of altering his voice),[9] and Hal Saunders stated that he telegrammed for money to pay for hospitalization in Hong Kong.[10] According to Saunders, Morton was on tour for about eighteen months. He was back in Australia in 1963 and appeared as a guest on John Laws's television program, *Showtime*,[11] which was broadcast in November, including the night of President Kennedy's assassination in Dallas.

KATH

Kathleen ("Kath") was Morton's final partner. She was introduced to the showman in 1963 by a mutual friend[12] and afterwards remained his constant companion for the next two decades, longer than any other female had. Quiet and unassuming, she looked after her partner, making his shirts, working the ticket box at his shows and acting as assistant for his shooting act.[13] Despite the ever-present possibility of an accident occurring as he shot cigarettes—sandwiched between her fingers, or held between her lips while bullets flew just centimeters from her face—she bravely remained unperturbed and confident in his abilities. She was often present at his late-night recording sessions and especially recalled producer Hal Saunders waxing lyrical about her partner's talents.[14] Her deep respect for her partner was nowhere demonstrated more than through the assistance she generously provided for this book.

MORE TOURING

In March 1965, Morton appeared in Canberra, once more hypnotizing a young damsel in a store to be revived that evening by a "prince charming."[15] Yet again, the public was warned that would-be pranksters and jokers would not be tolerated.[16] Morton was described (probably in his own words) as "an almost legendary figure for his many entertainment skills, including sharpshooting, singing and audience participation events."[17] Later that year, his show was at the Princess Theatre in Melbourne, advertised with a bevy of plaudits, quoted from reviews of his North American performances. A photograph showed him with a goatee beard, moustache, and a civilian-type hat; the focus of his show, it seemed, was hypnotism and not his golden hits of past years, although he was also singing and sharpshooting.[18]

Not all his live performances, however, were favorably received, as journalist Patrick Tennison retrospectively noted: "The Great Morton's show opened in Melbourne. At once he ran into trouble. On his opening night, someone stole his guitar and he had to fill in for more than an hour while police hunted the thief and friends scoured around for another one. The critics "panned" him sourly. They said he talked too much, the show was too slow and, anyway, it wasn't very bright or new entertainment."[19]

To which Morton, basking in the memories of some two decades previous, retorted: "The reporters they sent to interview me were too young to remember me from the old days. Just boys they were. Some still had pimples. And if one decides to get stuck into you, they all do."[20]

Morton recorded prolifically in 1965. In June, he put down tracks for the long-play album *Sing, Smile and Sigh*,[21] but to a large extent many of the songs were colorless, if effortless, re-workings of earlier favorites. Two albums of recitations followed: the double album *Robert (Tex) Morton's Reading Of Ginger Mick* and *The Sentiment And Humour Of Banjo Paterson, as read by Robert (Tex) Morton*.[22]

Later in 1966, he was back with his old recording company, EMI, essentially the same as Columbia. The current country-music hit "(The) Green, Green Grass Of Home," about a doomed prisoner awaiting execution, was an opportunity for him to narrate the second verse, even though his version was nowhere near as effective as recordings by American performers Johnny Darrell, Porter Wagoner and Jerry Lee Lewis, or Welsh pop star Tom Jones. In contrast, "Tex Morton's Protest Song (Burn Another Folkie)" was original and mildly humorous—in it, he ribbed fellow country singers like Slim Dusty, Athol McCoy and Kevin Shegog. It included veiled criticism of his old adversary, Buddy Williams.[23] A coupling of two songs from the album on a 45-rpm single sold a modest 908 copies from February 1967 until December 1968.[24] Morton rejuvenated a pair of his previous recordings, "Barnacle Bill the Sailor" and "I Got You (Right Out of My Mind),"[sic][25] but this time his over-the-top theatrics with the fair young maiden's voice on "Barnacle Bill the Sailor" were more comical than the 1937 recording, and he sang more verses on "I' Got You (Right Out of My Mind)" than he had on the 1953 Nashville recording. The later version progressively describes more of the singer's mental deterioration over the loss of his girlfriend, ending with the announcement that he had completely lost his mind. Although the accompaniment on the song was adequate, it paled in comparison to the performance of the Nashville session musicians.

Of greater interest were some fresh songs he had written. "Welcome to the Club" was a novelty composition that he dedicated to members of the numerous "stirrer's clubs" who would argue about practically anything, while drinking at their local hotel.[26] "Brass bands are beginning to use it," Morton optimistically wrote, "and many disc jockeys report ever-increasing requests for it to be played for their local 'clubs.'"[27] The poignant "21st Birthday" was one of two anti-war songs he composed and recorded when Australian troops fought in Vietnam. In it, Morton bitterly narrated the part of a grieving father who welcomed friends to what would have been his late son's twenty-first birthday. Morton said he knew the people involved in the composition.[28] "The Cream in Between," also known as "The Creamy,"[29] was about a "light colored person of mixed blood" and despite perhaps being mildly contentious in 1960s Australia, it was accepted by Indigenous and non-Indigenous people in outback camps and missions alike. In the United States in 1972, Merle Haggard created something of a controversy with his recording of "Irma Jackson," a track about interracial romance. Haggard's song had been held back by Capitol Records because it was feared that it might damage his image.[30] In contrast, Morton's effort didn't provoke controversy in Australia.

NORTH TO DARWIN

According to Jim Bowditch, who was editor of the *Northern Territory News*, Morton sent him a letter advising that he would be appearing in the Darwin Catholic Hall for three nights on certain dates that Bowditch was later unable to remember. Unfortunately, there was no advance publicity for the performances, although a local priest said he had invited some of his flock to the shows. Bowditch was astonished to find that, true to his word, Morton performed a full show for the modest audience that attended. "Tex gave the show his all," Bowditch recalled. "He could have been performing for an audience of thousands. The two plus me applauded with vigor." Morton even admitted latecomers, who had heard of the concert by word of mouth, for free. Bowditch remembered that Morton displayed many of his enormous talents, including whipcracking, conjuring, jokes, recitations and some hypnotism. His whipcracking was especially impressive: "He could cut a cigarette in half while in your mouth with this long whip," Bowditch wrote. He "was uncanny in his accuracy and had a way of putting people at ease and able to relax confidently while he struck with a whip, inches from their nose at full stretch." Bowditch himself clasped one end of a piece of paper between his lips while a female held the other end in her mouth. Morton sliced the paper in two with a single lash.[31]

Morton was drinking in the beer garden of the Victoria ("Vic") Hotel in Darwin with Bowditch, when he noticed cell windows only some thirty meters[32] from the tables and barbecue. When Bowditch told him the cells were part of the Darwin jail, Morton became annoyed. "What sadist would do this?" he asked, remarking that inmates would have smelt food cooking, heard laughter and drinking, possibly of their wives and girlfriends with other men, and listened to the merriment of the outside world. He became visibly angry, Bowditch recalled, and later wrote "The Jailhouse Window," also known as "Darwin Jailhouse Window,"[33] mentioning actual characters from the Territory, including Bowditch himself, Alan Stewart ("great white hunter"), Jack White ("Rum Jungle Jack"), and Robert Tudawali, an Indigenous actor who starred in the movie "Jedda." The mention of "Slim" on the jukebox most likely referred to Slim Dusty.[34] Morton also penned a description of the beer garden, stating, "Two hapless prisoners glumly watched through the bars of the local lock-up. I self-consciously moved my beer a foot or two out of their sight. I felt bad about that."[35] The hotel, in fact, was a popular watering hole frequented by crocodile shooters, buffalo hunters and mining prospectors, as well as local office workers and bank staff,[36] so Morton would have been in his element when drinking there. Despite Morton's rage at what he perceived as harsh—even cruel—treatment of incarcerated underdogs, "Darwin Jailhouse Window" had an up-tempo melody, enhanced by the uplifting clarinet accompaniment of jazz ace, Don Burrows.

THE MORTONS AND MCCOYS

Tasmanian-born country singer Athol McCoy's first encounter with Tex Morton, his hero, was in 1940 when he met the hillbilly star in Ulverstone. McCoy had followed Morton's career from the 1940s to the Acuff *Grand Ole Opry Tour* debacle—McCoy was then touring his home state with singer Reg Lindsay but flew to Sydney to meet his idol. Having recorded for Columbia, McCoy was by then a recognized country artist in his own right. About two years later, he was appearing in Mackay, and remembered with gratitude Morton's kindness in directing people, unable to attend Morton's show because it was packed out, to the Athol McCoy tent, "just down the road." In October 1963, they reunited at the Hobart Show (fair).[37]

Three years later, the two collaborated and performed together for some ten months.[38] "In 1966, I achieved my greatest ambition," McCoy later wrote. "Tex and I formed a partnership and toured Australia as 'The Mortons and McCoys.'" The name was a play on words from "The Martins and the Coys," which Morton had recorded in 1938. It was the reverse side of "Sergeant Small."[39] They started in Morven in southern Queensland, and traveled to Mount Isa, Alice Springs, through "dozens of Aboriginal missions," and then to Darwin, where they showed nightly for three weeks. They had originally intended to stay there for a fortnight, but Morton suggested they play another week because of the influx of people for the Darwin Show (fair). Slim Dusty was also in town, and he and guitarist Barry Thornton attended one of the performances. Then they drove to Western Australia, through Halls Creek, and finally finished the tour in Renmark, South Australia in December. "Tex handled all the radio stations," McCoy remembered. They had packed halls all the time, with Morton singing, sharpshooting and hypnotizing.[40] Recalling Morton's hypnotism, McCoy later wrote, "Every night on stage he did his very famous act and literally had people out like lights!" He remembered traveling with a fleet of cars and caravans, and Kath assisting with Morton's sharpshooting act, "chopping the ash off a lighted cigarette" which "had to be seen to be believed," though, he said, "it was no effort for Tex."[41]

"We had tremendous success," recalled McCoy, who described his mentor as "a wonderful man to work with," who didn't act "the big star" and was always generous and down-to-earth. He could make a cast of six people appear much larger, he remembered, describing Morton's ability to conjure fancy showbusiness nom-de-plumes for the cast. McCoy was in awe of Morton's ability and his enormous drawing power—audiences would drive hundreds of miles to see him, he said, echoing Dick Carr's memories of Morton's 1940s Wild West Shows.[42] McCoy later penned a poem to his friend, entitled "A Tribute to Tex." Joy McKean, Slim Dusty's wife and partner, recalled that she and Slim met Morton (most likely when he was with McCoy) when their paths crossed at Katherine, in the Northern Territory. The three were passing the time of day in Dusty's caravan, when Morton proposed they should travel to Montreal in Canada for "a big exhibition," most likely the Montreal Expo of

1967, also known as "The World's Fair." McKean wrote that Morton "was full of ideas.... He was enthusiastic about having us go with him and happened to mention, of course, for such a show I would have to dye my hair blonde. ... I think maybe Tex had a sly sense of humor hidden there somewhere and was having a lend of me. The small matter of funding was also of interest to me, but was airily waved aside by Tex who felt that was of little importance in the overall scenario."[43]

McKean described Morton as "a showman in the vein of the Skuthorpe rodeo family and the Foster family of traveling showmen" who could "talk the leg off an iron pot." She considered him to be "the most charismatic man, and a man of many and wide talents."[44]

MORTON ON RADIO

Journalist Colin Mackay recalled Morton twice appeared on the *Don Lane* television show, but he was most likely referring to *Tonight with Don Lane*, broadcast by TCN Nine from 1965 until 1969. The station's switchboard lit up like a Christmas tree, Mackay said. Once Morton went to Noumea, in New Caledonia, but wound up drunk and returned to Australia "wiped out." For that, he blamed the French mafia! Mackay also remembered that Morton claimed a bond with gypsies and sometimes cursed others with gypsy spells.[45] Nelson historian Alan Turley asserted that during a European tour, Morton had been "inducted into the ancient Romany tribes by being made a 'blood brother' of the then gypsy king" in a ceremony complete with traditional bloodletting,[46] but whether this is true, or just another fabrication by the showman, isn't clear. Nevertheless, it undoubtedly enthralled patrons at the Sydney bars Morton haunted, where he regaled audiences with his far-fetched stories.

Around 1966, Morton was broadcasting on radio in a series of 20-minute episodes. He also made longer radio programs for the ABC, in which he tended to play his older numbers from the 1930s and 1940s, frequently reminding listeners of his pivotal role in pioneering hillbilly music in Australia. Occasionally he spun discs by other artists, usually from the United States. Sometimes, such as with Hank Snow, he professed to have personally known famous country singers from his days in North America, and at times embellished fact with fantasy, like informing listeners that his recitation of "The Shooting Of Sam McGrew" had been recorded in freezing conditions in Alaska, whereas it most likely had been waxed in warmer climes.

Listening to these broadcasts, one gets the impression that Morton was ostensibly attempting to re-establish his credentials, in an era when other artists were better known, although his partner, Kath, said he didn't feel overlooked at the time.[47] Similarly, Kevin King, who knew him well during the 1970s, recalled that he was decidedly positive about the country music scene at the time.[48] On the other hand, Buck Carson, his acquaintance for over a decade, recalled that Morton was exceptionally bitter about country music in later years, and didn't want anything to do with it. Some of his acrimony might have been feigned, however: journalist and friend Colin Mackay thought that though Morton occasionally protested not liking country music, "he really loved it."[49] Sometimes he spoke disparagingly of fellow country music singers—and occasionally could even be rude to them, for instance, when he refused to autograph fiddler Alan Swanson's boomerang that had been signed by Australian country singers, and threw it on the ground.[50] On the other hand, he didn't appear to outwardly dislike other well-known country artists like Slim Dusty and Gordon Parsons, though privately he criticized others. Occasionally, his attitude could be disagreeable, even bordering on obnoxious. Once, in a fit of pique he testily hurled a microphone, set up to capture his guitar playing, across the stage. Another time, he airily snubbed a showgrounds committee that had patiently awaited his arrival.[51] One source recalled "he could also be a very arrogant and rude bastard to people at times." Another described him as sometimes being "like a grumpy old headmaster."[52] Garry Coxhead, who knew both Morton and Buddy Williams, thought that Morton, when he returned to Australia in 1959, especially resented Buddy Williams because his old challenger was then very popular, whereas Morton was no longer Australia's first-call country music star.[53] At the very least, Morton "didn't suffer fools lightly" recalled Trevor Day.[54]

According to Buck Carson, Morton, in a dressing gown, would regularly and lazily while away the days at his house in Sydney, greeting passing pedestrians in the morning and entertaining fellow artists afterwards.[55] He also would habitually hold court at either the Manly or Steyne Hotels,[56] showing scant interest in recording, appearing to be not only disinterested in country music but in other avenues of entertainment as well. Kevin King, Morton's friend, was at many of those daytime sessions both in Morton's house and hotels, and recalled Morton frequently sang songs he had never recorded commercially. Every now and then the two would embark on lengthy pub crawls (bar tours), he said.[57]

MORTON ON TELEVISION

In 1966, the showman was interviewed about his hosting a half-hour television series, *With Tex Morton*, on GTV6-Ballarat, described as his first venture into television. Morton was at pains to stress that he was "no hillbilly": "I sing country and western numbers for sure, and folk songs, and hobo and stockman songs," he asserted, "but I'm no hillbilly."[58] Sometime in the late 1960s, he was featured in a series of some fourteen television shorts, *Presenting Robert Morton*, which he introduced with a few notes of "Waltzing Matilda" on his guitar. Often wearing a white hat and suit, he sang songs including "Old Man Duff," "Wee Jeanie Hunter," "Tex Morton's Protest Song," "Billy Boy," "The Darwin Jailhouse Window," "Rye whisky," "In Eleven More Months and Ten More Days," "Peg-Leg Jack," an over-the-top rendition of "Barnacle Bill, The Sailor," "The Cat Came Back," and "Frankie and Johnny"; on other occasions he narrated Banjo Paterson's poems, "Clancy of the Overflow," "The Man From Ironbark," and "The Bush Christening." The snippets revealed a relaxed Morton revisiting, in the main, the old-time chestnuts that had made him famous some three decades earlier. Accompanying himself on guitar, he introduced each song by describing its origins, every so often demonstrating his flawless use of accents.

During the 1960s and 1970s, Columbia (then part of EMI) reissued songs from Morton's earlier years on several budget-priced albums[59] which sold well. *Songs Of The Outback*[60] comprised of a dozen favorites, including "Aristocrat," "The Story of Parson Joe," "Old Shep," and "The Drover's Wife" which he'd recorded as "The Neighbor's Wife" in Nashville in 1953. *Sentimental Tex* sold slightly over 2,000 copies (in monaural sound) between 1965 and 1971. On the other hand, fewer than 1,000 monaural copies of *Goin' Back To Texas* were bought between 1966 and 1968.[61] In 1987, EMI finally did justice to Morton's legacy by reissuing his entire Regal Zonophone recordings, first on a five-disc vinyl set, then on compact disc. Because the original master copies had been destroyed, EMI was forced to use pristine copies of the original 78s, provided by collectors, as masters.[62] Morton himself had previously overseen the reissue of his Rodeo/Tasman recordings in 1980, again using 78 rpm discs as masters;[63] and Peter Burgis's Kingfisher label reissued some Tex Morton radio shows from the 1940s.[64]

THE TEX MORTON STORY

In 1967, *Everybody's* magazine published a series of articles about Morton, penned by journalist Colin Mackay.[65] Mackay said he initially approached Morton about writing his life story and, to break the ice, Morton invited Mackay to go fishing with him, but the two wound up in a public bar instead. The articles were obviously based for the most part on Morton's own inflated narrative but made interesting reading all the same, and were among the first to treat Morton's life in reasonable detail, if not complete accuracy. Because *Everybody's* was a periodical intended to entertain the masses, and certainly not a scholarly publication, Mackay simply repeated Morton's anecdotes, even though he could see through his subject's penchant to stretch the truth.

In fact, Mackay took much of what the showman told him with a grain of salt but echoed it anyway, because he knew it would be attention-grabbing reading. He was particularly skeptical of Morton claiming to have a PhD at a respectable university, even advising the author not to bother looking for evidence of such a degree because there would be none. He also thought that his subject "bullshitted he was in some movies."[66] Nevertheless, Mackay and his colleagues enjoyed Morton's fanciful yarns and the effect they had on eager listeners. "It was all good, amusing stuff," he remembered, though he never knew if the showman's tales were fair dinkum (genuine). "If he saw you were interested, he'd lay it on thick," he added.[67] For his part, Morton was delighted with his "life story," undoubtedly reveling in the publicity it generated. Much later, he approached Mackay with the intention of having another series of quasi-autobiographical articles published, describing the *Everybody's* stories as "bullshit."[68]

Singer Aussie Laws (Ralph Bailey) recalled that Morton used to frequent Sydney's Kings Head Hotel. "It was a journalist's club in those days and after consuming a few glasses of Dr. Resch's finest elixir (beer) he would regularly tell us about his buckjumping prowess," Laws said. "But no one ever got to see him on a horse, so we can't tell . . . if he was as good as he claimed."[69] Journalist Jim Oram said that if a stranger asked for Morton, he was initially treated with suspicion, because "caution was necessary. There were those who wished to ask Tex about money owed or had a summons to present."[70]

18

NEW ZEALAND, 1967–1970

MORTON SHOWED IN New Zealand in late 1967 with rising country music star Maria Dallas, whose "Tumblin' Down" had been a hit the previous year.¹ Despite his aging years, Morton stole the show. Remembering his records of years gone by, audiences preferred his unplugged renditions of older numbers, devoid of "blaring amplified guitar" and "gimmicks"—songs like "Rocking Alone in an Old Rocking Chair" and "Old Shep."² A newspaper review asked rhetorically how many younger entertainers could perform as effectively.³ "His records have withstood the advent of bop, rock 'n' roll and what have you," a columnist contended.⁴

Newspapers of the late 1960s regularly ran articles about the showman, in which he recounted his nascent hillbilly days and his North American exploits, comparing him favorably with the newer generation of country music artists. He was, it seems, becoming acknowledged as the progenitor of Australasian country music and a fabulous, experienced performer in his own right.⁵ For his part, Morton seemed content to persevere with the same tried and trusted acts, outwardly lacking the creative drive that had characterized his earlier years, though generating much-needed income just the same. Even his hometown of Nelson welcomed its prodigal son. In January 1969, Morton was crowned king of the city's Mardi Gras, sponsored by the local Jaycees. Described as "the star of the evening," he presented prizes and entertained an estimated 9,000 paying fans. "His "biggest crowd pleasers were songs from the Depression," the local newspaper confirmed.⁶

"THE COUNTRY TOUCH"

In 1968[7] and 1969 Morton hosted a successful New Zealand television series, *The Country Touch*, produced in Auckland by Bryan Easte for the New Zealand Broadcasting Corporation. Easte recalled that he and Morton, who was touring at the time and had dropped in to meet him, conceived the show together. Easte hired the Hamilton County Bluegrass Band (HCBB) to provide instrumental accompaniment for the series after he had attended a gig at which the band was playing. While Morton remained on tour, Easte organized the square dancers and music for the series, and then contacted the touring showman.[8]

The Hamilton County Bluegrass Band furnished most of the accompaniment for the shows, as well as performing their own songs and instrumentals. Sometimes they were supplemented by a pianist and other guitarists.[9] The band consisted of Colleen and Paul Trenwith, David Calder, Leonard ("Len") Cohen, Alan Rhodes, and possibly Sandy McMillin as well.[10] Easte told a reporter that he hoped the show "will be the sort of program that will encourage people to kick off their shoes and relax."[11] Paul Trenwith recalled there was an initial seven-show series in 1968, then two series of thirteen shows each.[12] Each program ran for twenty-six minutes. Trenwith said the episodes were produced as "live" performances in two segments. He thought that programs from the first series were rehearsed on Saturdays for music, cameras and lighting, and then filmed on Sundays. The episodes were released a week apart, on Saturday nights.[13] Programs in the second series were recorded on weekends—one episode on a Saturday and another on the following Sunday. "Those were long days and if, during the filming of a show, someone made a mistake (HCBB, performer, dancer, cameraman, etc.), we went back to the start of that segment and filmed it again. We didn't like making mistakes!" he said. He thought that one show might have been broadcast from the Founders Theatre in Hamilton.[14]

Morton, in his early fifties, looking noticeably older than in his Regal Zonophone days, and sporting short hair and a moustache, introduced guest artists and sang the occasional song, like "Good Old Days." The Roy Acuff-style introduction with its "Howdy Neighbor, Howdy" theme, to the skillful accompaniment of the Hamilton County Bluegrass Band, firmly established the show's down-home atmosphere.[15]

Paul Trenwith had nothing but praise for Morton:

We always found him straight-forward to work with. He was quite specific in what he wanted as backing (which was all we did with him), and we respected his wishes, recognizing that he "knew what he wanted." In retrospect, I wish I'd researched more about his background, as I would have realized what a significant figure he was, in the beginning days of country music in New Zealand and Australia. I did talk to him a lot about the early days, and we also talked with Slim Dusty about those early days. Slim really respected the early work that Tex had done, and credited Tex with being his inspiration.[6]

The late Colleen Trenwith also recalled working with Morton on the set of *The Country Touch*:

My memory of Tex is of a unique, colorful entertainer with a big, warm personality. He was consistently interesting, always ready to tell stories about the things he had done in his life. In spite of that I was not sure how much were "stories for the sake of being entertaining," or absolute truth. It's not that I doubted his sincerity—it was more that I had never met anyone like him before, and to have done the things he had done, in Australia, the US and Canada was totally wild, and beyond my own sphere of thinking and life's expectations.

Tex was a snappy dresser, always immaculate and usually with a hat ... either his recognizable "cowboy hat" or a sporty ball cap of some kind. Paul and I visited him and his wife, Kath, at their camper in a campground in Auckland at the time when we were filming *The Country Touch* series. I felt as though he and Kath liked us and enjoyed us visiting them.

We were "on set" with Tex for the filming of at least twenty shows of *The Country Touch*. We took coffee breaks, and often all went out for lunch together with Tex, our band and others from the TV crew. He was always the center of attention because his stories were so colorful.

I am not clear about whether or not we actually accompanied him musically in his own songs on *The Country Touch*. I think he just sang them and played guitar on his own. However, when we went to Australia in 1971, to live with him and do some shows with him, I do remember playing fiddle with him on his songs. He played most songs with his capo on the first fret, using C chords, and as a result I had to learn to play in the key of C sharp—one of the worst keys on fiddle.[17]

Reviews for *The Country Touch* were mixed. One media critic described it as "a winner." "The setting is cozy, the faces are for the most part young and friendly and the songs are songs everybody knows—or at least sound very familiar," he wrote,[18] but another commentator decried its emphasis on American-style country music and panned it as "a visually inferior vehicle for noisy, insistent music."[19] Both critics, however, agreed that Morton was the star of the show. "The only good thing about this particular program was Tex Morton," conceded the second reviewer. "Among all the other pallid performances, his fairly shone with professionalism. He may be as antipodean as the rest of them, but his style, his personal aplomb, made him thoroughly acceptable in this setting."[20] Morton's role as host of the second series was also lauded: "Compared with other exponents of the art of the relaxed look, notably Perry Como, Andy Williams and Dean Martin, our Tex is as superbly casual, at least as likeable, and hardly as vain," waxed one appraisal. "Morton's casual expertise, smooth professionalism, was the key to a production which is undoubtedly the best thing the producer has given us yet."[21]

In mid-1968, Morton recorded four tracks for the extended-play album, *Tex Morton In New Zealand*, including the acerbic "Good Old Days," "(The) Eyes of Temptation" and the perennial favorites "Hallelujah, I'm a Bum" and "Rocking Alone in an Old Rocking Chair." The record sold 833 copies in Australia[22]

"TEX MORTON TODAY"

In 1970, still in New Zealand and accompanied by guitarist Peter Posa as well as the Hamilton County Bluegrass Band, he recorded the album *Tex Morton Today*, which was comprised of a refreshing blend of older chestnuts and modern compositions. "Freight Train Yodel," "There's a Bridle Hanging on the Wall," "The Black Sheep," "The Good Old Droving Days," "Don't Make Me Go to Bed (and I'll Be Good)" were all from an earlier era, whereas "The Transport Man," "Australia (A Song Poem)," "Miner's Luck," "The Shicer (Moaner's Luck)," "Bob The Log" and "The Travelling Showman" were recent compositions. The recitation "A Bush Christening" was from the pen of Banjo Paterson. Music historian Eric Watson was especially impressed with Morton's newer songs. Some tracks, however, like "There's a Bridle Hanging on the Wall," seem overproduced, with their full-on vocal choruses dominating. On the other hand, "The Transport Man," with its droll twist and narration to music, displayed an inventiveness which rivalled that of American

Shel Silverstein, author of Johnny Cash's "A Boy Named Sue."²³ "The Shicer" was equally effective. The comical composition was about a newly arrived pommy (English person) who bought a dunny (outside toilet), and then sold it without realizing it was on top of a rich nickel deposit. "The Travelling Showman" was doubtless autobiographical and expounded on the liberated, outdoor lifestyle of show-people like Morton. Perhaps he was recalling the halcyon years of his Wild West circuses of the 1940s. "Australia (A Song Poem)," replete with vocal chorus, was a nationalistic paean to Morton's adopted homeland, and not at all like much country music of the period. "Miner's Luck" told of the nationalities of miners from all over the world who had died searching for gold in soil that might have contained other minerals that were now desirable—perhaps it was a nod to the burgeoning acknowledgement of multiculturalism—and "Bob the Log" was a humorous, uptempo romp that added variety to the album.²⁴

Guitarist Peter Posa recalled the sessions: "Tex was a true gentleman and [was] gifted in so many ways. He was a perfectionist in the recording studio and spent quite a lot of time redoing parts of the record that he wasn't happy with."²⁵

Broadcaster John Minson wrote that *Tex Morton Today* was especially popular on radio. "I recall the album ... [it] was worn out and a second copy was needed. 'The Transport Man', 'Bob The Log', 'The Traveling Showman' and Tex's own anthem-offering 'Australia' seemed never to be off the turntable," he said. "The melody of 'Australia' was naggingly familiar, and when questioned about it Tex replied, 'I took the tune of 'The Wild Colonial Boy' and changed the tempo.'"²⁶ Another newspaper reported that three record shops in the town of Tamworth begged local station 2TM to stop playing the album because all their stocks of it were sold out and inquiries for it were driving them mad.²⁷ On the other hand, reviewer Gil Wahlquist—no fan of Morton's—described the album as catering to the world of prejudice, attitudes and platitudes, by weaving those themes into cynical, tongue-in-cheek tales. "Bob the Log," he asserted, "panders outrageously to an aspect of Australian folklore which leads to endless bragging," and "Don't Make Me Go to Bed (and I'll Be Good)," he added, "twists the arm of a mother/son situation which is so mawkishly sentimental as to be outrageous." Wahlquist conceded, however, that "Tex Morton is the most outstanding reader of [CJ] Dennis in this country."²⁸

During the late 1960s, again in New Zealand, Morton waxed *A Tex Morton Singalong*, with the somewhat intrusive "Teen Folk" Chorale, "Beautiful Queensland," the "Campfire Medley" ("Wagon Wheels," "Home on the Range," and "Carry Me Back to the Lone Prairie"), "Chinee Luck," "Rodeo Round-Up," a medley of his earlier buckjumping classics comprised of "Rocky Ned," "Aristocrat" and "Mandrake." The disc was released (maybe belatedly) in Australia in September 1971, and sold 2,029 copies.[29]

19

AUSTRALIA, 1970–1983

IN 1970, Bryan Easte was a worried man: the amiable host of his television show was quitting. In fact, Morton had gone missing "somewhere in the South Island." Easte sadly confessed that he couldn't envisage another television series without the showman.[1] When finally contacted, Morton implacably claimed he had received offers to tour South Africa and Canada but was still considering hosting the program.[2] He was being deceptive, however, and all along was intending to interest Australian television networks in a similar series,[3] with the Hamilton County Bluegrass Band. A newspaper stated the band would appear in an Australian-produced Tex Morton television show, but that didn't eventuate,[4] because Australian executives feared the venture wouldn't be popular in profitable urban areas, appealing only to "country hicks," despite a report that country music was especially well-liked on Sydney radio,[5] and another newspaper arguing that *The Country Touch* was "far superior to anything similar produced in Australia, and a damn sight better than most of the rubbish made in the United States."[6]

Regardless, Morton flew to Australia at the beginning of 1971, taking with him the Hamilton County Bluegrass Band, on the promise of getting the group gigs, based on his name and reputation. But after the television proposal foundered, the band was forced to find alternative work. They lived at first in Woy Woy and then in a large house in Balgowah, near Manly (in Sydney), remaining friendly with Morton and Kath, even picnicking with them on a beach north of the city, and for a while Morton organized performances for them.[7] "However, the gigs with Tex didn't eventuate," wrote Paul Trenwith.[8] A year later, the band signed with Slim Dusty and Joy McKean,[9] a move that upset Morton.[10] Trenwith, however, had nothing but respect for the New Zealand star. "I have always been impressed by his musical performances—he was a skilled guitarist, vocalist and of course his performances were high quality," he wrote.[11]

On Thursday October 14, 1971, Morton recorded two tracks for a single release, at EMI's studios in Sydney. "Dunmarra" is dedicated to the song's subject Noel Healey, one of the really colorful characters of the Northern Territory, who had died before the song was released, and describes how Healey's station, on the Stuart Highway some 860 kilometers[12] north of Alice Springs, came to be named "Dunmarra." (The name is a corruption of "Dan O'Mara," an overland telegraph linesman who disappeared in the region in the early 1900s.)[13] "Old Blue," a humorous ode to an aggressive canine companion, had been penned by Morton's comrade from New Zealand, Barry Crump, a professional crocodile and buffalo hunter, later a deer culler for the New Zealand government, television personality and widely-acclaimed author—"one of the funniest men I know," said Morton, who recalled that Crump gave him the song's lyrics while they were drinking together.[14] The single, "Old Blue" / "Dunmarra," was issued in December 1971 but was deleted a year later with sales of 665 copies.[15]

OLD RIVALS UNITE

In March 1972, in a bombshell move that startled the Australian country music industry, Morton and longtime rival Buddy Williams combined their shows and toured together. According to one report, Morton, having completed a series of stands at the Tamworth Centenary Show, just happened to drop in and pay a surprise visit to Williams's show, where Williams recognized him in the audience and invited him to perform on stage.[16] Also present was Mike Burraston, a devoted fan of both performers, who—as the story goes—pondered, half-joking, "Wouldn't it be a laugh if you both joined shows after all these years?"[17] Within twenty minutes, the joke had become reality, and the arrangements were finalized on Sunday, March 19. A photograph depicted an informally dressed Morton, wearing shorts and a baseball-type hat, shaking hands with Williams, dressed in hat, shirt and long trousers.[18]

In retrospect, Morton probably would have gained more from the reunion than Williams: he had left New Zealand seeking greener pastures, but his dream of a television production had evaporated, by then the Hamilton County Bluegrass Band was with Slim Dusty, and he wasn't touring as he had in days of yore, with a big-top, buckjumping acts and transport. In 1972, for example, a newspaper reported that "an estimated several thousand country and western fans failed to show up when the Tex Morton Circus came to Tamworth this week." Attendance was a mere 150, and "judging by the sporadic clapping after [Morton's] opening rendition of 'The Cat Came Back' few of them were ardent country and western followers." The review stated that many fans were disillusioned that the show was nothing like Morton's circuses of the 1940s: "Two horses and four dogs made a valiant attempt to uphold the traditions of the circus animal acts and well deserved the applause that greeted them. Somewhat predictable trapeze and trampoline routines and a slightly repetitive array of clown skits . . . rounded off the circus program."[19] Another show was plunged into darkness when the generator ran out of petrol and "Tex was left yodeling in the dark."[20]

Buddy Williams, on the other hand, was by that time an established country music act in his own right, with solid recording credentials and a large-scale touring show to -boot. Perhaps, then, the idea of reuniting might have been Morton's in the first place, and his friend Burraston was a willing intermediary. According to Kath, the old rivals got on well together. Williams, she recollected, would call on Morton in his caravan at night, habitually staying until the early hours of the morning.[21] Williams's daughter, Karen, remembered Morton as welcoming and friendly. He often assisted her with her homework and was sometimes up all night communicating on his ham radio.[22]

Morton, Williams and Sister Dorrie (then-reunited with her former partner) recorded "I Like Country Music (I Like Mountain Music)" in May of 1972, coinciding with Williams recording his album *Aussie On My Mind*.[23] "I Like Country Music" was an uptempo, semi-comedy number with entertaining repartee between Morton and Williams, ending with a deliberately flubbed Morton guitar run and amusing comments. "The Morton magic was still there," enthused broadcaster John Minson. "He even had the guitars tuned out of pitch with Dorrie's accordion to give it that old corny sound."[24] Morton later claimed that he had initially approached RCA about the idea for the recording as a single,[25] but in 1987 Williams criticized the company, declaring,

"It was never promoted, there was nothing done about it at all. RCA didn't get behind it. It was more or less a collector's item."[26] The record as a single was backed with Morton's composition, "The Widow Next Door," a well-crafted, caustic anti-Vietnam war original that also featured Dorrie.[27]

Morton and Williams toured for about six weeks,[28] but the affiliation ended abruptly. Williams said that Morton unexpectedly "shot through" (left unexpectedly) without a farewell.[29] Perhaps Williams realized he had been providing much of the infrastructure—chiefly the tent and trucks—whereas Morton didn't contribute much in that regard, but instead tended to "play the star."[30] Karen Williams recalled her father had great respect for Morton,[31] and thought the breakup was amicable, though in the end it probably benefited Williams more than his old rival.[32] Williams's friend Garry Coxhead confirmed that the two parted on amiable terms and remained friends afterwards. Williams, he said, would occasionally meet with Morton after the two had ceased touring together. Coxhead recalled that Williams would sometimes break out into a Tex Morton song while driving. And for twelve months after Morton had died, Williams would take his hat off at each show and say something along the lines of "in memory of a great Australian entertainer, the late Tex Morton" and sing "The Letter Edged in Black."[33]

A major factor in the severance was simple economics, because the addition of Morton to Williams's shows wouldn't have increased gate takings all that much, and most people who went especially to see Morton would also have attended Williams's show anyway. In a similar vein, Lynette Guest wrote: "Back in 1972, it was becoming hard for traveling shows to make a living, and Buddy and Tex came up with the idea to join forces on the road and see how it all went, but audience size wasn't improving and the start of entertainment in clubs . . . made it hard for the showies to compete."[34]

ON TOUR WITH SLIM NEWTON

In September 1972, Morton toured with Ralph Ernest ("Slim") Newton, who had notched a runaway country music hit with "The Redback [spider] On The Toilet Seat" for Hadley records.[35] The two were accompanied on tour by rope spinner Kid McCleod and Sister Dorrie, both from his Wild West shows of thirty years earlier, a Roughriders Band, and "the famous Hill Family" with their troupe of performing ponies, horses and dogs.[36] Newton said that

Dorrie "sang a bit," and described her as "a hard woman" who occasionally drank Scotch in Morton's car outside the hotels Morton frequented. "He drank like a fish," said Newton.[37] In 1995, Newton described the show as an "ill-fated rodeo circus" stating, "I don't think I've ever worked harder in my life." Newton recounted in detail:

> To move his "tent" to location and assemble it took all day. It consisted of a large oval side wall with a five-sheet "C"-shaped cover over the audience at one end and a circus ring assembled ... in the center, with two large "king" poles and overhead lights. A foyer was assembled at the front and a "knockem joint" from a carnival at the rear to serve as an entrance for the performers, [a] stage for singing and [a] sound-control area. The whole tent was held up with poles and ropes and car axles for pegs which entailed me swinging fifteen-pound sledge-hammers. All the sheets and canvas, front and rear, had to be laced together. The seats were of Oregon planks laced to RHS steel stringers and jacks which were, together with the chutes, all made by me in Brisbane before we started off.[38]

The equipment was transported on a single blue Bedford truck which broke its differential one day; "that caused us havoc," said Newton, who noted that the showman had a fascination with the color blue. "He had a blue Ford ranch wagon, blue Ford ex-ambulance and a blue 'Mr. Whippy' [icecream] type van with a lighting plant in the rear which always gave trouble on and off the road." Newton recalled the show was comprised of Morton, Dorrie, circus performers, George Hill who had a trick pony and dogs, "Big Chief Little Beaver," who spoke with an accent "like Harold Steptoe from the British television series," and himself. Kath, "a nice, tolerant lady," accompanied the show.[39]

To Newton, Morton was "an enigma": a wonderful showman, but also a conman. "He had the ability to get away with things that others couldn't," Newton thought. Once, Morton announced to a packed tent, "We're not showing tonight. You can all go and get your money back." And that was exactly what happened. Another time, Newton recounts, "a chap asked me [if there] were any vacancies for tent hands. Knowing we'd lost three men that day, I knocked on Tex's caravan door and told him what I wanted. He said, 'Sorry, we're full up' and shut the door in my face."[40] And, wrote Newton, "An acquaintance of his from way back one interval time told Tex he'd recently been married. Tex said he'd like to meet his wife after the show, so the bloke came over, introduced his lady and Tex said, 'hello, goodbye' and went on with what he was doing.[41] I could never work the man out," Newton concluded.

Newton's music teacher told him that "he had no time for Buddy Williams, but Tex was a different story. He reckoned that Morton was a larrikin (rowdy person) who'd been up for just about anything you could name, except murder. But he was honest!" Morton's storytelling fascinated Newton, too: "You could be talking to Tex in a bar or wherever and I've found out that I knew ... he was telling lies, yet I believed him. That was the way he was." He was particularly impressed by how Morton's voice could cut through the noise of a crowd.[42]

Newton's patience had its limits, though. After his caravan "collapsed a wheel bearing and buggered [broke] the hub" seven miles from the nearest town, Morton drove past and promised to help.[43] After Newton's family spent a night in the caravan with no power, lights, or assistance rendered, help eventually arrived later the next morning—but then, Newton and Morton quarreled over who would pay for the repairs. Eventually the showman agreed to foot the bill after Newton threatened to leave. Soon afterwards, Newton and his family quit, against Morton's wishes. He recalled he had only been with Morton for about nine weeks before he departed.[44] "I believe the show folded not long after that," he wrote. "Too many things went wrong all the time. The buckjump side of the show only lasted a couple of days, then folded up." The owner of the pony and dogs wrecked his caravan while towing it and lost nearly everything, but luckily his animals survived. "He ended up sleeping in the truck with the animals for the rest of the tour." In retrospect, Newton wrote: "I'm not sorry I worked for Tex. It was an education, but I was glad to get out."[45] He remembered that Morton was constantly borrowing money, reiterating his opinion that Morton was in serious financial straits at the time.[46]

Morton had seriously miscalculated when he left *The Country Touch*. His dream of hosting his own Australian television series had failed to materialize and, instead, he'd toured with shows that were mere shadows of his stirring Wild West circuses of yesteryear. The buckjumpers had deserted him, the pony-and-dog act would have been simply a novelty at the time, his transport was plagued by mechanical difficulties and, to exacerbate the situation, he could be surly and abrupt at times.

THE GOONDIWINDI GREY

Morton's fortunes were boosted, however, in 1973. "The Goondiwindi Grey (The Gunsynd Song)," released as a single and on the album *Tex Morton's*

Australia for Picture Records, hit the big time that year.[47] The song was about Gunsynd, the famous Australian grey-colored thoroughbred who won twenty-nine races and over a quarter of a million dollars in prize money between 1969 and 1973.[48] Recorded at the Old Corn Exchange Building in Sydney,[49] the song, released as a single, was backed by "Drinking with the Dead (The Glass on the Bar)," with photographs of Gunsynd on one side of the record and Morton on the other.[50] The up-tempo number later became "a massive hit,"[51] winning the 1974 song of the year award for its writers from the Australasian Performing Right Association (APRA).[52] Later, the album *Tex Morton's Australia* was again released by Festival as *Tex Morton's Goondiwindi Grey*, with a photograph of Gunsynd on the jacket cover.[53] In the main, the disc consisting of five bush-ballad-type recitations, interspersed with nine songs, was a hybrid of genres straddling Australian country music and older bush verse, demonstrating Morton's re-emergence as a gifted composer and arranger of Australian songs. The album was described as "perhaps the finest thing of its kind ever to be produced in Australia" and "the greatest piece of work Tex has ever done."[54]

"If ever there was a country classic, this was it," effused broadcaster John Minson, describing the release as "Fourteen tracks of humor, drama, sadness, a panoramic picture of Australia in verse and song."[55] The album comprised the last significant recordings Morton made, however. Afterwards, he drifted into television and feature-length movies, and never followed-up on these sessions, exasperating historian Eric Watson, who approached Morton to persuade him to record again, but was told that the singer was merely considering a return to the studio in the future. "I think he believes he's immortal," a frustrated Watson was reported as saying. Even though Ron Hirst of M-7 records made every effort to lure Morton onto his own label with tempting deals, he was unsuccessful, recalled Minson. "It wasn't for lack of material. Close friends told of lyrics he had prepared, even rough tapes he'd made at home."[56]

Showman Larry Dulhunty remembered Morton telling him that he was embittered with recording because he "couldn't get on a decent label" in Sydney. "All they have done is tie me up with a contract while they have been promoting somebody else," he told Dulhunty, probably around 1975.[57] It's conceivable that he was referring to an earlier period with EMI and Slim Dusty, then the label's premier country artist. Morton wouldn't have appreciated being accorded second-tier status while recording for EMI, and experiences like this might have disillusioned him with country music.

ON TOUR WITH BUCK CARSON

Buck Carson toured with Morton during early 1982, although he had known him earlier than that. Carson, a talented singer and guitarist as well as a country music historian of sorts, described his experiences with the traveling showman:

> He was magic! But apart from that he was hard to be around in-person at times. I found this out after mingling with him for a period of over eleven years at his home in Manly, Sydney, and doing a short tour with him. Tex was very well read and educated. He didn't tolerate mugs [fools] and he couldn't stand drunks ... although Tex liked a drink, he always behaved himself and always kept the Tex Morton facade up and running. And it was a facade playing Tex Morton.... Tex was always well rehearsed in everything he did and certainly knew that he was a star and would request the best of everything. One show I booked for him in Ipswich ... was back in early 1983. His fee was $1,200 for a single 45-minute spot, return air fare to Sydney (first class) $40 a day food expenses, plus open tab for refreshments. Booked into five-star accommodation ... open telephone line to anywhere in Australia and New Zealand, return taxi ... Ipswich to Brisbane, plus a contract with a rain-clause inserted, but with all this expense, Morton put bums on seats: over 2,000 patrons. "FULL HOUSE." ... I remember one time back in the 1970s when the family visited him at Smith Street. Tex was in the bathroom having a shave. He called my two small boys (two and four years [old]) up to the bathroom. When they came out Tex had painted their faces completely all over with shaving cream. Tex [was] always the entertainer.[58] "Tex was very talented and well-read. He was also gifted with a charismatic personality, but he was excessively self-important and fully absorbed in playing the part of being Tex Morton."[59]

Carson's recollections of Morton in his later years expose another side of the showman's personality that was also alluded to by Slim Newton and others: sometimes, Morton's behavior could be curt and even dismissive of associates, even though he could also be the affable and amiable persona of old. Perhaps this side of his character revealed an underlying bitterness that his contribution to Australian country music had been overlooked by others. Carson, for example, recalled Morton telling him, "Don't talk to me about country music. It'll break your f****** heart,"[60] although others close to the showman, like Kath Morton, stated there was nothing in his character that revealed sourness in his dealings with others. Trevor Day believed that Morton thought recording was futile, since radio would likely "only play [his records] at 4 am in the morning";[61] but Johnny Heap stated: "In our few meetings Tex never indicated any bitterness toward the business."[62] Terry Gordon, who knew Morton as well, also believed that Morton was not one to be disgruntled about his treatment by the Australian country music industry at the time.[63] To fellow country singer Dusty Rankin, Morton "was a terrific person" who was exceedingly generous to those less fortunate than himself.[64]

In the 1970s, Morton was used in a series of maverick television advertisements by John Singleton's SPASM agency,[65] which was promoting retailer David Holdings's supermarket sales outlets. A voice-over announced the retailer's prices before the irritating catch phrase spoken by Morton rasped, "Where d'yer get it?"[66] The commercial is still cited as one of the most grating advertisements of recent times, even achieving a level of cult status in several circles. In 1977 it won the Raw Prawn award for Australia's worst commercial.[67]

FORMALLY RECOGNIZED AT LAST

In 1976, author and historian Eric Watson published a brief account of Morton's life and influence on Australian country music in his pioneering book in two volumes, *Country Music in Australia*.[68] But Morton's embellishments and memory lapses—after all, his career stretched back some fifty years—posed problems. Watson was initially skeptical regarding several of his subject's claims, but was convinced of their veracity when Morton showed him documents, contracts, newspaper clippings and the like.[69] Watson, however, improbably affirmed that the entertainer had obtained a BA degree and a doctorate from "a Canadian university," had toured as a crowd warmer for Hank Williams, and had been "one of Hollywood's most sought-after television character actors." He also cited an incorrect date for Morton's birthday (although according to additional sources Morton habitually gave a misleading date when asked).[70] But since Watson's book was so influential, many of these myths went unchallenged for years. Watson clearly admired Morton and concluded his chapter on him with this fitting tribute:

> Tex Morton's great contribution to Australian country music lies firstly in the interest he stimulated in the form originally, and in the quality of his work; and secondly in that he set a very original style for a country music of our own, setting the ball rolling with which Buddy Williams, Slim Dusty and so many others ran so brilliantly and scored so heavily. His work so lit the imaginative fires of thousands of young Australians in the 1940s that they seized on his style and made it a national one, and by imitation, extension, and amalgamation with our previously established country-folk roots, created a commercial Australian country music which will always bear very heavily the imprint of his personality.[71]

During the late 1960s and early 1970s, the town of Tamworth increasingly became involved in recording and publicizing country music, to the extent that in 1969 it was named "Country Music Capital" by local radio station 2TM.[72] Tex Morton was the initial inductee into the Australasian Country Music Roll Of Renown, Tamworth's equivalent of Nashville's Country Music Hall Of Fame, whose first nominations included Morton's major influence, Jimmie Rodgers.[73] Author and historian Max Ellis, chief executive officer of the Roll of Renown awards, made the announcement, noting that Morton "astonished many of the young record executives who had little idea of his achievements and even less of his extraordinary talents and the magnetic personality that he projected."[74] The honor fittingly commemorated his seminal influence on the development of country music in Australasia. As Ellis recalled, Morton himself was especially thrilled with the award:

> When it was announced on stage at the Tamworth Town Hall my feeling was that Tex was very excited and hugely pleased. After I presented him with the citation, he launched into a long reminiscence about how he had been arrested for vagrancy for sleeping under the bridge at Tamworth and some other stories about the old days... He became very involved in the festival and my belief is he was extremely grateful for the recognition and huge respect he received from both his peers and the public. He was an astounding character—larger than life and always full of information and comments.[75]

Morton, at last, had formally received the recognition he had long deserved.

The Australasian Country Music Roll of Renown was created on the front lawns of Radio 2TM with 26 granite boulders brought from Fielders Farm near Kootingal.[76] In January 1977, Morton was at the presentation of his Roll of Renown plaque (the first to be awarded) which was attached to one of the boulders, but when it was unveiled before a huge, enthusiastic crowd of fans, he complained that his birth date—taken from Watson's book—was wrong.[77]

The plaque was later replaced with a better image of Morton and his correct date of birth.[78] The inscription fittingly read:

> Born Robert Lane August 30th 1916 in Nelson, NZ. Performed and recorded at the age of 16. Came to Australia in 1932. Pioneered the traveling country show and toured the world. Tex Morton the showman supreme, single handedly established the identity of Australasian country music.
>
> Australia's "Yodelling Boundary Rider" Tex Morton was born Robert Lane in Nelson, New Zealand, on August 30, 1916. In the years to come, this amazing man would develop a career and reputation as one of the most exciting and versatile performing artists on any stage in the world.
>
> As the first to record original country music in this nation, Tex is renowned as "the father of Australian country music."[79]

Morton was so taken by the award and his plaque that he drove out to it in the early hours of the morning the day after it was unveiled and read the inscription by torchlight.[80]

On Saturday January 29, 1977, Morton, Buddy Williams and Smoky Dawson were the first to be recognized by Tamworth's "Hands of Fame," another mark of respect to Australasia's country music pioneers. The trio placed their hands in wet concrete, with Tamworth's Lord Mayor looking on.[81] Undeniably, Morton's title of "the father of Australasian country music" was richly deserved; he appeared content to be regarded as the elder statesman of Australasian country music, reveling in the standing he was accorded, in interviews for radio, television and newspapers.

TEX MORTON: ACTOR

During the 1970s, Morton acted in television and movies, but this was offset by a dwindling interest in singing and recording. The songs and recitations on *Tex Morton's Australia*, later as *Tex Morton's Goondiwindi Grey*, were his last major recordings. Apart from odd, and at times seemingly ad-hoc, recordings made after 1973, he had finally turned his back on music. John Minson especially recalled his apathy: "Tex disliked everyone connected with recording. He had an enormous stock of material and just couldn't be bothered getting into [a] recording state, editing or composing melodies for the lyrics . . . yet Tex always insisted he was open to offers."[82]

His new career was acting, initially in television productions. He had a minor role in the Crawford Productions 1975 television crime series

Homicide,[83] and the following year he worked in *Rate of Exchange*, a full-length feature episode intended as a pilot for a television series.[84] Between 1975 and 1976, Morton appeared in three episodes of *Matlock Police*,[85] and in 1977, he performed in an episode of *Glenview High*.[86]

He then transitioned to minor roles in full-length movies, beginning in 1976 when he acted in a feature film, *The FJ Holden*, described as "a snapshot of the life of young teenage men in Bankstown ... in the 1970s." The film dealt with "the characters' difficulty in reconciling mateship with respect for a girlfriend." It was released in April 1977.[87] The same year, he acted in the television movie *Say You Want Me* (also known as *Breaking Point*),[88] and possibly appeared in an episode of *The Young Doctors*.[89] Morton listed other productions in a curriculum vitae, including: *Behind The Legend* (for the ABC), *Roadhouse* (a television plot), *Now And Then* (in which he played "Bob the ferrymaster"), the Film Australia documentary *Meeting*, and *Dead Easy*.[90] In 1978, he appeared in five episodes of the short-lived *Case for the Defence*.[91] In 1980 it was announced that he was to act in the crime series, *Bellamy*,[92] and in 1983, he was in the television series *Waterloo Station*, playing "an aging ex-alcoholic show-business personality who entertained troops during the war."[93]

Morton's major acting triumphs, however, were in three major feature movies in the 1980s. *Stir*, a realistic prison drama in which he played the jail's governor, had been inspired by the 1974 riots at Bathurst Jail (about 200 kilometers from Sydney). In 1982, he appeared alongside Angela Punch McGregor, Arthur Dignam and his good friend Tony Barry in *We Of The Never Never*, based on the 1908 book of the same name.[94] It described the travails of an upper-class socialite married to a Northern Territory station manager in the early twentieth century, and her relationship with local Indigenous people, and was described as "a minor masterpiece of Australian letters."[95] The movie, shot on-location at outback settings including a reconstructed Elsey Station, and Mataranka, the property in the novel, was released in November 1982.

Morton played a hotel proprietor. Tony Barry thought that Morton's wide experience of life enabled him to play all sorts of characters believably. "He could read people better than anyone I know," he said. The two met before filming began and shared a room on the set. Far from being just a bit player in the cast, Morton remained active even when not on screen, and his confidence and experience regularly ensured the smooth running of the movie. When the production manager was hospitalized, Morton stepped in and "kept the thing going behind the scenes with great subtlety and aplomb," Barry recalled.

Another time, the group had been given two-way radios that had a range of only forty kilometers—useless at times since crews could be separated from each other by as much as sixty kilometers. Using his ham-radio experience, however, Morton constructed a makeshift aerial which he hitched to the upper branches of a tree, enabling the crew to receive transmissions from distances much greater than the 40-kilometer range. He also knew many community personages from his early days of touring and was able to hire mechanics and the like. "He commanded respect from the locals," Barry remembered.[96]

Morton quickly sussed that he and Barry were being "tried out" with drinking sessions that lasted well into the night. After Barry returned drunk in the early hours of the morning, Morton would quiz him about the complaints from the locals. "Don't worry, we'll sort that out tomorrow," he would assure his friend—and he invariably did. Afterwards, Barry and Morton remained close friends until Morton's death in 1983. Barry had enormous respect for Morton's talents and personality. "He lived fourteen lifetimes," he said.[97]

Barry noted that there was an undercurrent of "red necked racism" towards Indigenous members of the cast and crew from some of the production staff and the local police, but he and Morton highlighted and ridiculed their bigotry, by demonstrating that Indigenous people were more intelligent than they were usually given credit for. Morton once sang "The Creamy" to the crew, with a derelict three-stringed guitar he had salvaged from nearby, while Aboriginal actor Donald Blitner looked on. Morton then handed him the guitar and had him sing the song. To the astonishment of the others, Blitner sang and played it almost perfectly. Another time, an ex-rodeo hand that Morton had known from way back described how he had saved Blitner's life, after Blitner had been attacked by a bull, by stitching a gash with horse hair. The crew thought this was yet another tall story, until Blitner lifted his shirt and revealed the scars from the wound.[98] Barry spoke highly of Morton and described him as "the most generous bloke I ever met in my life ... there are hundreds of stories going around to confirm what a great, open-hearted guy he was." He recalled Morton "didn't mind sharing his periodical financial successes with his down-and-out mates." According to Barry, Morton once placed a bag stuffed with cash on a hotel bar and told everyone they could take whatever they needed, but "not a quid more." Morton then moved to another part of the hotel and drank by himself, before reclaiming the bag. "[expletive], the bastards left us enough to drink," he reportedly said, on finding there were still some 3,000 pounds left.[99]

Morton's final movie role was as a corrupt politician in *Goodbye Paradise*. Leading actor Ray Barrett said Morton was a dedicated worker and superbly professional.[100] "Jobs didn't come easily," Barrett recalled. "We worked our arses [asses] off for sixpence. Tex was a pro in the sense that he got out and earned his quid."[101] By then, it seemed, Morton had his foot firmly in the door of a new career that would have been deemed as more respectable than that of a country singer. He seemed especially proud of his new profession as an actor—which he pointedly pronounced as "act-OR."[102] But sadly, he was in a coma, near death, when *Goodbye Paradise* was released with positive reviews of his performance. Although Morton only appeared in supporting roles in the four movies he made, three of those—*Stir*, *We Of The Never Never* and *Goodbye Paradise*—were listed among the seventy-five classic Australian films preserved by the National Film and Sound Archives,[103] and *Goodbye Paradise* won the award for best film at the inaugural Sydney Film Critics' Circle Awards in 1983.[104]

THE FINAL CONCERT

The aging showman's major singing finale was on Thursday January 21, 1982, at Tamworth, in a "big top" tent on the city's Number Three Oval (some months before *We Of The Never Never* was made).[105] As Morton was preparing for his performance, signing autographs, Smoky Dawson walked past him to wish him well. "It was Tex's night," he recalled. Acknowledging him, Morton said, "I was just thinking . . . the way things are going today, I think we old pioneers should call a meeting and get together to do something about this." Later, Dawson wrote a song about the "first wave" of Australian country music—"Tex, Buddy and Me."[106] Perchance Morton's mind was drifting back to Tamworth some decades earlier when he had camped and toured there in his hardscrabble days.

Then a relaxed Morton, dressed in a gray suit, wearing a hat, and now and then puffing on a cigarette, enthralled the crowd with some of his better-known numbers, including a reflective recitation of "You'll Never Be Missed"—oddly foreshadowing his death the following year—and an unnecessary jibe at Buddy Williams for his trill yodeling.[107]

Max Ellis, who was at the show, recalled the performance:

> In 1982 we decided to honor him as our most important pioneer. At a packed concert in the big top, Tex, the consummate showman, opened to thunderous

applause. He strolled on stage, spent some time to pull up a battered old box to sit on, then still without a word, he slowly rolled and lit a cigarette. The entranced audience stilled into absolute silence before he uttered a sound. He then stunned them with a superb performance demonstrating how he had become such a respected and admired star both here and overseas. Sadly, it was to be his last major concert.[108]

DEATH

On Saturday July 16, 1983, a doctor who had been called to Morton's house had the ailing entertainer taken to Sydney's Royal North Shore Hospital in an ambulance. He was diagnosed with pneumonia,[109] and was first placed on a hospital gurney and then in a ward, but not in intensive care, although afterwards it was privately conceded by a nurse that he should have been.

Tony Barry was with him early that week. Morton announced he was going to give up smoking, to which Barry replied it was far too late for that. Barry tried to organize a marriage celebrant to formally marry Morton and Kath, insisting that Morton make a will so that Kath would be provided for, afterwards, but the "professor in charge" (as Barry derisively called the supervising specialist) smugly refused to allow it declaring the family "bow to his judgment," since Morton could be kept on life support almost indefinitely. He was soon proved wrong.[110]

Kath recalled that Morton was stoic to the last: while in the hospital he hadn't been overly concerned that death was imminent, she said.[111] Siblings Barbara and Kim, who flew from New Zealand to be by his side, arrived on the evening of Wednesday July 20, and brother Rex was there too, but the showman lapsed into a coma early the following day, and slipped away on the morning of Saturday July 23, before his son Bob, enroute from Western Australia, could be with him. He was only sixty-six years old. His death resulted from years of excessive smoking, and lung disease was the likely cause.

According to Tony Barry, when Morton realized the end was near, he exclaimed, "I don't know what I've done right, but I must have done something right to get Kath."[112] She had been his devoted partner for some twenty years—much longer than Marjorie, Dorrie or "Wolf Girl" in Canada.

Some months before he was rushed to the hospital, Morton had taken his old partner Dorrie to a journalists' club in Sydney and driven her home. Afterwards, about three weeks before he died, he phoned to tell her he wasn't well. They spoke for some time, then he said, "Goodbye, love." A sixth sense warned her that he knew he might soon die and was saying farewell to her for the final time. It unsettled her, and she was too distraught to visit him in the hospital later.[113]

The funeral for Australia's greatest showman was held in Sydney's Northern Suburbs Crematorium. Performers drove sometimes thousands of kilometers for the ceremony: "The word flashed around the bush telegraph, "Morton is dead... the king is gone," wrote Kim Lane: "Several carloads of them drove nonstop from up there down to Manly for the funeral, or just to have a farewell session in the old showmen's oasis, the Kings Head."[114]

But the funeral was a private affair, with only family and a few close friends present.[115] Morton was cremated in Australia, and his remains were returned to New Zealand. Afterwards, there was another service in Nelson, attended by his family, and his ashes were buried there, alongside the unadorned plots of his parents. He had finally and permanently returned to the place where his fabulous career had begun, some half-century earlier. The epitaph in Marsden Cemetery, in Stoke (a suburb of Nelson), said it all: "A millionaire in the experience of life,"[116] for to list all his achievements would have required a much larger monument. The plaque, set in the ground alongside those of his parents, read:[117]

> ROBERT WILLIAM LANE
> "Tex Morton"
> FATHER OF AUSTRALIAN COUNTRY
> MUSIC — A MILLIONAIRE IN THE
> EXPERIENCE OF LIFE
> NELSON 30·8·16 — SYDNEY 23·7·83

In Sydney, a wake was held by friends and comrades on the Saturday following his death.

In 1985, several New Zealand country music clubs joined forces to raise funds for a Tex Morton memorial. Subsequently, a plaque honoring Nelson's famous son was erected in Trafalgar Square by the Nelson Country Music Club, but in 2009 it was vandalized, torn from the stone to which it was anchored. Barbara Lane was photographed near what was left of the memorial, promoting calls for appropriate recognition of one of the city's "greatest sons and achievers."[118] Some two years afterwards, though, a few Nelson citizens, like history buff and former councillor Alan Turley, were still lamenting the city's indifference in recognizing Morton.[119] A display board honoring the showman was later erected in the Trafalgar Centre nearby, but was removed afterwards.[120] The staff of Trafalgar Centre informed the author in late 2017 that there was no display featuring Morton, about whom they knew nothing.[121] Nelson has shown scant interest in commemorating Morton, maybe because of a cultural aversion to country music.[122] Kim Lane wrote: "Vigorous attempts to have some form of tangible memorial here in his home town have all been greeted with ill-concealed scorn."[123] In stark contrast, there is a statue of Nelson's revered son, Lord Rutherford, and a memorial to the scientist at Brightwater.[124] Morton's alma mater, Nelson College, on the other hand, has a section devoted to its erstwhile student in the school's museum.[125] Ironically perhaps, the impatient student- turned- showman who left prematurely in 1931 is now a captive—in spirit anyway—of the College which commendably has not forgotten him.

IN MEMORY OF THE SHOWMAN

There was no such apathy in recognizing the "father of Australasian country music" in the "Country Music Capital" of Tamworth, New South Wales, however. The Tex Morton Memorial Association, founded about 1985, raised finances for a monument of Morton by selling medallions. They were sent to buyers in a cardboard slip with a note, signed by author and historian Eric Watson, acknowledging the purchaser was "one of the honored contributors whose generosity and devotion to the memory of the late Tex Morton has made the erection of his memorial in Tamworth possible."[126] By December 1985, there were enough finances to erect the bust. Watson optimistically reported the association was reviewing sketches by leading sculptors in Melbourne and Sydney. Watson stressed the need for a "tasteful and fitting" memorial, and a spokesperson for the Tamworth City Council advised the concept had been approved in principle but more information would be required before final permission would be given.[127]

Finally, the bust, sculptured by Canberra-based Peter Latona, was unveiled by Eric Watson on Wednesday, January 24, 1990, in Tamworth's Bicentennial Park during the city's annual country music festival. On this occasion, Watson eulogized Morton, and others in attendance shared memories of him. Kath was photographed alongside her partner's image.[128] Although the bust was intended to be life-size, Latona had sculpted a bigger one because, he said, Morton was larger than life.[129]

The monument was again dedicated at 3pm on Tuesday July 23, 1991 (the eighth anniversary of Morton's death). Fittingly, its inscription read: [130]

> Just say there's no gold at the end of the rainbow
> Tell him a rolling stone gathered no moss,
> A wink and a smile and those merry eyes twinkle
> "Moss would grow should I work for a boss!"
>
> Oh how I envy the showman his treasures
> Far from the city's oppressions and schemes,
> Did he but know it he's rich beyond measure
> For he has wealth beyond his wildest dreams.
>
> Yes now I envy the traveling showman,
> His friend is as big as the wide land he roams,
> Thinks like a king, has the heart of a gypsy.
> And the whole of the wonderful country's his home.
>
> verses from "The Traveling Showman" by
> TEX MORTON
> 1916–1983
>
> A gift from the
> Tex Morton Memorial Association
> To All People Who Admired And Loved
> His Many Talents
> 23rd July, 1991

AFTERWORD

ALTHOUGH THIS BIOGRAPHY, as much as possible, has avoided indulging in speculative conclusions in interpreting Morton's actions, there are, nevertheless, some tentative reflections and impressions that might have had a bearing on his life.

From the outset, Morton was intelligent, as evidenced by his primary school education, though not academically inclined. But his lectures on hypnosis and hypnotherapy showcased his ability to use terminology to impress others, including those who were themselves intellectual—the students at McGill University, for example, or the Canadian doctors who readily accepted him. Reading Morton's notes, too, one is regularly struck by his flair with the English language and his command of vocabulary. But there is no persuasive evidence of his having legitimately achieved the tertiary and postgraduate qualifications that he later claimed were his. Morton undoubtedly possessed what might be termed "musical intelligence": he at first imitated and then adapted the hillbilly music he heard while growing up, fusing the styles of a variety of artists—Vernon Dalhart, Carson Robison, Jimmie Rodgers, Goebel Reeves and Harry Torrani, for example—to create his own thoroughly authentic style that was founded on, though not wholly derivative of, American country music. His most important influence was Jimmie Rodgers, whom he later credited with kickstarting country music in Australia, though Morton modestly understated his own influence. From merely singing American compositions verbatim, he moved to writing original songs that included

Australian place names, occupations and themes that eventually endowed his compositions with a unique identity.

By and large, much of the "cowboy" music that Morton recorded was not traditional music but professionally written songs by Tin Pan Alley–type composers like Carson Robison, or British writers such as Michael Carr and Jimmy Kennedy, who romanticized a largely fictional view of the West that afforded a degree of escapism for audiences at the time. This was further mirrored by Hollywood's version that every now and then was populated by cowboys who intermittently burst into song. Though Morton drew heavily on the recordings of citybilly performers like Vernon Dalhart and Carson Robison, he performed their music in a harder, Jimmie Rodgers type of manner that imbued his works with a distinct edge. Although his style was technically simple, he sang with feeling—a characteristic associated with premier country vocalists—and enhanced his music with unique guitar runs and exceptional yodeling.

Because he influenced Australian country singers who followed, like Buddy Williams and Slim Dusty, Morton's role as the "father of Australasian country music" is assured. For some years after his return from North America, though, he appeared to some to have been disappointed, even bitter, that his contribution to the genre had largely gone unnoticed, so he especially cherished his elevation to the Roll of Renown in Tamworth.

Morton was multi-talented: a recording artist, trick shooter, whip-cracker, stage hypnotist, memory expert, reciter of verse, and actor. Songwriter and producer Hal Saunders even described him as a genius. But in his later years especially, he seemed to lose the will and ambition to succeed. Colin Mackay, who knew him well, described him as "brilliant"—"he could do everything,"—but his attitude destroyed any hope of becoming a star in any one field because he kept changing careers. He could have made it "big" but "didn't try," Mackay thought,[1] referring to the Tex Morton of the 1960s and 1970s. But his comments wouldn't have applied to the aspiring hillbilly singer of the 1930s and the Wild-West star of the ensuing decade, when Morton's relentless urge to succeed drove him to become Australia's premier country singer and showman. Nowhere was his later disinterest more evident than after 1973, the year in which *Tex Morton's Australia* (later *The Goondiwindi Grey*) album was released and received enthusiastic plaudits from all and sundry in the country music field. What might have been a revival of his writing and singing fizzled to virtual silence.

His combative attitude with Arch Kerr did him no good in the long run, either, though Columbia also lost out when he quit the company. He had "cut off his nose to spite his face" because in his pique he left himself no alternative: there was no other recording company in town, though he might have rationalized his decision by the success of his Wild West circus, even when wartime conditions restricted its income.

It has been said that creativity burns brightest in youth: some scientists believe that imagination in the sciences and the arts increases during the mid-twenties, climaxes around the late thirties and early forties, and then undergoes a slow decline.[2] Though this is only a hypothesis, it does match Morton's career. Commencing as a raw entertainer in New Zealand as a teenager, Morton had achieved an apex of musical stardom by 1943, when he was still in his twenties. During his thirties, 1946–1956, he was still at the top of his game as a showman and hypnotist, but on his return to Australia, by his early forties he had outwardly lost interest in country music. And so, he embarked on several career-changing moves instead, from recitation artist to actor, but always relied on his stage acts to ensure a stable income. He seemed content, too, to resume his nomadic role as a traveling showman, though his popularity was nowhere near the zenith it had reached in his golden days of the 1940s.

Perhaps Morton's career changes reflected an underlying desire to achieve a status, each more worthy—in his parents' eyes at least—than its predecessor. A question might be whether Morton's career shifts were, in some profound psychological sense, reparations for the disappointment his parents felt when he abandoned his home. Although he was a star of Australian entertainment during the late 1930s and 1940s, his chosen occupation was a hillbilly singer, then regarded as lowbrow. Likewise, his more lucrative role as a showman was tainted by images of unruly circus hands, an unstable lifestyle, mothers steering their sons away from his shows, and by rumors of immorality. Stage hypnotism, especially when presented with faux academic qualifications, was a step up, but the advent of television oversaw a declining interest in live entertainment. In his twilight years, he pursued an acting career in television and movies, which he welcomed because the profession was, in his eyes, respectable.

On the other hand, Morton claimed it was simply boredom and a never-ending thirst for new vocations that inspired him to morph from one profession to another: "I've always done what I had in mind. I wanted a circus, I got it, but the novelty wore off. I was fascinated with hypnotism and so I went into that field. I toured the country several times and got sick of the rodeo-circus thing. I mean, once you've done it a few times there's no challenge or future in it. I've never stayed too long at anything. I have to try new things."[3]

It has been suggested that on returning to Australia in 1959, he recognized that Slim Dusty was the premier Australian country music performer and, never content to be in second place, he downplayed his singing and adopted other vocations.[4] Dusty was, after all, singing Australian bush ballads, a genre in which Morton had tried to interest Columbia during the 1940s. He seemed to lose interest in country music, doubtless because, for a while he had run out of ideas, but staying with it also might have been, in his eyes, a retrograde step—he would have had to compete against a new crop of country artists, unlike his halcyon days when he had the field almost to himself. He further distanced himself from those days by appearing to be openly critical of the name "Tex Morton," even though he had conceived it himself in 1934, occasionally exhibiting feigned disinterest in country music, while quietly resenting what he perceived as the public's ignorance of his pivotal role in pioneering the genre in Australia. He was perhaps envious even of his own popularity of days gone by, though all the while resorting to country music every now and then, like the odd new album and his television show *The Country Touch*.

In his formative years Morton possessed a drive to succeed that overshadowed private relationships, especially with Marjorie and the twins, where he placed his personal ambitions above his family, leaving his young wife to raise their children by herself, and content to send her maintenance funds as a *pater in absentia*. He could be self-centered, stubborn and even arrogant at times, although Dorrie was able to deal with his moods, even when he was inconsiderate and disregarded her feelings. Surprisingly, she and Marjorie didn't harbor enduring grudges against him, and Dorrie even wept when thinking of her old partner, long after they had ceased touring together.

Morton had special attachments to his parents and siblings. Despite having upset his family by leaving home to become that *bête noire*—a hillbilly singer—he avoided, as much as possible, bringing shame on his parents, even changing his name to prevent later embarrassment. But he wouldn't have been the first headstrong teenager to defy his parents, and later he patched up differences with his father and mother, both of whom were proud of his achievements. He was especially close to his brothers and sister, all of whom spoke glowingly, honestly and warmly of him. For two decades he lived an affectionate and peaceful life with Kath, who has always spoken fondly of him.

An unanswered question is: where did all his money go? Morton died in humble circumstances despite the fabulous fortunes he had made, and lost, in his heyday. There are stories of his leaving cash-filled bags on hotel bars, instructing patrons to take what they needed (but no more), and then retrieving what (if anything) was left. When the author questioned several who knew him, they were mystified, too, and could only say he was both careless with money and an easy touch. Some funds might have gone to help others, given that he was associated with numerous charities throughout his career,[5] and he was known to have given cash to less-fortunate strugglers. But, almost certainly much of his earnings were frittered away on spur-of-the-moment impulse buying, instead.[6] Perhaps he invested some of his money, as he did with Bob Geraghty, a leading Surfers Paradise property developer. Financially, though, he lived for the moment, oblivious to long-term fiscal planning. Might this attitude have been shaped by his early years of grinding poverty and empathy with others during the Depression? We will never know, although the following lines from a poem Morton wrote might offer some insight:

> You can hoard your money all your life or put it in a bank
> Please listen to these words of wisdom, for I'll be very frank
> You can't take your money with you
> There's no pockets in a shroud
> For you don't need dough in Heaven
> In fact it's not allowed.[7]

Undeniably, Morton was a showman extraordinaire. Some of his talent might be attributed to a type of hyperactivity described by his sister—he became restless after a few days in the one place, for example, and talked incessantly. His well-known ability to exaggerate and embellish indisputably was an asset, too, as it enabled him to bolster his status and impress audiences. To Colin Mackay, his tall tales were a necessary aspect of the showman's lifestyle. Exaggerating was illusion, thought Mackay, and illusion was a component of showmanship. It might even be that Morton developed what psychologists call "imagination inflation," in which he came to believe his recall of events that had been embellished in the first place,[8] akin to believing his own yarns, though this is also speculative. But at times Morton contradicted himself, or he became evasive, such as asserting that his "doctorate" had been awarded by "a Canadian university," yet had it been authentically gained through a prestigious academy, being vague would have been counterproductive.

As entertaining as Morton's fanciful claims were, there was no imperative for him to exaggerate, for his reputation stands on its own. Undeniably he was Australia's first country music star, irrefutably his influence permeated the works of others who, inspired by him, followed in his footsteps, and incontrovertibly he was a resounding sensation with Australian and North American audiences. Memorials erected to his memory refer, not to his asserted credentials or largely exaggerated exploits, but to his pivotal role in Australian country music and it is this achievement for which he is justifiably remembered. So, his reputation is intact.

The history of country music in Australia is inextricably linked with Tex Morton. It was Morton who played a central role in being first to transplant the music of American hillbilly and Western singers to Australasian shores, it was Morton who initially adapted this music to an Australasian setting, and it was Morton who paved the way for other local country artists to follow. Indisputably, Tex Morton was the major founding figure of Australasian country music

DISCOGRAPHY

Compiled by David Crisp and David Hardy with the assistance of Lance Anderson, Hedley Charles, and Robert Platt.

Record Company Abbreviations Used

ABC Records, Sydney, NSW, Australia
ABC = ABC compact disc
Armed Forces Radio Service
W-711 = 16" transcription disc
Attitude
ATT = Attitude compact disc
Australian Bush Balladeers Association
TRIB = Australian Bush Balladeers Association Compact Disc
Australian Record Company, Sydney, NSW, Australia
10 = Rodeo, 78 rpm, single play
R = Rodeo, 78 rpm, single play
Bear Family (Germany)
BCD = Bear Family
British Archive of Country Music (UK)
D-101 = BACM, compact disc
Castle Communications (Australia) Limited
PCD = Premium Masters compact disc
PMC = Premium Masters cassette tpe
STARCD = Startel CD
Chrome Dreams, New Malden, Surrey, UK
CD CD = Chrome Dreams compact disc
Columbia Broadcasting System, USA
Ok = Okeh, 78 rpm, single play
Col C = Columbia, Canada, 78 rpm, single play
Columbia Graphophone (Aust.) Ltd, Sydney, NSW, Australia

Prefix:
G = Regal Zonophone, 78 rpm, single play

Columbia Graphophone Co. Ltd. London, England
FB = Columbia, 78 rpm, single play

Country Stars
CTS = Country Stars compact disc

Cypbell Pty Limited, Port Macquarie, NSW
AUS = Kingfisher audio cassette

Delta
Delta = Delta 26156 compact disc "Yodelin' Crazy"

Dingo Track Records, Australia
DTR004CD = compact disc

E.M.I. Sydney, NSW, Australia
DO = Columbia, 45 rpm, single play
SEGO = Columbia, 45 rpm, extended play
OSX, OEX = Columbia, 33 rpm, long play
SCXO = Columbia, 33 rpm, stereo long play
DRUM = DRUM, 33 rpm, long play
AX = AXIS 33 rpm, long play
R = Regal compact disc
TC,FA,C = cassette tape
TVS = Capitol, 33 rpm, stereo long play
EME = EMI 33 rpm, long play
CART = 8-track cartridge.

E.M.I. New Zealand
DNZ = Columbia, 45 rpm, single play
HR = His Master's Voice, 45 rpm, single play
SEGM, ESGM = Columbia, 45 rpm, extended play
MSX = Columbia, 33 rpm, long play
SCXM = Columbia, 33 rpm, stereo long play

Festival Records, Sydney, NSW, Australia
FWA = Festival, 45 rpm, single play
FK = Festival, 45 rpm, single play
FX = Festival, 45 rpm, extended play
FL, L = Festival, 33 rpm, long play
Cal R66 = Calendar, 33 rpm, long play

SRA = Universal Summit, 33 rpm, long play
HZ, SH = Horizon, 33 rpm, long play
F, CS = cassette tape
Festival Records, New Zealand
FL, L = Festival, 33 rpm, long Play
R67 = Calendar, 33 rpm, Long Play
Golden Editions Ltd, New Zealand
4CBS = Golden Editions, 33 rpm, long play.
Hughes Leisure Group.
BUD-CD-3 = compact disc, 3 CD set
BUD-CD-25 = Lucky Country, compact disc
Jasmine Records (UK)
JAS, JASMCD = Jasmine, compact disc
K-Tel International (Aust) Limited, Sydney, NSW, Australia
NA = K-tel, 33 rpm, long play
Larrikin Records, Sydney, NSW, Australia
LRF, LAR = Larrikin, 33 rpm, long play
LRH = compact disc)
Majestic Products Limited, Sydney, NSW, Australia
CG = Majestic Records (CBS Special Products), 33 rpm, long play
WA = Majestic Records, 33 rpm, long play
Music For Pleasure Group, Sydney, NSW, Australia
MFP = Music For Pleasure, 33 rpm, long play
Music World Ltd, New Zealand
MALPS, MWSP = Music World, 33 rpm, long play
Philips Electrical Industries, Sydney, NSW, Australia
P AUST = Philips, 78 rpm, single play
Philips Electrical Industries, New Zealand
P NZ = Philips, 78 rpm, single play
Philips Electrical Industries, South Africa
P SA = Philips, 78 rpm, single play
Picture Records, Sydney, NSW, Australia
PRS = Picture Record, 45 rpm, single play
CLP = Picture Record, 33 rpm, long play
Popular Record Club, Sydney, NSW, Australia
E = Popular Record Club, 33 rpm, long play

250 DISCOGRAPHY

<u>Radio Corporation of America, Sydney, NSW, Australia</u>
RCA = RCA, 45 rpm, single play
VAL1 = RCA, 33 rpm, long play
<u>Rajon, Australia</u>
CDR = Rajon compact disc
<u>Readers Digest Records Australia</u>
RD4–239 = Readers Digest 5 LP set
<u>Recording Corporation of New Zealand</u>
TA = Tasman, 78 rpm, single play
<u>Revive (Europe)</u>
REVCD = Revive two-compact-disc set
<u>Rouseabout</u>
RRH = Rouseabout compact disc
<u>Scandinavian Columbia Graphophone Company Ltd</u>
GD = Columbia, 78 rpm, Single Play
<u>Selection Records, Sydney, NSW, Australia</u>
PRL, PRML, = Selection, 33 rpm, long play
CRC, PRMC = Selection, cassette
PCD = Selection, compact disc
<u>Sony Australia.</u>
Sony Aust = Sony, compact disc
<u>Tempo, Australia</u>
DMCD-230 = Tempo, compact disc
<u>The International Music Company, Hamburg, Germany</u>
PC205521 202 = International Music Company compact disc
<u>Timeless/Warner Music, Sydney, NSW, Australia</u>
MUSIDISK = MUSIDISK compact disc
<u>Universal Record Club, Sydney, NSW, Australia</u>
UM, U = Universal Record Club, 33 rpm, long play
<u>University Of Melbourne</u>
AHS = University Of Melbourne compact disc
<u>World Record Club, New Zealand</u>
SLZ = World Record Club, 33 rpm, long play
<u>World Record Club, Sydney, NSW, Australia</u>
WRC = World Record Club, 33 rpm, long play

*<u>Underlined</u> text denotes artist credits as printed on record labels.

Private Speak-O-Phone Recordings

Ca. 1934, Wellington, New Zealand. Tex Morton (vocal, guitar). Privately recorded Speak-O-Phone discs, currently held by the National Film and Sound Archives (NFSA) in Canberra, Australia. No other Speak-O-Phone discs are currently known to exist. Each disc is approximately four minutes in length and contains two songs (both on the same side of each disc).

	NFSA Title Number
MEXICAN YODEL / THE LAST ROUNDUP	585973
AT THE END OF THE HOBO'S TRAIL / THE INSULT	585981
AT THE END OF THE HOBO'S TRAIL / THE INSULT	585986

Commercially Released Recordings

This section lists all known commercial releases to October 2021.

TUESDAY FEBRUARY 25, 1936, COLUMBIA STUDIOS, PARRAMATTA ROAD AND COLUMBIA LANE, HOMEBUSH, SYDNEY, NSW, AUSTRALIA

The Yodelling Boundary Rider. (Tex Morton) Vocal with Yodelling and Guitar Accompaniment

Matrix	Song Title	Release Catalog Number
T-1413	TEXAS IN THE SPRING	G22714; OSX/MSX 7766; MFP A8130; OEX 10257; DRUM 8143; MUSIDISK 5310521002; DMCD-230; D-101; EME.1098/2
T-1414	GOIN' BACK TO TEXAS	G22714; OSX/MSX 7766; MFP A8130; OEX 10257; DRUM 8143; MUSIDISK 5310521002
T-1415	HAPPY YODELER*	G22715; Sony Aust 76096021; DMCD-230; EMI CASS 8140904; CD 8140902
T-1416	SWISS SWEETHEART	G22715; Sony Aust 76096021

*Spelt "Yodeller" on reissues.

TUESDAY MARCH 3, 1936, COLUMBIA STUDIOS, PARRAMATTA ROAD AND COLUMBIA LANE, HOMEBUSH, SYDNEY, NSW, AUSTRALIA

The Yodelling Boundary Rider. (Tex Morton) Vocal with Yodelling and Guitar Accompaniment

T-1417	WYOMING WILLIE	G22716; OSX/MSX 7766; MFP A8130; OEX 10257; DRUM 8143; MUSIDISK 5310521002; D-101
T-1418	YOU'RE GOING TO LEAVE THE OLD HOME, JIM¹	G22716; OSX/MSX 7749#; AX 1041#; TC-AX-1041#; MUSIDISK 5310521002; TC-AX 701279#; (CA-17147–1)*
T-1419	THE OREGON TRAIL*	G22717; Col FB-2068; OSX/MSX 7766##; MFP A8130; OEX 10257; DRUM 8143; PRIMO CD 6039+; MUSIDISK 5310521002; JASBOX13–4**; D-101
T-1420	CARRY ME BACK TO THE LONE PRAIRIE	G22717; OSX/MSX 7766; MFP A8130; OEX 10257; DRUM 8143; Sony Aust 76096021

*Matrix / Control number used on English Pressing was CA-17147–1, artist credit as TEX MORTON (The Yodelling Boundary Rider) With His Guitar).
**Jasmine various artist CD "A Cowboy's Life Is Good Enough For Me" (2005)
#titled "The Tramp's Mother."
##titled "The Oregon Train."
+Czech Republic various artist CD titled "All Time Great Singing Cowboys."

WEDNESDAY JULY 1, 1936, COLUMBIA STUDIOS, PARRAMATTA ROAD AND COLUMBIA LANE, HOMEBUSH, SYDNEY, NSW, AUSTRALIA

The Yodelling Boundary Rider. (Tex Morton) Vocal with Yodelling and Guitar Accompaniment.

CT-1449²	THE PRAIRIE IS A LONESOME PLACE AT NIGHT	G22872; OSX/MSX 7766; MFP A8130; OEX 10257; DRUM 8143; MUSIDISK 5310521002
CT-1450	SING, YOU COWBOY	G22872; WARNER 5249875355*

* Warner various artist CD "Finest Australian Vintage Country Vol 2" (2011).

THURSDAY AUGUST 20, 1936, COLUMBIA STUDIOS, PARRAMATTA ROAD
AND COLUMBIA LANE, HOMEBUSH, SYDNEY, NSW, AUSTRALIA

The Yodelling Boundary Rider. (Tex Morton) Vocal with Yodelling and Guitar Accompaniment

CT-1460	RAGTIME COWBOY JOE	G22905; MUSIDISK 5310521002
CT-1461	THE WANDERING STOCKMAN	G22904; Sony Aust 76096021
CT-1462	OLD SHIP O' MINE (The Sailors' Hillbilly)	G22905; MUSIDISK 5310521009
CT-1463	WRAP ME UP IN MY STOCKWHIP AND BLANKET (The Dying Stockman)	G22904; OSX/MSX 7631; WRC R04444; PRL/PRML 034*; Sony Aust 76096021; DMCD-230; PRMC 034*

* Selection various artist LP/CASSETTE "Country Radio Request Hour Vol 7," (1982).

THURSDAY OCTOBER 15, 1936, COLUMBIA STUDIOS, PARRAMATTA ROAD
AND COLUMBIA LANE, HOMEBUSH, SYDNEY, NSW, AUSTRALIA

The Yodelling Boundary Rider. (Tex Morton) Vocal with Yodelling and Guitar Accompaniment, Mouth Organ by Harry Thompson

CT-1474	JUST DRIFTING ALONG	G22950; FB 1918*; MUSIDISK 5310521002
CT-1475	THE YODELLING BAG MAN	G22950; FB 1918*; LRF2 011**; SEL PRD-003**; MUSIDISK 5310521002; DMCD-230; CD 5007***

*Artist credit, TEX MORTON (The Yodelling Boundary Rider) with Guitar (Mouth Organ by Harry Thompson).
**Larrikin/Selection various artist double LP sets. "Country Music in Australia". Early Larrikin issues were un-numbered (1977).
*** "Maverick Country", 4 CD set released in the UK by Chrome Dreams, as "The Yodelling Bagman".

TUESDAY OCTOBER 20, 1936, COLUMBIA STUDIOS, PARRAMATTA ROAD
AND COLUMBIA LANE, HOMEBUSH, SYDNEY, NSW, AUSTRALIA

The Yodelling Boundary Rider. (Tex Morton) Vocal with Yodelling and Guitar Accompaniment

CT-1476   ON THE GUNDAGAI LINE   G22951; SEGO/SEGM-70088; AX 1041; TC-AX-1041; Sony 76096021; D-101; TC-AX 701279

CT-1477   ALL SET AND SADDLED*   G22951; FB-2068; OSX/MSX 7766; MFP A8130; Sony Aust 76096021; MUSIDISK 5310521002; D-101; JASMCD-3552**; REVCD008

* Matrix / Control number used on English pressing was CA-17146–1, artist credit as "TEX MORTON (The Yodelling Boundary Rider) With His Guitar."
** Jasmine various artist CD "Yodelling Mad! The Best Of Country Yodel Volume One" (2002).

TUESDAY FEBRUARY 23, 1937, COLUMBIA STUDIOS, PARRAMATTA ROAD AND COLUMBIA LANE, HOMEBUSH, SYDNEY, NSW, AUSTRALIA

The Yodelling Boundary Rider. (Tex Morton) Vocal with Yodelling, Accordion and Guitar Accompaniment

CT-1496   LONESOME VALLEY SALLY   G23058; MUSIDISK 5310521002
CT-1497   TAKE ME BACK TO DREAM BY THE OLD MILL STREAM   G23058; MUSIDISK 5310521002

FRIDAY MARCH 5, 1937, COLUMBIA STUDIOS, PARRAMATTA ROAD AND COLUMBIA LANE, HOMEBUSH, SYDNEY, NSW, AUSTRALIA

The Yodelling Boundary Rider. (Tex Morton) Vocal with Yodelling and Guitar Accompaniment

CT-1499   THE BLACK SHEEP   G23064; OSX/MSX 7749; AX 1041; TC-AX-1041; Sony Aust 76096021; PCD-090***; BUD-CD-3; DMCD-230; D-101; PRML 004/LRF 025*; TC-AX 701279; PRMC 004*

CT-1500   YOU ONLY HAVE ONE MOTHER   G23064; OSX/MSX 7749; AX 1041; TC-AX-1041; TC-AX 701279; PRL/PRML 027**; MUSIDISK 5310521002

* Larrikin/Selection various artist LP/CASSETTE, "Country Radio Request Hour Vol 1" (1977).
** Selection various artist LP "Country Radio Request Hour Vol 6" (1981).
*** Selection various artist CD "Country Radio Request Hour Vol 9" (1998).

SATURDAY JUNE 5, 1937, COLUMBIA STUDIOS, PARRAMATTA ROAD AND COLUMBIA LANE, HOMEBUSH, SYDNEY, NSW, AUSTRALIA

The Yodelling Boundary Rider. (Tex Morton) Vocal with Yodelling and Guitar Accompaniment

CT-1517	OLD PAL OF MY BOYHOOD DAYS	G23145; MUSIDISK 5310521002; D-101
CT-1518	ACROSS THE GREAT DIVIDE	G23145; MUSIDISK 5310521002; D-101
CT-1519	WHY SHOULD I WORK?	G23146; DMCD-230
CT-1520	THE END OF A HOBO'S TRAIL	G23146; MUSIDISK 5310521002; D-101

THURSDAY JULY 1, 1937, COLUMBIA STUDIOS, PARRAMATTA ROAD AND COLUMBIA LANE, HOMEBUSH, SYDNEY, NSW, AUSTRALIA

The Yodelling Boundary Rider. (Tex Morton) Vocal with Yodelling and Guitar Accompaniment

CT-1521	BARNACLE BILL, THE SAILOR (No.2)	G23167; BUD-CD-3
CT-1522	PEG-LEG JACK	G23167; PRL/PRML 034*; BUD-CD-3
CT-1523	THE RAILROAD BUM	G23166; MUSIDISK 5310521002
CT-1524	FANNY BAY BLUES	G23166; MUSIDISK 5310521002

* Selection various artist LP "Country Radio Request Hour Vol 7." (1982).

TUESDAY OCTOBER 26, 1937, COLUMBIA STUDIOS, PARRAMATTA ROAD AND COLUMBIA LANE, HOMEBUSH, SYDNEY, NSW, AUSTRALIA

The Yodelling Boundary Rider. (Tex Morton) Vocal with Yodelling and Guitar Accompaniment

| CT-1539 | THE BIG ROCK CANDY MOUNTAINS+ | G23278; Col FB 1948; LRF 026*; GD 254; MUSIDISK 5310521002; CDP-7986562#; PCD-090##; BUD-CD-3; DMCD-230; PRL/PRML 005*; CRC-501; PRMC 005*; CDR-0332^; CDR-0609^^; PC 205521 202%%; TIMELESS 5186592032@; DER 1046###; EMI CDP 7986562++ |

CT-1540	MY SWEETHEART'S IN LOVE WITH A SWISS MOUNTAINEER	G23278; Col FB 1948; GD 254; OEX 9746***; DRUM 8142***; TC-DRUM-8142; MUSIDISK 5310521002; DM 26516%; BUD-CD-3; WRC 12491; TC-OEX-9746; 8X-OEX-9746 (CT); DER 1046###; CTS 55551; Delta 26516
CT-1541	ROCKIN' ALONE IN AN OLD ROCKING CHAIR	G23279; PRL/PRML 027**; BUD-CD-3; Sony Aust 76096021; PRMC 027**
CT-1542	THERE ARE TEAR STAINS ON YOUR LETTER MOTHER DEAR	G23279; MUSIDISK 5310521002

On English pressing Col FB 1948, artist credit as TEX MORTON (The Yodelling Boundary Rider) with Guitar.
On Scandinavian pressing GD 254, artist credit as TEX MORTON The Yodelling Boundary Rider with Guitar.
+ Titled "The Big Rock Candy Mountain" on LRF 026; PRL/PRML 005 and CRC 501.
++ EMI "Yodelling Crazy."
* Larrikin/Selection various artist LP/CASSETTE, "Country Radio Request Hour Vol 2" (1977).
** Selection various artist LP/CASSETTE "Country Radio Request Hour Vol 6" (1981).
*** Columbia Records various artist LP "Australian Country Yodellers."
# EMI (UK) various artist CD "Yodelling Craze" (1992).
Selection various artist CD "Country Radio Request Hour Vol 9" (1998).
Deroy DER 1046 "That's How The Yodel Was Born."
% Delta Music various artist CD "Yodellin' Crazy: 25 Original Country Yodellin' Classics" (2006).
%% The International Music Company CD titled "The History of Pop Radio, Volume 7" (2000).
^ Rajon various artist 3 CD Set "The Great Australian Vintage Country" (2004).
^^ Rajon various artist 3 CD Set "The Great Australian Vintage Country" (2006).
@ Timeless Music Co. various artist 3 CD Set "Finest Australian Vintage Country" (2010).

THURSDAY MARCH 10, 1938, COLUMBIA STUDIOS, PARRAMATTA ROAD AND COLUMBIA LANE, HOMEBUSH, SYDNEY, NSW, AUSTRALIA

The Yodelling Boundary Rider. (Tex Morton) Vocal with Yodelling and Guitar Accompaniment

CT-1571	THE GREATEST MISTAKE OF MY LIFE	G23382; MUSIDISK 5310521002
CT-1572	I'M DREAMING TONIGHT OF THE OLD FOLKS	G23382; OSX/MSX 7749; AX 1041; TC-AX-1041; Sony Aust 76096021; TC-AX 701279

| CT-1573 | THE LETTER EDGED IN BLACK | G23383; SEGO/SEGM-70048; OSX/MSX 7631; WRC R04444; PRL/PRML 027*; MUSIDISK 5310521002; DMCD-230 |
| CT-1574 | THE YELLOW ROSE OF TEXAS | G23383; SEGO/SEGM-70048 |

* Selection various artist LP "Country Radio Request Hour Vol 6" (1981).

TUESDAY APRIL 12, 1938, COLUMBIA STUDIOS, PARRAMATTA ROAD AND COLUMBIA LANE, HOMEBUSH, SYDNEY, NSW, AUSTRALIA

Tex Morton & Harry Thompson. (Tex Morton & Harry Thompson Vocal Duet with Yodelling, Guitar and Mouth Organ*) (Tex Morton & Harry Thompson Vocal Duet with Yodelling and Guitar#)

CT-1576	MY BLUE RIDGE MOUNTAIN HOME*	G23415; Col FB 2211; MUSIDISK 5310521002
CT-1577	WHEN IT'S NIGHT TIME IN NEVADA#	G23416; OSX/MSX 7766; MFP A8130; OEX 10257; DRUM 8143; MUSIDISK 5310521002
CT-1578	WEEPING WILLOW TREE*	G23415; MUSIDISK 5310521002
CT-1579	RED RIVER VALLEY*	G23416; OSX/MSX 7766; MFP A8130; OEX 10257; DRUM 8143; MUSIDISK 5310521002

CT-1576 On English pressing Col FB 2211, artist credit as "TEX MORTON The Yodling Boundary Rider (with Guitar) HENRY THOMPSON on The Mouth Organ."

WEDNESDAY JULY 27, 1938, COLUMBIA STUDIOS, PARRAMATTA ROAD AND COLUMBIA LANE, HOMEBUSH, SYDNEY, NSW, AUSTRALIA

The Yodelling Boundary Rider. (Tex Morton) Vocal with Yodelling and Guitar Accompaniment

| CT-1593 | THE MARTINS AND THE COYS | G23493, G23529; D-101; MUSIDISK 5310521002 |
| CT-1594 | SERGEANT SMALL | G23493; SEGO/SEGM-70088; LRF2 011*; PRD-003*; Fest D-30696**; WARNER 5249875355***; DMCD-230; Sony Aust 76096021; CDR-0332^; CDR-0609^^; TIMELESS 5186592032@ |

| CT-1595 | I LEFT MY HEART IN RED RIVER VALLEY | G23494; MUSIDISK 5310521002; D-101 |
| CT-1596 | BIRD IN A GILDED CAGE+ | G23494; OSX/MSX 7749; AX 1041; TC-AX-1041; Sony Aust 76096021; CDR-0332^; CDR-0609^^; TIMELESS 5186592032@ |

^ Rajon various artist 3 CD Set "The Great Australian Vintage Country" (2004).
^^ Rajon various artist 3 CD Set "The Great Australian Vintage Country" (2006).
+ Titled "Bird In a Guilded Cage" on Sony Aust 76096021.
* Larrikin/Selection various artist, double LP sets. "Country Music in Australia". Early Larrikin issues were un-numbered. (1977).
** Festival various artist CD "Sleepers and Rails: A Musical Trip Through Time on Australian Railways" (1991).
*** Warner various artist CD "Finest Australian Vintage Country Vol 2" (2011).
@ Timeless Music Co. various artist 3 CD Set "Finest Australian Vintage Country" (2010).

TUESDAY SEPTEMBER 6, 1938, COLUMBIA STUDIOS, PARRAMATTA ROAD AND COLUMBIA LANE, HOMEBUSH, SYDNEY, NSW, AUSTRALIA

The Yodelling Boundary Rider. (Tex Morton) Vocal with Yodelling and Guitar Accompaniment

| CT-1611 | MOVE ALONG BALDY | G23529; Col FB 2211; D-101 |

CT-1611 on English pressing Col FB 2211, artist credit as "TEX MORTON The Yodelling Boundary Rider with Guitar."

MONDAY NOVEMBER 21, 1938, COLUMBIA STUDIOS, PARRAMATTA ROAD AND COLUMBIA LANE, HOMEBUSH, SYDNEY, NSW, AUSTRALIA

The Yodelling Boundary Rider. (Tex Morton) Vocal with Yodelling and Guitar Accompaniment

CT-1635	OLD MAN DUFF	G23682; D-101
CT-1636	DREAMING WITH TEARS IN MY EYES	G23631; BCD 16863
CT-1637	YOUNG PAT MALONEY	G23582
CT-1638	DYING DUFFER'S PRAYER	G23582; OSX/MSX 7631; WRC R04444

CT-1639	CRIME DOES NOT PAY	G23682; OSX/MSX 7749; AX 1041; TC-AX-1041; Sony Aust 76096021; BUD-CD-3; D-101; CDR-0332*; CDR-0609**; TC-AX 701279; TIMELESS 5186592032***
CT-1640	MY OLD CRIPPLED DADDY	G23631; OSX/MSX 7749; AX 1041; TC-AX-1041; TC-AX 701279

* Rajon various artist 3 CD Set "The Great Australian Vintage Country" (2004).
** Rajon various artist 3 CD Set "The Great Australian Vintage Country" (2006).
*** Timeless Music Co. various artist 3 CD Set "Finest Australian Vintage Country" (2010).

TUESDAY MAY 9, 1939, COLUMBIA STUDIOS, PARRAMATTA ROAD AND COLUMBIA LANE, HOMEBUSH, SYDNEY, NSW, AUSTRALIA

The Yodelling Boundary Rider. (Tex Morton) Vocal with Yodelling and Guitar Accompaniment

CT-1662	BONNY BLUE EYES	G23756
CT-1663	MY OLD BUNKHOUSE BUDDIES	G23756; OSX/MSX 7766; MFP A8130; OEX 10257; DRUM 8143
CT-1664	TRAVEL BY TRAIN	G23757; SEGO/SEGM-70088; AX 1041; TC-AX-1041; Sony Aust 76096021; BUD-CD-3; DMCD-230; TC-AX 701279
CT-1665	MURRUMBIDGEE JACK	G23757; OSX/MSX 7631; WRC R04444; CDR-0332*; CDR-0609**; TIMELESS 5186592032***

* CDR-0332 Rajon various artist 3 CD Set "The Great Australian Vintage Country" (2004).
** CDR-0609 Rajon various artist 3 CD Set "The Great Australian Vintage Country" (2006).
*** Timeless Music Co. various artist 3 CD Set "Finest Australian Vintage Country" (2010).

MONDAY SEPTEMBER 11, 1939, COLUMBIA STUDIOS, PARRAMATTA ROAD AND COLUMBIA LANE, HOMEBUSH, SYDNEY, NSW, AUSTRALIA

The Yodelling Boundary Rider. (Tex Morton) Vocal with Yodelling and Guitar Accompaniment

CT-1684	DREAMS OF SILVER (AND MEMORIES OF GOLD)	G23849

CT-1685	ROCKY NED (The Outlaw)	G23849; OSX/MSX 7631; WRC R04444; PRL/PRML 009*; BUD-CD-3; D-101; JASMCD3586**
CT-1686	I'LL BE HANGED IF THEY'RE GONNA HANG ME	G23853; SEGO/SEGM-70088; BUD-CD-3
CT-1687	I'M GONNA YODEL MY WAY TO HEAVEN	G23853; BUD-CD-3

* Selection various artist LP "Country Radio Request Hour Vol 4". (1979).

** Jasmine various artist CD "Old Faithful-Songs From The Saddle."

MONDAY NOVEMBER 20, 1939, COLUMBIA STUDIOS, PARRAMATTA ROAD AND COLUMBIA LANE, HOMEBUSH, SYDNEY, NSW, AUSTRALIA

The Yodelling Boundary Rider. (Tex Morton) And Pat Fraley (The Wrestling Cowboy) Singing and Yodelling with Guitars–1. (Tex Morton) Vocal with Yodelling and Guitar Accompaniment*

CT-1718	HAND ME DOWN MY WALKING CANE-1	G23896
CT-1719	LET THE REST OF THE WORLD GO BY-1#	G23896; C-01916 (AC)
CT-1720	THE ORIGINAL NED KELLY SONG*	G23895; OSX/MSX 7637*; WRC R-01916*; WRC-C-01916 (AC); Sony Aust 76096021; BUD-CD-3; D-101
CT-1721	THE DAY I LEFT DADDY ALONE	G23895; OSX/MSX 7749**; AX 1041**; TC-AX-1041**; TC-AX 701279

On later pressings of CT-1720 the title was shortened to THE NED KELLY SONG.

* Australia/New Zealand Columbia-World Record Club various artist LP "Country Style Vol 2.."

** Titled "The Day I Left My Daddy Alone."

\# Probably also Dick Carr-steel guitar.

THURSDAY NOVEMBER 30, 1939, COLUMBIA STUDIOS, PARRAMATTA ROAD AND COLUMBIA LANE, HOMEBUSH, SYDNEY, NSW, AUSTRALIA

The Yodelling Boundary Rider. (Tex Morton) Vocal with Yodelling and Guitar Accompaniment

CT-1734	BILLY BRINK THE SHEARER	G23933; Sony Aust 76096021; DMCD-230
CT-1735	LITTLE SWEETHEART OF DAYS GONE BY	G23933
CT-1736	WHEN THE BLOOM IS ON THE SAGE	G23934; OSX/MSX 7766; MFP A8130; OEX 10257; DRUM 8143
CT-1737	SLEEPY HOLLOW	G23934

FRIDAY MARCH 29, 1940, COLUMBIA STUDIOS, PARRAMATTA ROAD AND COLUMBIA LANE, HOMEBUSH, SYDNEY, NSW, AUSTRALIA

The Yodelling Boundary Rider. (Tex Morton) Vocal with Yodelling and Guitar Accompaniment

CT-1751	FREIGHT TRAIN YODEL	G23995; OSX/MSX 7599*; WRC 5720; WRC0635 (AC);PCD-086**; DMCD-230; D-101
CT-1752	ARISTOCRAT	G23995; OSX/MSX 7631; WRC R04444; Sony Aust 76096021; DMCD-230; JASMCD3586***

* Australia/New Zealand Columbia various artist LP "Country Style."
** Selection various artist CD "Country Radio Request Hour Vol 8" (1997).
*** Jasmine various artist CD "Old Faithful-Songs From The Saddle."

MONDAY MAY 13, 1940, COLUMBIA STUDIOS, PARRAMATTA ROAD AND COLUMBIA LANE, HOMEBUSH, SYDNEY, NSW, AUSTRALIA

The Yodelling Boundary Rider. (Tex Morton) Vocal with Yodelling and Guitar Accompaniment

CT-1753	SHE CAME ROLLING DOWN THE MOUNTAIN	G24029; SEGO/SEGM-70048; D-101
CT-1754	IF YOU PLEASE MISS GIVE ME HEAVEN	G24030; OSX/MSX 7749; AX 1041; TC-AX-1041; TC-AX 701279
CT-1755	JUST PLAIN FOLKS	G24030; OSX/MSX 7749; AX 1041; TC-AX-1041; PRL/PRML 027**; TC-AX 701279; JASMCD3587++
CT-1756	THE STOCKMAN'S LAST BED	G24031; OSX/MSX 7637#; WRC R 01916#; WRC C 01916 (AC); DMCD-230;

CT-1757	BEAUTIFUL QUEENSLAND	G24029; SEGO/SEGM-70048; PRL/PRML 008*; Col TVS4##; Sony Aust 76096021; DMCD-230; PRMC 008*
CT-1758	OLD BOKO AND ME	G24031; OSX/MSX 7836***; OEX 10109***; TC OEX 10109; AXIS 1112***; TC AX 1112; DRUM 8071***; TC DRUM 8071; AHS 07; DMCD-230; JASMCD3586+

Matrix CT 1757 "BEAUTIFUL QUEENSLAND" was adapted, with wording changes, from W. Lee O'Daniel's "BEAUTIFUL TEXAS."
* Selection various artist LP/CASSETTE "Country Radio Request Hour Vol 3" (1979).
** Selection various artist LP "Country Radio Request Hour Vol 6" (1981).
*** Columbia/Axis/Drum various artist LP "A History of Australian Country Music."
# Australia/New Zealand Columbia-World Record Club various artist LP "Country Style Vol 2."
Columbia various artist LP "Country Spectacular."
+ Jasmine various artist CD "Old Faithful-Songs From The Saddle."
++ Jasmine various artist CD "Just Plain Folks-Songs of the Old Folks at Home."

MONDAY NOVEMBER 18, 1940, COLUMBIA STUDIOS, PARRAMATTA ROAD AND COLUMBIA LANE, HOMEBUSH, SYDNEY, NSW, AUSTRALIA

The Yodelling Boundary Rider. (Tex Morton) Vocal with Yodelling and Guitar Accompaniment

CT-1801	OLD ROVER (DEDICATED TO A FAITHFUL FRIEND)	G24172
CT-1802	YOU'LL NEVER BE MISSED (Monologue with Guitar)	G24172; LRF 232*

* Larrikin various artists LP "That's Australia."

THURSDAY MARCH 13, 1941, COLUMBIA STUDIOS, PARRAMATTA ROAD AND COLUMBIA LANE, HOMEBUSH, SYDNEY, NSW, AUSTRALIA

The Yodelling Boundary Rider and Sister Dorrie (Tex Morton, vocal with Yodelling and Guitar Accompaniment) (and Sister Dorrie, Vocal Duet with Yodelling and Guitar Accompaniment only on CT-1821)

CT-1818	THE DROVER'S WIFE	G24263; SEGO/SEGM 70039; OSX/MSX 7631; WRC R04444; D-101

CT-1819	COME BACK TO THE VALLEY	G24314
CT-1820	IN THE LUGGAGE VAN AHEAD	G24263; SEGO/SEGM 70039; OSX/MSX 7749; AX 1041; TC AX 1041; Sony Aust 76096021; DCMD-230
CT-1821	(HONEY, I'VE GOT) EVERYTHING BUT YOU	G24314

WEDNESDAY MAY 28, 1941, COLUMBIA STUDIOS, PARRAMATTA ROAD AND COLUMBIA LANE, HOMEBUSH, SYDNEY, NSW, AUSTRALIA

Tex Morton & Sister Dorrie with Tex Morton's Roughriders. [Tex Morton-vocal, guitar; Sister Dorrie (Dorothy Carroll)-duet vocals; Dick Carr-steel guitar; possibly Tom Wallis-bass; possibly Al Kinloch-fiddle; possibly Herbie Marks-accordion] The personnel of the Roughriders is taken from John Edwards' Morton discography. A knowledgeable source indicates that Sister Dorrie sometimes played piano accordion and that George Raymond played fiddle. Personnel in the band most likely changed over the years.

CT-1837	OLD SHEP	G24376; OSX/MSX 7599**; OSX/MSX 7631; WRC R04444; WRC 5720; WRC 0635 (AC); SCA 010; CD EMI SCA 010***; DMCD-230
CT-1838	THROUGH THE SIN OF A SON	G24376; OSX/MSX 7749; AX 1041; TC-AX-1041; LRF2 011*; PRD-003*; PCD-086#; TC-AX 701279
CT-1839	WHEN THE CACTUS IS IN BLOOM	G24394; OSX/MSX 7766; MFP A8130; OEX 10257; DRUM 8143; D-101
CT-1840	DON'T SAY GOODBYE	G24345; SEGO/SEGM-70039; DTR004CD##

* Larrikin/Selection various artist, double LP sets. "Country Music in Australia". Early Larrikin issues were unnumbered (1977).
** Australia/New Zealand Columbia various artist LP "Country Style."
*** EMI various artist LP "Country Fantastic."
\# Selection various artist CD "Country Radio Request Hour Vol 8" (1997).
\#\# Edited version with vocals removed, used as background music on Bob Morton's track "Ode To Dad" issued on CD "Tex Morton Souvenir Album Volume 1" Dingo Track Records DTR004CD.

Tex Morton And His Roughriders. [Personnel as above except for Sister Dorrie (Dorothy Carroll) who was not present; unknown-harmonica on CT-1841]

CT-1841	ROVER NO MORE	G24394; OSX/MSX 7631; WRC R04444
CT-1842	MANDRAKE	G24345; SEGO/SEGM-70039; OSX/MSX 7631; WRC R04444; PRL/PRML 009*; PRMC 009* DMCD-230; Sony Aust 76096021; JASMCD3586**; MID 29***

* Selection various artist LP/CASSETTE "Country Radio Request Hour Vol 4". (1979).
** Jasmine various artist CD "Old Faithful-Songs From The Saddle."
*** New Zealand various artist LP "Twenty New Zealand Country Hits" (1980).

WEDNESDAY APRIL 21, 1943, COLUMBIA STUDIOS, PARRAMATTA ROAD AND COLUMBIA LANE, HOMEBUSH, SYDNEY, NSW, AUSTRALIA

Tex Morton & His Roughriders. (Tex Morton-vocal, guitar; Dick Carr-steel guitar, possibly Tom Wallis-bass; possibly Al Kinloch-fiddle; possibly Herbie Marks-accordion; unknown-harmonica)

CT-2046	THE STORY OF PARSON JOE	G24731; OSX/MSX 7631; WRC R04444; JASBOX 13-4**; D-101
CT-2047	THE FLOWERS NEVER BLOOM IN LONESOME VALLEY	G24731
CT-2048	'NEATH THE SILVER WILLOW TREE	G24732
CT-2049	THE GOOD OLD DROVING DAYS	G24732; OSX/MSX 7631***; WRC R04444; Sony Aust 76096021; DMCD-230; MUSIDISK 5249823462*; D-101

* Warner Music, 3 CD various artist set (2011).
** Jasmine various artist CD "A Cowboy's Life Is Good Enough For Me" (2005). This has the full track with opening guitar run and yodel, not present on all subsequent reissues of the song.
*** On early pressings titled "Good Old Roving Days."

LABEL CREDITS

CT-1837, CT-1838, CT-1839, CT-1840   Tex Morton and Sister Dorrie

CT-1841, CT-1842, CT-2046, CT-2047,   Tex Morton and his Roughriders
CT-2048, CT-2049

COLUMBIA REISSUE LPS

OSX 7631   "Songs Of The Outback", later issued on World Record Club RO 4444

OSX 7749   "Sentimental Tex", later issued on Axis AX 1041 and TC-AX-1041/TC-AX 701279 as "The Black Sheep"

OSX 7766   "Goin' Back To Texas" later issued on Music For Pleasure A8130 as "Red River Valley"

In 1987, all 93 masters on the Regal Zonophone label were re-released by EMI in Sydney. For this release of a 5 LP boxed set, titled "Regal Zonophone Collection", the Regal Zonophone label was re-instated in the catalog. Catalog number for this set is EMBB 430051 (On Cover)

Record One: EMEB–430051
Record Two: EMEB–430052
Record Three: EMEB–430053
Record Four: EMEB–430054
Record Five: EMEB-430055

The "Regal Zonophone Collection" was also issued on a set of 4 cassette tapes. Set Number TC-EMBB–430051

Cassette One: TC–430051
Cassette Two: TC–430052
Cassette Three: TC–430053
Cassette Four: TC-430054

(Housed in an Early Style VHS Video Tape Unit.)

This material was later released on 2 double CD issues
EMI 814202-2 "The Regal Zonophone Collection Volume One"

Disc One:-814203–2
Disc Two:-814204–2

(First and Second reprints have same numbering system.)

EMI 814205-2 "The Regal Zonophone Collection Volume Two 1938–1943"

    Disc One:-814206–2
    Disc Two:-814207–2

Reprinted set has Regal Zonophone Label on discs.
Set Number-814205–2

    Disc One:-814205–2
    Disc Two:-814205–2

Reprinted set has same number on discs as set number. It is not known if any more reprints were done.

Radio Transcriptions, Sydney, NSW, Australia

"Covered Wagon" program recorded in 1938, Pagewood Studios, Sydney, NSW, Australia; other dates unknown, 1940s

TEX MORTON "SHOWTIME RADIO"

"The Yodelling Boundary Rider" vocal, guitar, yodelling, with the Rough Riders Band. (The Kingfisher releases spell the band as "Rough Riders", so it is spelled this way in the relevant sections of the discography.)

(Personnel on the "Covered Wagon" program: Tex Morton-vocal, guitar; Harry Thompson-harmonica. Personnel of the Rough Riders band on the other broadcasts is unknown, but might be: Dick Carr-steel guitar; Tom Wallis-bass; Al Kinloch-fiddle; Herbie Marks-accordion).

With Sister Dorrie (Dorothy Carroll), vocal *, and Harry Thompson, Mouth Organ Solo **.

COVERED WAGON PROGRAM

(a) Theme	AUS-7; LRH-446; RRH 26
(b) My Blue Ridge Mountain Home	AUS-7; LRH-446; RRH 26
(c) Wyoming Willie	AUS-7; LRH-446; RRH 26
(d) Liebestraum**	AUS-7; LRH-446; RRH 26
(e) Wah Hoo	AUS-7; LRH-446; RRH 26
(f) Theme	AUS-7; LRH-446; RRH 26

4BH BRISBANE SHOW PROGRAM

(a) Dialogue	AUS-7; LRH-446; RRH 26
(b) Hand Me Down My Walkin' Cane*	AUS-7; LRH-446; RRH 26

TEX MORTON RODEO BROADCAST (QLD)
- (a) Introduction — AUS-7; LRH-446; RRH 26
- (b) When The Cactus Is In Bloom* — AUS-7; LRH-446; RRH 26
- (c) Rio Grande (monologue) — AUS-7; LRH-446; RRH 26
- (d) Conclusion — AUS-7; LRH-446; RRH 26

COVERED WAGON PROGRAM
- (a) Theme — AUS-7; LRH-446; RRH 26
- (b) South American Joe** — AUS-7; LRH-446; RRH 26; ABC 2790923+
- (c) Weeping Willow Tree — AUS-7; LRH-446; RRH 26
- (d) Texas In The Spring — AUS-7; LRH-446; RRH 26
- (e) Ragtime Cowboy Joe — AUS-7; LRH-446; RRH 26
- (f) Theme — AUS-7; LRH-446; RRH 26

BROADCAST
- (a) Barnacle Bill The Sailor — AUS-7; LRH-446; RRH 26
- (b) Hobo Bill — AUS-7; LRH-446; RRH 26
- (c) Roll Along Covered Wagon — AUS-7; LRH-446; RRH 26

LRH-445 and LRH-446 are CD issues on the LARRIKIN LABEL.

Radio Transcriptions, Sydney, NSW, Australia, 1942

Tex Morton, vocal and yodelling, with the Rough Riders Band lead by Dick Carr. Featuring Sister Dorrie, * Dan Agar as Shorty [Tex Morton-vocal, guitar; Sister Dorrie (Dorothy Carroll)-vocal; personnel of the Rough Riders is unknown, but might be: Dick Carr-steel guitar; Tom Wallis-bass; Al Kinloch-fiddle; Herbie Marks-accordion]

I LIKE MOUNTAIN MUSIC	AUS-32
SLEEPY HOLLOW	AUS-32
THE YODELLING BAG MAN	AUS-32
CLANCY OF THE OVERFLOW	AUS-32
CRIME DOES NOT PAY	AUS-32
COME BACK TO THE VALLEY	AUS-32
GOING TO THE BARN DANCE TONIGHT*	AUS-32
THE STOCKMAN'S LAST BED	AUS-32
TEXAS IN THE SPRING	AUS-32
MOONLIGHT AND SKIES	AUS-32
WHEN IT'S NIGHT TIME IN NEVADA*	AUS-32

I'LL BE HANGED IF THEY'RE GONNA HANG ME	AUS-32
ROCKIN' ALONE IN AN OLD ROCKING CHAIR	AUS-32
OLD MAN DUFF	AUS-32
MY LITTLE BUCKAROO	AUS-32
CAN I SLEEP IN YOUR BARN TONIGHT, MISTER?*	AUS-32
OLD SHEP*	AUS-32
SHE CAME ROLLING DOWN THE MOUNTAIN	AUS-32
ROCKY NED	AUS-33
THE BLACK SHEEP	AUS-33
MOTHER, THE QUEEN OF MY HEART	AUS-33
THE LITTLE OLD CHURCH IN THE VALLEY*	AUS-33
MY BLUE RIDGE MOUNTAIN HOME	AUS-33
YOU AND MY OLD GUITAR	AUS-33
THE WANDERING STOCKMAN	AUS-33
MY LITTLE LADY	AUS-33
WRAP ME UP WITH MY STOCKWHIP AND BLANKET	AUS-33
MY SWEETHEART'S IN LOVE WITH A SWISS MOUNTAINEER	AUS-33
JUST PLAIN FOLKS	AUS-33
WEEPING WILLOW TREE*	AUS-33
THE LETTER EDGED IN BLACK	AUS-33
PEG LEG JACK	AUS-33
THE VALLEY, THE HOMESTEAD AND YOU	AUS-33
COWBOY	AUS-33
WHEN THE BLOOM IS ON THE SAGE	AUS-33
WYOMING WILLIE	AUS-33

Radio Transcriptions, Sydney, NSW, Australia, 1942

Tex Morton, vocal and yodelling, with the Rough Riders Band lead by Dick Carr [Tex Morton-vocal, guitar; Sister Dorrie (Dorothy Carroll)-vocal; Dick Carr-steel guitar; other personnel of the Rough Riders band might be Tom Wallis-bass; Al Kinloch-fiddle; Herbie Marks-accordion]

CLANCY OF THE OVERFLOW	AUS–1; STARCD1004
WALTZING MATILDA	AUS–1; STARCD1004

STARCD1004 Manufactured and distributed by Startel Entertainment, a division of Castle Communications (Australia) Limited (1994).

Radio Transcriptions, Sydney, NSW, Australia, 1942
Tex Morton, vocal with the Rough Riders, duet with Sister Dorrie *; Dan Agar as Shorty [Tex Morton-vocal, guitar; Sister Dorrie (Dorothy Carroll)-vocal; personnel of the Rough Riders band is unknown, but might be: Dick Carr-steel guitar; Tom Wallis-bass; Al Kinloch-fiddle; Herbie Marks-accordion]

THEY CUT DOWN THE OLD PINE TREE	AUS-31; PCD 10124; PMC 10124
SING YOU COWBOY	AUS-31; PCD 10124; PMC 10124
DADDY AND HOME	AUS-31; PCD 10124; PMC 10124
EVERYTHING BUT YOU*	AUS-31; PCD 10124; PMC 10124
ON THE GUNDAGAI LINE	AUS-31; PCD 10124; PMC 10124
FRANKIE AND JOHNNY	AUS-31; PCD 10124; PMC 10124
LET THE REST OF THE WORLD GO BY*	AUS-31; PCD 10124; PMC 10124
THE NED KELLY SONG	AUS-31; PCD 10124; PMC 10124
YODELLING COWBOY	AUS-31; PCD 10124; PMC 10124
MY OLD PAL	AUS-31; PCD 10124; PMC 10124
BILLY BRINK, THE SHEARER	AUS-31; PCD 10124; PMC 10124
CARRY ME BACK TO THE LONE PRAIRIE	AUS-31; PCD 10124; PMC 10124
MOVE ALONG BALDY	AUS-31; PCD 10124; PMC 10124
I'VE ONLY LOVED THREE WOMEN	AUS-31; PCD 10124; PMC 10124
BONNY BLUE EYES*	AUS-31; PCD 10124; PMC 10124
THE TRAMP'S MOTHER	AUS-31; PCD 10124; PMC 10124
GOIN' BACK TO TEXAS	AUS-31; PCD 10124; PMC 10124
FREIGHT TRAIN YODEL	AUS-31; PCD 10124; PMC 10124

AUS prefixes are Kingfisher cassette tapes. PCD 10124 is a Premium Masters CD and PMC 10124 is a Premium Masters audio cassette issued by Castle Communications (Australasia) Limited (1994).

Radio Transcriptions, Sydney, NSW, Australia, 1940s
Tex Morton "All Set And Saddled" radio show Episodes 1-4. [Tex Morton-vocal, guitar; Sister Dorrie (Dorothy Carroll)-vocal; other personnel unknown]

EPISODE 1

THEME AND INTRODUCTION	AUS-28
RAGTIME COWBOY JOE	AUS-28
FREIGHT TRAIN YODEL	AUS-28
GUARDIAN SOAP COMMERCIAL	AUS-28

STEAK AND POTATOES	AUS-28
DR. HODGKISSES' GOLD MINE	AUS-28
THE STOCKMAN'S LAST BED	AUS-28
GUARDIAN SOAP COMMERCIAL	AUS-28
WHEN THE CACTUS IS IN BLOOM	AUS-28
THEME AND CONCLUSION	AUS-28

EPISODE 2

THEME AND INTRODUCTION	AUS-28
WYOMING WILLIE	AUS-28
DEEP IN THE HEART OF TEXAS	AUS-28
GUARDIAN SOAP COMMERCIAL	AUS-28
WRAP ME UP WITH MY STOCKWHIP AND BLANKET	AUS-28
SAVING MISS MONA	AUS-28
CARRY ME BACK TO THE LONE PRAIRIE	AUS-28
GUARDIAN SOAP COMMERCIAL	AUS-28
RED RIVER VALLEY	AUS-28
THEME AND CONCLUSION	AUS-28

EPISODE 3

THEME AND INTRODUCTION	AUS-29
ROCKY NED	AUS-29
BONNY BLUE EYES	AUS-29
GUARDIAN SOAP COMMERCIAL	AUS-29
ARE YOU THINKING OF ME TONIGHT?	AUS-29
MISTAKEN IDENTITY	AUS-29
ROCKING ALONE IN AN OLD ROCKING CHAIR	AUS-29
GUARDIAN SOAP COMMERCIAL	AUS-29
HAND ME DOWN MY WALKING CANE	AUS-29
THEME AND CONCLUSION	AUS-29

EPISODE 4

THEME AND INTRODUCTION	AUS-29
I'M GONNA YODEL MY WAY TO HEAVEN	AUS-29
GUARDIAN SOAP COMMERCIAL	AUS-29
THE OLD APPLE TREE	AUS-29
THE WRONG MR. HOPKINS	AUS-29
MY LITTLE BUCKAROO	AUS-29
ROVER NO MORE	AUS-29
GUARDIAN SOAP COMMERCIAL	AUS-29

| WHEN THE BLOOM IS ON THE SAGE | AUS-29 |
| THEME AND CONCLUSION | AUS-29 |

Each of the "All Set And Saddled" radio show episodes is a complete show with no break.

Radio Transcriptions, Sydney, NSW, Australia, 1948

Tex Morton "On Air 1948." "The Yodelling Boundary Rider" vocal, guitar, yodelling, with The Rough Riders Band. [Tex Morton-vocal, guitar; Sister Dorrie (Dorothy Carroll) vocal *, vocal only ***; personnel of the Rough Riders band is unknown, but might be: Dick Carr-steel guitar; Tom Wallis-bass; Al Kinloch-fiddle; Herbie Marks-accordion]

HAND ME DOWN MY WALKIN' CANE*	AUS–8; LRH–445; RRH 9; ABC 2790923+
MY LITTLE LADY*	AUS–8; LRH–445; RRH 9
MANDRAKE	AUS–8; LRH–445; RRH 9; ABC 2790923+
DEEP IN THE HEART OF TEXAS***	AUS–8; LRH–445; RRH 9
SOLDIER'S SWEETHEART	AUS–8; LRH-445; RRH 9
I'LL BE HANGED IF THEY'RE GONNA HANG ME	AUS–8; LRH-445; RRH 9
BEAUTIFUL QUEENSLAND	AUS–8; LRH-445; RRH 9
OLD ROVER	AUS–8; LRH-445; RRH 9
WYOMING WILLIE	AUS–8; LRH-445; RRH 9
RED RIVER VALLEY*	AUS–8; LRH-445; RRH 9
THE BIG ROCK CANDY MOUNTAIN	AUS–8; LRH-445; RRH 9
THROUGH THE SIN OF A SON*	AUS–8; LRH-445; RRH 9
ROVER NO MORE	AUS–8; LRH-445; RRH 9
SLEEPY HOLLOW	AUS–8; LRH-445; RRH 9
THE MARTINS AND THE COYS***	AUS–8; LRH-445; RRH 9
ALONG THE STOCK ROUTE (MONOLOGUE)	AUS–8; LRH–445; RRH 9; ABC 2790923*
SHE'LL BE COMIN' ROUND THE MOUNTAIN*	AUS–8; LRH-445; RRH 9
THE YELLOW ROSE OF TEXAS*	AUS–8; LRH-445; RRH 9
THE BLACK SHEEP	AUS–8; LRH-445; RRH 9
RAGTIME COWBOY JOE*	AUS-8; LRH-445; RRH 9

*ABC 2 CD set "Down The Overlander's Trail."

Ca. October 1949, Australian Record Company,
probably 29 Bligh Street, Sydney, NSW, Australia

Tex Morton & Sister Dorrie, with his Roughriders. [Tex Morton, vocal, guitar only-1; Sister Dorrie (Dorothy Carroll), duet vocal-2; personnel of the Roughriders band is unknown, but might have been: Dick Carr-steel guitar; Tom Wallis-bass; Al Kinloch-fiddle; Herbie Marks or Dorothy Carroll-accordion.] The following recording sessions are at variance with Morton's later assertion that all songs released on the Rodeo and Tasman labels were recorded at one marathon recording session in Auckland. Recent evidence suggests that some sides were probably recorded in Sydney with the balance recorded in Auckland. Releases were on the ARC's Rodeo label and the New Zealand Tasman label.

M-28561-A	ONE HAS MY NAME, THE OTHER HAS MY HEART*	10–0001, R-001; TA 001; Fest 19815
M-28561-B	DON'T MAKE ME GO TO BED AND I'LL BE GOOD*	10–0002, R-002; R-02; TA 002; Fest 19815; TRIB 4; JASMCD3714
M-28562-A	MY DADDY IS ONLY A PICTURE-2**	10–0003; TA 003; Fest 19815; JASMCD3714
M-28577-A	YOU AND MY OLD GUITAR-2#	10–0003; TA 003; JASCD466; Fest 19815; Sony Aust 76096021
M-28577-B	MY LITTLE LADY-2##	10–0004; TA 004; Fest 19815
M-28578-A	FRANKIE AND JOHNNY-1%	10–0002, R-002; R-02; TA 002; Fest 19815; JASMCD3714
M-28578-B	STOCKMAN'S PRAY'R-1# %%	10–0004; TA 004; Fest 19815; WARNER 5249875355%
M-28579-A	SOLDIER'S SWEETHEART, PART 1 –1#	TA 005; Fest 19815
M-28579-B	SOLDIER'S SWEETHEART, PART 2-1#	TA 005; Fest 19815
M-28580-B	HE HOLDS THE LANTERN -1% (While his Mother Chops the Wood)	R 10–0001; TA 001; JASMCD3714 Fest 19815
M-28580-A	A ROLLING STONE (Unissued)	

Tasman and Rodeo Label Credits:
* Tex Morton With His Roughriders.

DISCOGRAPHY 273

** Tex Morton With Sister Dorrie, And His Roughriders.
# Tex Morton With His Guitar.
Tex Morton With Sister Dorrie And Guitar.
% Tex Morton With Guitar.
%% Warner various artist CD "Finest Australian Vintage Country Vol 2" (2011) titled "A STOCKMAN'S PRAYER."

Ca. January–March 1950, Astor Studios, 74 Shortland Street, Auckland, New Zealand

Some evidence suggests it is likely there was more than one session for these recordings. Tex Morton & Sister Dorrie, with his Roughriders. [Tex Morton-vocal, guitar only-1; Sister Dorrie (Dorothy Carroll) duet vocal-2; possibly Will Jeffs, Tommy Kahi, Bill Sevesi-steel guitar (at different sessions); Johnny Bradfield-guitar; George Campbell-bass; possibly Sister Dorrie (Dorothy Carroll)-accordion]

MX-30680	WHEN YOU HAVE NO ONE TO LOVE YOU-2 (LINDA DARLIN')	#10–0006; TA-006; Fest 19815; JASMCD3714
MX-30711	TEARDROPS IN MY HEART*	10–0006; TA-006; Fest 19815; JASBOX 13–4%%
MX-33811	ROSE OF SHENANDOAH VALLEY-2**	10–0010; TA-010; Fest 19815; Sony Aust 76096021^
MX-33812	SLIPPIN' AROUND-2**	JASMCD 10–0007; TA-007; Fest 19815; JASMCD3714***
MX-33813	WHEN MY BLUE MOON TURNS TO GOLD AGAIN-2**	10–0012; TA-009; Fest 19815 (MX-33813 on label-MX-30712 on record)
MX-33814	I'LL NEVER SLIP AROUND AGAIN-2**	10–0009; TA-008; Fest 19815; JASMCD3714
MX-33964	TREASURE UNTOLD-1%	10–0008; TA-008; Fest 19815; BCD 16673+
MX-33965	WAITING FOR A TRAIN-1%	10–0010; TA-009; Fest 19815; Sony Aust 76096021; JASMCD3714
MX-33966	ONE GOLDEN CURL-1%	10–0012; TA-011; Fest 19815; JASMCD3714
MX-33967	A ROLLING STONE-1%	10–0007; TA-007; Fest 19815; Sony Aust 76096021^^
MX-33968	ROCK MY CRADLE (ONCE AGAIN)-2##	10–0009; TA-012; Fest 19815
MX-34249	JUST BECAUSE*	10–0011; TA-012; Fest 19815; JASMCD3714

| MX-34250 | WABASH CANNON BALL* | 10–0011; TA-011; Fest 19815; JASMCD3714^^^ |
| MX-34251 | THIS COLD WAR WITH YOU-2** | 10–0008; TA-010; Fest 19815 |

Tasman and Rodeo Label Credits:
% Tex Morton With His Guitar.
%% Jasmine various artist CD "A Cowboy's Life Is Good Enough For Me" (2005).
* Tex Morton and his Roughriders.
** Tex Morton With Sister Dorrie, And His Roughriders.
*** Titled "Slipping Around."
# Tex Morton With Sister Dorrie, And Guitar And Bass.
Tex Morton With Sister Dorrie, And His Guitar.
^ titled "Rose of Sheivendoah Valleys" on Sony Aust 76096021.
^^ titled "I'm a Rolling Stone" on Sony Aust 76096021.
^^^ titled "Wabash Cannonball."
+ Bear Family various artist CD (BCD 16673 AR, 2003) "I Am Sad And Weary-Jimmie Rodgers Revisited", "Treasures Untold."

The Australian Record Company initially released these recordings in its Rodeo 10–0000 series, but at R-068 (ca. 1956) switched to the R000 series for new pressings. However, most Tex Morton new pressings continued to use the "10" prefix, apart from the two known exceptions of R-001, (one side) and R-002/R-02. The only proven unissued title is 28580A "A ROLLING STONE". Many copies of Rodeo 100007 were mistakenly released as Rodeo 10–0006.

ARC mx numbers were allocated on the day of processing and covered all product either local or imported from worldwide sources. Some of these numbers may represent actual recording masters but most would appear to be control or stamper numbers covering thousands of items each year from all aspects of recorded sound. MX 34769 to MX 34772 (by Dusty Rhodes) were recorded on 31 May 1950, and MX 30708 and MX 30709 (Bela Kanitz Trio, per Jack Mitchell) were recorded in October 1949 (their matrixes adjoin Tasman TA06.)[3]

In 1981 Tex Morton arranged for Festival in Australia and Interfusion in New Zealand to reissue these on his Rodeo label as a 2LP gatefold set L45823/4 and twin cassette C45823/4.

Friday, March 6, 1953, Castle Studio, Tulane Hotel,
206 8th Avenue North, Nashville, Tennessee, USA

Tex Morton. [Tex Morton-vocal, guitar; probably Walter ("Hank") Garland-guitar; Gerald Lester (Jerry) Byrd-steel guitar; Ernest (Ernie) Newton-bass; Thomas Lee (Tommy) Jackson-fiddle; Owen Bradley-piano/organ]⁴

CO 49080	I'VE KNOWN THE TRUTH	OK 18014; Col C 2241; P-24505-H AUST; P-24505-H NZ; P-24505-H SA; JASMCD3714
CO 49081	THE NEIGHBOR'S WIFE	Sony Aust 76096021***
CO 4908	I'VE GOT YOU (RIGHT OUT OF MY MIND) #	OK 18020; Col C 2338; P-24506-H AUST; P-24506-H SA; P-24506-H NZ; Sony Aust 76096021; Columbia DO8303; JASMCD3714; Columbia OEX 10078
CO 49083	CIRCUS BOY	Sony Aust 76096021
CO 49084	KIWI SONG ##	Sony Aust 76096021
CO 49085	RAILROAD BOOMER	OK 18020; Col C 2338; P-24506-H AUST; P-24506-H SA; P-24506-H NZ; PRML 016*; PRMC 016* Sony Aust 76096021; JASMCD3714
CO 49086	I WAS BORN IN OLD WYOMING ###	OK 18014; Col C 2241; P-24505-H AUST; P-24505-H NZ; P-24505-H SA; PRML 016*; JASMCD3554**; Sony Aust 76096021; W-711+

* Selection various artist LP/CASSETTE "Country Radio Request Hour Vol 5." (1980)
** Jasmine various artist CD "I Love To Yodel" (2004), from US Columbia 78.
*** Sony Music 76096021 label shows SONY MUSIC-BIG JO-KE "The Essential" 2 CD Set (2009).
 Spine of the CD case shows 88697 60960 2.
\# Titled "I've Got You (Right Out Of My Head)" on Sony Aust 76096021.
\#\# Titled "Kiwi Songs" on Sony Aust 76096021.
\#\#\# Titled "I Was There in Old Wyoming" on Sony Aust 76096021.
\+ USA Armed Forces Radio Service 16" Transcription, various artists.

1954–1958, various locations throughout Canada and the USA

Tex Morton. LP titled "The Tex Morton Story," release date April/May 1959.#
(Tex Morton-vocal, narration, guitar; Ian Barrie-organ)

These recordings were mastered by Robert Iredale at Festival recording studios, 223-229 Harris Street, Pyrmont, Sydney, NSW, Australia, from tapes provided by Morton, who said they were made at Carnegie Hall. Carnegie

Hall, however, was unable to provide a precise date for Morton's two reported performances there, nor is there any listing of the event in the New York Times. It is possible that Morton's performances at Carnegie Hall were at a private function—hence there was no listing in the Times—and were held in one of the smaller recital halls seating around 260 rather than the main hall. It is also possible that the Carnegie Hall setting is an embellishment by Morton, and the recordings are non-studio tapes. In some cases, the applause was added later (in Australia) to simulate live recordings.

RIO GRANDE	FL-7093; FX-10548; FL 30,121; E-251; UM-446; SRA 250,098; R66–6074
THE SHOOTING OF DAN McGREW (ALOUETTE)	FL-7093; FX-10545; SRA 250–176; E-251; UM-446; L-25364; L45207; SR66–9795; HZ 33; SRA 250,098; R66–6074; FL 371; L-15045; FL 30,121; F 3371
THE CREMATION OF SAM McGEE/TENNESSEE WALTZ*	FL-7093; FX-10545; SRA 250–176##; UM-446
(THE CREMANATION OF SAM McGEE on 2LP sets) TENNESSEE WALTZ*	FL 372##; L37708; L45208##; HZ 33; SR66–9795; L-15045; FL 30,121; E-251; UM-446; SRA 250,098; R66–6074; F 3372## SR66–9795
DON'T GO DOWN THE MINE DAD	FL-7093; FX 10,356; FL 30,121; E-251; UM-446; SRA 250,098; R66–6074
YOU'LL NEVER BE MISSED	FL-7093; FL 30,121; E-251; UM-446; SRA 250,098; R66–6074
I BELONG TO GLASGOW	FL-7093; FX-10546; FL 30,121; E-251; UM-446; SRA 250,098; R66–6074
THE COWBOY'S PRAYER/ HOME ON THE RANGE	FL-7093; FX-10547; L37708; E-251; UM-446; FL 30,121; SRA 250,098; R66–6074
CLANCY OF THE OVERFLOW	FL-7093; FX-10548; FL-31,673***; R66–257***; MUSICDISK 5249823462** MUSICDISK 5249899055**; FL 30,121; E-251; UM-446; SRA 250,098; R66–6074
WALTZING MATILDA#	FL-7093; FX-10546; SRA 250–176; E-251; UM-446; L45208; HZ 33; FL 372; MUSICDISK 5249899055** SRA 250,098; R66–6074; F 3372 FL 30,121; L-15045
CHANT PAGAN	FL-7093; FX-10547; FL 30,121; E-251; UM-446; SRA 250,098; R66–6074

| FACE ON THE BAR ROOM FLOOR | unissued in Australia |

"The Tex Morton Story" FL-7093/FL-30,121 was also issued by Popular Record Club, E-251 and Universal Record Club, UM-446; Reissued by Festival, on Universal Summit, SRA 250,098; Reissued by Festival, on Calendar R66-6074.
* This was cut from "The Cremation of Sam McGee/Tennessee Waltz" and issued as a single 8 second track on SR66-9795.
** Warner 3 CD various artist set. (2011)
*** Festival/Calendar various artist LP "The Lights of Cobb & Co."
# Possibly recorded at Carnegie Hall, New York.
The guitar introduction "Tennessee Waltz" edited out.

1959, Festival recording studios, 223-229 Harris Street, Pyrmont, Sydney, NSW, Australia

Tex Morton (Tex Morton-vocal, guitar)

YOU AND MY OLD GUITAR	FWA-117; FX-5113; FX-10,211; FL-30,935; L-15031; L-25364; R66–589; R67–6130; JASMCD3714
DREAMS OF SILVER	FWA-117; FL-30,935; L-15031; R67–6130; R66–589
WRAP ME UP WITH MY STOCKWHIP AND BLANKET	FWA-118; FX-5115; FX-10,213 FL-30,935; SR66–9,830; U 785; L-15031; SRA 250–176; L45208; L-25364; R67–6130; SR66–9795; R66–589; FL-31673**; R66–257**; HZ 33; K-TEL NA454#; FL 372; L-15045; C15104; Cal L 15060; F 3372; JASMCD3714
FLOWERS NEVER BLOOM IN LONESOME VALLEY	FWA-118
TREASURES UNTOLD	FX-5113; FX-10,211; FL-30,935; R67–6130 SR66–9,830; U 785; L-15031; R66–589; C15104; Cal L 15060; JASMCD3714***
PARSON JOE	FX-5113; FX-10,211; FL-30,935; R67–6130; SR66–9,830; U 785; L-15031; R66–589; C15104; Cal L 15060; JASMCD3714###
BILLY BOY	FX-5113; FX-10,211; FL-31152; L37708; R66–9,699; L15034; FL 30,400; FL 7257; R66–669
THEY CUT DOWN THE OLD PINE TREE	FX-5115; FX-10,213; FL-30,935; R67–6130; JASMCD3714 L-15031; L-25364; R66–589
MAY I SLEEP IN YOUR BARN TONIGHT, (MISTER)##	FX-5115; FX-10,213; FL-30,935; R67–6130; L-15031; R66–589; JASMCD3714

SLEEPY HOLLOW   FX-5115; FX-10,213; SR66–9,830; U 785; L-15031; SRA 250–176; L-25364; C15104; L45207; FL 371; R66–589; SR66–9795; SRA 250–090*; HZ 33; L-15045; SCD 499–086; FL 30,935; Cal L 15060; F 3371

FL 30,935 / R66–589 "The Versatile Tex Morton". FL 30,935 also issued by Festival Records New Zealand Calendar R67–6130 "The Versatile Tex Morton" issued by Festival Records, New Zealand
SR66–9,830, Cal L 15060, Universal Record Club U 785 and cassette C15104 "Australian Ballads"
SR66–9795 "Best of Tex Morton."
Festival Extended Plays, FX 5113, FX 5115, FX 10,110 and FX 10356 were also issued by Festival Records New Zealand.
* Summit various artist LP "Country and Western Showcase."
** Festival/Calendar various artist LP "The Lights of Cobb & Co."
*** As "Treasure Untold"
# K-TEL LP "True Blue Songs of Australia."
Titled "May I Sleep In Your Barn Tonight, (Mister)?" on some issues.
Titled "The Story Of Parson Joe."

December 1960, Festival recording studios, 223-229 Harris Street, Pyrmont, Sydney, NSW, Australia
Tex Morton. "Tex Morton Looks Back" (Tex Morton-vocal, guitar)

IN ELEVEN MORE MONTHS	FL-31,152; FX 10,356; SRA 250.156; R66–699; L45207; L-25364; R66–9,699; FL 7257; SH66–94069; FL 371; L-15034; SH66–94069; FL 30,400; R67–6074; E-203; F 3371; JASMCD3714****
THE TRAMP'S MOTHER	FL-31,152; SRA 250.156; L45207; R66–699; L37708; R66–9,699; FL 7257; L-15034; E-203 R67–6074; SH66–94069; FL 30,400; FX-10,356; FL 371; R66–9,969; F 3371
FRANKIE AND JOHNNIE	FL-31,152; FX 10,357; SRA 250.156; R66–699; L45207; R66–9,699;FL 7257; L-25364; SH66–94069; FL 371; L-15034; FL 30,400; R67–6074; E-203; R66–9,969; F 3371
THE STOCKMAN'S LAST BED	FL-31,152; FX-10,110; SRA 250.156; R66–699; L45207; L-25364; R66–9,699; FL 7257; F 3371 SH66–94069; FL 371; L-15034; FL 30,400; R67–6074; E-203; R66–9,969
HALLELUJAH I'M A BUM	FL-31,152; FX 10,357; SRA 250.156; R66–699; L45207; L37708; R66–9,699; SH66–94069; FL 371; FL 7257; SRA 250 153##; L-15034; SH66–94069; FL 30,400; R67–6074; E-203; SMX 44271###; CS 1153####; R66–9,969; F 3371; JASMCD3714***

ABDULLA BUL-BUL AMEER[5]	FL-31,152; FX-10,110; R66–699; SRA 250.156; L45207; FL 371; R66–9,699; FL 7257; L-25364; SH66–94069; L-15034; SH66–94069; FL 30,400; R67–6074; E-203; R66–9,969; F 3371
THE CAT CAME BACK	FL-31,152; FX 10,356; FK-3170; R66–699; Cal R66,438**; C15025**; L45208; L-25364; R66–9,699; FL 7257; SRA 250 176*;SRA 250 177#; HZ 33; FL 372; SR66–9795; L-15034; FL 30,400; L-15045; CS 1177 (AC); R67–6074; E-203; F 3372; JASMCD3714
SHE WAS HAPPY TILL SHE MET YOU	FL-31,152; FX-10,110; SR66–9795; R66–699; L45208; L37708; R66–699; FL 7257; FL 372; L-15034; FL 30,400; R67–6074; E-203;R66–9,969; F 3372; JASMCD3714
OLD MAN DUFF	FL-31,152; L37708; R66–9,699; R66–699; FL 7257; FX-10,110; L-15034; FL 30,400; R67–6074; E-203; R66–9,969; JASMCD3714
RYE WHISKEY	FL-31,152; FX 10,357; L37708; R66–699; R66–9,699; FL 7257; FK-3170 L-15034; FL 30,400; R67–6074; E-203; R66–9,969
THE LETTER EDGED IN BLACK	FL-31,152; FX 10,357; FK-259; L37708; R66–9,699; FL 7257; R66–699; L-15034; FL 30,400; R67–6074; E-203; R66–9,969; JASMCD3714

FL-7257/FL-31,152 titled "Tex Morton Looks Back" also issued on Popular Record Club E-203

L-15034 Calendar "Tex Morton Looks Back" on some copies label shows catalog number.

R66–9,969, also issued by Festival New Zealand as Calendar R67–6074 (Calendar R66–9,699 has green label, Calendar R66–699 has orange label).

* Spoken introduction edited out.
** Calendar various artist LP/cassette "Sorta Country" (Nov 1974).
*** As "Medley: Hallelujah I'm a Bum / The Great American Bum (We Are Three Bums)/ Don't Work For A Living."
**** titled "In Eleven More Months and Ten More Days."
\# Universal Summit various artist LP "Sorta Country."
\## Universal Summit various artist LP "Australia's Country Greats."
\### Summit various artist LP "Australia's Country Greats."
\#### Summit various artist cassette "Australia's Country Greats."

1961, Festival recording studios, 223-229 Harris Street, Pyrmont, Sydney, NSW, Australia

Robert (Tex) Morton. "The Sentimental Bloke by C. J. Dennis" (Tex Morton-vocal)

INTRODUCTION BY THE ARTIST	FL-30,092/3; Cal R66–496; Cal BR66–496
A SPRING SONG	FL-30,092/3; Cal R66–496; Cal BR66–496
THE INTRO	FL-30,092/3; Cal R66–496; Cal BR66–496
THE STOUSH O'DAY	FL-30,092/3; Cal R66–496; Cal BR66–496
DOREEN	FL-30,092/3; Cal R66–496; Cal BR66–496
THE PLAY	FL-30,092/3; Cal R66–496; Cal BR66–496
THE STROR'AT COOT	FL-30,092/3; Cal R66–496; Cal BR66–496
THE SIREN	FL-30,092/3; Cal R66–496; Cal BR66–496
MAR	FL-30,092/3; Cal R66–496; Cal BR66–496
PILOT COVE	FL-30,092/3; Cal R66–496; Cal BR66–496
HITCHED	FL-30,092/3; Cal R66–496; Cal BR66–496
BEEF TEA	FL-30,092/3; Cal R66–496; Cal BR66–496
UNCLE JIM	FL-30,092/3; Cal R66–496; Cal BR66–496
THE KID	FL-30,092/3; Cal R66–496; Cal BR66–496
THE MOOCH O'LIFE	FL-30,092/3; Cal R66–496; Cal BR66–496

1962, Festival recording studios, 223-229 Harris Street, Pyrmont, Sydney, NSW, Australia

Tex Morton (Tex Morton-vocal, guitar)

KEVIN BARRIE	FL-30,935; SR66–9,830; U 785; L-15031; R66–589; R67–6130;C15104; Cal L 15060
THE DISQUALIFIED JOCKEY	FL-30,935; FK-259; Cal R66, 438*; C15025*; L-15031; SRA 250–176; L37708; R67–6130; L45207; R66–589; FL-31,673**; R66–257**; SR66–9795; FL 371; F 3371; SRA 250 177***; HZ 33; L-15045; CS 1177 (C)

* Calendar various artist LP/cassette "Sorta Country."
** Festival/Calendar various artist LP "The Lights of Cobb & Co."
*** Universal Summit various artist LP "Sorta Country."

1962, Festival recording studios, 223-229 Harris Street, Pyrmont, Sydney, NSW, Australia

"Tex Morton Reads Banjo Paterson" (Tex Morton-vocal)

PRELUDE	
DROVING DAYS	FL-30,876/7; L45923/4*
A BUSH CHRISTENING	FL-30,876/7; L45923/4
THE PEARL DIVER	FL-30,876/7; L45923/4
ANTHONY CONSIDINE	FL-30,876/7; L45923/4
CLANCY OF THE OVERFLOW	FL-30,876/7; L45923/4
THE MAN FROM SNOWY RIVER	FL-30,876/7; L45923/4
FRYING PAN'S THEOLOGY	FL-30,876/7; L45923/4
THE GREAT CALAMITY	FL-30,876/7; L45923/4
THE FIRST SURVEYOR	FL-30,876/7; L45923/4
OVER THE RANGE	FL-30,876/7; L45923/4
FATHER REILLY'S HORSE**	FL-30,876/7; L45923/4
JIM CAREW	FL-30,876/7; L45923/4
THE MAN FROM IRONBARK	FL-30,876/7; L45923/4
MAORI'S WOOL	FL-30,876/7; L45923/4
THE SWAGMAN'S REST	FL-30,876/7; L45923/4
JOHNSON'S ANTIDOTE	FL-30,876/7; L45923/4
CONROY'S GAP	FL-30,876/7; L45923/4

* L45923/4 issued as "A.B.("Banjo") Paterson's The Man From Snowy River and other Poems Read by Tex Morton."
** On L45923/4 "FATHER RILEY'S HORSE."

June 1965,* Festival recording studios, 223-229 Harris Street, Pyrmont, Sydney, NSW, Australia
Tex Morton. "Sing, Smile and Sigh" (Tex Morton-vocal, guitar)

YOUNG MAN FROM THE COUNTRY	L45208; L37708; Cal R66–258; FL 31,720 SRA 250156; FL 372; F 3372 AUS-1 B**; HZ SH66–94069
WEE JEANIE HUNTER	L45208; L37708; Cal R66–258; FL 31,720; SRA 250156; HZ SH66–94069; FL 372; F 3372
YOUNG PAT MALONEY	L-25364; L45207; SR66–9795; SRA 250176; Cal R66–258; HZ 33; SRA 250156; FL 31,720; SRA 250–176; HZ SH66–94069; FL 371; L-15045; F 3371
I'VE KNOWN THE TRUTH	L45208; L37708; Cal R66–258; SRA 250156; FL 31,720; HZ SH66–94069; FL 372; F 3372

THE MAN ON THE FLYING TRAPEZE (BILL) BRINK THE SHEARER "(BILLY)" on some issues	L45208; L-25364; Cal R66–258; SRA 250156; FL 31,720; HZ SH66–94069; FL 372; F 3372 L45208; L37708; Cal R66–258 FL 31,720; SRA 250156; HZ SH66–94069 AUS-1 B**; FL 372; F 3372
LITTLE BROWN JUG	L-25364; L45207; SR66–9795; L-15045; SRA 250176; Cal R66–258; SRA 250156; HZ 33; HZ SH66–94069; FL 31,720; SRA 250–176; FL 371; F 3371
(THE) BALLAD OF NED KELLY	SRA 250176; L45207; SR66–9795; F 3371 Cal R66–258; SR66 9665#; L-25364; SRA 250–179#; HZ 33; FL 371; L-15033+; SR66–9,830; FL 31,720; L-15045; AUS-1 B**; Cal L 15060; U 785; HZ SH66–94069
(AT)THE END OF THE OLD HOBO'S TRAIL	L37708; L45208; SR66–9795; L-15045; Cal R66–258; SR66–9,830; U 785; HZ 33; FL 31,720; SRA 250–176; FL 372; C15104; Cal L 15060; HZ SH66–94069; F 3372
AFTER THE BALL	Cal R66–258; SR66–9,830; U 785; C15104; FL 31,720; L37708; Cal L 15060; HZ SH66–94069
THE DROVER'S WIFE	SRA 250179; L37708; L45208; L-15045; Cal R66–258; SR66–9,830; U 785; HZ 33; FL 372; SR66–9795; CG-200***; C15104; FL 31,720; SR66 9665#; SRA 250–176#; L-15033+; Cal L 15060; HZ SH66–94069; F 3372
SOLDIER'S SWEETHEART	Cal R66–258; SR66–9,830; U 785; C15104; FL 31,720; L37708; AUS-1**; Cal L 15060; HZ SH66–94069

* FL 31,720 and SR66–9,830 state a recording date of June 1965 for the LP FL 31,720/R66–258 titled "Sing, Smile and Sigh."

SR66–9795 titled "Best of Tex Morton", has photo (some only) reversed and "Tennessee Waltz"; all the other 11 tracks are the same as SRA 250–176.

SRA 250–176 and L-15045 titled "Best of Tex Morton" (1970), has "Waltzing Matilda."

SRA 250–156 and SH66–94069 titled "Laugh and Sing With Tex Morton" (1974).

L45207/8; FL 371/2 are 2LP sets titled "Hallelujah I'm a Bum" also on cassette F 3371/2 and 45207/8 L-25364 titled "20 Golden Greats."

L37708 titled "50th Anniversary Album" also issued by Festival Records, New Zealand.

** AUS-1 is a 2 LP, (one LP type cover) various artist Custom Recording, produced by Festival titled "Songs and Poems of Australia. Both discs are number AUS-1. "Soldier's Sweetheart" is on the first disc and the remaining titles are on the second disc. The first LP MX29111/MX29112) was issued, the second LP (MX28755/MX28756) remains possibly unissued.

Sticker on one side over AUS-1 is R66–577. Sticker (2½" x 1½") on other LP over Australian Festival is Calendar; it is unknown if either LP was issued as such.

*** CG 200 is a CBS Special Products "20 Country Greats Volume 3."

+ L-15033 Calendar various artist LP titled "Australia's Country Music Stars."

\# Calendar/Universal Summit various artist LP "Australia's Country Music Stars."

1965, Festival recording studios, 223-229 Harris Street, Pyrmont, Sydney, NSW, Australia

"Robert 'Tex' Morton's Reading of Ginger Mick" (Tex Morton-vocal)

DUCK AND FOWL	FL-31,685
WAR	FL-31,685
THE CALL OF STOUSH	FL-31,685
RABBITS	FL-31,685
TO THE BOYS WHO TOOK THE COUNT	FL-31,685
THE GAME	FL-31,685
A GALLANT GENTLEMAN	FL-31,685
THE PUSH	FL-31,686
SARI BAIR	FL-31,686
GINGER'S COBBER	FL-31,686
THE SINGING SOLDIERS	FL-31,686
IN SPADGER'S LANE	FL-31,686
THE STRAIGHT GRIFFIN	FL-31,686
A LETTER TO THE FRONT	FL-31,686

1965, Festival recording studios, 223-229 Harris Street, Pyrmont, Sydney, NSW, Australia

Tex Morton. "The Sentiment and Humour of Banjo Paterson, as read by Robert (Tex) Morton" (Tex Morton-vocal)

SALTBUSH BILL	FL-31,696
THE ROAD TO OLD MAN'S TOWN	FL-31,696
ON KILEY'S RUN	FL-31,696
BEEN THERE BEFORE	FL-31,696
HOW GILBERT DIED	FL-31,696
SANTA CLAUS IN THE BUSH	FL-31,696
THE TRAVELLING POST OFFICE	FL-31,696
MULGA BILL'S BICYCLE	FL-31,696
STORY OF MONGREL GREY	FL-31,696
A BUNCH OF ROSES	FL-31,696
WHEN DAVEY RODE THE MULE	FL-31,696
AS LONG AS YOUR EYES ARE BLUE	FL-31,696

PASSING OF GUNDAGAI	FL-31,696
HOW McGINNIS WENT MISSING	FL-31,696
LOST	FL-31,696
BOTTLE-O	FL-31,696

1965, Sydney, NSW, Australia

Tex Morton, Narration on "Peter Scriven's ORIGINAL TINTOOKIES SOUNDTRACK." (Tex Morton-vocal)

I LIKE LOOKING AT PLANETS-The Astronomer	FL-31,758

Late 1966, EMI recording studios, 301 Castlereagh Street, Sydney, NSW, Australia.

Tex Morton (Tex Morton-vocal, guitar; Don Burrows-clarinet on "Darwin Jailhouse Window"; other instrumentation includes bass, piano, drums, organ and electric guitar but the musicians are not known). The record was released on February 23, 1967, suggesting a recording date of late 1966 (DC, email to AS, September 7, 2021).

(THE) GREEN, GREEN GRASS OF HOME	DO-4762; OSX 7799; OEX-10078; AX 6327; AX 1107***; DRUM 8001***; SPR1***; EMI TC-FA-157009; EMI 1572002; EMI 1572004 (C); TC-SPR-1; 8X-SPR-1 (CART); TC-DRUM 8001/SPR1+; TC-AX-1107; WRC SLZ-8190; AX 701293***; TC-AX-701293; TC AXIS 6327
TEX MORTON'S PROTEST SONG (BURN ANOTHER FOLKIE)*	DO-4762; OSX 7799; OEX-10078; AX 6327; EMI TC-FA-157009; TC AXIS 6327; EMI 1572002; EMI 1572004 (C);
THE CREAM IN BETWEEN (THE "CREAMY")*	DO-4785; OEX-10078; MFP A 8113**; AX 6327; EMI TC-FA-157009; EMI 1572004 (C); EMI 1572002; TC AXIS 6327
21st BIRTHDAY	DO-4785; OEX-10078; EMI 1572004 (C); AX 6327; TC AXIS 6327; MFP 8074; EMI TC-FA-157009; EMI 1572002; MFP A 8074###

THE JAILHOUSE WINDOW (DARWIN JAILHOUSE WINDOW)*	DO-5031; SEGO 70179#; OEX-10078; HR-10484; AX 6327; EMI TC-FA-157009; EMI 1572004 (C); EMI 1572002; TC AXIS 6327; ABC-EMI 524618-2/ABC-UNIVERSAL 10032/ABC-WARNER 2558302923/ABC-UNIVERSAL 1777785%
BARNACLE BILL THE SAILOR	DO-5031; OEX-10078; AX 6327; HR-10484; EMI 1572004 (C); MFP 8044##; TC AXIS 6327; EMI TC-FA-157009; EMI 1572002
WELCOME TO THE CLUB	DO-8303; OEX-10078; AX 6327; TC AXIS 6327; EMI TC-FA-157009; EMI 1572002; R 157002; EMI 1572004 (C)
I GOT YOU (RIGHT OUT OF MY MIND)	DO-8303; OEX-10078; AX 6327; TC AXIS 6327; EMI TC-FA-157009; EMI 1572002; EMI 1572004 (C)

"I'VE" on some issues

* Song title variations on OEX-10078 "Tex Morton Encores", AXIS 6327 also TC AXIS 6327.
** Music For Pleasure various artist LP "Dusty Road" track titled "(The) Cream In Between."
*** EMI Records LP "Our Kinda Country."
# Columbia 45rpm EP "Four of The Best", Track titled "Jailhouse Window."
Music For Pleasure various artist LP "Australian Style."
Music For Pleasure various artist LP "My Home on the Sunburnt Plains."
% ABC Records CD "Rules Of The Road"-Tex Morton dubbed duet with Lee Kernaghan (2000).
Released as ABC-EMI 524618-2/ABC-UNIVERSAL 10032/ABC-WARNER 2558302923/ABC-UNVERSAL 1777785 as a result of ABC Records changing contracts with different record companies.
AX 6327 also on cassette TC AXIS6327.
+ DRUM 8001 on covers only (SPR1).

Mid-1968, Auckland, New Zealand

Tex Morton "Tex Morton In New Zealand" (Tex Morton-vocal, guitar; other instrumentation includes electric bass guitar and harmonica, but the musicians are not known)

GOOD OLD DAYS	SEGO-70171; DNZ10574; EMI TC-FA-157009; EMI 1572002; EMI 1572004 (C)
(THE) EYES OF TEMPTATION	SEGO-70171; EMI TC-FA-157009; EMI 1572002; EMI 1572004 (C)
HALLELEUJAH, I'M A BUM	SEGO-70171; EMI TC-FA-157009; EMI 1572002; EMI 1572004 (C)

| ROCKING ALONE IN AN OLD ROCKING CHAIR (ROCKIN' ALONE*) | SEGO-70171; EMI TC-FA-157009;EMI 1572002*; DNZ10574; EMI 1572004 (C); MID 29* |

* New Zealand various artist LP "Twenty New Zealand Country Hits", Track titled "Rockin' Alone" (1980).

Ca. 1970, New Zealand.

Tex Morton with 'Teen Folk' Chorale. "A Tex Morton Singalong" (Tex Morton-vocal, guitar; Teen Folk Chorale, vocal; instrumentation includes steel guitar, organ, electric guitar and drums, but the musicians are not known). "A Tex Morton Singalong" was released in Australia on September 2, 1971, but was probably recorded earlier, when Morton was still in New Zealand.

BEAUTIFUL QUEENSLAND	SEGO-70194; EMI TC-FA-157009; EMI 1572002; EMI 1572004 (C)
CAMPFIRE MEDLEY (WAGON WHEELS, HOME ON THE RANGE, CARRY ME BACK TO THE LONE PRAIRIE)	SEGO-70194; EMI TC-FA-157009; EMI 1572002; EMI 1572004 (C)
RODEO ROUND-UP (ROCKY NED, ARISTOCRAT, MANDRAKE)	SEGO-70194; EMI TC-FA-157009; EMI 1572002; EMI 1572004 (C)
CHINEE LUCK	EMI 1572002; EMI 1572004 (C) EMI 1572002

"In The Good Old Days" (1991 reissue)

1970, New Zealand

"Tex Morton Today." Tex Morton with Peter Posa and the Hamilton County Bluegrass Band (Tex Morton-vocal, guitar; Peter Posa-guitar; Alan Rhodes-guitar; Paul Trenwith-banjo; Dave Calder-mandolin; Len Cohen-harmonica and Dobro; Lyndsay Bedogni-bass; Colleen Trenwith-fiddle; Country Touch Singers-backing vocals; Brian Hirst-chorale leader)

| FREIGHT TRAIN YODEL | SCXO/SCXM-7933; AX 6415; AX 701277; AX 1033; SLZ 850; S5406 |
| THERE'S A BRIDLE HANGING ON THE WALL | DO-10256, SCXO/SCXM-7933; AX 6415; AX 1033; AX 701277; SLZ 850; S5406 |

THE TRANSPORT MAN	SCXO/SCXM-7933; AX 6415; AX 701277; AX 1033; EGSM 1002; DO-9025; AX 701327##; NA 497+++; SLZ 850; MID 29%; S5406
THE BLACK SHEEP	EGSM 1002; DO-9025; EMI 1572004 (C); OEX-10078; AX 6327; TVS-6###
A BUSH CHRISTENING	SCXO/SCXM-7933; AX 6415; AX 701277; AX 1033; AHS-07+; SLZ 850; S5406
AUSTRALIA (A SONG POEM)	SCXO/SCXM-7933; OEX-10078; AX 6415; AX 1033; AX 701277; EMI 1572004 (C)++; SLZ 850; S5406 (an abridged version appeared on AX 6327, TC AXIS 6327; AUST 1–2#; R 157001; EMI/Thorn TC-FA157009; EMI 1572004 (C)and on EMI 1572002)
THE GOOD OLD DROVING DAYS	SCXO/SCXM-7933; AX 6415; AX 701277; AX 1033; SLZ 850; S5406
MINER'S LUCK	SCXO/SCXM-7933; AX 6415; AX 701277; AX 1033; EGSM 1002; SLZ 850; S5406
THE SHICER (MOANER'S LUCK)	SCXO/SCXM-7933; AX 6415; AX 701277; AX 1033; DO-9489; SLZ 850; S5406;
DON'T MAKE ME GO TO BED (AND I'LL BE GOOD)	SCXO/SCXM-7933; AX 6415; AX 701277; AX 1033; EGSM 1002; SLZ 850; S5406
BOB THE LOG	DO-9489; DO-10256; SCXO/SCXM-7933; AX 6415; AX 701277; AX 1033; SLZ 850; S5406
THE TRAVELLING SHOWMAN	SCXO/SCXM-7933; AX 6415; AX 701277; AX 1033; AX 1061*; 7243-8-54639-2-1**; SLZ 850; S5406

SCXO-7933 "Tex Morton Today" issued 1970, also issued on World Record Club, Australia, S5406 and World Record Club New Zealand, SLZ 850. On AXIS 701277; AXIS 6415; AXIS 1033 and 814-209-2 (CD) is titled "The Travelling Showman."

+ Titled "The Bush Christening."
++ Titled "Australia (So Wide And Grand)."
+++ Titled "Transport Man" on label for "24 GREAT TRUCK DRIVIN' SONGS" KTEL.
* Axis various artist LP "We Can Sing a Country Song."
** ABC Records various artist CD "MACCA ON AIR: A Music Selection From Australia All Over" (1996).
# Australiana Collection, 2 LP set.
Axis various artist LP "Long Lonesome Highway."
TVS6 (CAPITOL) "20 Country Tracks."
% New Zealand various artist LP "Twenty New Zealand Country Hits", track titled "Transport Man" (1980).

Thursday October 14, 1971, EMI recording studios,
301 Castlereagh Street, Sydney, NSW, Australia
Tex Morton (Tex Morton-vocal and rhythm guitar; Dave Bridge-lead guitar; Kevin King-rhythm guitar; Ron Martin-acoustic bass; Colleen Trenwith-fiddle)

OLD BLUE	DO-9764; OEX-10078; AX 6327; TC AXIS 6327; EMI TC-FA-157009; EMI 1572002; EMI 1572004 (C)
DUNMARRA	DO-9764; OEX-10078; AX 6327; TC AXIS 6327; EMI TC-FA-157009; EMI 1572002; EMI 1572004 (C)

1972, RCA recording studios, Sussex Street, Pyrmont, Sydney, NSW, Australia
Tex Morton with Sister Dorrie and Buddy Williams [Tex Morton-vocal, guitar; Buddy Williams-vocal, guitar; Sister Dorrie (Dorothy Carroll)-accordion; Ron Martin-bass; Ken Kitching-Dobro; possibly George Raymond-fiddle; unknown-banjo; Lynette Guest, Karen Williams-background vocals]

I LIKE COUNTRY MUSIC	RCA 102109; VPL1 0555*;
(I Like Mountain Music)	TC AX 701410;
The Buddy Williams Family Get Together with Tex Morton, Sister Dorrie and the Rough Riders' Band.	PMC 10193; WARNER 3984293092 (CD); PCD 10193; TC VPL1 0555; AXIS 701410*
THE WIDOW NEXT DOOR	RCA 102109; VAL1 0577**

Tex Morton (Guitar), Sister Dorrie (Auto Harp) and the Rough Riders' Band.
* Nicholls N Dimes various artist LP "Our Buddy" (1985) and later reissued by EMI on AXIS 701410 (1988).
** RCA various artist LP titled "Songs Of The Soldiers And The Band Played Waltzing Matilda."

1973, Copperfield recording studios, Surrey Hills, Sydney, NSW, Australia
Tex Morton's Australia. (Picture Record) (Tex Morton-vocal, guitar; George Raymond-fiddle; other instrumentation includes accordion, piano and bass but the musicians are not known)

THE GOONDIWINDI GREY (The Gunsynd Song)+	PRS-001; CLP-3000; L-36,173; RD4–239++; L-25364; VAL2 0364*; MAJ WA-342**; MALPS 380; MALPS 399%; 2MS 044%; 4CBS 1008#; CO/SONY 492991; MWSP-18##; MALPS-399+; Philips 6037030%%
DRINKING WITH THE DEAD (THE GLASS ON THE BAR)	PRS-001; Philips 6037030%%
ANDY'S GONE WITH THE CATTLE	CLP-3000; L-36,173; MALPS 380; L37708
THE COACHMAN'S TALE	CLP-3000; L-36,173; MALPS 380
LASCA	CLP-3000; L-36,173; MALPS 380
THE BUSHRANGERS	CLP-3000; L-36,173; MALPS 380; L37708
BULLOCKY BILL	CLP-3000; L-36,173; MALPS 380; L-25364
MICK DOOLEY'S PANTS	CLP-3000; L-36,173; MALPS 380; L-25364
GLASS ON THE BAR	CLP-3000; L-36,173; MALPS 380; L-25364
I'M BETTING THE ROLL ON ROMA	CLP-3000; L-36,173; MALPS 380
THE GREAT AUSTRALIAN ADJECTIVE	CLP-3000; L-36,173; MALPS 380; L-25364
DALEY'S DORG*	CLP-3000; L-36,173*; MALPS 380
A SATISFIED LIFE	CLP-3000; L-36,173; MALPS 380
BOKO	CLP-3000; L-36,173; MALPS 380
HOLY DAN	CLP-3000; L-36,173; MALPS 380; L-25364

+ "The Gunsynd Song" added to later pressings.
The first pressings of PRS 001 were un-numbered 7-inch 45 rpm records.
In the picture, the spindle hole changed from his mouth to throat on later pressings.
CLP-3000, MALPS 380 titled "Tex Morton's Australia". MALPS 380 also pressed in New Zealand.
L-36,173 titled "Tex Morton's Goondiwindi Grey."
L-37708 titled "Tex Morton's 50th Anniversary Album.
L-25364 titled "20 Golden Greats."
* RCA various artist LP/cassette (VAK 2–0364) "The Winners."
** Majestic various artist LP "The Good Times in Country Music.
# Golden Editions 4LP Box Set.
Music World 3 LP set "Country's Greatest."
% Music World 2 LP sets.
%% New Zealand release.
+ Music World various artist LP "Delux Best of Country Music."
++ Readers Digest 5 LP Set.

Saturday, March 10–Sunday, March 11, 1979, Wandong, Victoria, Australia
Tex Morton. "Wandong Country" various artists (Tex Morton-vocal, guitar)

FRANKIE AND JOHNNY   BLT 12003; BUD-CD-25

Tex Morton "The Tamworth Tapes", Rich River Records

FRANKIE AND JOHNNY (non-Country backing)   TAR 1989; AWCM00404

Undated Home Recordings
FIREBALL DAN   PCD 716; TRIB 4
TUMBA BLOODY RUMBA   ATT 0102
THE FLYING DOCTOR POEM   ATT 0102

*With spoken introduction by Eric Watson.
**Different from the "Lasca" in "Tex Morton's Australia" album.

NOTES

It has not been possible to identify all sources cited in these notes, since some clippings referenced were from unidentified newspapers and magazines, and sometimes dates and page numbers also were not present. This is particularly the case with documents in the archival collection, "The Papers of Tex Morton," housed at the National Library of Australia, and for xeroxed clippings of newspaper articles sent to the author during the 1980s and the early 1990s. Also, some cited sources are from newspapers and magazines that are currently not accessible online.

Much of the cited material is currently in the possession of private collectors like David Crisp, David Hardy and Peter Burgis, and a small portion of that has been subsequently donated to the National Library of Australia (NLA) and the National Film and Sound Archive (NFSA).

Transcripts of the interview with Morton by "Roxburgh, Garth Gibson and Francis Steel," held in the NFSA, were published in early editions of *Country & Western Spotlight*, (referenced as *CWS*, with page numbers). Garth Gibson gave David Crisp permission for a copy of the same interview to be used for research purposes, well before the NFSA acquired it. It has subsequently been released commercially on the Lyric label as CDL539, under the title *Tex Morton The Travelling Showman*. The original NFSA title is possibly incorrect, as Gibson interviewed Morton *at* (not *with*) Roxburgh, New Zealand. The author accessed Gibson's transcript of the interview ("The Tex Morton Story") in *CWS* or a tape copy provided by David Crisp.

Archived newspapers were searched online from these internet sites:

trove.nla.gov.au, (Trove Collection, NLA)

paperspast.natlib.govt.nz, (Papers Past Collection, National Library
  of New Zealand)

newspaperarchive.com, (Newspaper Archive, Canada)

Discographical references are generally for Australian releases only, and were sourced from Tony Russell's *Country Music Records A Discography*,

1921–1942 (New York: Oxford University Press, 2008), in which David Crisp cited Australian releases of recordings made in the USA; and from a xeroxed copy of David Crisp's annotated discography of Columbia Graphophone's Regal Zonophone label, generously provided to the author by him. David's discographies of Australian Panachord and Brunswick, published in issues of *CWS*, were equally indispensable. The Tex Morton discography in this book, compiled by David Crisp and David Hardy, was used for recordings of Tex Morton. For this, Bob Pinson and John Rumble, from the Country Music Foundation, and musician Bob Moore assisted with information about Morton's 1953 Nashville recordings. John Edwards's unpublished Tex Morton discography (ca. 1957) should be acknowledged here, too. Occasionally, discographical information from *Praguefrank's Country Music Discographies*, an online resource compiled with the assistance of several people involved with this book, has been used, although the Tex Morton discography at Praguefrank's site (accessed at: https://countrydiscography.blogspot.com/2011/11/tex-morton.html) currently requires correcting and updating.

Introduction

1. For a discussion of "The Big Bang of Country Music," see Ted Olson, *We Shall All Be Reunited: The Bristol Sessions: What They Weren't, and Why That Matters*, booklet accompanying the CD, *We Shall All Be Reunited: The Bristol Sessions 1927–1928*, Bear Family CD, BCD 17592. The entire recordings are on *Historic Sessions: The Bristol Sessions—The Big Bang Of Country Music*, Bear Family 5-CD set, BCD16094.

2. Vernon Dalhart, recording artist, "The Wreck on The Southern Old 97," Edison label 51361 (disc) Edison 4898 (cylinder). These were distributed in Australia for Edison (USA).

3. "Historical Population of Australia, 1788 to Future," *ChartsBin*, accessed April 26, 2022, at: http://chartsbin.com/view/eoo.

4. Jocelyn Neal, *Country Music: A Structural and Stylistic History* (New York: Oxford University Press, 2013): 325.

5. The late American folklorist W.K. McNeil told AS by letter ca. 1990s that he considered the Australian bush ballad to be a legitimate sub-genre of country music.

6. Jocelyn Neal, *Country Music: A Structural and Stylistic History* (New York: Oxford University Press, 2013): 325.

7. William ("Bill") Malone, *Country Music USA Revised Edition* (Austin: University of Texas Press, 1985): 141; Ivan Tribe. *Country: A Regional Exploration* (Westport: Greenwood Press, 2006): 46.

8. Ivan Tribe, "Tex Morton," in Barry McCloud, editor, *The Ultimate Encyclopedia of Country Music and its Performers* (New York: Bumper Books, 1995): 567–68; Barry Mazor, *Meeting Jimmie Rodgers* (New York: Oxford University Press, 2009): 99–100.

9. The entry mistakenly states that he recorded *I'd Like To Have A Beer With Duncan*, which was a hit for Slim Dusty. Richard Waterhouse "Tex Morton," *Australian Dictionary of Biography*, National Centre of Biography, Australian National University, 2012, accessed August 6, 2017, at: http://adb.anu.edu.au/biography/morton-tex-15027/text26223.

10. AS, "Tex Morton and His Influence on Country Music in Australia during the 1930s and 1940s," in Charles Wolfe and James Akenson *Country Music Annual 2002*, Lexington: University Press of Kentucky, 2002): 82–103; AS, "The Yodeling Cowgirls: Australian Women and Country Music," in Charles Wolfe and James Akenson, *The Women of Country Music: A Reader* (Lexington: The University Press of Kentucky 2003): 186–201. The *Journal of Country Music* also published an article about early Australian country music: AS, "Cowboys and Hillbillies Down Under: The First Wave of Australian Country Music," *Journal of Country Music* 13, no. 2, 1990: 16–23.

Chapter 1

1. "News of the Day," *The Colonist* 72, issue 15284 (January 26, 1920).
2. CM, "I Should Have Been a Presbyterian Minister," *EM Magazine*, (July 19, 1967).
3. Copy of birth certificate, Registrar of Births and Deaths, Nelson, issued January 25, 1996; sent to AS by BL.
4. Mildred Lane died in 1977 (BL, telephone conversation with AS, May 31, 2017) and Bernard Lane in 1981; "Bernie Lane's full life ends," *Nelson Evening Mail* (December 9, 1981).
5. David Mitchell, "Tex Morton—much more than a country singer," *Nelson Evening Mail* (August 1983).
6. KL to PB, letter ca. 1990s or early 2000s.
7. TM, ABC radio program, 1960s, DC private collection.
8. TM, handwritten lyrics of "Wee Jeanie Hunter," PTM Collection, NLA.
9. "Bernie Lane's full life ends," *Nelson Evening Mail* (December 9, 1981).
10. RL, interview by RW, NLA, ORAL TRC 6124/22, August 13, 2010.
11. BL, interview by RW, NLA, ORAL TRC 6124/25, October 12, 2010.
12. RL, interview by RW, NLA, ORAL TRC 6124/22, August 13, 2010.
13. Ibid.
14. "The 1920s," *New Zealand History*, accessed August 2017, at: https://nzhistory.govt.nz/culture/the-1920s/overview.
15. BL, interview by RW, NLA, ORAL TRC 6124/25, October 12, 2010; RL, interview by RW, NLA, ORAL TRC 6124/22, August 13, 2010.
16. BL, interview by RW, NLA, ORAL TRC 6124/25, October 12, 2010.
17. TM, *MLS, RPA Magazine* (March 1, 1939): 36–37.
18. TM, *MLS, RPA Magazine* (April 1,1939):37, 57. The *Lurline* was not commissioned until 1932, when Lane would have been about 16.
19. CM, conversation with AS, July 17, 1990.
20. TM's mother quoted by BL in Gordon Spittle, *TMS* (Auckland: GWS Publications, 2008): 96.

21. "Education in Nelson," *TheProw*, accessed online April 6, 2022, at: http://www.theprow.org.nz/society/education-in-nelson/.

22. BL stated Morton attended Central School: BL, interview by RW, NLA, ORAL TRC 6124/22, October 12, 2010; BL, telephone conversation with AS, May 31, 2017.

23. Reference from Nelson Central School, May 29, 1933, copy given to AS by KM.

24. Letter from Acting Chief Postmaster to "Master B Lane" (TM), December 16, 1929, copy given to AS by KM.

25. 3 km = 1.9 miles

26. Robert Gear to AS, letter, January 8, 1996.

27. Alan Turley, telephone conversation with AS, November 27, 2018; "A Period of Educational Reform," *Te Ara - the Encyclopedia of New Zealand*, accessed July 2019, at: https://teara.govt.nz/en/1966/education-evolution-of-present-system/page-3.

28. Scobie J. McKenzie to AS, letter, March 7, 1989.

29. BL, telephone conversation with AS, May 31, 2017.

30. Gordon Spittle, *TMS* (Auckland: GWS Publications, 2008): 104.

31. TM, handwritten note, n.d., PTM Collection, NLA. Lane studied English, Composition and Literature; French; Commercial (Book-Keeping, Economics and Geography); Mathematics (Arithmetic, Algebra, Geometry and Trigonometry); and Science (Physics, Chemistry and Electricity) in 1930 (Copies of TM's five school reports from Nelson College given to AS by KM, 2021).

32. Copies of TM's five school reports from Nelson College, given to AS by KM, 2021.

33. Photograph of letter from Nelson College, 1931, copy given to AS by KM.

34. Gordon Spittle, *TMS* (Auckland: GWS Publications 2008): 7.

35. TM, handwritten note, n.d., PTM Collection, NLA.

36. CM, "I Should Have Been a Presbyterian Minister," *EM Magazine* (July 19, 1967).

37. TM, *MLS, RPA Magazine* (May 1, 1939): 39, 56.

38. CM, "I Should Have Been a Presbyterian Minister," *EM Magazine* (July 19, 1967).

39. Will Fyfe was a Scottish music hall performer. "Will Fyfe," *Wikipedia*, accessed April 6, 2022, at: https://en.wikipedia.org/wiki/Will_Fyffe; "Will Fyfe Is Born," *Masonrytoday*, accessed April 6, 2022, at http://www.masonrytoday.com/index.php?new_month=02&new_day=16&new_year=2016.

40. KL cited from KL to PB, letter, ca. late 1990s or early 2000s. Goebel Reeves did not record "The Letter Edged in Black."

41. Robert Gear to AS, letter, January 8, 1996.

42. GG, "The Tex Morton Story Part One," *CWS Magazine*, 65 (November 1969): 9.

43. TM, handwritten note, n.d., PTM Collection, NLA.

44. Arch Barclay, "Tex Got Country Music Going," unidentified newspaper, n.d., ca. 1970s.

45. David Mitchell, "Tex Morton—much more than a country singer," *Nelson Evening Mail* (August 1983); handwritten notes by TM, PTM Collection, NLA.

46. GG, "The Tex Morton Story Part One," *CWS Magazine*, 65 (November 1969): 10.

47. TM, handwritten note, n.d., PTM Collection, NLA.

48. TM, interview by GG, 1969.

49. Unidentified article, probably by Alan Turley, n.d., cited from KL to PB, letter ca. 2002; reference from McKay's store (described as a "draper, dressmaker, and college outfitter",) May 29, 1933, copy given to AS by KM.

50. GG, "The Tex Morton Story Part One," *CWS Magazine*, 65 (November 1969): 10.

51. Reference from AG Pinson, May 30, 1933, copy given to AS by KM.

52. Reference from Ernest Wood, May 29, 1933, copy given to AS by KM.

53. CM, "I Should Have Been a Presbyterian Minister," *EM Magazine* (July 19, 1967): 21.

54. CM, "I Should Have Been a Presbyterian Minister," *EM Magazine* (July 19, 1967); Jazzer Smith, editor, *The Book of Australian Country Music 1* (Gordon, NSW: Berghouse Floyd Tuckey Publishing Group, 1984): 13; Gordon Spittle, *TMS* (Auckland: GWS Publications, 2008,): 9.

55. Advertisement, *Waihi Daily Telegraph* 33, issue 8588 (March 8, 1934): 3. 1/ = 1 shilling = 10 cents.

56. "P and T annual dance," *Waihi Daily Telegraph* 33, issue 8614 (May 10, 1934): 3.

57. "Waihi to Nelson distance," accessed June 2017, at: https://www.google.com.au/search?q=Waihi+to+Nelson+distance&ie=utf-8&oe=utf-8&client=firefox-b&gfe_rd=cr&ei=mcRAWemDLPTc8wesj7KICg .

58. Pat Ware, "Tex Morton's Triumphant Return To Australia," *Tempo and Television Magazine* (January-February 1959): 5–6.

59. "Country Music Pioneer," *New Zealand Listener Magazine* (June 21, 1968). 1 shilling (12 pence) = 10c.

60. Jazzer Smith, editor, *The Book of Australian Country Music 1* (Gordon, NSW: Berghouse Floyd Tuckey Publishing Group, 1984): 13; CM, "I Should Have Been a Presbyterian Minister," *EM Magazine* (July 19, 1967); AS, "Cowboys and Hillbillies Down Under: The First Wave of Australian Country Music," *Journal of Country Music* 13, no. 2, 1990: 17.

61. Alan Turley to AS, letter and telephone call, August 1, 2017; "Mortons Garage Waihi", *VYMaps.com*, accessed April 8, 2022, at: https://vymaps.com/NZ/Mortons-Garage-Waihi-136632/.

62. RL, interview by RW, NLA, ORAL TRC 6124/22, August 13, 2010.

63. Numerous Sydney journalists, interviews by AS , May 1990.

64. "Hospital Concert," *Auckland Star* (March 27, 1934).

65. Advertisements, *Waikato Independent* 34, issue 3207 (September 15, 1934): 5.

66. EW *CMA*, 1(Sydney: Angus and Robertson Publishers 1982): 13.

67. "Turkey Time," *Waikato Independent* 34, issue 3207 (September 15, 1934): 5.

68. "Hill-Billy Married. Tex Morton's Romance, Not Wanted in Hamilton," *Waikato Times* 121, no. 20388 (December 31, 1937): 13.

69. GG, "The Tex Morton Story Part One," *CWS Magazine*, 65 (November 1969): 10.

70. *Wireless Weekly Magazine* (February 21, 1936): 48.

71. "Speak-O-Phone Record Cutter Phonograph," YouTube, accessed April 8, 2022, at: https://www.youtube.com/watch?v=Ivozh45ttXQ.

72. TM, handwritten note, n.d., PTM Collection, NLA. Two shillings = 20 cents.

73. This was stated in a display of one Speak-O-Phone disc at the Australian Country Music Hall of Fame, in Tamworth; Max Ellis, email to AS, January 16, 2019. See also, "Tex Morton's Discs Found 71 Years Later in Australia," *News Archive*, accessed April 7, 2022, at: https://celebrityaccess.com/caarchive/tex-mortons-discs-found-71-years-later-in-australia/. The songs on these Speak-O-Phone discs were not the first country-music recordings made outside the USA, as some people have claimed.

74. Eric Scott, email to AS, August 31, 2016. Scott, a recording engineer, stated that recorded versions currently issued as mp3 files may be "playing back slow".

75. The Texas Drifter Goebel Reeves, "At The End of the Hobo's Trail," Panachord label, Panachord 12047. Panachord was a Brunswick (Australia) label; Ross Laird, *Sound Beginnings: The early record industry in Australia* (Sydney: Currency Press, 1999): 83.

76. "The Insult," *Songs Of the Cattle Trail & Cow Camp*, accessed April 15, 2022, at: http://www.traditionalmusic.co.uk/songs-cattle-trail-cow-camp/songs-of-the-cattle-trail-and-cow-camp%20-%200237.htm

77. Harry Torrani, recording artist, "Mexican Yodel," Regal Zonophone label, Regal Zonophone G21644, released in Australia in June 1933.

78. Dorothy Horstman, *Sing Your Heart Out Country Boy: Classic Country Songs and Their Inside Stories by the People who Wrote Them* (Toronto and Vancouver: Clarke, Irwin & Company Limited, 1975): 299.

Chapter 2

1. GG, "The Tex Morton Story Part One," *CWS Magazine*, 65 (November 1969): 10–11. TM named the showmen as Albert Russell, Percy Blackman and Lex MacDonald ("The Boy Soprano").
2. EW, *CMA*, 1 (Sydney: Angus and Robertson Publishers, 1982): 13.
3. GG, "The Tex Morton Story Part Two," *CWS Magazine*, 66 (1970): 41.
4. TM, MLS, *RPA Magazine* (June 1, 1939): 64.
5. "Tex Morton Denies He Neglected Wife," Sydney *Daily Mirror* (September 27, 1946).
6. "Australia's Cowboy New Zealand-Born," New Zealand *Evening Post*, October 1, 1949, PTM Collection, NLA; "Tex Morton Ballad Singer," unidentified newspaper, n.d., PTM Collection, NLA.
7. TM, MLS, *RPA Magazine* (June 1, 1939): 64.
8. David Mitchell, "Tex Morton—much more than a country singer," *Nelson Evening Mail* (August 1983).
9. "Superstar Tex Morton," Historical Feature, *Daily Telegraph-Mirror* (July 23, 1991); "Legend of show biz began long career as street busker," Historical Feature, Sydney *Daily Mirror* (September 28, 1983): 56.
10. "Wirth's Circus," Mackay *Daily Mercury* (June 25, 1932): 41.
11. RL, interview by RW, NLA, ORAL TRC 6124/22, August 13, 2010.
12. TM, MLS, *RPA Magazine* (June 1, 1939), 47–64. The *Monowai* regularly shuttled between New Zealand and Australia during the 1930s. "Photograph of Monowai," accessed

October 2017 at: http://www.nzmaritime.co.nz/monowai/monowai.htm. Mention of the Auckland Show might suggest, however, that his first trip to Australia was in 1934, when he was perhaps a member of The Gaieties and living in the North Island, and it was followed soon afterwards by a second voyage to Australia, possibly in early 1935.

13. "From Hobo Street Singer to ABC Headliner," *Band News Magazine* (December 26, 1939): 9.

14. "Community Sing To-Morrow Evening," *Nelson Evening Mail* 66 (June 7, 1934), 9; "Community Sing At School Of Music," *Nelson Evening Mail* 66 (June 8, 1934): 2; "Community Sing An Enthusiastic Audience," *Nelson Evening Mail* 66 (June 9, 1934): 2; "Reappearance of Tex Morton Who created a furore last Friday," *Nelson Evening Mail* 66 (June 12, 1934): 1.

15. TM's parents might have given him a watch. Perhaps Sergeant Small took the watch in 1935, as MM later suggested: MM, interviewed by HC, August 28, 1994.

16. Gordon Spittle, *TMS* (Auckland: GWS Publications, 2008): 14, 107.

17. TM, handwritten note, n.d., PTM Collection, NLA.

18. CM and other journalists interviews by AS, July 17, 1990.

19. TM, MLS, *RPA Magazine* (July 1, 1939): 47.

20. Ibid.

21. "Sorlie's Musical Revue," Rockhampton *Morning Bulletin* (June 12, 1935): 12; "Geo. Sorlie's Musical Revue," *Bowen Independent* (July 1, 1935): 3.

22. "Cossacks Arrive," Rockhampton *Evening News* (June 11, 1935): 12.

23. TM, MLS, *RPA Magazine* (August 1, 1939): 42. One guinea = £1 and 1 shilling = $2.10.

24. Gordon Spittle, *TMS* (Auckland: GWS Publications, 2008): 17.

25. "Assaulted Policeman: Youth Convicted," Rockhampton *Morning Bulletin* (June 25, 1935). £1= $2.

26. TM, MLS, *RPA Magazine* (September 1, 1939): 25.

27. TM, MLS, *RPA Magazine* (October 1, 1939): 36–37.

28. TM, MLS, *RPA Magazine* (November 1, 1939): 36–37.

29. Application for radio license, 1968, PTM Collection, NLA. Morton's height was about 176.5 cm

30. Paul McKenna Davis, "Hip Hypnotist," *Montreal Star* (January 22, 1972), PTM Collection, NLA. 165 pounds = 75 kilograms.

31. SDD, interview by AS, April 30, 1989.

32. Sydney journalists, interviews by AS, Sydney, May 1990.

33. BL quoted in Gordon Spittle, *TMS* (Auckland: GWS Publications, 2008): 96.

34. Norbert Batchelor, telephone conversation with AS, February 3, 1996.

35. William France to AS, letter, July 23, 1992.

36. Norbert Batchelor, telephone conversation with AS, February 3, 1996.

37. TM, interview by Nigel Lovell, ABC, 1972.

38. CM, "I Made Good Without Knowing It," *EM Magazine* (July 26, 1967).

39. Ibid.

40. TM comment cited in Jim Bennett to AS, letter, January 15, 1996.

41. Jazzer Smith, "The Tex Morton Story," *Across Country*, no 6 (February 1979): 5.
42. "2KY Sydney The First," *Radio Heritage Foundation*, accessed April 20, 2022, at: https://www.radioheritage.com/story73/; "Racing Radio," *Workers Online*, accessed April 20, 2022, at: http://workers.labor.net.au/77/c_historicalfeature_racing.html. The station had trade-union affiliations.
43. "'Uncle Russ' Sells Heenzo and Presents Clever Radio Turn Now Visiting Perth," Perth *Mirror*, April 2, 1938: 7.
44. TM, interview by Nigel Lovell, ABC, 1972.
45. "Finals—Uncle Rus Radio Trials," *SMH* (August 10, 1936): 36; "Uncle Rus Radio Trials," *SMH* (August 26, 1936): 2. Internet searches of archived newspapers, failed to find reports of TM winning radio talent quests in 1935, 1936 or 1937.
46. Advertisement for radio program, *Wireless Weekly Magazine* (February 21, 1936): 48.
47. "The Mills Brothers, recording artists, "How Am I Doin'," Brunswick (Australia) label, Brunswick 6269. The Mills Brothers toured Australia in 1939 (PB, email to AS, April 20, 2019).
48. "Turn on the Wireless," Grafton *Daily Examiner* (February 21, 1936): 7; "Broadcasting Programmes for the Week Saturday, February 22, 3LO, Melbourne," Melbourne *Weekly Times* (February 22 ,1936): 2; "Broadcasts This Week Monday, February 24," Broken Hill *Barrier Miner* (February 24, 1936): 4; "Over the Air To-day's Programmes," Grafton *Daily Examiner* (February 25, 1936): 7; "2BL Sydney," *Newcastle Morning Herald and Miner's Advocate* (February 25, 1936): 5.
49. SDD, interview by AS, April 30, 1989.
50. TM, *MLS, RPA Magazine*, February 1, 1939: 35. (The article refers to Rodgers as "Billy Rogers.")
51. GG, "The Tex Morton Story Part One," *CWS Magazine*, 65 (November 1969): 11.
52. SDD, interview by AS, April 30, 1989.
53. RWI to AS, letter, May 3, 1989. Since Britain declared war on Germany on September 3, 1939, it's likely that Tyler returned to England sometime around or after September 1939.
54. RWI, *Reminiscing In Tempo: A personal recollection of jazz music and the record business in Australia, 1923–1993* (privately published, 1993): 86.
55. Buck Carson, telephone conversation with AS, February 1, 2020.
56. Spelled "Yodeller" on reissues.
57. TM, recording artist, "Texas in the Spring" / "Goin' Back to Texas", Regal Zonophone label, Regal Zonophone G22714; TM, recording artist, "Happy Yodeler" / "Swiss Sweetheart", Regal Zonophone label, Regal Zonophone G22715.
58. Martin & Roberts (Fox & Wilson), recording artists, "The Roundup in the Spring": Regal Zonophone label, Regal Zonophone G22247.
59. Frank Luther and Carson Robison, recording artists, "Goin' Back to Texas," Brunswick (Australia), Brunswick 4296 and Panachord label, Panachord 12250.
60. Bill Malone, *Country Music USA*, revised edition (Austin: University of Texas Press,1985): 141.

61. Athol and Eileen McCoy, interview by RW and Kevin Bradley, NLA 186493, 1993–1994. McCoy stated that Morton was a brilliant yodeler and had, arguably, the highest yodel of all the Australian hillbilly artists.

62. Nolan Porterfield to AS, letter, November 2, 1995.

63. George Payne, telephone conversation with AS, February 17, 2018.

64. Bart Plantenga, *Yodel-Ay-Ee-Oooo: The Secret History of Yodelling Around the World*. (New York: Routledge, 2004): 15.

65. Ibid.

66. John Edwards, "Old Time Singers No. 9: The Mystery of the 'Texas Drifter.'" *CWS Magazine* 10: 31, in GG *CWS Special Edition* (collection of articles by John Edwards that were originally published in CWS) n.d.

67. TM, interview by GG, 1969.

68. GG, "The Tex Morton Story Part Two," *CWS Magazine*, 66 (1970): 40. "Kiwi" is Australian slang for a New Zealander.

69. Sales figures of 14796 for Regal Zonophone label, Regal Zonophone G22714 ("Texas in the Spring"/" Goin' Back to Texas") compared with 9839 for Regal Zonophone label, Regal Zonophone G22715 ("Happy Yodeller"/" Swiss Sweetheart"). The ratio of 14 796:9839 = 1.5, suggesting that for every G22715 disc sold, an average of 1.5 RZ G22714 discs were sold. These are not initial sales figures, but instead are accumulated sales figures, over the years the discs remained in the Regal Zonophone catalog.

70. Carson J Robison and his Pioneers, recording artists, "I Was Born in Old Wyoming," Zonophone / Regal Zonophone label, Zonophone/Regal Zonophone Zo/RZ 6136.

71. Charles Nabell, recording artist, "There's a Mother Always Waiting You at Home Sweet Home", OKeh label, OK 40418.

72. Guthrie T. Meade, Jr, with Dick Spottswood and Douglas S. Meade, *Country Music Sources: A Biblio-Discography of Commercially Recorded Traditional Music* (Chapel Hill: Southern Folklife Collection, 2002): 328.

73. Goebel Reeves, recording artist, "The Tramp's Mother," Panachord label, Panachord 12242.

74. AS, "Cowboys and Hillbillies Down Under: The First Wave of Australian Country Music." *Journal of Country Music* 13, no. 2 (1990): 17.

75. The New Zealand press frequently identified him as "Bob Lane"; see "Nelson Boy's Success As Gramophone Star," *Nelson Evening Mail* 70 (May 5, 1936): 4. The article stated that Morton had appeared at Nelson's Regent Theatre to "assist funds for the unemployed about two winters ago, where he was an instant success."

76. Advertisement, *Warwick Daily News* (May 2, 1936): 8; advertisement, *Dubbo Liberal and Macquarie Advocate* (May 19, 1936): 4; advertisement Goulburn *Evening Penny Post* (May 21, 1936): 2.

77. AS, "Cowboys and Hillbillies Down Under: The First Wave of Australian Country Music," *Journal of Country Music* 13, no. 2 (1990): 19; TM, interview by GG, 1969.

78. TM, recording artist, "The Prairie is a Lonesome Place at Night" / "Sing, You Cowboy", Regal Zonophone label, Regal Zonophone G22872.

79. The Hill Billies, recording artists, "The Prairie Is a Lonesome Place at Night" / "Sing, You Cowboy," Regal Zonophone label, Regal Zonophone G22357. (This is the British, not the American, group.)

80. TM, recording artist, "Wrap Me Up in My Stockwhip and Blanket (The Dying Stockman)" / "The Wandering Stockman," Regal Zonophone label, Regal Zonophone G22904; TM, recording artist, "Old Ship O' Mine" / "Ragtime Cowboy Joe" Regal Zonophone label, Regal Zonophone G22905.

81. This song is sometimes known as "Wrap Me Up **with** My Stockwhip and Blanket." Generally, the title in the text matches the title used on record or in relevant texts.

82. "Dying Stockman," *Australian Folk Songs*, accessed April 6, 2022, at http://folkstream.com/034.html

83. William (Bill) Scott, *Complete Book of Australian Folk Lore* (Sydney: Lansdowne Publishing, 2000): 138; Hugh Anderson, *The Story Of Australian Folksong 3rd edition*. (Melbourne: Hill Of Content, 1970): 233.

84. Frank Crumit, recording artist, "Wrap Me Up in My Tarpaulin Jacket," HMV label, HMV B.8032.

85. TM, interview by Nigel Lovell, ABC, 1972; His Masters Voice (HMV) was the British Gramophone's Australian branch, and issued hillbilly discs from 1926 to 1936 in its EA series. From 1931 onward, its discs were pressed by Columbia Graphophone.

86. Graham Seal, *Banjo Paterson's Old Bush Songs: Music and Verse Selected and Annotated by Graham Seal* (Sydney: Angus & Robertson Publishers, 1983): 138.

87. Slim Dusty, recording artist, "The Dying Stockman," EMI label, EMI 33-OSX-7745.

88. Slim Dusty, recording artist, *Australian Bush Ballads And Old Time Songs* EMI label, 33-OSX-7745; Slim Dusty, recording artist, *Australia Is His Name* (EMI label, EMI 7946582; Slim Dusty, recording artist, *Lands of Lots Of Time*, EMI label, EMI 8148742, 1997; Slim Dusty and his Bushlanders, recording artists, *Another Aussie Sing Song*, EMI label, EMI SCXO7689.

89. "Wrap Me Up with My Stockwhip and Blanket"[sic], *Australian Screen*, NFSA website, accessed April 20, 2022, at: https://aso.gov.au/titles/music/wrap-me-stockwhip-and-blanket/ (the title is listed as "Wrap Me Up with My Stockwhip And Blanket".)

90. TM, recording artist, "Just Drifting Along" / "The Yodelling Bagman", Regal Zonophone label, Regal Zonophone G22950.

91. Ray Grieve, *A Band In A Waistcoat Pocket: The Story Of The Harmonica In Australia*. (Paddington: Currency Press, 1995): 77–79.

92. "Tivoli Show," *Smith's Weekly* (October 9, 1937): 23.

93. Harry Thompson to DC, letter, April 18, 1987; Ray Grieve, *A Band In A Waistcoat Pocket: The Story Of The Harmonica In Australia* (Paddington: Currency Press, 1995): 77–79; "Jacaranda Festival," *Grafton Daily Examiner*, October 30, 1937: 4; "Bright A.B.C. Concert," Sydney *Labor Daily*, November 18, 1937: 12.

94. Ray Grieve, *A Band In A Waistcoat Pocket: The Story Of The Harmonica In Australia* (Paddington: Currency Press, 1995): 79.

95. MM, interview by HC, August 28, 1994.

96. Ray Grieve, *A Band In A Waistcoat Pocket: The Story Of The Harmonica In Australia* (Paddington: Currency Press, 1995): 80.

97. EW, *CMA, 1* (Sydney: Angus and Robertson Publishers, 1982): 18; EW liner notes to compact disc album *The Tex Morton Collection, Vol. 1, 1936–1938*, 1993, EMI label, EMI 8142022.

98. TM, recording artist, "On the Gundagai Line" / "All Set and Saddled, Regal Zonophone label, Regal Zonophone G22951; Jimmie Rodgers, recording artist, "Hobo Bill's Last Ride", Zonophone label EE213.

99. One penny = about one cent. £5 = $10.

100. Contract details, cited from copy of letter advising of Columbia Graphophone contract, December 21, 1936, provided by PB. n.d. The date the contract commenced was October 29, 1936.

101. £100 = $200.

102. Contract details cited from copy of letter advising of Columbia Graphophone contract, January 3, 1939, provided by PB, n.d.

103. "Sunday Night Harbour Tour," *SMH* (October 10, 1936): 13; "Sunday Night Harbour Cruise," *SMH* (October 24, 1936).

104. "Advertising," *SMH* (October 17, 1936): 3.

105. "Advertising," *SMH* (May 29, 1937): 3.

106. TM, *MLS, RPA Magazine* (January 1, 1939): 41. 30 shillings = $3.

107. "Crudity at the Tivoli," Sydney *Truth* (November 8, 1936): 31.

108. "Tivoli Revue," *SMH* (November 7, 1936): 18; Sydney *Truth* (November 8, 1936): 1.

109. CM, "I Made Good Without Knowing It," *EM Magazine* (July 26, 1967).

110. "Laugh, Town Laugh," Sydney *Labor Daily* (November 9, 1936): 8; "Advertising," Sydney *Sun* (November 15, 1936): 27; "Advertising," *SMH* (January 23, 1937): 3; "Advertising," Newcastle *Sun* (January 28, 1937): 11; "Broadcasting," *SMH* (April 24, 1937): 12; "Broadcasting Programmes for the Weekend," *Daily Telegraph* (May 8, 1937): 19.

Chapter 3

1. CM, "I Made Good Without Knowing It," *EM Magazine* (July 26, 1967).

2. PB email to AS, April 20, 2019.

3. Apparently, Marjorie's mother was then using the name Elizabeth Thornhill instead of her married name (Brisbane) or her maiden name (Mathieson). MM might have been a descendant of Sir Thomas Brisbane, the colonial governor of New South Wales from 1821 to 1825, cited from MM, interviewed by HC, August 28, 1994.

4. BL, interview by RW, NLA ORAL TRC 6124/25, October 12, 2010; RM, *Facebook* message to AS, April 29, 2018.

5. MM, interview by HC, August 28, 1994.

6. "Street Singer to Radio Star, Tex Morton's Amazing Career" *RPA Magazine* (May 1, 1938): 46.

7. MM, interview by HC, August 28, 1994.

8. RM, *Facebook* message to AS, March 8, 2019.

9. Gordon Spittle, *TMS* (Auckland: GWS Publications, 2008): 40; Transcript of marriage certificate, NSW marriage records, registration number 17150/1937. Transcript

provided by Joy Murrin, September 2016. Presumably, Marjorie's mother would have needed to give her consent, since Marjorie would have been under the age of 21 at the time. Morton would have turned 21 the previous August.

10. "Another Radio Romance," *SMH* (December 1, 1937): 13; "Radio Topics," *Sydney Labor Daily* (November 23, 1937): 8.

11. "Street Singer to Radio Star, Tex Morton's Amazing Career," *RPA Magazine* (May 1, 1938): 12.

12. Marjorie stated they traveled to New Zealand two days after their wedding, but Morton was still with Jim Davidson until later in 1937. The date might have been sometime in December.

13. EW. *CMA, 1* (Sydney: Angus and Robertson Publishers, 1982): 11.

14. CM, "I Should Have Been a Presbyterian Minister," *EM Magazine* (July 19, 1967).

15. BL, interview by RW, NLA, ORAL TRC 6124/25, October 12, 2010.

16. Ibid.

17. KL to PB, letter ca. late 1990s or early 2000s.

18. RM, interview by RW, NLA, BIB ID 4582970, December 4, 2008.

19. MM interview by HC, August 28, 1994.

20. Transcript of divorce certificate, NSW Registry of Births, Deaths and Marriages. Registration number 17150, suit no S3788/79. Transcript provided by Joy Murrin. The marriage was dissolved on August 11, 1979.

21. RM, *Facebook* message to AS, December 13, 2017.

22. EW, *CMA 1* (Sydney: Angus and Robertson Publishers, 1982): 14.

23. SDD, interview by AS, April 30, 1989.

24. Unidentified article, probably by Alan Turley, sent to PB by KL, ca. 2002.

25. Dick Carr to AS, letter, August 22, 1988.

26. "Lionel Bibby and His Son Jim are Crack Marksmen," *Film Australia Collection*, NFSA, accessed July 2018 at: https://faclibrary.com/Title-Details.aspx?tid=26&titlename=Lionel+Bibby+and+His+Son+Jim+are+Crack+Marksmen.

27. Hal Saunders to AS, letter, July 22, 1990.

28. Reg Goodwin to AS, letter, January 8, 1996. 20 meters = 65 feet.

29. CM, "I Should Have Been a Presbyterian Minister," *EM Magazine* (July 19, 1967).

30. PB, email to AS, April 21, 2019; cited dates are from Peter Valenti, *Errol Flynn: A Bio-Bibliography* (London: Greenwood Press, 1983).

31. "Errol Flynn," *Wikipedia*, accessed May 2017 at: https://en.wikipedia.org/wiki/Errol_Flynn.

32. TM, recording artist, "Lonesome Valley Sally" / "Two Cowgirls on the Lone Prairie," Regal Zonophone label, Regal Zonophone G24359.

33. The Girls of the Golden West, "Lonesome Valley Sally," Regal Zonophone label, Regal Zonophone G24359. The songwriter credits for Morton's recording were "Kennedy/Sandford/McConnell."

34. Dick Robertson, "Lonesome Valley Sally," Regal Zonophone label, Regal Zonophone G22468.

35. "Take Me Back to Dream by the old Mill Stream," cited in advertisement headlined "America's Greatest Catalog of Cowboy, Hillbilly and Native Popular Ballads," for *American Music Catalog* (Hollywood: American Music, Inc., 1942), in *Billboard Magazine*, 54, no. 42, (October 17, 1942).

36. TM, "Take Me Back to Dream by the old Mill Stream," Regal Zonophone label, Regal Zonophone G23058; cited in *Album of 21 Hill-Billy Songs Including Numbers Composed And Featured By Tex Morton The Yodelling Boundary Rider* (Sydney: Nicholson's Pty Ltd. ca. 1938): 14. The Cantrell Brothers Dance Orchestra, recording artists, "Take Me Back to Dream (By the Old Millstream)," Regal Zonophone label, Regal Zonophone G23102.

37. "The black sheep loves you best of all," sheet music, *Library of Congress*, accessed April 20, 2022, at: https://www.loc.gov/item/ihas.100005799/; Guthrie T. Meade, Jr, with Dick Spottswood and Douglas S. Meade, *Country Music Sources: A Biblio-Discography of Commercially Recorded Traditional Music* (Chapel Hill: Southern Folklife Collection, 2002): 290.

38. AS, "Cowboys and Hillbillies Down Under: The First Wave of Australian Country Music," *Journal of Country Music* 13, no. 2 (1990), 22.

39. Tex Morton, recording artist, "The Black Sheep," Regal Zonophone label, Regal Zonophone G23064.

40. "Historic Population of Australia, 1788 to Future," *ChartsBin*, accessed April 5, 2022, at: chartsbinhttp://chartsbin.com/view/e00

41. DC, emails to AS, July 11, 2016; January 27, 2019, and October 13, 2021. Crisp wrote: "The Sheltons 'The Black Sheep' was released on Decca De 5219. At the time Columbia Graphophone was pressing Deccas locally from both the Y and X series. US Decca would have sent over crates of items, and the local experts would have only selected certain items to issue here. The surplus would have been dumped or given out to local artists, or staff."

42. Vince Courtney, "The Black Sheep," Broadcast de Luxe W.618. One of six titles recorded in Melbourne in 1930.

43. TM, recording artist, "You Only Have One Mother", Regal Zonophone label, Regal Zonophone G23064. Morton sings the song as "You'll Only Have One Mother," and it is titled as such in one unidentified songbook (Sydney: D. Davis & Co, 1938); Trevor Day, telephone conversation with AS, May 6, 2019.

44. The Hill Billies, recording artists, "Across the Great Divide," Regal Zonophone label, Regal Zonophone G23238.

45. TM, recording artist, "Old Pal of my Boyhood Days" / "Across the Great Divide", Regal Zonophone label, Regal Zonophone G23145; TM, recording artist, "Why Should I Work," Regal Zonophone label, Regal Zonophone G23146.

46. TM, recording artist, "The End of a Hobo's Trail", Regal Zonophone label, Regal Zonophone G23146. Goebel Reeves recorded "At The End of the Hobo's Trail" three times in 1930; two versions were released. The first wasn't issued in Australia, the second was rejected (unissued), and the third was released in Australia on the Panachord label, Panachord 12047.

47. TM, recording artist, "Barnacle Bill, the Sailor (No.2) / "Peg-Leg Jack", Regal Zonophone label, Regal Zonophone G23167. Frank Luther (and Carson Robison), recording artists, "Barnacle Bill, the Sailor," Brunswick (Australia) Brunswick 4180 and Panachord

Australia label, Panachord 12293; Frank Luther and Carson Robison, recording artists, "Barnacle Bill the Sailor," Panachord Australia label, Panachord A2779; Frank Luther (with Carson Robison), recording artist, "Barnacle Bill, The Sailor—No 2" / "Peg-Leg Jack," Brunswick (Australia), Brunswick 4371. Carson Robison & His Pioneers, recording artists, "Peg Leg Jack," Regal Zonophone label, Regal Zonophone G21447; Bud & Joe Billings (Frank Luther and Carson Robison), recording artists, "Barnacle Bill the Sailor—No.2", Zonophone label, Zo/RZ EE266.

48. Art Leonard, recording artist, "Barnacle Bill the Sailor," Regal / Regal Zonophone label, Re/RZ G20498.

49. GG, "The Tex Morton Story Part One," *CWS Magazine*, 65 (1969): 9.

50. "Barnacle Bill the Sailor," *Wikipedia*, accessed April 5, 2022, at: https://en.wikipedia.org/wiki/Barnacle_Bill_%28song%29.

51. CM, "I Made Good Without Knowing It," *EM Magazine* (July 26, 1967).

52. "Richard Tauber Leaves For Australia," Burnie *Advocate* (May 30, 1938): 2; "Tauber in Australia" newsreel on YouTube, accessed April 5, 2022, at: https://www.youtube.com/watch?v=QNDz8OmABOA.

53. Robert Coltman, "Carson Robison: First of the Rural Professionals," *Old Time Music Magazine* no 28 (1978): 8.

54. Goebel Reeves's "Railroad Bum" was not the later song "A Railroad Bum," as recorded by Jim Reeves, *The Country Side of Jim Reeves*, RCA recording label, Camden CAS 686. Goebel Reeves and Jim Reeves were not related.

55. Goebel Reeves, recording artist, "Railroad Boomer," Panachord label, Panachord 12242.

56. TM, recording artist, "The Railroad Bum", / "Fanny Bay Blues", Regal Zonophone label, Regal Zonophone G23166, TM, interview by GG. TM.

57. TM, recording artist, "My Sweetheart's in Love with a Swiss Mountaineer" / "The Big Rock Candy Mountains," Regal Zonophone label, Regal Zonophone G23278. The original title on Morton's Regal Zonophone disc was "The Big Rock Candy Mountains," but subsequent reissues were sometimes titled "The Big Rock Candy Mountain" (DC, email to AS, December 12, 2019). DC wrote, "'The Big Rock Candy Mountains' is correct in the 78 era—on RZ G23278/Co FB1948/GD254 anyway. But the numerous re-issues over the years in various formats are sure to be a mixed bag."

58. Harry McClintock, recording artist, "The Big Rock Candy Mountain", Zonophone label, Zonophone EE125; Stuart Hamblen, recording artist, "The Big Rock Candy Mountains", Zonophone label, Zonophone EE258; Goebel Reeves, recording artist, "The Big Rock Candy Mountain", Banner label, Banner 33309 was unissued in Australia but Morton might have heard it from an imported disc.

59. Art Leonard, recording artist, "The Big Rock Candy Mountain," Regal Zonophone label, Regal Zonophone G20416.

60. Athol and Eileen McCoy, interview by RW and Kevin Bradley, NLA 186493, 1993–1994.

61. TM, recording artist, "Rocking Alone in an Old Rocking Chair" / "There Are Tear Stains on Your Letter Mother Dear," Regal Zonophone label, Regal Zonophone G23279.

62. Dorothy Horstman, *Sing Your Heart Out Country Boy: Classic Country Songs and Their Inside Stories by the People who Wrote Them* (Toronto and Vancouver: Clarke, Irwin & Company Limited, 1975): 223; "Rockin' Alone (in an Old Rockin' Chair), *SecondHandSongs*, accessed May 5, 2022, at: https://secondhandsongs.com/work/134852/all

63. Jack Savage, recording artist, "Rockin' Alone (in an old rockin' chair)," Decca label, Decca F.6079; "Jack Savage," *Praguefrank's Country Music Discographies*, accessed April 6, 2022, at: http://countrydiscography.blogspot.com.au/2012/02/jack-savage.html (May 4, 2022); Kevin Coffey, *Facebook* message, December 13, 2016.

64. Jack Savage, recording artist, "Rocking Alone in an Old Rocking Chair," Decca label Decca X1288; DC, email to AS, December 12, 2016. Morton especially seems to have copied the spoken lines from the Savage disc.

65. "Arch Kerr Talks Of Early Recordings." *Australasian Country Music Annual 1981* (Sydney: Maxwell Printing 1981): 18.

66. DC, email to AS, December 13, 2016; DC, email to AS, December 20, 2019. DC wrote, "Jack Savage X1288 'Rockin' Alone (in an Old Rockin' Chair)' took 9 years (1937–1946) to sell just over 1000 copies. Many Decca X's were poor sellers even though they were the same quality and price as RZ's."

67. PB email to AS, January 6, 2018.

68. "Community Concert," *Katoomba Daily* (October 29, 1937): 3.

69. "Broadcasting Programmes," *Newcastle Sun* (August 14, 1937): 2; "Detailed Lists, Results, Guides," Maitland *Daily Mercury* (August 14, 1937): 10.

70. "With ABC Band," *Newcastle Sun* (November 8, 1937): 8.

71. untitled notice, Grafton *Daily Examiner* (November 1, 1937): 6.

72. TM, interview by Nigel Lovell, ABC, 1972.

73. "Davidson's Dance Band and Gladys Moncrieff," Brisbane *Telegraph* (November 1, 1937): 7.

74. "Broadcasting," Brisbane *Courier Mail* (November 6, 1937): 18.

75. "Broadcasting Programmes for the Week Saturday," Melbourne *Weekly Times* (March 19, 1938): 2; "Four Well-Known Stars," *Katoomba Daily* (April 8, 1938): 1.

76. "Banjo Club's Review," *SMH* (March 12, 1938): 6.

77. "Tex Morton Returns," *Katoomba Daily* (March 17, 1938): 2. £150 = $300.

78. "From Street Singer To Radio Star," Broken Hill *Barrier Miner* (September 17, 1938): 3.

79. "Tex Morton Returns," *Katoomba Daily* (March 17, 1938): 2.

80. "Tex Morton," *Katoomba Daily* (September 6, 1938): 2.

81. "Tex Morton Booked By ABC For Ten-Week Season," *Australian Music Maker and Dance Band News Magazine* (November 1, 1939): 3.

82. "On the Air," *Bowen Independent* (December 8, 1939): 8.

83. "Tex Morton Coming to Pittsworth," *Pittsworth Sentinel* (August 31, 1940): 2.

84. " March of Troops in City," *SMH* (December 1, 1939): 13.

85. "The Woman's Bureau," Melbourne *Weekly Times* (August 13, 1938): 38.

86. "Tex Morton for England Bob Lyon for Australia," *Tempo Magazine* (May-June 1939): 9.

87. PB, email to AS, January 6, 2018.

88. TM, recording artist, "The Greatest Mistake of My Life", Regal Zonophone label, Regal Zonophone G23382; Jim Davidson and His Band, recording artists, "The Greatest Mistake of My Life," Regal Zonophone label, Regal Zonophone G23306; BP, to AS, letter, June 13, 2017.

89. Tony Russell, *Country Music Records: A Discography, 1921-1942* (New York: Oxford Press, 2004): 526. Cary Ginell and Kevin Coffey list "I'm Dreaming Tonight of My Blue Eyes (writer Tex Morton)" as at the same session, but this is a misprint; Cary Ginnell and Kevin Coffey, *Discography of Western Swing and Hot String Bands 1928–1942* (USA: Greenwood, 2001). Dickie McBride, recording artist, "I'm Dreaming Tonight of the Old Folks," Decca label, Decca 5734.

90. TM, recording artist, "The Letter Edged in Black" / "The Yellow Rose of Texas," Regal Zonophone label, Regal Zonophone G23383; Vernon Dalhart, recording artist, "The Letter Edged in Black," Brunswick (Australia) label, Brunswick 2900, 2911; Bradley Kincaid, recording artist, "The Letter Edged in Black," Regal Zonophone label, Regal Zonophone G22499; Gene Autry & Jimmy Long, recording artists, "The Yellow Rose of Texas," Regal Zonophone label, Regal Zonophone G22166. Guthrie T. Meade, Jr, with Dick Spottswood and Douglas S. Meade, *Country Music Sources: A Biblio-Discography of Commercially Recorded Traditional Music* (Chapel Hill: Southern Folklife Collection, 2002): 290.

91. Vernon Dalhart and Carson Robison, recording artists, "My Blue Ridge Mountain Home," HMV label, HMV EA295.

92. TM & Harry Thompson, recording artists, "My Blue Ridge Mountain Home" / "Weeping Willow Tree", Regal Zonophone label, Regal Zonophone G23415; TM & Harry Thompson, recording artists, "When It's Night Time in Nevada" / "Red River Valley," Regal Zonophone label, Regal Zonophone G23416; Frank Luther & Carson Robison, recording artists, "When It's Night Time in Nevada," Regal Zonophone label, Regal Zonophone G21055.

93. The Singing Stockmen (Norm & Arthur Scott), recording artists, "When It's Night Time in Nevada," Regal Zonophone label, Regal Zonophone G23534.

94. Lester McFarland & Robert A. Gardner, recording artists, "Weeping Willow Tree," Panachord label, Panachord 12180 and Brunswick (Australia) 3787; Art Leonard, recording artist, "Weeping Willow Tree", Regal Zonophone label, Regal Zonophone G21554.

95. The Hill Billies, recording artists, "Old Shep" / "Red River Valley," Regal Zonophone label, Regal Zonophone G22494. Their version of "Old Shep" is different from the better known Red Foley song, although both are about having to put a pet dog down. Art Leonard, recording artist, "The Red River Valley," Regal Zonophone label, Regal Zonophone G21555.

96. Bob Dyer, recording artist, "The Martins and the Coys," Regal Zonophone label, Regal Zonophone G24115; The Hoosier Hot Shots, recording artists, "The Martins and the Coys," Vocalion and OKeh labels Vo/OK 05214: Gene Autry, "The Martins and the Coys," from the movie *The Big Show*, YouTube, accessed April 15, 2022, at: https://www.youtube.com/watch?v=_8INqY7mSis.

97. "The Martins and the Coys," *Database of Popular Music*, accessed April 5, 2002, at: http://www.dbopm.com/link/index/4002/59893. April 5, 2022; "The Big Show (1936 film)," *Wikipedia*, accessed April 15, 2022, at: https://en.wikipedia.org/wiki/The_Big_Show_(1936_film); "The Martins and the Coys," YouTube, accessed April 15, 2022, at: https://www.youtube.com/watch?v=qz6uKOKPLL0.

98. Guthrie T. Meade, Jr, with Dick Spottswood and Douglas S. Meade, *Country Music Sources: A Biblio-Discography of Commercially Recorded Traditional Music* (Chapel Hill: Southern Folklife Collection, 2002): 147.

99. TM, recording artist, "I Left My Heart in Red River Valley" / "Bird in a Gilded Cage," Regal Zonophone label, Regal Zonophone G23494; Frank & James McCravy (The McCravy Brothers), recording artists, "A Bird in as Gilded Cage," Brunswick (Australia), Brunswick 4335.

100. Elzie Floyd & Leo Boswell, recording artists, "She's Only a Bird in a Gilded Cage," Regal Zonophone label, Regal Zonophone G20355.

101. TM, recording artist, "Sergeant Small" / "The Martins and the Coys," Regal Zonophone label, Regal Zonophone G23529; TM, interview by GG.

102. MM, interview by HC, August 28, 1994. Might the watch that MM mentioned have been given to TM by his parents when he returned to Nelson in 1934?

103. "Street Singer to Radio Star, Tex Morton's Amazing Career" *RPA Magazine* (May 1, 1938): 12.

104. TM, ABC radio program, 1960s.

105. Daphne Caine to AS, letter, January 19, 1996. Two shillings = 20c.

106. Statement regarding Sergeant Small threatening to sue TM cited from: "Sergeant Small," An Australian Folk Song A Day, accessed April 20, 2022, at: http://ozfolksongaday.blogspot.com/2011/04/sergeant-small.html.

107. Ken Blanch, "Swaggie Saga—One Of Convenience", *CWS Magazine*, new series no 33 (November 1982): 3–4; Originally published in the *Brisbane Courier Mail* (November 18, 1982.)

108. CM, "I Had Two Trains to Call My Own," *EM Magazine* (August 2, 1967)": 28.

109. MM, interview by HC, August 28, 1994.

110. "Tex For Broken Hill, Hit Song Banned" *Tempo Magazine* (September 1938): 10. "Sergeant Small" must have been withdrawn from sale very shortly after its release, since Columbia Graphophone kept monthly sales figures for records in its catalog, and there are no sales figures at all for "Sergeant Small."

111. TM, interview by Nigel Lovell, ABC, 1972; Gordon Spittle, *TMS* (Auckland, GWS Publications, 2008): 32.

112. TM, recording artist, "Move Along Baldy," Regal Zonophone label, Regal Zonophone G23529; TM, ABC radio program, 1960s.

113. Frankie Marvin, recording artist, "Old Man Duff," Zonophone label, Zo EE296 and Panachord label, Panachord 12224.

114. TM, recording artist, "Dreaming With Tears in My Eyes" / "My Old Crippled Daddy," Regal Zonophone label, Regal Zonophone G23631; TM, recording artist, "Dreaming With Tears in My Eyes," *The Influence Of Jimmie Rodgers*, Bear Family compact disc, BCD 16863 FH. 2008.

115. TM, recording artist, "Old Man Duff" / " Crime Does Not Pay." Regal Zonophone label, Regal Zonophone G23682; "Crime Does Not Pay" was also the title of a different song recorded by the Frank Luther Trio, written by Bob Miller and recorded in 1934, though Luther's disc wasn't released in Australia. It was released in the United States on several labels. "Bluey" is Australian slang for a male with red hair.

116. TM, recording artist, "Dying Duffer's Prayer" / "Young Pat Maloney," Regal Zonophone label, Regal Zonophone G23582; Frank Luther, recording artist, "That Silver Haired Daddy of Mine," Regal Zonophone label, Regal Zonophone G22123 . In the United States, several artists had recorded the song but Luther's was the only one issued in Australia at the time.

117. Sixteen inches = 41 centimeters.

118. Eric Cleburne to AS, recorded letter, 1990; Eric Cleburne to AS, letter, 1990.

119. Ray Grieve to AS, letter, January 22, 1990; DC, email to AS, January 27, 2019.

120. Eric Cleburne to AS, recorded letter, 1990; Eric Cleburne to AS, letter April 2, 1990.

121. Hal Saunders to AS, letter, July 22, 1990.

122. A synchronous motor is a special type of electric motor that runs at an extremely precise speed. See: David Herres, "Induction motor vs synchronous: What's the difference?" *Test&MeasurementTips*, accessed April 15, 2022, at: https://www.testandmeasurementtips.com/difference-between-synchronous-and-asynchronous-induction-motors-faq/.

123. Reference to "American production" cited from PB email to AS, 1989; notes to *Tex Morton: Australia's Yodelling Boundary Rider*, Larrikin Entertainment CD, Larrikin label LRH 446, 1996; PB email to AS, July 13, 2016.

124. Ray Grieve, *A Band In A Waistcoat Pocket: The Story Of The Harmonica In Australia* (Paddington: Currency Press, 1995): 79.

125. "Do You Know," *RPA Magazine* (September 1, 1942): 29.

126. Carr's birth name was Reginald Blyth confirmed by Joy Kirkpatrick, who knew him, (Joy Kirkpatrick, email to AS, August 8, 2020) and his granddaughter, Melissa Blyth, (*Facebook* message to AS, August 8, 2020).

127. Dick Carr to AS, letter, August 22, 1988.

128. Ibid.

129. Ibid. £50 = $100.

130. Ibid.

131. Ibid.

132. EW, *CMA* 2 (Sydney: Angus and Robertson Publishers, 1983): 147.

133. "Recording Pioneer Passes Away," *Capital News* 20, no. 7 (July 1995): 6.

134. Joy Kirkpatrick, email to AS, February 19, 2019.

Chapter 4

1. "Why Be Serious," *Auckland Star* (December 3, 1938); "Frank Neil's Revue 'Why Be Serious,'" *Press* (January 25, 1939): 5; "Why Be Serious", *Evening Post* (January 9, 1939): 4; J.C. Williamson Revue," *Evening Star* (January 28, 1939): 11.

2. "Newsreel, 1938—Tex Morton With Will Mahoney Show," *Australian Music Maker and Dance Band News Magazine* (January 1, 1939): 9.

3. Their ship was the *Awatea*. Photograph of TSS *Awatea*, Smaritime.com, accessed April 5, 2022, at: http://www.ssmaritime.com/Awatea.htm.

4. £12 = $24.

5. "William James Mahoney," in *Australian Dictionary of Biography* 15; accessed April 6, 2022, at: http://adb.anu.edu.au/biography/mahoney-william-james-will-11038.

6. PB to AS, letter, June 13, 2017.

7. Copy of contract for the 1938–1939 New Zealand *Why Be Serious* tour, JC Williamson Collection, Victorian Arts Centre, 1938.

8. "Why Be Serious," *Auckland Star* (December 3, 1938).

9. Gordon Spittle, *TMS* (Auckland: GWS Publications, 2008): 25.

10. TM, recording artist, "Bonny Blue Eyes" / "My Old Bunkhouse Buddies," Regal Zonophone label, Regal Zonophone G23756; TM, recording artist, "Travel by Train" / "Murrumbidgee Jack," Regal Zonophone label, Regal Zonophone G23757; EW. *CMA, 1* (Sydney: Angus and Robertson Publishers, 1982): 19. See also "Frank Coughlin," *Wikipedia*, accessed April 5, 2022, at: https://en.wikipedia.org/wiki/Frank_Coughlan. EW started that Coughlin had co-authored the song, but the songwriter credits on reissue albums credit Coughlan with sole authorship.

11. Max Ellis, "Sad Songs," unpublished article, April 13, 2017; Max Ellis, email to AS, April 13, 2017.

12. Frankie Marvin, recording artist, "I'm Gonna Yodel My Way to Heaven," Panachord label, Panachord 12224.

13. Johnny Marvin, recording artist, "I'm Gonna Yodel My Way to Heaven," Zonophone / Regal Zonophone label, Zonophone / Regal Zonophone Zo/RZ EE384.

14. The Hill Billies, recording artists, "I'm Gonna Yodel My Way to Heaven," Regal Zonophone label, Regal Zonophone G22511.

15. TM, recording artist, "Dreams of Silver (and Memories of Gold)" / "Rocky Ned", Regal Zonophone label, Regal Zonophone G23849; TM, recording artist, "I'll Be Hanged if They're Gonna Hang Me" / "I'm Gonna Yodel my Way to Heaven," Regal Zonophone label, Regal Zonophone G23853.

16. "Australian rodeo," *Wikipedia*, accessed April 6, 2022, at: https://en.wikipedia.org/wiki/Australian_rodeo; Jenny Hicks, *Australian Cowboys Roughriders & Rodeos* (Sydney: Angus & Robertson, 2000):78.

17. J. Gill, on-air telephone conversation with John Laws, 2SM-Sydney June 15, 2009.

18. Garry Coxhead, *Facebook* post (September 28, 2016).

19. PB, "Rocky Ned the 1st & Rocky Ned the 2nd—Buckjump History," *Australian Bush Balladeers Association Newsletter* 6, no. 3 (July 2005): 22.

20. "Rocky Ned," *The West Wyalong Advocate* (April 29, 1938): 2. American saddles were larger than Australian saddles, and arguably easier for buckjumping.

21. TM, ABC radio program, 1960s, DC private collection.

22. "Last of Rocky Ned," *The Dandenong Journal* (April 9, 1941): 12; "Rocky Ned Killed,"

Kilmore Free Press (April 3, 1941): 4. McConville valued Rocky Ned at £500 ($1000) at the time.

23. PB, "Rocky Ned the 1st & Rocky Ned the 2nd—Buckjump History," *Australian Bush Balladeers Association Newsletter* 6, no. 3 (July 2005): 22.

24. "Pat Fraley v Hansen," Melbourne *Age* (June 5, 1939): 4. "Cowboy Wrestler Pat Fraley Arrives," Melbourne *Age* (June 7, 1939): 12.

25. Photograph of Brother Jonathan by Tom Lennon, Powerhouse [Museum], Collection, accessed April 4, 2022, at: https://collection.maas.museum/object/390359; "Brother Jonathan & Brother Frank," *Arizona Pro Wrestling History*, accessed April 6, 2022, at: http://azwreshistory.blogspot.com/2011/06/brother-jonathan-brother-frank.html.

26. TM, interviewed by GG, 1969 ; "Cowboy Wrestler Talks of Chaps And Six Shooters," *Brisbane Telegraph*, July 31, 1939: 19.

27. Robert Murillo, *Pro Wrestling: The Fabulous, The Famous, The Feared And The Forgotten: 'Irish Pat Fraley'* (Turnover Scissors Press. Amazon Kindle e-book).

28. Gordon Spittle, *TMS* (Auckland: GWS Publications, 2008): 56.

29. CM and other journalists, interview by AS, July 17, 1990.

30. MM, interview by HC, August 28, 1994.

31. Inferred from Robert Murillo, *Pro Wrestling: The Fabulous, The Famous, The Feared And The Forgotten: 'Irish Pat Fraley'* (Turnover Scissors Press: Amazon Kindle e-book).

32. TM and Pat Fraley (The Wrestling Cowboy), recording artists, "Hand Me Down My Walking Cane" / "Let The Rest of the World Go By", Regal Zonophone label, Regal Zonophone G23896; Marion Evelyn Cox and Harvey Hindermeyer, recording artists, "Hand Me Down My Walking Cane," Edison cylinder 3955 and disc 50–629. PB email to AS, January 16, 2018.

33. Lester McFarland and Robert A. Gardner, recording artists, "Let the Rest of the World Go By," Brunswick (Australia), Brunswick 3780.

34. Bob Nichols & Riley Puckett, recording artists, "Let the Rest of the World Go By," Regal / Regal Zonophone labels, Regal / Regal Zonophone G20665.

35. Was "The Original" part of the title to claim precedence over Blinkhorn's Ned Kelly song? Morton wouldn't have liked being upstaged by a migrant from Canada writing a song about Australia's infamous bushranger.

36. TM, recording artist, "The Day I Left Daddy Alone" / "The Original Ned Kelly Song," Regal Zonophone label, Regal Zonophone G23895; TM, recording artist, "Hand Me Down My Walking Cane" / "Let The Rest of the World Go By," Regal Zonophone label, Regal Zonophone G23896.

37. TM ABC radio program, 1960s, DC private collection.

38. TM, recording artist, "The Day I Left Daddy Alone" / "The Ned Kelly Song," Regal Zonophone label, Regal Zonophone G23895, sold 13812 copies. Smilin' Billy Blinkhorn, recording artist, "Poor Ned Kelly" / "Sweetheart Yodel," Regal Zonophone label, Regal Zonophone G23882, sold 6837 copies. DC. email to AS, October 27, 2016.

39. "Bluey Brink," *Mainly Norfolk: English Folk and Other Good Music* accessed April 5, 2022, at: https://mainlynorfolk.info/lloyd/songs/blueybrink.html.

40. Jimmie Rodgers, recording artist, "My Old Pal", Zonophone label, Zonophone EE150. This song was especially popular in Australia at the time.

41. TM, "Billy Brink the Shearer" / "Little Sweetheart of Days Gone By," Regal Zonophone label, Regal Zonophone G23933; TM, recording artist, "When the Bloom is on the Sage" / "Sleepy Hollow," Regal Zonophone label, Regal Zonophone G23934.

42. The Happy Chappies (assisted by the Ramblers), recording artists, "When the Bloom Is on The Sage," Regal Zonophone label, Regal Zonophone G20974.

43. Carson Robison, recording artist, "Sleepy Hollow," Brunswick (Australia), Brunswick 478 (recorded October 1930); Regal Zonophone / Zonophone label, Regal Zonophone Re/RZ G21146 (recorded December 1930).

44. Advertisement, *RPA Magazine* (November 1, 1939): 6.

45. "Intimate Glimpse of Life Among the Screen Stars," Hobart *Mercury* (January 18, 1940): 14.

46. MM, interview by HC, August 28, 1994.

47. "Neglect of Local Talent: Visiting Showman's Frank Criticism," unidentified newspaper or magazine, n.d. (ca. 1940s).

48. "Tex Morton Had A Guardian Angel," Melbourne *Sporting Globe* (December 27, 1941): 4.

49. Advertisement in *Australian Music Maker and Dance Band News Magazine* (January 1940): 20. The advertisement stated that the tour would commence on January 8, 1940.

50. CM, "I Made Good Without Knowing It," *EM Magazine* (July 26, 1967).

51. Article in *Australian Music Maker and Dance Band News Magazine* (April 1, 1940): 14.

52. Advertisement, Burnie *Advocate* (January 27, 1940).

53. 100 km= about 62 miles.

54. Athol McCoy, interview by HC, September 9, 1989.

55. "Tex Morton at Home," *Australian Music Maker Magazine* (January 1940): 20.

56. Advertisement for William Scott, *Tempo* Magazine (December 1939–January 1940): 26.

57. Dorothy Carroll, interview with JMe, November 20, 1986; JMe to AS, letter, October 20, 1992.

58. "Vaud Stars in the News," *Tempo Magazine* (May-June 1939): 15; "Tex Morton Back in Sydney," *Tempo Magazine* (May-June 1939): 15.

59. Death notice for Bill Scott, *Billboard* (April 8, 1950): 57.

60. SDD, interview by AS, April 30, 1989.

61. Ibid.

62. Arthur Bussey to AS, letter, February 21, 1990.

63. William Scott, quoted in "Neglect of Local talent: Visiting Showman's Frank Criticism," unidentified, newspaper or magazine, n.d. (ca. early 1940s).

64. "Arch Kerr," *History of Country Music in Australia*, accessed April 7, 2022, at: https://countrymusichalloffame.com.au/the-hands-of-fame-inductees/.

65. Announcement of Arch Kerr's death (on-air broadcast), *Hoedown*, 2TM-Tamworth, November 22, 1988.

66. "Popular Leader for Sydney," Brisbane *Telegraph* (June 22, 1938): 22.

67. Jazzer Smith editor, *The Book of Australian Country Music 1* (Gordon: Berghouse Floyd Tuckey Publishing Group, 1984): 85.

68. RWI, *Reminiscing In Tempo: A personal recollection of jazz music and the record business in Australia, 1923–1993* (privately published, 1993): 86. £6 = $12.

69. RWI to AS, letter, May 3, 1989.

70. Arch Kerr, interview by JM, 1978.

71. Ibid.

72. RWI to AS, letter, May 3, 1989.

73. Ibid.

74. "Supreme commander reference" is from "The Rain Tumbles Down in July," YouTube, accessed April 10, 2022, at: https://www.youtube.com/watch?v=ERkZfL8lob8.

75. Slim Dusty and Joy McKean, interview by AS, June 4, 1991.

76. SDD, interview by AS, April 30, 1989.

77. Ibid.

78. Arch Kerr, interview by JM, 1978; Buck Carson, telephone conversation with AS, August 2017.

Chapter 5

1. TM, recording artist, "21st Birthday," Columbia (EMI) label, Columbia DO-4785; TM, recording artist, "The Widow Next Door," RCA label, RCA 102109,

2. TM, recording artist, "Freight Train Yodel" / "Aristocrat," Regal Zonophone label, Regal Zonophone G23995.

3. "The Aristocrat of Buckjumpers," Rockhampton *Morning Bulletin* (June 20, 1939): 13. £10 = $20.

4. Photograph of poster advertising "Skuthorpe's New Sensational Circus and Rodeo," National Library of New Zealand, accessed April 6, 2022, at: http://mp.natlib.govt.nz/detail/?id=8466&l=en. £20 = $40.

5. TM, handwritten note, n.d., PTM Collection, NLA.

6. "Tex Morton's Songs—How He Writes Them On Serviettes," *RPA Magazine* (September 1, 1942): 16.

7. TM, ABC radio program, n.d. ca. 1960s.

8. TM, recording artist, "Beautiful Queensland" / "She Came Rolling Down the Mountain," Regal Zonophone label, Regal Zonophone G24029; TM, recording artist, "If You Please Miss Give Me Heaven" / "Just Plain Folks," Regal Zonophone label, Regal Zonophone G24030; TM, recording artist, "Old Boko and Me" / "The Stockman's Last Bed," Regal Zonophone label, Regal Zonophone G24031.

9. Guthrie T. Meade, Jr, with Dick Spottswood and Douglas S. Meade, *Country Music Sources: A Biblio-Discography of Commercially Recorded Traditional Music* (Chapel Hill: Southern Folklife Collection, 2002): 274; "Charles K. Harris," *Wikipedia*, accessed April 15, 2022, at: https://en.wikipedia.org/wiki/Charles_K._Harris.

10. For example: "Toy telephone" (the Singing Kettles, Hadley HS-10); "Royal telephone" (Jimmy Little, Festival 453; Burl Ives, Australian Festival label, Festival FL-30, 152; "No Telephone in Heaven," The Carter Family, Zo/RZ EE240. The McFarland and Gardner disc was issued as "Hello, Central! Give Me Heaven, Brunswick (Australia), Brunswick 479. The McCravy Brothers also recorded "Hello Central, Give Me Heaven" (OKeh label OK 45135) but this wasn't released on an Australian label.

11. Bradley Kincaid, recording artist, "Just Plain Folks", Regal Zonophone label, Regal Zonophone G22554.

12. Philip Hayward, "Folk from Country: the Localisation of Hillbilly and Country Music on Lord Howe Island," in Philip Hayward and Geoff Walden, *Roots and Crossovers: Australian Country Music, Volume 2* (Gympie: aicmPress, 2002): 69.

13. Valerie Kent, "Lavater, Louise Isidore (1867–1953)," in *Australian Dictionary of Biography, Vol. 10*, accessed April 6, 2022, at: http://adb.anu.edu.au/biography/lavater-louis-isidore-7107.

14. "The Stockman's Last Bed," *The Institute of Australian Culture*, accessed April 6, 2022, at: http://www.australianculture.org/the-stockmans-last-bed-1905/; The Stockman's Last Bed," *An Australian Folk Song a Day*, accessed April 6, 2022, at: http://ozfolksongaday.blogspot.com.au/2011/02/stockmans-last-bed.html; "Maria and Bessie Gray and *The Stockman's last bed*," *Australharmony*, The University of Sydney, accessed April 6, 2022, at: http://sydney.edu.au/paradisec/australharmony/gray-maria-and-bessie-and-the-stockmans-last-bed.php.

15. TM, recording artist, "Old Boko and Me," Regal Zonophone label, Regal Zonophone G24031.

16. TM, recording artist, "Old Rover" / "You'll Never Be Missed," Regal Zonophone label, Regal Zonophone G24172. It's interesting that Morton recorded only two songs at this session. Had he run out of material or were there arguments with Kerr?

17. PB email to AS, October 31, 1992. "Dorrie Crescent," in Canberra, was probably named after her.

18. EW stated that Dorrie's family were "entertainers who toured extensively in Northern NSW and southern Queensland," but Dorothy made no mention of this in either of two interviews she gave that were accessed by AS. EW, *CMA, 1* (Sydney: Angus and Robertson Publishers, 1982): 19.

19. Dorothy Carroll, interview by JMe, November 20, 1986.

20. Dorothy Carroll, interview by JM, 1985.

21. Ibid.

22. MM, interview by HC, August 28, 1994.

23. Dorothy Carroll, interview by JMe, November 20, 1986.

24. Ibid.

25. Dorothy Carroll, interview by JM, 1985.

26. Dorothy Carroll, interview by JMe, November 20, 1986.

27. TM and Sister Dorrie, recording artists, "(Honey, I've Got) Everything but You", Regal Zonophone label, Regal Zonophone G24314.

28. Dorothy Carroll, interview by JMe, November 20, 1986. Dorothy recorded "(Honey, I've Got) Everything but You" with Morton on March 13, 1941. Morton was on tour in Forbes on March 31, 1941, suggesting that Dorothy didn't join Morton's show "the next day," as she said, but about two weeks later.
29. Dorothy Carroll, interview with JM, 1985.
30. TM, interview by JM, broadcast on 2TM-Tamworth, ca. 1970.
31. Dorothy Carroll, interview by JMe, November 20, 1986.
32. Ibid.
33. Ibid.
34. KM, telephone conversation with AS, June 7, 2017.
35. Dorothy Carroll, interview by JM, 1985.
36. KL to PB, letter, ca. late 1990s or early 2000s.
37. Dorothy Carroll, interview by JM, 1985.
38. R. Harris to AS, letter, January 8, 1996.
39. CM and other journalists, interviews by AS, July 17, 1990.
40. Roger Carroll, cited in PB email to AS, October 31, 1992.
41. Patrick Tennison, "Morton Rides Again," *The Bulletin Magazine* (October 2, 1965).
42. Their reunion is described in Chapter 19 of this book.
43. CM and other journalists, interview by AS, July 17, 1990.

Chapter 6

1. TM, recording artist, "In the Luggage Van Ahead" / "The Drover's Wife," Regal Zonophone label, Regal Zonophone G24263; TM, recording artist, "Come Back to the Valley" / "(Honey, I've Got) Everything but You," Regal Zonophone label, Regal Zonophone G24314.
2. TM, ABC radio program, 1960s; Information on Bluett is at: Martha Rutledge, "Bluett, Frederick George (Fred) (1876–1942), in *Australian Dictionary of Biography, Supplemental, Volume 2005*, accessed April 6, 2022, at: http://adb.anu.edu.au/biography/bluett-frederick-george-fred-12806.)
3. Norm Cohen, *Long Steel Rail: The Railroad In American Folksong* (Urbana: University of Illinois Press, 1981): 304–15.
4. Vince Courtney, recording artist, "In the Luggage Van Ahead," Regal label, Regal G20235.
5. DC, email to AS, July 21, 2016. Crisp stated that Dalhart's recording was issued on Lincoln 2374 in the USA, and copies of the Lincoln disc were imported into Australia. Lincoln records sold well in Australia prior to 1927. Dalhart's version was titled "In the Baggage Coach Ahead," whereas Courtney's version referred to a "luggage van." Morton's version is strikingly similar to Courtney's recording.
6. Dorothy Carroll, interview by JM, 1985.
7. TM, recording artist, "Come Back to the Valley", Regal Zonophone label, Regal Zonophone RZ 24314; Frankie Marvin, recording artist, "Come Back to the Hills," Regal Zonophone label, Regal Zonophone G22218 and Panachord label, Panachord 12139.

8. John Edwards, discography, *The Yodelling Boundary Rider, Tex Morton: A Discography*, Southern Folklife Collection, Wilson Library, University of North Carolina, Chapel Hill, NC. Provided courtesy of the John Edwards Foundation.

9. TM, recording artist, "Mandrake" / " Don't Say Goodbye," Regal Zonophone label, Regal Zonophone G24345; TM, recording artist, "Old Shep" / "Through the Sin of a Son," Regal Zonophone label, Regal Zonophone G24376; TM, recording artist, "When the Cactus is in Bloom" / "Rover No More," Regal Zonophone label, Regal Zonophone G24394; Dick Carr to AS, letter, August 22, 1988.

10. TM, interview by GG, 1969.

11. Dorothy Carroll, interview by JMe, November 20, 1986.

12. RWI to AS, letter, May 3, 1989.

13. TM, interview by Bill Burraston, ca. 1970, provided by DC.

14. TM, interview by GG, 1969.

15. TM & Sister Dorrie, "Old Shep"/ "Through the Sin of a Son," Regal Zonophone label, Regal Zonophone G24376.

16. David Hardy, email to AS, January 22, 2022.

17. The Hill Billies, recording artists, "Old Shep"/ "Red River Valley, Regal Zonophone label, Regal Zonophone G22494.

18. Vince Courtney, recording artist, "Through the Sin of a Son," Regal Zonophone label, Regal Zonophone G20216; Vince Courtney, "Through the Sin of a Son," image of sheet music, accessed April 10, 2022, at: http://nla.gov.au/nla.obj-168347544/view#page/n4/mode/1up).

19. Jimmie Rodgers, recording artist, "When the Cactus is in Bloom," Zonophone/Regal Zonophone label EE345.

20. "Tex Morton's Songs—How He Writes Them On Serviettes," *RPA Magazine* (September 1, 1942): 16. A serviette is a napkin.

21. "The Wild Rover", *Wikipedia*, accessed April 14, 2022, at: https://en.wikipedia.org/wiki/The_Wild_Rover; TM, ABC radio program, 1960s.

22. Dorothy Carroll, interview by JMe, November 20, 1986.

23. "John William (Jack) Carey b. 4th November 1912, Tamworth NSW, d. 13th May 1990," *eHive* (from the Australian Stockman's Hall of Fame and Outback Heritage Centre), accessed April 10, 2022, at: https://ehive.com/collections/3492/objects/77667.

24. Kathryn M. Hunter, "Rough riding: Aboriginal participation in rodeos and traveling shows to the 1950s," accessed April 10, 2022, at: http://press-files.anu.edu.au/downloads/press/p74381/pdf/ch0553.pdf.

25. TM, ABC radio program, 1960s, DC private collection. 30 shillings = $3.

26. CM and other journalists, interview by AS, July 17, 1990.

27. TM, interview by JM, broadcast on radio station 2TM-Tamworth, ca. 1970.

28. Ian Hands, *Ambassadors Of Country Music* (Archerfield: privately published by Ian Hands, 1984): 2.

29. Ibid.

30. Ibid.

31. CM and other journalists, interview by AS, July 17, 1990.

32. PB email to AS, July 2016.

33. Gordon Spittle, *TMS* (Auckland, GWS Publications, 2008), 38; TM, interview by JM, broadcast on 2TM-Tamworth, ca. 1970.

34. "Rodeo Horses Killed in Road Smash," *Gloucester Advocate* (May 10, 1949): 2; TM, interview by JM, ca. 1970s.

35. "Five Injured in Trailer Smash," *Newcastle Morning Herald and Miner's Advocate* (July 3, 1945): 2; "Rodeo Van Crashes: Five Injured at Jessmond," *Newcastle Sun* (July 27, 1945): 3; 6 meters = 20 feet.

36. Gladys Ward to AS, letter, January 16, 1996.

37. "Busker Tex Morton Now A Favourite Artist And A Proud Family Man," Murray Bridge *Standard* (July 21, 1942): 30.

38. "Tex Morton's Twins," *RPA Magazine*, n.d. The date of this article was probably ca. late 1941, since the article stated the twins were two months old; 3000 miles = 4 800 km.

39. "Tex Morton's Twins," *RPA Magazine*, n.d.

40. "Busker Tex Morton Now A Favourite Artist And A Proud Family Man," Murray Bridge *Standard* (July 21, 1942): 30; Busker Tex Morton Now a Favourite Artist and a Proud Family Man," *Grenfell Record and Lachlan District Advertiser* (July 16, 1942): 4; "The Tex Morton Twins," Broken Hill *Barrier Daily Truth* (July 30, 1942): 3. 30miles an hour = 48 km per hour.

41. Ros Highfield to AS, letter, January 7, 1996.

42. "Maintenance Claim", Mackay *Daily Mercury* (September 18, 1946), 4; MM, interview by HC, August 28, 1994.

43. Joan Martin Hundley to AS, letter, May 29, 1991.

44. "Showman Says Wife Lived with Yodeller," Sydney *Truth* (July 16, 1950): 10.

45. "Bruce Carroll's Wife Seeks Maintenance Order But Denies Romance with Hill-Billy Tex Morton" Perth *Mirror* (July 15, 1950): 1.

46. SDD, interview by AS, April 30, 1989.

47. CM and other journalists, interviews by AS, July 17, 1990.

48. BL, interview with RW, NLA, ORAL TRC 6124/25, October 12, 2010. BL could not recall the years in which Marjorie and the twins lived in Nelson, but it was most likely in 1947 and 1948.

49. "New Show," *Adelaide Advertiser* (August 25, 1942): 5.

50. RM (*Facebook* message to AS, August 9, 2019) stated that MM changed her and the twins' names from "Lane" to "Morton". "It caused a bit of confusion when I was in the Army and had to show my birth certificate."

51. Legal form, January 25, 1950, PTM Collection, NLA.

52. RM *Facebook* message to AS, August 9, 2019.

53. KM, telephone conversation with AS, June 4, 2019; KM, telephone conversation with AS, January 24, 2022.

54. BL telephone conversation with AS, January 24, 2022.

55. TM, recording artist, "The Flowers Never Bloom in Lonesome Valley" / "The Story of

Parson Joe," Regal Zonophone label G24731; TM, recording artist, "The Good Old Droving Days" / "Neath the Silver Willow Tree," Regal Zonophone label, G24732.

56. EW, *CMA, 1* (Sydney: Angus and Robertson Publishers, 1982): 19.

57. TM, recording artist, *The Tex Morton Regal Zonophone Collection*, 5 long-play vinyl records, EMI label, EMI EMBB 430051. The set was reissued on compact disc in 1993 on two double compact disc sets: TM, recording artist, *The Tex Morton Regal Zonophone Collection, Volume 1 (1936–1938)*, EMI label, EMI 8142022; TM, recording artist, *The Tex Morton Regal Zonophone Collection, Volume 2 (1938–1943)*, EMI label, EMI 8142052.

58. RWI to AS, letter, May 3, 1989.

59. Ibid.

60. EW to AS, letter, March 18, 1990.

61. TM, quoted in GG 1969. "The Tex Morton Story Part Two," *CWS*, 66 (1970): 42.

62. "Arch Kerr Talks Of Early Recordings," *Australasian Country Music Annual 1981* (Sydney: Maxwell Printing, 1981): 18.

63. SDD, interview by AS, April 30, 1989.

64. Ibid. Kerr insisted that hillbilly performers audition, for him, their songs for the next recording session. Both Buddy Williams and Slim Dusty, Ron Wills said, found this irksome. TM, it seems, refused to audition songs for Kerr.

65. SDD, interview by AS, April 30, 1989.

66. TM, interview by GG, 1969.

67. Bernie Burnett to AS, letter, March 12, 1994.

68. Arch Kerr, quoted from interview, ca. 1981, on *Country Closeup*, television series, Australia; AS, "Cowboys and Hillbillies from Down Under: The First Wave of Australian Country Music," *Journal of Country Music* 13, no.2 (1991): 21.

69. GG, "The Tex Morton Story Part Two," *CWS*, 66 (1970): 41.

70. RWI, *Reminiscing In Tempo: A personal recollection of jazz music and the record business in Australia, 1923–1993* (privately published 1993): 146; PB to AS, letter, September 22, 2017.

71. "The Life and Times of Buddy Williams," *Capital News* (January 1987): 2-3; JM, to AS, letter, October 14, 1990.

72. Karen Williams, telephone conversation with AS, September 12, 2017.

73. Bernie Burnett to AS, letter, March 12, 1994.

74. HC, telephone conversation with AS, ca. 2016.

75. TM, jacket notes; *Tex Morton Encores*, long-play album, EMI label, EMI AXIS 6327. "Tex Morton's Protest Song" was also released as a single-play 45, EMI label, Columbia (EMI) DO-4762.

Chapter 7

1. EW, *CMA, 1* (Sydney: Angus and Robertson Publishers, 1982): 29.

2. Trevor Day, telephone conversation with AS, May 6, 2019.

3. TM, interview by GG, 1969 .
4. These figures include "Sergeant Small".
5. DC to AS, letter, May 14, 1989.
6. DC, email to AS, January 31, 2019.
7. PB, email to AS, April 29, 2019.
8. GG, "The Tex Morton Story Part Two," *CWS*, 66, 1970: 42.
9. Goebel Reeves's recordings that were released in Australia comprise the following five discs—a surprisingly small number considering the influence he had on TM: The Texas Drifter "The Cowboy's Prayer" / "The Drifter's Buddy," Decca X 1226; The Texas Drifter (Goebel Reeves), "At The End of the Hobo's Trail" / "The Oklahoma Kid," Panachord label 12047; The Texas Drifter (Goebel Reeves), "The Tramp's Mother" / "Railroad Boomer," Panachord label, 12242; The Texas Drifter, "The Hobo and the Cop" / "The Cowboy's Lullaby," Regal Zonophone label, Regal Zonophone G22336; Goebel Reeves, The Texas Drifter, "The Cowboy's Prayer" / "Hobo's Lullaby," Regal Zonophone label, Regal Zonophone G22363. TM recorded "At the End of the Hobo's Trail," "The Tramp's Mother" (as "You're Going to Leave the Old Home, Jim," and "Railroad Boomer" (as "The Railroad Bum").
10. GG, "The Tex Morton Story Part One," *CWS*, 65 (November 1969): 11.
11. Colin Escott, *The Story of Country Music* (London: BBC Worldwide, Ltd, 2003): 33.
12. "Arch Kerr Talks Of Early Recordings," *Australasian Country Music Annual 1981* (Sydney: Maxwell Printing, 1981): 20.
13. Ibid.
14. Veronica Mratinich, 1978. *The Songs Of Goebel Reeves—Collection and Analysis* (unpublished term paper), cited from Fred Hoeptner, 1994, booklet accompanying *Goebel Reeves Hobo's Lullaby*, Bear Family compact disc, Bear Family label BCD 15 680 AH.
15. Tony Russell, "Bush & Range: Australian Old-Time," *Old Time Music Magazine*, 29 (Summer 1978): 23.
16. SDD, interview by AS, April 30, 1989.
17. AS, 1990. "Cowboys and Hillbillies Down Under: The First Wave of Australian Country Music." *Journal of Country Music* 13, no. 2 (1990): 22; Buddy Williams, interview on *Country Closeup* television program ca. 1981.
18. Dusty Rankin interview by RW and John Harple, NLA Oral TRC 3388/109, July 22, 1997.
19. Classifications were based solely on the judgment of the author, so others may disagree with some results.
20. The likeability index (L) is calculated as follows: $L = \log_e(A/N)$ where A = average sales (per disc) for songs comprising the attribute; N = average sales (per disc) for songs not comprising the attribute. Euler's Number, e, is the base of the natural logarithms and is approximately equal to 2.7. If A = N (ie there is no decided preference for songs with the attribute present compared with those without it, and average sales for both are equal) then A/N = 1, and $\log_e(1) = 0$. If L > 0 it suggests that songs with the attribute were preferred by buyers over those without it and, conversely, if L < 0 it suggests that songs with the at-

tribute were not especially popular with buyers. Since the scale is logarithmic, it is truncated at the extremes. Generally, where the percentage of all sales exceeds the percentage of titles, L > zero (i.e., 0). L should be treated with caution, however, as it assumes that record buyers equally preferred both sides of a disc. The notation $\log_e(x)$ is generally written as $\ln(x)$.

21. There is no reasonable method to determine what side of a disc the public bought a record for. Generally, however, Columbia featured two sentimental, or two comedy, numbers on the one disc, and much of Morton's recordings were essentially "average" in quality, suggesting there was no overall preference for one side or the other for many of Morton's records.

22. TM, interview by by GG, 1969.

23. Ibid.

24. GG, "The Tex Morton Story Part Two," *CWS*, 66, 1970: 41.

25. John Berry, "No Hill-Billy Tag For Tex," *Sunday News* (May 19, 1968).

26. Since the "Other" category is not included in these analyses, the percentages for "All Australian" and "All Foreign" do not sum to 100. If the category "Other" is considered, however, the percentages add to 100, allowing for rounding errors.

27. "Population Of Australia," *The Canberra Times* (July 26, 1940): 2.

28. DC, email to AS, December 20, 2016.

29. GG, "The Tex Morton Story Part One," *CWS* 65 (November 1969): 9.

30. TM, interview by GG, 1969.

31. Barry Mazor, *Meeting Jimmie Rodgers* (New York: Oxford University Press, 2009): 99–100.

32. "TM, recording artist, "Treasures Untold," on *I Am Sad and Weary: Jimmie Rodgers Revisited*, BCD16673 AR (Bear Family, 2003), and "Dreaming With Tears in My Eyes," on *Let Me Be Your Sidetrack: The Influence of Jimmie Rodgers*, BCD16863 FH (Bear Family, 2008). Both songs were previously recorded by Jimmie Rodgers.

33. GG, "The Tex Morton Story Part One," *CWS*, 65 (November 1969): 9.

34. Mike Paris and Chris Comber, *Jimmie the Kid: The Life of Jimmie Rodgers* (London: Eddison Press, 1977): 148. The Greenway paper referred to is "Folksong Discography," *Western Folklore* XXI: 1, January 1960: 71.

35. Barry Mazor, *Meeting Jimmie Rodgers* (New York: Oxford University Press, 2009): 99.

36. Tony Russell, *Country Music Originals: The Legends And The Lost* (New York: Oxford University Press, 2010): 69.

37. Analysis provided by Dr Damien Kingston, University of Tasmania, March 2017; revised April 2017.

38. EW, "Eric Watson Reports From NSW," *CWS*, 28, October/November/ December 1959.

39. Clinton Walker, *Buried Country: The Story of Aboriginal Country Music*, revised edition (Portland OR: Verse Chorus Press, 2014): 58–59.

40. Clinton Walker, *Buried Country: The Story of Aboriginal Country Music*, revised edition (Portland OR: Verse Chorus Press, 2014): 169.

41. Clinton Walker, *Buried Country: The Story of Aboriginal Country Music*, revised edition. Portland OR: Verse Chorus Press, 2014): 111.

42. Clinton Walker, *Buried Country: The Story of Aboriginal Country Music*, revised edition (Portland OR: Verse Chorus Press, 2014): 273.

43. TM, interview by Nigel Lovell, ABC, 1972.

44. Graham Seal, "Tex Morton Sings an Australian Song," *Verandah Music*, accessed April 10, 2022, at: http://verandahmusic.blogspot.com.au/p/articles.html.

45. Ibid.

46. "Arch Kerr Talks Of Early Recordings," *Australasian Country Music Annual 1981* (Sydney: Maxwell Printing, 1981): 20.

47. Tony Russell, "Bush & Range: Australian Old-Time." *Old Time Music* 29 (Summer 1978): 23.

48. Graeme Smith, "The Gendered Voice of Australian Country Music," *Context* 35/36, 2011: 30.

Chapter 8

1. Kevin Coffey, *Facebook* message to AS, February 27, 2017.

2. Jenny Hicks, *Australian Cowboys Roughriders & Rodeos* (Sydney: Angus & Robertson, 2000): 57–88.

3. "Tex Morton Had A Guardian Angel," Melbourne *Sporting Globe* (December 27, 1941): 4.

4. "Tex Morton at the Show," Grafton *Daily Examiner* (April 9, 1940): 2.

5. "Advertising," Ipswich *Queensland Times* (May 18, 1940): 10; "Tex Morton's Wild West Rodeo," Ipswich *Queensland Times* (May 18, 1940): 9.

6. William F. Scott, letter to Prime Minister John Curtin, November 5, 1941. M1415/l, 26, National Archives Of Australia (NAA), Canberra, cited in Toby Martin, *Yodelling Boundary Riders: Country Music in Australia since the 1920s* (Melbourne: Lyrebird Press, The University of Melbourne, 2015): 126–27.

7. "Tex Morton's Wild West Show," Leeton *Murrumbidgee Irrigator* (March 25, 1941): 3.

8. "Street Singer to Radio Star," *RPA Magazine* (May 1, 1938): 12.

9. "Intimate Glimpse of Life Among the Screen Stars," Hobart *Mercury* (January 18, 1940): 14.

10. "Tex Morton Hobo," Cairns *Post* (July 23, 1940): 3.

11. Ibid.

12. Jenny Hicks, *Australian Cowboys Roughriders & Rodeos* (Sydney: Angus & Robertson, 2000): 34.

13. Jenny Hicks, *Australian Cowboys Roughriders & Rodeos* Sydney: Angus & Robertson, 2000): 5. Six feet = 2 meters; 300 feet = 100 meters.

14. Morton stated that Skuthorpe rode "Wallace" for the feat. TM, ABC radio program, 1960s, DC private collection.

15. Lance Skuthorp, "The Champion Bullock Driver," *The Bulletin* 42, no. 2164 (August 4, 1921).

16. Violet Skuthorpe, interview by Peter MacGregor, ABC radio, 1958. Copy provided by the ABC, courtesy Colin Munro.

17. Jenny Hicks, *Australian Cowboys Roughriders & Rodeos* (Sydney: Angus & Robertson,

2000): 69.

18. Jack Pollard, *The Horse Tamer: The Story of Lance Skuthorpe* (Wollostencroft, NSW: Pollard Publishing Co, 1970): 127.

19. Jack Pollard, *The Horse Tamer: The Story of Lance Skuthorpe* (Wollostencroft, NSW: Pollard Publishing Co, 1970): 132.

20. Ibid.

21. Jenny Hicks, *Australian Cowboys Roughriders & Rodeos*.(Sydney: Angus & Robertson, 2000): 80; "Champion Bareback Rider Violet Skuthorpe Will Join Cowboy Team," *Daily Telegraph Home Magazine* (February 28, 1938): 3.

22. Clarrie Neal, "Lance Skuthorp and the Skuthorp Family," *Riverstone Historical Society*, accessed April 22, 2022, at: https://www.riverstonehistoricalsociety.org.au/blog/?page_id =1429. The original spelling of the family name was "Skuthorp" but Lance Jr changed it to "Skuthorpe."

23. Jack Pollard, *The Horse Tamer: The Story of Lance Skuthorpe* (Wollostencroft, NSW: Pollard Publishing Co, 1970): 147.

24. "Tim McCoy," *The Old Corral*, Curator Chuck Anderson, et.al., 1. Accessed April 20, 2022, at https://www.b-westerns.com/mccoy.htm.

25. Copy of "The Giant of Brady's Gap," n.d., PTM Collection, NLA.

26. CM and other journalists interviews by AS, July 17, 1990.

27. Smoky Dawson, *Smoky Dawson, A Life* (Sydney: George Allen & Unwin, 1985): 125.

28. Jenny Hicks, *Australian Cowboys Roughriders & Rodeos* (Sydney: Angus & Robertson, 2000): 82.

29. Statements about Kitty Gill and the Gill brothers cited from "Tex Morton's Wild West Rodeo," *Johnstone River Advocate and Innisfail News* (July 23, 1940): 4.

30. "Rodeo and Circus: Stan Gill's Entertaining Show," The *Braidwood Dispatch and Mining Journal*, December 10, 1948: 1; 50 feet = 15 meters.

31. Jenny Hicks, *Australian Cowboys Roughriders & Rodeos* (Sydney: Angus & Robertson, 2000): 80

32. Jenny Hicks, *Australian Cowboys Roughriders & Rodeos* (Sydney: Angus & Robertson, 2000): 59.

33. Hessian (known as burlap in the United States) is a coarse, woven fabric made from the skin of the jute plant or sisal fibres; see "Hessian fabric," *Wikipedia*, accessed April 20, 2022, at: https://en.wikipedia.org/wiki/Hessian_fabric.

34. Don Webb to AS, letter, February 14, 1996.

35. Slim Dusty and Joy McKean, interview by AS, June 4, 1991.

36. Slim Dusty, "Recollections of Tex Morton." Cassette tape made by Slim Dusty for AS and sent to AS by Joy McKean, 1991.

37. TM, recording artist, "The Travelling Showman," on the album *Tex Morton Today*, EMI label SCXO-7933, 1970, subsequently reissued as the long-play vinyl album, TM, recording artist, *The Travelling Showman*, EMI label AXIS 6415.

38. CM and other journalists, interviews by AS, July 17, 1990.

39. Dick Carr to AS, letter, August 22, 1988.

40. Morton apparently didn't show on Sunday nights.

41. Vince Walker, telephone conversation with AS, January 7, 1996.
42. "Some Snaps Of Tex's Wild West Show," TM songbook, *Tex Morton's Wild West & Rodeo Song Album No. 5 (Sydney:* Nicholson's Pty Ltd, 1940).
43. "Tex Morton's Wild West Show," *Townsville Daily Bulletin,* July 18, 1940: 9; 20 feet = 6 meters.
44. Gordon Spittle, *TMS* (Auckland: GWS Publications, 2000): 104.
45. KL to PB, letter, ca. late 1990s or early 2000s.
46. David Mitchell, "Tex Morton—much more than a country singer," *Nelson Evening Mail* (August 1983).
47. 15 feet = 4.6 meters; 40 feet = 12 meters.
48. "Tex Morton's Wild West Show," *Townsville Daily Bulletin* (July 18, 1940): 9.
49. "Publisher's Note," TM songbook *Tex Morton's Wild West & Rodeo Song Album No. 5,* (Sydney: Nicholson's Pty Ltd. 1940).
50. "Tex Morton's Rodeo Is Swell!," *Music Maker Magazine* (November 30, 1940): 3.
51. "Varied Entertainment At Tex Morton's Wild West Circus," Rockhampton *Morning Bulletin* (June 7, 1941): 8.
52. "Tex Morton's Rodeo May Be Forced Off Road! No Petrol!," *Music Maker Magazine* (November 20, 1941): 3.
53. "Wild West Show Tex Morton Entertains," *Cairns Post* (June 28, 1941): 3.
54. "Country News," Lithgow *Mercury* (February 3, 1941): 3. £6000 = $12 000; 40 feet = 12 meters.
55. Joe Ellul to AS, letter, February 2, 1996; Joe Ellul, interview by AS, February 1996.
56. D. Webb to AS, letter, February 13, 1996.
57. Delores and John Balaam, interview by Mike O'Malley, September 1991.
58. Ibid.; W. Ball, telephone conversation with AS, February 3, 1996; D. Thorp to AS, letter, January 9, 1996.
59. Brief note about TM, *Tempo Magazine* (November-December 1940): 6.
60. Leon Becker, transcription of cassette tape sent to PB, January 7, 1996.
61. Neville Pellitt, *A Country Voice 55+ Years on Air* (Golden Square: Moonlight Publishing, 2002): 11.
62. £1 = $2.
63. "Adjourned: Rodeo Star Fined For Non-Attendance As Witness," *Werribee Shire Banner,* March 26, 1942: 2. £1= $2.
64. "Tex Morton In Suburbs," Melbourne *Sporting Globe* (February 14, 1942): 3.
65. "Tex Morton's Rodeo," *Rockhampton Morning Bulletin* (January 17, 1944): 4; "Tex Morton's Rodeo," *Rockhampton Morning Bulletin,* January 18, 1944): 5.
66. Rosemary Van den Berg, *Clogs and Bare Feet* Google e-book, Dorrance publishing, 2010: 112–13.
67. "Camp Rockhampton," *Queensland WWII Historic Places,* Queensland Government, accessed April 8, 2022, at: http://www.ww2places.qld.gov.au/places/?id=1314.
68. CM and other journalists, interviews by AS, July 17, 1990.

69. "Advertising," Brisbane *Courier Mail*, October 23, 1943: 6.
70. "Battle of Brisbane," *Wikipedia*, accessed April 10, 2022, at: https://en.wikipedia.org/wiki/Battle_of_Brisbane.
71. CM, "I Had Two Trains To Call My Own," *EM Magazine* (August 1967): 28.
72. Gordon Spittle, *TMS* (Auckland: GWS Publications, 2008), 44; CM, "I Had Two Trains To Call My Own," *EM Magazine* (August 1967): 28. £1000 = $2000.
73. "Advertising," *Nambour Chronicle and North Coast Advertiser* (February 25, 1944): 2.
74. Three or four shillings = 30 or 40 cents; one shilling and sixpence = 15c.
75. Guide to costs and wages, *State Library of Victoria*, accessed April 8, 2022, at: http://guides.slv.vic.gov.au/whatitcost/earnings.
76. Calculations from *Thom Blake Historian*, accessed April 8, 2022, at: http://www.thomblake.com.au/secondary/hisdata/calculate.php.
77. "Rodeo Show Coming to Werribee," *Werribee Shire Banner* (November 1, 1945): 2; "Wild West Rodeo," *Camperdown Chronicle* (November 9, 1945): 2.
78. "Topics of the Day," *Newcastle Morning Herald and Miner's Advocate* (March 29, 1946): 2.
79. "Tex Morton Rodeo," *Murrumburrah Signal and County of Hardin Advocate* (March 28, 1946): 4. 90 feet is approximately 30 meters; 150 feet is approximately 50 meters—the length of an Olympic swimming pool. £1000 = $2000.
80. "Tex Morton's Rodeo," Deniliquin *Independent* (October 17, 1946): 3.
81. "Tex Morton receives warm welcome at Gawler," Gawler *Bunyip* (January 4, 1946): 4. The admission cost was nearly 50 cents.
82. Jenny Hicks, *Australian Cowboys Roughriders & Rodeos* (Sydney: Angus & Robertson, 2000): 76.
83. Doug and Phyllis Ashton, interviews by AS, February 10, 1994.
84. "George Melrose Comes To Town," *Cessnock Eagle and South Maitland Recorder* (March 6, 1945): 1; "Advertising," Glen Innes *Examiner* (April 21, 1945): 3; "Advertising," Lismore *Morning Star* (November 27, 1944): 3; "Advertising," Townsville *Daily Bulletin* (June 6, 1944): 4.
85. "Coming to Clare," Clare *Northern Argus* (August 21, 1947): 5.
86. "Pipers Piped the Wrong Man," *Whyalla News* (August 1, 1947): 4; "Tex Morton's Circus," Clare *Northern Argus* (August 21, 1947): 5; "Tex Morton Circus," *Kalgoorlie Miner* (July 1, 1947): 1.
87. "Tex Morton Circus," *The Kalgoorlie Miner* (April 5, 1947): 1. 1000 kilometers = 620 miles.
88. Ibid.
89. "Circus Travels by Road From W.A.," *Adelaide Advertiser* (August 27, 1947): 8 ; Pipers Piped the Wrong Man," *Whyalla News* (August 1, 1947): 4.
90. 200 miles = 322 kilometers.
91. KL to PB, letter, ca. late 1990s or early 2000s.
92. "Freaks, Fun, Fantasy of Sideshow Alley," Brisbane *Courier Mail* (August 11, 1947): 4.
93. "Advertising," Brisbane *Courier Mail* (August 9, 1947): 8.

94. "Advertising," Brisbane *Courier Mail* (August 7, 1947): 8.
95. "Advertising," Brisbane *Courier Mail* (August 13, 1947): 8.
96. "Advertising," Brisbane *Telegraph* (August 15, 1947): 14.
97. "Tex Morton Circus," Burnie *Advocate* (March 4, 1948): 6.
98. Article about TM, *RPA Magazine* (July 1948): 32.
99. "Australia Outlook Greatest—Morton Wild West Show," *Billboard Magazine* (June 17, 1950): 63.
100. "Tex Morton's Fine Show," *Gundagai Independent* (February 13, 1941): 4; advertising, *Queensland Times* (March 10, 1944): 5; "Tex Morton's Rodeo," *Gloucester Advocate* (February 23, 1945): 2.
101. Liner notes to TM, *Tex Morton: The Regal Zonophone Collection, Vol. 1*, compact disc collection, EMI label, EMI CD 8142022.
102. Reg Lindsay, interview by AS, July 6, 1990.
103. Slim Dusty and Joy McKean, *Another Day, Another Town* (Sydney: Pan Macmillan, Australia, 1996): 122–23.
104. SDD, interview by AS, April 30, 1989.
105. Frank Daniel to AS, letter, January 7, 1996.
106. "Stan Gill's Rodeo and Circus," Clare (SA) *Northern Argus* (October 10, 1946): 9 (this article reports "letting the buckjumpers into the ring out of a stall"); F. Daniel to AS, letter, January 7, 1996.
107. Ian Hands, *Ambassadors of Country Music* (Archerfield: privately published by Ian Hands): 2.
108. O. Gentry, *The Jackaroo* (Wellington: Wakefields Digital [e-book], 2002): 160.
109. Jim Bennett to AS, letter, January 15, 1996.
110. Reg Harris to AS, letter, January 8, 1996.
111. "Seating Collapses at Rodeo," Mount Gambier *Border Watch* (November 22, 1945): 3.
112. Stuart Wallace, telephone conversation with AS, January 7, 1996.
113. G. Ward to AS, letter, January 16, 1996.
114. "Singing Cowboy," *New Zealand Listener* (October 21, 1949), PTM Collection, NLA.
115. Gordon Spittle, *TMS* (Auckland: GWS Publications. 2008): 54. At the time, Morton was possibly wearing Australian Akubra (not Stetson) hats.
116. Slim Dusty, "Recollections of Tex Morton." Cassette tape made by Slim Dusty for AS and sent to AS by Joy McKean, 1991.
117. Smoky Dawson, *Smoky Dawson, A Life* (Sydney: George Allen & Unwin, 1985): 127.
118. Smoky Dawson, interview by Robin Hughes for The *Australian Dictionary Of Biography*, 1994, accessed December 2016, at: http://www.australianbiography.gov.au/subjects/dawson/interview10.html. This link is no longer active but Dawson's life is described in "Australian Biography: Smoky Dawson," *NFSA*, accessed April 10, 2022, at: https://www.nfsa.gov.au/collection/curated/australian-biography-smoky-dawson.
119. Slim Dusty and Joy McKean, interview by AS, June 4, 1991.
120. Jenny Hicks, *Australian Cowboys Roughriders & Rodeos* (Sydney: Angus & Robertson, 2000): 89.

121. Untitled newspaper article, *Tumut and Adelong Times* (March 26, 1946): 2.
122. Neville Pellitt to HC, letter, September 9, 1990. Several (but not all) newspapers reported the man's name as "Bell," (for example the *Charleville Times*, February 28, 1947, and the *Queensland Times*, January 27, 1947) but Pellitt said it was "Dell."
123. "Brawl At Rodeo," *Cairns Post* (January 27, 1947): 1.
124. "Legend of show biz began long career as street busker," historical feature about TM, Sydney *Daily Mirror* (September 28, 1983): 56.
125. Neville Pellitt to HC, letter September 9, 1990.
126. Dell's comments cited from Neville Pellitt to HC, letter, September 9, 1990.
127. "Crowds Demonstrate At Wonthaggi Presentation," *Naracoorte Herald* (January 30, 1947): 3; £12 = $24.
128. Neville Pellitt to HC, letter September 9, 1990.
129. Cec O'Leary, interview by Mike O'Malley, September 1991.
130. Peter Colman to AS, letter, September 5, 1990.
131. Tex Croft, interview by HC, August 28, 1994.
132. Jenny Hicks, *Australian Cowboys Roughriders & Rodeos* (Sydney: Angus & Robertson, 2000): 81.
133. Doug and Phyllis Ashton, interviews by AS, February 10, 1994.
134. Slim Dusty and Joy McKean, interview by AS, June 4, 1991.
135. "The Orchante Saga #83", *New Zealand's MagicNZ*, accessed April 6, 2022, at: http://www.magicnewzealand.com/ezine-archive/2001-Jan-to-Dec-2001/077-Jun10–2001.txt.
136. Ray Cotton to AS, letter, January 28, 1996.
137. Noel Edlington, telephone conversation with AS, January 1996.
138. Reg Harris to AS, letter, January 8, 1996.
139. "Tex Morton lives in Jimmy's Songs," *Geraldton Guardian* (September 8, 1995): 6.
140. Mike Burraston, cited from PB to AS, letter, June 13, 2017.
141. Dorothy Carroll, interview by JM, 1985.
142. "Advertising," Perth *Mirror* (April 19, 1947): 14.
143. Jim Muldoon, telephone conversation with AS, January 1996.
144. Mary Schlue to AS, letter, January 25, 1996.
145. Kevin King, telephone conversation with AS, March 24, 2019.
146. Pat Hodda to AS, letter, March 20, 1997. 5 shillings = 50c.
147. TM, radio show, recorded from radio; DC Collection.
148. "Tex Morton Failed," Goulburn *Evening Post* (April 26, 1944): 2.
149. "Boys Stage A Rodeo," *Cobram Courier* (April 16, 1941): 3.
150. Ian Hands, *Ambassadors of Country Music* (Archerfield: privately published by Ian Hands, 1984): 2.

Chapter 9

1. Tex Banes, interview by AS, May 13, 1996. Arguably, however, Melbourne-based Smoky Dawson would have been better known than Banes at the time.

2. "Yodelling—So What," *Australian Music Maker and Dance Band News Magazine* (May 1937).
3. "Advertising," *SMH* (November 24, 1937): 21.
4. "Advertising," *SMH* (May 22, 1937): 30.
5. Advertisement, *Australian Music Maker Magazine* (May 31, 1941): 17.
6. £14 and ten shillings = $29.
7. TM, *Tex Morton Home Study Course for Hill-Billy, Spanish Guitar*, xeroxed notes. n.d.
8. Ibid.
9. Advertisement, *Australian Women's Mirror Magazine* (March 24, 1948).
10. Advertisement, *Australian Women's Mirror Magazine* (September 29, 1948).
11. Ian Hands to AS, letter, February 15, 2005.
12. Advertisements for TM guitars, *Hoofs and Horns Magazine* (May, June, July and August 1951).
13. Jimmie Rodgers, recording artist, "Daddy and Home," Zonophone label, Zonophone EE159.
14. Tex Banes to AS, letter, August 21, 1996.
15. EW, *CMA*, 2 (Sydney: Angus and Robertson Publishers, 1983), 109–110; James Akenson, "Tex Banes: Early Australian country music and Australian—US interaction," *Roots and Crossovers: Australian Country Music, Volume 2* Philip Hayward & Geoff Walden, editors (Gympie: aicmPress, 2004): 47; liner notes to *Tex Banes & The Hayseeds* (Cattle Records LP 127).
16. *Tex Morton's First Song Album*, songbook (Sydney: Nicholson's Pty. Ltd., n.d.); *Album of 21 Original Hill-Billy Songs*, songbook (Sydney: Nicholson's Pty. Ltd., n.d.); *Tex Morton's Australian Bush Ballads & Old Time Songs*, songbook, (Melbourne: Allan & Co., n.d.); *Tex Morton's Wild West & Rodeo Song Album No. 5*, songbook (Sydney: Nicholson's Pty. Ltd., 1940.); *Tex Morton's Song Album No. 7*, songbook, (Sydney: Nicholson's Pty. Ltd., n.d.). Some of these sonbooks featured other songs not associated with TM.
17. "Tex Morton's wild west comics," catalogue held at NLA, accessed April 10, 2022, at: http://catalogue.nla.gov.au/Record/4981359. The author compiled a listing of all known TM comics from both the NLA and DC, but did not include the list in this book. The words to a TM song was published in nearly every issue. These included (with volume number and issue number): "Crime Does Not Pay" (1,1), "Young Pat Maloney" (1,2), "The Flying Doctor (poem)" (1,3); "The Ned Kelly Song" (1,4); "I Left My Heart in Red River Valley" (1,5); "Mandrake" (1,6); "Aristocrat" (1,7); "King of Kalgoorlie (poem)" (1,8); "On the Gundagai Line" (1,9); "The Yodelling Bagman" (1,10); "All Set and Saddled" (1,11); "The Stockman's Prayer (poem)" (1,12); "Move Along Baldy" (2,1); "The Dying Duffer's Prayer" (2,2); "Travel by Train" (2,3); "Bonnie Blue Eyes:" (2,4); "My Old Bunkhouse Buddies" (2,5); "Rocky Ned the Outlaw" (2,6 and 2,12); "Good Old Droving Days" (2,7); "Boko" (2,9); "Swanky Cowboy" (2,10); "'Neath the Willow Tree" (2,11); "Winner of Squatter's Cup" (3,2). Issues (2,8) and (3,4) did not contain song lyrics.
18. TM comic 2, no. 7, DC Collection. 1 shilling = 10c.

Chapter 10

1. "Woke To Face Charge of Rape," *Sydney Daily Mirror* (July 31, 1945): 2.
2. "Woman Questioned In Rape Charge," *Newcastle Sun (August 1, 1945)*: 2; "Showmen on Rape Charge," *The Cessnock Reader and South Maitland Reporter* (July 20, 1945) reported bail was for £80 each, whereas "Girl's Story of Wild Night," *Truth* (August 5, 1945) stated it was £300 each.
3. SDD, interview by AS, April 30, 1989.
4. MM, interview by HC, August 28, 1994.
5. SDD, interview by AS, April 30, 1989.
6. MM, interview by HC, August 28, 1994.
7. Lisa Featherstone, email to AS, August 4, 2016.
8. "Immoral Claim in Rape Case," Sydney *Daily Telegraph* (August 2, 1945): 24.
9. "Said Complainant Had 'Record,'" *Newcastle Morning Herald and Miner's Advocate* (August 1, 1945): 4.
10. "Girl's Story of Wild Night," Sydney *Truth* (August 5, 1945): 16.
11. "Girl's Story of Wild Night," 16.
12. "Bob Slessor, A Pretty Woman Had 2 showmen arrested," Sydney *Sunday Telegraph* (August 5, 1945): 24.
13. Dorothy E. Doyle, quoted in "Girl's Story of Wild Night," Sydney *Truth* (August 5, 1945): 5. The duration of the struggle was reported in "Girl's Story of Wild Night," Sydney *Truth*, August 5, 1945: 16.
14. Bob Slessor, "A Pretty Woman Had 2 Showmen Arrested," Sydney *Daily Telegraph* (August 5, 1945): 24.
15. "Yodelling Cowboy On Grave Charges With Rough Rider," Sydney *Truth* (August 4, 1945): 13.
16. "Girl's Story of Wild Night," Sydney *Truth* (August 5, 1945): 16.
17. "Double Rape Alleged," *Perth Daily News* (August 1, 1945): 2.
18. "S.M. Sends Showmen for Trial," clipping from unidentified newspaper (July 1945).
19. "A Pretty Woman Had 2 Showmen Arrested," Sydney *Daily Telegraph* (August 5, 1945): 24.
20. "Girl's Story of Wild Night," Sydney *Truth* (August 5, 1945): 16.
21. "Two Showmen to Stand Trial," Lismore *Northern Star* (August 3, 1945); "Showmen For Trial on Serious Charge," Grafton *Daily Examiner* (August 3, 1945): 3.
22. "Girl's Story of Wild Night," Sydney *Truth* (August 5, 1945): 16.
23. "Yodelling Cowboy On Grave Charges With Rough Rider," *Truth* (August 4, 1945).
24. TM, quoted in Bob Slessor, "A Pretty Woman Had 2 Showmen Arrested," Sydney *Daily Telegraph* (August 5, 1945): 24.
25. Bob Slessor, "A Pretty Woman Had 2 Showmen Arrested," Sydney *Sunday Telegraph* (August 5, 1945): 24.
26. MM, interview by HC, August 28, 1994.

27. "Yodelling Cowboy On Grave Charges With Rough Rider," *Truth* (August 4, 1945); "Girl's Story of Wild Night," *Sydney Truth* (August 5 ,1945): 16; £30 = $60.

28. "Yodelling Cowboy On Grave Charges With Rough Rider," *Truth* (August 4, 1945); "Girl's Story of Wild Night," *Sydney Truth* (August 5, 1945).

29. "Girl's Story of Wild Night," *Sydney Truth* (August 5, 1945): 16.

30. MM, interview by HC, August 28, 1994.

31. "Girl's Story of Wild Night," *SydneyTruth* (August 5, 1945): 16.

32. Ibid.

33. "No Bill Filed Against Showmen," Newcastle *Morning Herald and Miners' Advocate* (August 18, 1945): 4. "No Case Against Two Showmen," *SMH*(August 19, 1945): 4. "Grave Charge: No True Bill On Two Men," Brisbane *Truth* (August 19, 1945): 18.

34. MM, interview by HC, August 28, 1994.

35. "Woke to Face Charge of Rape," Sydney *Sun* (July 31, 1945): 2.

36. SDD, interview by AS, April 30, 1989.

37. CM and other journalists, interviews by AS, July 17, 1990. A "quid" in this context means "money."

38. MM, interview by HC, August 28, 1994.

39. Lisa Featherstone, email to AS, August 4, 2016.

40. HC, email to AS, July 28, 2016.

41. MM, interview by HC, August 28, 1994.

42. "Wants Law to Rope Her Cowboy," Sydney *Truth* (September 22, 1946): 33.

43. MM, interview by HC, August 28, 1994.

44. BL, telephone conversation with AS, March 29, 2017.

45. CM and other journalists, interview by AS, July 17, 1990.

46. "Tex Morton's Guitar Plays a New Note," Brisbane *Courier Mail* (September 18, 1946): 3; "Tex Morton Rodeo," *Gippsland Times* (October 18, 1945): 2.

47. "Advertising," Bordertown *Border Chronicle* (November 30, 1945): 8.

48. Twins Bernard and Robert ("Bob") were born Brisbane on Sept 8, 1941; MM, interview by HC, August 28, 1994.

49. "Tex Morton's Wife Wants Him Lassoed," Adelaide *Truth* (September 28, 1946).

50. £3 = $6.

51. "Wants Law to Rope Her Cowboy," *Sydney Truth* (September 22, 1946): 33. £20 = $40; £25 = $50.

52. "Cowboy Tex Denies Wife's Charges," Sydney *Truth* (September 29, 1946): 36; £1= $2.

53. "Tex Morton Denies He Neglected Wife," *Daily Mirror* (September 27, 1946).

54. "Cow Boy Saddle Was Emptied Out," Brisbane *Courier Mail* (September 27, 1946): 3. £2 = $4.

55. £5000 = $10 000.

56. "Yodeller to Pay £8 Per Week," Brisbane *Courier Mail* (October 4, 1946): 5. £8 = $16.

57. "Tex Morton's Wife Wants Court to Lassoo Him," Brisbane *Truth* (September 22, 1946): 24. £10 = $20.

58. "1945 Rodeo Show Coming to Werribee," *Werribbee Shire Banner* (November 1, 1945): 2; "Wild West Rodeo," *Camperdown Chronicle* (November 9, 1945): 2.

59. "Tex Morton's Wife Claiming Support," Townsville *Daily Bulletin* (September 18, 1946): 1. £3000 = $6000.

60. "Wants Law to Rope Her Cowboy," *Sydney Truth* (September 22, 1946): 33. £17 = $34.

61. "Tex Morton Tells Court: His Answers To Wife," Brisbane *Truth* (September 29, 1946): 30.

62. "Morton's Wife Wins Suit," *Brisbane Truth* (October 6, 1946): 33. £8 = $16.

63. "Tex Morton Wins Against Wife," *Townsville Daily Bulletin* (December 21, 1946): 1; "Tex Morton Wins Appeal," *Rockhampton Morning Bulletin* (December 21, 1946): 6.

64. MM, interview by HC, August 28, 1994.

65. Ibid.

66. Ibid. The author telephoned MM later in 1994 and she also stated that she was committed to caring for her children. She never remarried following her divorce from TM in 1979.

67. Jenny Hicks, *Australian Cowboys Roughriders & Rodeos* (Sydney: Angus & Robertson): 81. "Sheila" is Australian slang for a female.

68. "Circus Proprietor Fined £5," Launceston *Examiner* (January 9, 1948): 6. £5 = $10.

69. "Apology...," Launceston *Examiner* (January 9, 1948): 6.

70. Advertisement, Launceston *Examiner* (January 9, 1948): 6.

Chapter 11

1. Nearly all surviving episodes of *All Set and Saddled* were released on two cassettes on the Kingfisher Cassette label: TM, *All Set and Saddled*, Kingfisher AUS 28 and TM, *All Set and Saddled*, Kingfisher AUS 29. The NLA has copies of the Kingfisher programs at "Catalogue," NLA, TM, *All set and saddled*, accessed April 12, 2022, at: https://catalogue.nla.gov.au/Record/1854407; 16 inches = 41 cm.

2. Advertisement, Adelaide *Advertiser* (November 21, 1942).

3. "Camera Shots: Radio News in Pictures," *RPA Magazine* (January 1, 1943): 45.

4. "All Set and Saddled," *Tempo Magazine* (December 1942—January 1943): 3.

5. Cassette tape of radio broadcast by TM and Sister Dorrie, ca.1946.

6. Nolan Porterfield to AS, letter, November 2, 1995.

7. TM, handwritten note, PTM Collection, NLA.

8. "Wisemans Ferry," *Windsor and Richmond Gazette* (September 29, 1948): 9.

9. 60 kilometers = about 37 miles.

10. "Advertising," Penrith *Nepean Times* (October 7, 1948): 4.

11. Ibid.

12. "Advertising," *SMH* (November 16, 1948): 12.

13. "Advertising," *SMH* (January 29, 1949): 8.

14. "Advertising," *SMH* (April 1, 1950): 26.

15. Ian Hands, *Tex Morton's Dude Ranch* (unpublished document, 2002) Ian Hands, telephone conversation with AS, February 15, 2005.

16. "Advertising," *SMH* (August 2, 1949): 10. 35 acres = 0.14 square kilometers.

17. MM and RM, interview by HC, August 28, 1994.

18. "Names Tex Morton As His Wife's Lover: Man's Charge," Brisbane *Truth* (July 16, 1950): 2; MM and RM, interview by HC, August 28, 1994.

19. This might have been at the nearby Castlereagh Hall.

20. RM, interview by HC, August 28, 1994.

21. "Personal," Penrith *Nepean Times* (October 28, 1948): 4.

22. "Penrith Talent Entertains at 'Yaralla,'" Penrith *Nepean Times* (November 4, 1948): 7.

23. "Entertainment at Dude Ranch," Penrith *Nepean Times* (November 25, 1948) : 6. £75 = $150.

24. "Deaf And Dumb Children Entertained," Penrith *Nepean Times* (November 18, 1948): 3. Terms like "deaf and dumb" to describe disabilities have not been in common use in Australia since the early 1970s.

25. KL to PB, letter, ca. late 1990s or early 2000s.

26. "The Dude Ranch and the Senior Citizens," Penrith *Nepean Times* (July 2, 1959): 6.

27. Gordon Spittle, *TMS* (Auckland: GWS Publications, 2008): 42–43.

28. Monique Peer, quoted from diary entry, January 15, 1949, xeroxed copy of a transcription, sent by Ralph Peer II to AS, March 25, 1996. Mrs Peer gives the day as Thursday January 15, 1949, but January 15, 1949, was a Saturday. January 15, 1948, was a Thursday. Since the Peers were in Sydney in 1949, the meeting most likely occurred on a Saturday. It has been asserted, for example by EW, *CMA 1* (Sydney: Angus and Robertson Publishers, 1982): 20, that Peer stated: "Tex had single-handedly created and pioneered in Australia, a country music industry which compared more than favorably with some of our best areas in America. . . . He is the Jimmie Rodgers of Australia." An online search of archived newspapers failed to find such a report, though. TM did have an unsourced typewritten copy of the statement in his personal possessions (PTM Collection, NLA).

29. "Ralph Peer," *Country Music Hall of Fame*, accessed April 19, 2022, at: https://countrymusichalloffame.org/artist/ralph-peer/; "Ralph Sylvester Peer," *Hillbilly Music Source & Symbol*, accessed April 19, 2022, at: https://exhibits.lib.unc.edu/exhibits/show/hillbilly_music/biographies/peer; "Ralph Peer," *Wikipedia*, accessed April 19, 2022, at: https://en.wikipedia.org/wiki/Ralph_Peer. For further reading, see Barry Mazor, *Ralph Peer and the Making of Popular Roots Music* (Chicago: Chicago Review Press, 2015); "The Story of Ralph S. Peer," YouTube, accessed April 6, 2022, at: https://www.youtube.com/watch?v=VkhwoP9ke-Y.

30. "His Ear To The Ground For Music," *Sydney Sun* (December 22, 1948): 11.

31. Barry Mazor, *Ralph Peer and the Making of Popular Roots Music* (Chicago: Chicago Review Press, 2015): 234–35.

32. Mazor, *Ralph Peer and the Making of Popular Roots Music*, 234–35.

33. Ibid. Ralph Peer II to AS, letter, March 25, 1996.

34. Bernard Harte, *When Radio Was The Cat's Whiskers* (Adelaide: Rosenberg Publishing, 2002): 177; see also "Allan Crawford in conversation with Colin Nicol", *The Pirate Radio Hall of Fame*, accessed April 5, 2022, at: http://www.offshoreradio.co.uk/odds37.htm. (Some sources spell Crawford's first name as "Alan", and others as "Allan.")

35. Bernard Harte, *When Radio Was The Cat's Whiskers* (Adelaide: Rosenberg Publishing, 2002): 178; "The Rodeo Label," *Australian Record and Music Review Magazine* no 25, April 1995: 3.

36. EW *CMA*, 2 (Sydney: Angus and Robertson Publishers, 1983): 31.

37. EW, *CMA*, 2 (Sydney: Angus and Robertson Publishers, 1983): 222–23; Eric Cleburne, to AS letter, April 2, 1990. Cleburne was the recording engineer for Rodeo. As previously mentioned, he had previously engineered TM's "Covered Wagon" shows.

38. "Owing to Overseas Engagements Tex Morton Offers For Sale," Sydney *Daily Telegraph* (February 10, 1949): 12, 1949. The sale was advertised for February 12, 1949.

39. "Advertising, *SMH* (August 2, 1949): 10.

40. "Advertising," *SMH* (April 1, 1950): 27.

41. "Advertising," *SMH* (May 31, 1950): 25.

42. "Dude Ranch Change-Over", Penrith *Nepean Times* (June 8, 1950): 6.

43. "Singing Cowboy," *New Zealand Listener* (October 21, 1949), PTM Collection, NLA.

44. "Legend of show biz began long career as street busker," Historical feature about TM, Sydney *Daily Mirror* (September 28, 1983): 56.

45. SDD, interviewed by AS, April 30, 1989.

Chapter 12

1. BL did not recall Morton spending Christmas with the family in 1949, though she was trying to recall events some 70 years later; BL, cited from BL, telephone conversation with AS, June 24, 2021.

2. Unidentified itinerary, Joyce Stephens to HC, letter, June 24, 1989.

3. Advertisements in unidentified New Zealand newspapers. n.d. Seven shillings = 70c; five shillings = 50c.

4. BL interview by RW, NLA, ORAL TRC 6124/25, October 12, 2010.

5. PB email to AS, May 17, 2019. PB stated: "New Zealand's Tasman label was amongst the first record companies in New Zealand, with TANZA, HMV, Tempo, and Stebbing. Record presses were second-hand machines brought from Australia in 1948. Tasman was founded in early 1949 and had links to Rodeo in Australia through links with the Recording Corporation of New Zealand, which published Tasman discs. The Recording Corporation of New Zealand was a Wellington company, founded in 1932. All Tasman Tex Morton releases identify them as "Rodeo Series"; conversely, their Australian Rodeo series labels do not mention Tasman."

6. TM, recording artist, "He Holds the Lantern / One Has My Name (The Other Has My Heart)" Rodeo label, Rodeo 10-0001; TM recording artist, "Don't Make Me Go to Bed and I'll be Good" / "Frankie and Johnny," Rodeo label, Rodeo 10-00021; "You and My Old Guitar" / "My Daddy is Only a Picture," Rodeo label, Rodeo 10-0003; TM, recording artist, "Stockman's Prayer" / "My Little Lady," Rodeo label, Rodeo 10-0004; TM, recording artist, "Soldiers Sweetheart" parts 1 and 2, Tasman label, Tasman TA 005; TM, recording artist, "When You Have No One to Love You (Linda Darlin')" / "Teardrops in My Heart," Rodeo

label, Rodeo 10-0006; "TM, recording artist, "A Rolling Stone" / "Slippin' Around" , Rodeo label, Rodeo 10-0007; TM, recording artist, "This Cold War with You" / Treasure [sic] Untold," Rodeo label, Rodeo 10-0008; TM, recording artist, "I'll Never Slip Around Again" / "Rock My Cradle," Rodeo label, Rodeo 10-0009; TM, recording artist, "Waiting for a Train" / "Rose of Shenandoah Valley," Rodeo label, Rodeo 10-0010; TM, recording artist, "Just Because" / "Wabash Cannon Ball," Rodeo label, Rodeo 10-0011; TM, recording artist, "One Golden Curl" / "When My Blue Moon Turns to Gold Again," Rodeo label, Rodeo 10-0012.

7. Chris Bourke, email to AS, June 24, 2021.

8. Chris Bourke, *Blue Smoke: The Lost Dawn of New Zealand Popular Music 1918–1964* (Auckland: Auckland University Press, 2010): 84; Chris Bourke, email to AS, email, June 24, 2021. Bourke stated that other steel guitarists might have been Tommy Kaihi and Bill Sevesi. He stated that Kaihi was due to play on a session but Morton was too drunk to perform.

9. GG, "The Tex Morton Story Part Two," *CWS Magazine*, no 66, 1970: 41.

10. Gordon Spittle, *TMS* (Auckland: GWS Publications, 2008): 55.

11. Gordon Spittle, *TMS* (Auckland: GWS Publications, 2008): 56.

12. Chris Bourke, *Blue Smoke: The Lost Dawn Of New Zealand Popular Music 1918–1964* (Auckland: Auckland University Press, 2010): 84.

13. "John Edwards, discography, *The Yodelling Boundary Rider, Tex Morton: A Discography*, Southern Folklife Collection, Wilson Library, University of North Carolina, Chapel Hill, NC. Provided courtesy of the John Edwards Foundation.

14. Eric Cleburne to AS, letter, April 2, 1990.

15. "Tex Morton," *Praguefrank's Country Music Discographies*, accessed April 5, 2002, at: http://countrydiscography.blogspot.com/2011/11/tex-morton.html, states: "The matrices for the Tasman/Rodeo sessions are listed as given by John Edwards. Edwards notes that M-28562-B and M28580-A from the Sydney sessions are untraced. Based on the matrices, it looks like there were two recording sessions in Sydney and as many as five sessions in Auckland. Some collectors maintain that the Tasman and Rodeo labels have different versions for eight of the titles B items 095, 104, 108, 109, 111, 112, 114 and 118 B and thereby speculate that Morton recorded some songs in both Sydney and Auckland. It is possible, but there is no documentation to support this speculation. Some sources indicate that R-006 and R-007 were recorded on May 25, 1949, and that R-008 through R-012 were recorded on February 17, 1950, but the matrices for these recordings suggest that not all the recordings were made on the above dates. Rodeo initially released these recordings in its 10-0000 series, but at some undetermined point switched to its R-000 series for its re-pressings. Some records have extant copies in both series, and some only in the R-000 series."

16. David Hardy, email to AS, June 20, 2021. Hardy's analysis was used in compiling this book's discography of TM's recordings.

17. Some sides with band accompaniment feature a steel guitar, whereas others don't. The ones without steel guitar were probably recorded in Sydney, whereas it's generally accepted that the New Zealand session(s) featured steel-guitar accompaniment.

18. Ralph Peer II to AS, letter, March 25, 1996.

19. Rodgers recorded the song as "Treasures Untold:" Jimmie Rodgers, recording artist,

"Treasures Untold," Zonophone / Regal Zonophone label, Zonophone/Regal Zonophone EE1239.

20. Frank Crumit, recording artist, "Frankie and Johnnie," HMV label, HMV EA.227.

21. TM, recording artist, "Treasures Untold", Bear Family compact disc. *I Am Sad And Weary: Jimmie Rodgers Revisited*, Bear Family label, Bear Family BCD 16673 AR. 2003.

22. "Country singer Cecil Smith dies of heart failure," *Minneapolis Star and Tribune* (February 18, 1987).

23. "Hank Williams—part 1," *Praguefrank's Country Music Discographies*, accessed April 5, 2022, at: http://countrydiscography.blogspot.com.au/2009/08/hank-williams-part-i.html; Williams recorded the number in between January and May 1949, at the KWKH-Shreveport radio-station studio.

24. Johnny Bond, recording artist, "Rock My Cradle Once Again," U.S. Columbia, Columbia label 37529.

25. "Billy Folger: Louisiana's Boyfriend," *Old Time Country Magazine* 9, nos. 3 & 4: 8.

26. Eddie Dean, recording artist, "One Has My Name (The Other Has My Heart)," Crystal label, Crystal CRS 180.

27. Floyd Tillman, recording artist, "This Cold War With You" / "I'll Never Slip Around Again," Columbia label, Columbia 20615.

28. Floyd Tillman, recording artist, "Slippin' Around," Columbia label, Columbia DO3333.

29. The Carter Family, recording artists, "Wabash Cannonball," Regal Zonophone label, Regal Zonophone G24157.

30. The Pine Ridge Boys, recording artists, "When You Have No One To Love You," Regal Zonophone label ,Regal Zonophone G25114.

31. Roy Acuff, recording artist, "Wabash Cannon Ball," Vocalion/OKeh 04466 (1936); Roy Acuff, recording artist, "Wabash Cannon Ball," Columbia label, Columbia 37008 (1947); The Sons of The Pioneers, recording artists, "Teardrops in My Heart," Regal Zonophone label, Regal Zonophone G25191; The Pine Ridge Boys, recording artists, "When You Have No One To Love You," Regal Zonophone label, Regal Zonophone G25114; Wilf Carter, recording artist, "One Golden Curl," RCA Victor label, RCA 20–3152 (1947); Eddy Arnold, recording artist, "My Daddy is Only a Picture," Regal Zonophone label, Regal Zonophone G25280. TM's recording of "Wabash Cannon Ball" appears to be based on Acuff's version.

32. Roy Acuff, recording artist, "Don't Make Me Go to Bed and I'll Be Good," OKeh label, OKeh OK 6704; Dorothy Horstman, *Sing Your Heart Out Country Boy: Classic Country Songs and Their Inside Stories by the People who Wrote Them* (Toronto and Vancouver: Clarke, Irwin & Company Limited, 1975): 74.

33. Ralph Peer II to AS, letter, March 25, 1996.

34. Hal Saunders to AS, letter, July 22, 1990.

35. Delores and John Balaam, interview by Mike O'Malley, September 1991.

36. DC, email to AS, October 25, 2017.

37. Dorothy Carroll, interview by JM, 1985.

38. TM cited from "Cowboy Takes To Trances," *Charleville Times* (23 March 1950): 9; "Cowboy Takes To Trances," Sydney *Sun* (March 12, 1950): 3.

39. TM, cited from "Cowboy Takes To Trances," *Charleville Times* (March 23, 1950): 9; TM, cited from "Cowboy Takes To Trances," Sydney *Sun* (March 12, 1950): 3. £50 000 = $100 000.

40. TM, cited from Cowboy Takes To Trances," *Charleville Times* (March 23, 1950): 9; TM, cited from "Cowboy Takes To Trances," Sydney *Sun* (March 12, 1950): 3.

41. CM "My Mate Sold Elvis Presley," *EM* Magazine (August 9, 1967).

42. "Latest News," *Magic New Zealand e-zine* no 129, accessed April 6, 2022, at: http://www.magicnewzealand.com/ezine-archive/2002-Jan-to-Dec-2002/129-Aug04-2002.txt; "Latest News," *Magic New Zealand e-zine* no 77, accessed April 5, 2022, at: http://www.magicnewzealand.com/ezine-archive/2001-Jan-to-Dec-2001/077-Jun10-2001.txt; Spittle, *TMS* (Auckland: GWS Publications, 2008): 104. Some spell the name as "Braemer."

43. Public notice in unidentified Gore (New Zealand) newspaper (October 25, 1949), PTM Collection, NLA.

44. TM cited in Athol McCoy, interview by HC, September 9, 1989; post (now deleted) in internet forum *The Magic Café*, accessed April 5, 2022, at: http://themagiccafe.com/forums/viewtopic.php?topic=560630&forum=22&start=0.

45. Cited from reports of TM's shows, newspaper advertisements from unidentified source, advertising Morton's shows, PTM Collection, NLA. The day and month are shown, and from these the year can be ascertained.

46. "Greymouth Audience Enthralled by Tex Morton Show," unidentified newspaper report, n.d., PTM Collection, NLA.

47. Quoted from "Tex" (caption above photograph of TM), *Tempo Magazine* (March 1950): 10.

48. Quoted from TM poster, National Library of New Zealand, accessed April 5, 2022, at: http://natlib.govt.nz/records/23019301?search%5Bi%5D%5Bsubject%5D=Morton%2C+Tex%2C+1916-1983&search%5Bpath%5D=items.

49. Joyce Stephens to HC, letter, June 24, 1989.

50. Joyce Stephens to AS, letter, September 2, 1989.

51. BL, telephone conversation with AS, June 24, 2021. BL told AS that TM traveled to America twice: he was in the United States briefly (presumably in 1949) in order to assess the entertainment scene there, before leaving on a much more extensive tour there. She especially recalled his bringing her a special biro (new at the time) from the United States. Such a trip would have most likely have been in 1949 prior to (or even during) the New Zealand tour, or else early in 1950. In over 30 years of researching TM, the author had never heard of, or read about, such a trip until 2021.

52. "Tex Morton was a 'recent arrival' in Hollywood cited from The *Joplin Globe* June 6, 1950: 10, PTM Collection, NLA. The article stated that Morton had been born in an Australian town called "Texas"—hence the sobriquet of "Tex"—and that Ralph Peer had brought him to the USA as both a performer and composer, with intentions of Morton starring in a Hollywood movie.

53. Slim Dusty, and Joy McKean, interview by AS, June 4, 1991.
54. PB to AS, letter, October 31, 1992. Roger's birth date was April 25, 1934.
55. "Bruce Carroll's Wife Seeks Maintenance Order But Denies Romance With Hill-Billy Tex Morton," Perth *Mirror* (July 15, 1950): 1. In Australia, "maintenance" refers to both child support and alimony.
56. "Names Tex Morton As His Wife's Lover: Man's Charge," Brisbane *Truth* (July 16, 1950): 2. £15 = $30.
57. "Bruce Carroll's Wife Seeks Maintenance Order but Denies Romance with Hill-Billy Tex Morton," Perth *Mirror* (July 15, 1950): 1. The term "missus" is Australian slang for "wife."
58. "Mrs Carroll's Claim Misses," Perth *Mirror* (July 22, 1950): 16.
59. "Last Curtain in Love Drama," Sydney *Truth* (October 8, 1950): 9.
60. Dorothy Carroll, interview by JM, 1985.
61. "Australian Country Music Hands of Fame," *Australian Country Music Hall of Fame*, accessed April 17, 2022, at: https://countrymusichalloffame.com.au/the-hands-of-fame-inductees/.
62. "Obituary," Melbourne *Age* (May 1, 1952): 2.
63. MM, interview by HC, August 28, 1994. Most likely, the incident would have been at Easter, 1949 (that year, Good Friday was April 15).
64. £400 = $800.
65. RM interview with RW, NLA, BIB ID 4582970, December 4, 2008.
66. RM telephone conversation with AS, March 8, 2019. 1200 kilometers = 750 miles.
67. RM interview with RW, NLA, BIB ID 4582970, December 4, 2008.
68. RM *Facebook* message, December 13, 2017.
69. RM has recorded a tribute to his father: RM, "Ode to Dad, Tex Morton and Bob Morton," YouTube, accessed April 18, 2022, at: https://www.youtube.com/watch?v=gojeAS466tU.

Chapter 13

1. Morton authority Pat Ware told PB that he had seen a letter from Autry to Morton. Ware also stated at other times that the two corresponded with each other. (PB to AS, letter, August 8, 1990).
2. Marva Felchin (Director, Libraries and Archives of the Autry Museum of the American West), email to AS, December 8, 2017. Marva Felchin also stated that the Autry archives were still being cataloged, raising the possibility that there still may be evidence that Autry and Morton corresponded with each other.
3. CM, "My Mate Sold Elvis Presley," *EM Magazine* (August 9, 1967). There were unconfirmed rumors that Fraley was later employed by the Los Angeles Police Department as an instructor, but enquiries by the author were fruitless.
4. Gordon Spittle, *TMS* (Auckland: GWS Publications, 2008): 59.
5. "Smokey [sic] A Hard Act To Follow," *Herald Sun*, March 1992; SDD, interview by AS, April 30, 1989.

6. "Christie-Drake Hotel 1950," *Hollywood Historic Photos*, accessed April 2, 2022, at: http://hollywoodhistoricphotos.com/product_info.php/products_id/7100.
7. SDD, interview by AS, April 30, 1989.
8. Ibid.
9. C.J. McKenzie, "Now It's Tex the governor," *Sunday Telegraph* (August 31, 1980).
10. SDD, interview by AS, April 30, 1989.
11. BL, telephone conversation with AS, April 27, 2018.
12. CM, "My Mate Sold Elvis Presley," *EM*, August 9, 1967.
13. Ibid.
14. RWI 1993. *Reminiscing In Tempo: A personal recollection of jazz music and the record business in Australia, 1923–1993*, (privately published, 1993): 242; "Joseph, A. Hugh," *The Canadian Encyclopedia*, accessed April 20, 2022, at: https://www.thecanadianencyclopedia.ca/en/article/a-hugh-joseph-emc.
15. CM, "My Mate Sold Elvis Presley," *EM Magazine* (August 9, 1967). 600 kilometers = 375 miles. From then on, Morton was primarily based in Canada but occasionally made brief forays into the United States to comply with USA visa regulations.
16. CM, "My Mate Sold Elvis Presley" *EM Magazine* (August 9, 1967).
17. "Leading Hypnotist Plans Show Here," *Lethbridge Herald* (June 9, 1951): 13.
18. "Tex Morton at Center," *Lethbridge Herald* (June 18, 1951): 6.
19. Jack Litchfield, cited from Jack Litchfield to PB, letter, December 5, 1996.
20. Keith Titterington, "'Dixie' Bill Hilton and the Calgary Range Riders," *Country Musical Trails Less Traveled Magazine* 1, nos. 4, 3, 7, (1990).
21. Keith Titterington, "'Dixie' Bill Hilton and the Calgary Range Riders," *Country Musical Trails Less Traveled Magazine* 1, no. 4, 7, (1990). It's possible that Hilton misremembered the dates, however. An exhaustive search of the PTM Collection, NLA, failed to find any documents showing Hilton opening TM's shows in 1954 or 1955. Perhaps he opened shows for TM earlier than 1954.
22. Rod Olstad, email to AS, December 12, 1999.
23. Keith Titterington, "'Dixie' Bill Hilton and the Calgary Range Riders," *Country Musical Trails Less Traveled Magazine* 1, no. 4, 7 (1990). The problem with this statement is that neither place is listed in chronologies of Hank Williams' appearances in Canada. In addition, an online search of archived Canadian newspapers failed to locate a reference of Morton performing with Hilton and the Calgary Range Riders, but the newspapers that were sourced generally reported very little related to country music.
24. "Dixie" Bill Hilton, interview by Keith Titterington, December 10, 1983.
25. Rod Olstad, "Fred Lang and His Travels," *Canadian Folk Music Bulletin* 29, no. 3, 10 (1995); Rod Olstead, email to AS, December 12, 1999. 100 kilometers is approximately 62 miles.
26. Rod Olstad, email to AS, December 12, 1999.
27. 600 km = 370 miles.
28. Rod Olstad, email to AS, December 12, 1999.
29. "Dixie" Bill Hilton, interview by Keith Titterington, December 10, 1983.

30. "50's Star 'Dixie' Bill Hilton Passes On," *Country Music News Magazine* (March 1991).

31. Shirley Field to AS, letter, June 13, 1996.

32. "B.C.'s Country Sweetheart," *Country Musical Trails Less Traveled Magazine* 4, no. 4 (July/August 1993): 3

33. Pee Wee King's birth name was Julius Frank Kuczynski.

34. Pee Wee King to AS, letter, September 21, 1989.

35. Pee Wee King to AS, letter, November 1989.

36. Advertisement for Pee Wee King, "The Nation's #1 C & W Band Leader," *Billboard Magazine* (May 23, 1953): 156.

37. Barry McCloud, editor, "J. L. Frank," in *Definitive Country: The Ultimate Encyclopedia of Country Music and Its Performers* (New York: Bumper Books, 1995): 304.

38. Bob Pinson to AS, letter, May 25, 1990.

39. John Rumble, email to AS, February 10, 2017.

40. EW, liner notes to *The Tex Morton Collection, Vol. 1, 1936–1938*, LP and CD sets. Vinyl release EMBB-430051 (the actual discs were numbered consecutively, from 430051 to 430052); EW, *CMA, 1* (Sydney: Angus and Robertson Publishers, 1982): 23.

41. EW to AS, letter, March 15, 1990.

42. Pee Wee King to AS, letter, November 1989.

43. SDD, interview by AS, April 30, 1989.

44. "Big Bill Lister," *Praguefrank's Country Music Discographies*, accessed April 19, 2022, at: http://countrydiscography.blogspot.com/2010/05/big-bill-lister.html.

45. Don Helms cited in David Burley, email to AS, April 15, 2002. Burley acted as an intermediary between Helms and the author.

46. For example, Bill Olson (a collector who was at a Hank Williams concert) to AS, letter, 1990s.

47. CM, "My Mate Sold Elvis Presley," *EM Magazine* (September 9, 1967); Morton might have been confused. Parker took over management of Presley (cutting Hank Snow out of any arrangement) and sold him to RCA for a sum approximating $35 000 plus $5000 to repay royalties that Sun Records owed Presley.

48. "Jim Denny," *Country Music Hall of Fame*, accessed April 25, 2022, at: https://countrymusichalloffame.org/artist/jim-denny/.

49. Colin Escott, with George Merritt and William MacEwan, *I Saw The Light: The Story of Hank Williams* (New York: Bay Back Books, 2004): 227–56.

50. The recording sheet for TM's March 6, 1953, Nashville session states that TM's manager was Oscar Davis.

51. Gordon Spittle, *TMS* (Auckland: GWS Publications, 2008): 64.

52. Bob Pinson to AS, letter, July 28, 1988.

53. Colin Escott, email to AS, n.d.

54. Colin Escott, with George Merritt, and William MacEwan, *I Saw The Light: The Story of Hank Williams* (New York: Bay Back Books, 2004): 236.

55. Betty Walker (Billy Walker's wife), email to AS, ca. 2005.

56. Colin Escott to AS, various emails, n.d. Also: David Kent, owner of the rights to the show in 1990, did not reply to letters written to him by the author.

57. Bob Pinson, file cards of Hank Williams' life, held in the Nashville Public Library, provided by librarian Kathleen Feduccia, email to AS, August 27, 2021; "Hank Williams Timeline," accessed August 30, 2021, at:, https://leeharrisonline.tripod.com/hankwilliams/. Williams also performed in Canada on September 13, 1949, and October 27, 1949, but these dates predated Morton's move to North America. A search of online Canadian newspaper archives at *NewspaperArchive*, accessed September 2021, at: https://newspaperarchive.com/, however, failed to show any articles or advertisements for Hank Williams appearing with either Tex Morton or "Dixie" Bill Hilton, although this doesn't necessarily discount Morton appearing as a warm-up act (with Hilton) for Williams. Also, Jack Litchfield to PB, letter, December 5, 1996, was unable to find any references to Morton and Williams at the Toronto concert.

58. TM, recording artist, "I've Known the Truth" / "I Was Born in Old Wyoming," Philips label, Philips P 24505 ; TM, recording artist, "Railroad Boomer" / "I've Got You Right Out of My Mind," Philips label P 24506; TM, recording artist, "The Neighbor's Wife", "Circus Boy", "Kiwi Song"- not released on 78 rpm discs in Australia.

59. Ronnie Pugh, email to AS, March 26, 2017.

60. Norman Perry, quoted from Norman Perry, email to AS, August 20, 2021: Perry stated that he recorded at the Castle studios only about a month before Morton, and described the studios as: "Very unimpressive. Nothing more than a couple of small rooms in the hotel that had been converted into make-shift recording studios. They were very small with an elongated see-through glass for the engineer and the musicians to see each other. The room with the musicians was sound-proofed with various sound boards. Frankly, it was a bit cramped. There were no amplifiers. The instruments were plugged through to the control board. We were not able to see the control board or the recorders." See also: Brian Ward and Patrick Huber, *AS&R Pioneers: Architects of American Roots Music on Record* (Nashville: Vanderbilt University Press, 2018): 290–93.

61. Bob Pinson to AS, letter and xeroxed copy of TM's Nashville recording session sheet, ca. 1990. The sheet stated that Oscar Davis was TM's manager.

62. Bob Moore, cited in Kittra Moore, email to AS, July 31, 2005.

63. Norm Van Maastright, *Paul Yandell: Second To The Best* (Atglen, PA: Schiffer Publishing, Ltd, 2016): 94.

64. Morton later described the song as "just one of those songs a writer records and forgets. . . . I honestly don't think it's the best song I ever wrote" (TM, liner notes to *Tex Morton Encores*, EMI label, EMI AXIS 6327).

65. Kittra Moore, email to AS, July 31, 2005.

66. Advertisement, unidentified newspaper, n.d., PTM Collection, NLA; Gordon Spittle, *TMS* (Auckland: GWS Publications, 2008): 69.

67. John Rumble, email to AS, February 10, 2017.

68. "Catalog of Copyright Entries 1953 Jan—Dec 30," *archive.org*, accessed April 6, 2017, at: https://archive.org/stream/catalogofcopyrig375lib/catalogofcopyrig375lib_djvu.txt.

69. RWI. *Reminiscing In Tempo: A personal recollection of jazz music and the record business in Australia, 19231993* (privately published, 1993): 243.
70. RWI to AS, letter, May 3, 1989.
71. Bob Pinson to AS, letter including a xeroxed copy of Morton's Nashville recording session sheet, ca. 1990.
72. TM, recording artist, "I've Known the Truth" / "I Was Born in Old Wyoming," Philips label, Philips P-24505-H; TM, recording artist, "I've Got You Right Out Of My Mind" / "Railroad Boomer," Philips label, Philips P-24506-H.
73. DC and David Hardy, *The Tex Morton Discography*: 15.
74. TM, *The Essential Tex Morton*, Sony label, Sony 76096021.
75. "Wide Variety In Hit Numbers," Adelaide *Advertiser* (March 27, 1954): 12.
76. "Gold in them thar hillbilly records," Adelaide *News* (April 27, 1954): 19.
77. DC, email to AS, August 28, 2021. Although there are no official sales figures for Rodeo records, DC noted the preponderance of Morton's Rodeo records in collections of 78s he had purchased. For example, DC had 35 duplicate copies of Rodeo 001 and 30 duplicates for Rodeo 003, far exceeding the duplicate copies for other Rodeo artists in his collection.
78. Robert Feldman, "Tex Morton Has 'Em Swooning In The Aisles," Sydney *Daily Telegraph* (June 28, 1953): 44; PTM Collection, NLA; "The Great Morton—Hypnotism," The *Post-Record* (August 18, 1953): 3, PTM Collection, NLA.
79. The line "the cards are on the table" is in "I've Known the Truth," recorded in Nashville.
80. L. Edgar, "The Great Morton Adventurer ... Poet," Montreal *McGill Daily* (February 26, 1953): 2, PTM Collection, NLA.
81. Julianna Jenkins, email to AS, June 16, 2017.
82. Hank Snow with Jack Ownbey and Bob Burris, *The Hank Snow Story* (Chicago: University of Illinois Press, 1994).
83. TM cited by Gordon Spittle, *TMS* (Auckland: GWS Publications, 2008) 88; TM, interview by GG, 1969.
84. Hank Snow and Anita Carter, recording artists, "Down the Trail of Achin' Hearts" / "Bluebird Island", RCA label, RCA 48–0441.
85. PB to AS, letter, n.d. ca. 1990s.
86. Fred Hoeptner, email to AS, September 17, 2017.
87. "Post-Hypnosis Part of Morton's Method," unidentified newspaper, September 4, 1951, PTM Collection, NLA; Bruce Taylor, "Victim of Hypnosis Catches a Sailfish," Montreal *Herald* (September 4, 1951): 18, PTM Collection, NLA; "Morton Mixes Science, Fun," Montreal *Herald* (September 6, 1951): 19, PTM Collection, NLA; "Great Morton Opens Show Here Tonight," *Gazette* (September 8, 1951), PTM Collection, NLA.
88. Advertisement, unidentified publication, 1951, PTM Collection, NLA.
89. "Great Morton Acclaimed by Canadian Press," Montreal *Herald* (August 31, 1951), PTM Collection, NLA.
90. Paul McKenna Davis, "Hip Hypnotist," *Montreal Star* (January 22, 1972), PTM Collection, NLA.

91. Jack Litchfield cited from Jack Litchfield to PB, letter, December 5, 1996.

92. Erskine Johnson, "Hollywood," Montreal *Herald* (September 13, 1951): 16, PTM Collection, NLA; "Hypnotist Entertains Fridolin," *Montreal Star* (September 19, 1951); photograph of TM with Fridolin, PTM Collection, NLA; article about Fridolin (Gratien) Galenas, *Billboard* Magazine (March 3, 1951).

93. Unidentified newspaper report, n.d., PTM Collection, NLA; "Ethel Smith (organist)," *Wikipedia*, accessed April 24, 2022, at: https://en.wikipedia.org/wiki/Ethel_Smith_(organist).

94. "Great Morton Opens Show Here," unidentified newspaper, n.d., PTM Collection, NLA.

95. Howard Huston, "Around The Clock In Montreal," Montreal *Herald* (September 1, 1951): 4, PTM Collection, NLA.

96. John Minson, "Australian Pioneer's Colourful Past," *Capital News* (July 1993): 5.

97. Driving while blindfolded appears to have been another act of Morton's. For example, the article "The Great Morton Has An Accident," *Steinbech Carillon* (November 14, 1958): 5, reported "the Great man who once drove down Portage Avenue blindfolded...."

98. Gerry Taylor, "The Amazing Great Morton And Sweet Sounds With Balloons," New Brunswick *Daily-Gleaner (August 29, 2014)*: 1–4. Article sent by Fred Isenor, email to AS, July 25, 2017.

99. Unidentified article, *Gazette* (September 1, 1951), PTM Collection, NLA.

100. Pat Pearce, "Spotlight On Stage And Screen," Montreal *Herald* (October 4, 1951): 16, PTM Collection, NLA.

101. Bruce Taylor, "Victim Of Hypnosis Catches A Sailfish," Montreal *Herald* (September 4, 1951): 18, PTM Collection, NLA.

102. TM, Mother's Day Card, 1951, PTM Collection, NLA.

103. BL to AS, letter, March 30, 1990.

104. Ray Munro and Les Wedman, "Crows Like Rooster, Ssh, Sleeps On Job," *Vancouver Daily Province* (April 6, 1951), PTM Collection, NLA.

105. "Esquire Boston Dr Robert Morton," *Variety* Magazine (June 25, 1952), annotations next to clipping probably in TM's handwriting, PTM Collection, NLA.

106. Jack Litchfield, cited from Jack Litchfield to PB, letter, December 5, 1996.

107. "Hypnotist Morton's Wow $25,800 in Toronto 3", *Variety Magazine* (May 7, 1952), annotations next to clipping probably in TM's handwriting, PTM Collection, NLA.

108. "Hypnotist Morton's Wow in Toronto 3," *Variety Magazine* (June 25, 1952), PTM Collection, NLA.

109. Two photographs, n.d., PTM Collection, NLA; one photograph reproduced in EW *CMA, 1* (Sydney: Angus and Robertson Publishers 1982): 23.

110. TM, writing near newspaper clipping, PTM Collection, NLA.

111. Ibid.

112. Tex Morton and Seville Theatre, contract (October 1952), PTM Collection, NLA.

113. Ibid.

114. TM, handwritten note, 1952, PTM Collection, NLA.

115. Numerous photographs in PTM Collection, NLA.

116. "Morton Gives A Great Show," *The News Of The North*, n.d.: 8, PTM Collection, NLA; "Another First In Yellowknife," *NWT Archives*, accessed April 6, 2022, at: https://www.nwttimeline.ca/1950/1951Morton/Images/NNJuly131951001.pdf.

117. Untitled photographs of Virginia Shea, Boston, either 1952 or 1958 (based on matching day of month as shown on photograph with year), PTM Collection, NLA.

118. Gordon Spittle, *TMS* (Auckland: GWS Publications, 2008): 74-75.

119. Advertising poster, accessed April 20, 2022, at: https://www.nwttimeline.ca/1950/1951Morton/Images/NNJuly131951002.pdf.

120. Numerous photographs of TM in Canada, PTM Collection, NLA; photograph of TM advertising poster, *NWT Archives*, accessed April 6, 2022, at: https://www.nwttimeline.ca/1950/1951Morton/Images/NNJuly131951002.pdf.

121. Various photographs, n.d., PTM Collection, NLA.

122. Ormond McGill, *The New Encyclopedia of Stage Hypnotism* (Carmathen, Wales: Crown Publishing Ltd, 1996): 383.

123. Various headlines, from newspaper reviews, n.d., PTM Collection, NLA.

124. "Best Show Here In Years' Is Verdict On Great Morton," unidentified Manitoba newspaper (December 2, 1954), PTM Collection, NLA.

125. Gordon Spittle, *TMS* (Auckland: GWS Publications, 2008): 80.

126. HC, citing statements made by TM, in HC email to AS, May 24, 2017.

127. BL, telephone conversation with AS, May 31, 2017.

128. Jack Litchfield cited from Jack Litchfield to PB, letter, December 5, 1996.

129. Advertisement, *Toronto Daily Star* (January 22, 1953), PTM Collection, NLA.

130. *Variety Magazine* (January 31, 1953): 51, PTM Collection, NLA.

131. Charles Trowbridge, "Rubes (Our Man Too) Howl At Stage Hypnotist," unidentified newspaper, n.d., PTM Collection, NLA.

132. "Hocus-Pocus," *Billboard Magazine* (September 29, 1951): 82.

133. Jack Litchfield to PB, letter, December 5, 1996.

134. Photograph of TM poster, *Pinterest*, accessed April 10, 2022, at: https://au.pinterest.com/pin/520869513139853683/.

135. "The Great Morton," report in unidentified Chicago newspaper, n.d., PTM Collection, NLA.

136. BL, telephone conversation with AS, May 31, 2017.

137. "Hypnotist Great Morton Booked for Six Days at Grand," *Evansville Press* (February 27, 1953), PTM Collection, NLA; "Hypnotist Will Open at Grand March 10," *Evansville Courier* (February 25, 1953), PTM Collection, NLA.

138. James Palmer, "Clinical Air Marks Show by Hypnotist," *Evansville Courier* (March 11, 1953): 24, PTM Collection, NLA.

139. Sears Roebuck Company, quoted from catalog, item description text, n.d., PTM Collection, NLA; "Sears Sleep Show" advertisement, *Sunday Courier and Press* (March 6, 1953), PTM Collection, NLA.

140. PTM Collection, NLA; "Apollo Theatre," *Wikipedia*, accessed April 6, 2022, https://en.wikipedia.org/wiki/Apollo_Theater.

141. "House Reviews," *Variety Magazine* (June 17, 1953), PTM Collection, NLA.

142. Advertisements in *The Telegram* (Toronto) and *Toronto Daily Star* (July 20, 1953), PTM Collection, NLA.

143. "Hypnotist, Folk Singer Shoots Kangaroos Too," *Hamilton Review* (July 16, 1953), PTM Collection, NLA; "Versatile Hypnotist Has Enjoyed Varied Life," *Hamilton Spectator* (July 16, 1953), PTM Collection, NLA.

144. "The Great Morton—Hypnotism," *The Post-Record* (August 18, 1953), PTM Collection, NLA. The name "Severne" does not appear on any of Morton's reports from Nelson College.

145. BL, interview with RW, NLA ORAL TRC 6124/25, October 12, 2010.

146. Various photographs of TM hypnotizing subjects, n.d., PTM Collection, NLA; a search of online newspaper archives, however, failed to find any reference to Morton in England, but this was most likely owing to the newspapers that were archived.

147. Photograph of Joe Brown, PTM Collection, NLA; EW *CMA, 1* (Sydney: Angus and Robertson Publishers, 1982): 24.

148. "'Best Show Here in Years' Is Verdict On Great Morton," unidentified Manitoba newspaper (December 2, 1954), PTM Collection, NLA.

149. "Great Morton Astonishes Big Crows With All-Round Show," *Brandon Daily Sun* (December 7, 1954): 13, PTM Collection, NLA.

150. Review of performance by TM, *Brandon Daily Sun* (December 8, 1954): 4, PTM Collection, NLA.

151. "The Great Morton Show Is Held Over," unidentified newspaper, Fort William (October 28, 1954), PTM Collection, NLA.

152. Advertisement, unidentified newspaper (January 15, 1957), PTM Collection, NLA.

153. "50's Star 'Dixie' Bill Hilton Passes On," *Country Music News* (March 1991). Hilton died February 1, 1991.

154. Advertisement, unidentified newspaper (January 15, 1957), PTM Collection, NLA; advertisement, unidentified newspaper, ca. 1957, mentioning "Harbour Street" in Kingston," PTM Collection, NLA; receipt for a hat at the English Shop, Kingston & Montego Bay, Jamaica, January 18, 1957, PTM Collection, NLA.

155. Jack Litchfield, cited from Jack Litchfield to PB, letter, December 5, 1996.

Chapter 14

1. "Master Hypnotist Thrills All—The Great Morton Opens 2½ Hour Show Tonight," Hamilton Review (July 23, 1953), PTM Collection, NLA; unidentified Edmonton Newspaper, ca. 1955, based on matching day and date of the month with year, PTM Collection, NLA. That this statement appeared in different newspapers might suggest that it was composed by TM, himself.

2. TM, cited from Insurance policy, occupational information, 1958, PTM Collection, NLA.

3. Gordon Spittle, *TMS* (Auckland: GWS Publications, 2008): 7; "Huge Audiences Nelson Entertainer in U.S.," unidentified newspaper, n.d., PTM Collection, NLA.

4. Gordon Spittle, *TMS* (Auckland: GWS Publications, 2008): 77.

5. Alan Turley to AS, letter, August 1, 2017.

6. "Our Cover," *Journal of Hypnotism* 3, no. 1 (September–October 1953): 15.

7. Mike Burraston, cited from PB to AS, letter, December 10, 1990.

8. Gordon Spittle, *TMS* (Auckland: GWS Publications, 2008):77.

9. Gordon Spittle, *TMS* (Auckland: GWS Publications, 2008): 78.

10. Gordon Spittle, *TMS* (Auckland: GWS Publications, 2008): 77; "The Fabulous Tex Morton," *Tempo & Television* (January-February, 1959): 7; "Tex Morton," *Australian Country Music Hall of Fame*, accessed April 12, 2022, at: https://ehive.com/collections/200851/objects/1461088/tex-morton /; Alan Turley, "Tex Morton," *Nelson Historical Society Journal* 6, issue 01, 1996, accessed April 12, 2022, at: http://nzetc.victoria.ac.nz/tm/scholarly/tei-NHSJ06_01-t1-body1-d5.html; "The Fabulous Tex Morton," *Tempo & Television Magazine* (January-February 1959)": 7.

11. Gordon Burr, email to AS, July 26, 2017.

12. L. Edgar, "The Great Morton—Adventurer, Poet," *McGill Daily* (February 26, 1953): 2, PTM Collection, NLA.

13. Julianna Jenkins, email to AS, July 28, 2017.

14. University of California (Los Angeles), *1950–1951 General Catalog*, accessed April 12, 2018, at: https://registrar.ucla.edu/file/b21f64a4-4d88-4f22-bae9-2451e083973c.

15. Cecil McKenzie, "Now It's Tex the governor," *Sunday Telegraph* (August 31, 1980).

16. "Western University of Health Sciences," Wikipedia, accessed April 12, 2022, at: https://en.wikipedia.org/wiki/Western_University_of_Health_Sciences. There is also a Pacific Western University, located in San Diego. (Morton claimed to have been awarded a doctorate from this institution in one newspaper article.) The university, however, appears to be an unaccredited distance-learning university founded in late 1976. In 1988 it offered a "nine-months-to-a-Ph.D." degree for US $1675. There is no solid evidence in Morton's papers in the NLA that suggests he gained a properly certified degree or higher degree.

17. BL, telephone conversation with AS, August 6, 2018.

18. Map of McGill University, accessed April 12, 2022, at: http://www.physics.mcgill.ca/gen/campus.html; McGill University Campus map, accessed April 12, 2022, at: http://maps.mcgill.ca/?zoom=16&lat=45.50537766786356&lng=-73.5779481927205&campus=DWT&txt=EN&theme=&id=.

19. Gordon Spittle, *TMS* (Auckland: GWS Publications, 2008): 81.

20. Stephen Steiner, cited from Gordon Spittle, *TMS* (Auckland: GWS Publications, 2008): 81.

21. "The Rather Amazing Mr. Morton," advertising booklet or program, n.d., PTM Collection, NLA; Gordon Spittle, *TMS* (Auckland: GWS Publications, 2008): 81.

22. Barbara Nathan, "McGill Mummies Mesmerised as Morton Molds Masses," *McGill Daily* 42, no. 46 (December 4, 1952); press clipping, unidentified source, n.d., PTM Collection, NLA.

23. L. Edgar, "The Great Morton-Adventurer . . . Poet," *McGill Daily* (February 26, 1953): 2, PTM Collection, NLA.

24. "Popular Hypnotist Here," clipping, unidentified Hong Kong newspaper, n.d., PTM Collection, NLA.

25. TM, typewritten essay, PTM Collection, NLA. In another document, TM stated, "I'm a Christian, and I believe in the teachings of Christ", TM, typewritten essay, n.d., PTM Collection, NLA.

26. BL and KM, telephone conversations with AS, January 24, 2022.

27. Robert Genter, "'Hypnotizzy' in the Cold War: The American Fascination with Hypnotism in the 1950s," *Journal of American Culture* 29, no 2 (2006), accessed April 10, 2018, at: http://onlinelibrary.wiley.com/doi/10.1111/j.1542-734X.2006.00326.x/full; "The Bridey Murphy Saga: Yesterday's News, Vol. V," *Denver Public Library Genealogy, African American & Western History Resources*, accessed April 15, 2022, at: https://history.denverlibrary.org/news/bridey-murphy-saga-yesterdays-news-vol-v.

28. Derren Brown, *Tricks of the Mind* (London: Channel 4 Books, 2006): 126–27.

29. "Pipes for Pitchmen," *Billboard Magazine* (July 17, 1948): 94.

30. "National Guild of Hypnotists," *Wikipedia*, accessed April 8, 2022, at: https://en.wikipedia.org/wiki/National_Guild_of_Hypnotists.

31. Martin Keily, quoted from "Resources: NGH, About us," *MartinKeilyHypnosis.com*. Accessed April 2017, at: http://martinkielyhypnosis.com/about-national-guild-of-hypnotists/.

32. Rexford L. North, "The Case for Stage Hypnotism," *Journal of Hypnotism* 1, no. 4 (November 1951): 11–12.

33. Gordon Spittle, *TMS* (Auckland: GWS Publications, 2008): 83.

34. Harry Arons, "How to Make Money with Hypnotism," *Journal of Hypnotism* 1, no. 1 (May 1951) : 3; "Anyone Can Develop Hypnotic Ability," *Journal of Hypnotism* 1, no. 1 (May 1951): 5, 18.

35. Herbert Charles, "Man Loses Savings—Hypnotism to Blame?," *Journal of Hypnotism* 2, no. 3 (May 1951): 9–11,

36. "Our Cover Personality," *Journal of Hypnotism* 3, no. 1 (September-October 1953): 15.

37. "National Guild of Hypnotists," *Wikipedia*, accessed April 12, 2022, at: https://en.wikipedia.org/wiki/National_Guild_of_Hypnotists.

38. Pat Pearce, "Spotlight on Stage and Screen," Montreal *Herald* (October 4, 1951), PTM Collection, NLA.

39. Patrick Tennison, "Morton Rides Again," *The Bulletin* (October 2, 1965): 28. Morton's comments were made over 50 years ago, and some would not be appropriate today.

40. Terence Watts, quoted from "Stage Hypnosis—How and Why It Works," *selfhypnosis.com*, accessed April 6, 2022, at: http://www.selfhypnosis.com/stage-hypnosis/; "Terence Watts, Writer Innovator & Trainer", Terence Watts home page, accessed April 26, 2022, at: https://terencewatts.com/.

41. Advertisement in unidentified newspaper, n.d., ca. 1970, PTM Collection, NLA.

42. Amanda Barnier, quoted from Wendy Zuckerman, "Science vs podcast looks into the world of hypnotism, and if it's really legitimate, *news.com.au*, accessed June 2017, at: http://www.news.com.au/technology/science/science-vs-podcast-looks-into-the-world-of-hypnotism-and-if-its-really-legitimate/news-story/51d625b7a7f207500fd29ea2639f9bd8.

43. Barbara Nathan, "McGill Mummies Mesmerised as Morton Molds Masses," *McGill Daily* 42, no. 46 (December 4, 1952); press clipping, unidentified source, n.d., PTM Collection, NLA.

44. James Palmer, "Clinical Air Marks Show by Hypnotist," *Evansville Courier* (March 11, 1953): 24, PTM Collection, NLA.

45. "The Great Morton Captive Audience Applauds Skill," Hongkong [sic] *South China Morning Post* (June 23, 1962), PTM Collection, NLA.

46. Gerry Taylor, quoted from "The Amazing Great Morton And Sweet Sounds With Balloons," New Brunswick *Daily-Gleaner* (2014); Fred Isenor, email to AS, July 25, 2017

47. "Esquire, Boston", *Variety Magazine* (May 7,1954), with penciled notes about recent takings, PTM Collection, NLA.

48. "World's Greatest Hypnotist Had Amazing Career," *Atikokan Progress* (November 11, 1954), PTM Collection, NLA.

49. "Association, Imagination and Location," *AcademicTips.olrg*, accessed April 2017, at: https://www.academictips.org/memory/assimloc.html.

50. "How Your Learning Style Affects Your Use of Mnemonics," *AcademicTips.org*, accessed April 6, 2022, at: https://www.academictips.org/memory/mnemlsty.html.

51. Mike Burraston, cited from PB email to AS April 30, 2017.

Chapter 15

1. Press report, *Illinois State Register* (February 15, 1955): 12, PTM Collection, NLA.
2. PB to AS, letter, December 10, 1990.
3. 1957 insurance policy, copy, PTM Collection, NLA.
4. BL interview, with RW, NLA, ORAL TRC 6124/25, October 12, 2010.
5. BL, telephone conversation with AS, May 31, 2017.
6. Ken Brumley, quoted from Ken Brumley to AS, letter, January 8, 1996.
7. Robert Feldman, "Tex Morton Has 'Em really Swooning In The Aisles," Sydney *Telegraph* (June 28, 1953), PTM Collection, NLA.
8. "Service Department," *CWS Magazine*, no. 20 (Oct-Nov-Dec 1957): 34.
9. EW, "Australian News", *CWS Magazine*, no. 22 (April-May-June 1958): 16.
10. Copy of contract, PTM Collection, NLA.
11. Herbert Whittaker, "The Fifty Glorious Years of the Royal Alexandra's Reign," *The Globe Magazine* (August 24, 1957): 25, PTM Collection, NLA. TM's photograph was displayed in a gallery of star performers, including Yul Brynner, Mae West, Orson Welles, Raymond Massey, Helen Hayes, Margot Fonteyn and Ethel Barrymore.
12. "The Great Morton—Hypnotism," unidentified newspaper, probably New Brunswick, n.d., PTM Collection, NLA.
13. "'The Great Morton' Is Master Showman," unidentified Canadian newspaper, Fort William, n.d., PTM Collection, NLA.
14. "Great Morton Pleases Audience; Repeats Tonight," unidentified newspaper, n.d., PTM Collection, NLA.

15. TM, radio interview by Bill Burraston, ca. 1970.

16. "Audience Members Put To Sleep By Hypnotist Morton," unidentified newspaper, n.d., PTM Collection, NLA.

17. TM, recording artist, "The Cremation of Sam McGee" and "The Shooting of Dan McGrew" were on the album *The Tex Morton Story*, Festival label FL7093, FX-10548. There are reportedly different versions of these that were also recorded in North America: see "Tex Morton," Praguefrank's Country Music Discographies, accessed April 12, 2022, at: http://countrydiscography.blogspot.com.au/2011/11/tex-morton.html. Hank Snow recorded an album consisting mainly of Service's poetry in 1968, some years after Morton's narrations: Hank Snow, recording artist, *Tales of the Yukon*, RCA recording label RCA Victor, LSP-4032.

18. Review of TM show, *The Russell Banner*, Manitoba (March 6, 1958): 1, PTM Collection, NLA.

19. Wally Davis, "Dr Morton's Show Proves Big Hit," Flin Flon *Daily Reminder* 35, no. 48 (March 19, 1958): 1, PTM Collection, NLA.

20. BL, telephone conversation with AS, July 20, 2017; "Dr Morton's Show Proves Big Hit," Flin Flon *Daily Reminder* 35, no. 48 (March 19, 1958): 1, PTM Collection, NLA.

21. "Marjolaine Hebert Biography," *IMDb*, accessed April 6, 2022, at: http://www.imdb.com/name/nm0405692/bio?mode=desktop&ref_=m_ft_dsk; "Marjolaine Hebert," *Wikipedia*, accessed April 5, 2022, at: https://fr.wikipedia.org/wiki/Marjolaine_H%C3%A9bert.

22. Photograph of TM with Hebert in Canada, unidentified newspaper, n.d., PTM Collection, NLA; Viageds Estriens, "Marjolaine Hebert," *pressreader*, accessed April 6, 2022, at: https://www.pressreader.com/canada/la-tribune2636/20170617/282600262870314.

23. BL, telephone conversations with AS, September 6, 2019, and January 21, 2020.

24. CM, "My Mate Sold Elvis Presley," *EM Magazine* (September 9, 1967).

25. "Tex of all Trades," unidentified newspaper, n.d., PTM Collection, NLA.

26. "Many Mr. Mortons," *ABC Weekly* (September 1959): 13, PTM Collection, NLA.

27. TM discography, *Praguefrank's Country Music Discographies*, accessed January 19, 2019, at: http://countrydiscography.blogspot.com/2011/11/tex-morton.html.

28. Brendan Hancock, and Matthew Schelle, "The Festival Records Story, accessed April 6, 2022, at: http://shamanalternative.com/site/wp-content/uploads/2015/08/FESTIVAL_RECORDS_STORY_PART_1.pdf.

29. Hal Saunders to PB, letter, August 30, 1989.

30. TM, recording artist, *The Tex Morton Story*, Festival label, Festival FL-7093, FX-10548.

31. Hal Saunders to PB, letter, August 30, 1989.

32. Goebel Reeves, recording artist, "The Cowboy's Prayer," Regal Zonophone label, Regal Zonophone G22363.

33. Carson Robison Trio, recording artists, "Home on The Range," Regal Zonophone label, Regal Zonophone G21835.

34. copies of TM's ham radio licences, PTM Collection, NLA; photograph of TM with call sign "VE2AHZ," accessed April 20, 2022, at: https://www.audioculture.co.nz/profile/tex-morton; Gordon Spittle, *TMS* (Auckland: GWS Publications 2008): 92.

35. "The Great Morton Has An Accident," *Steinbach Carillon* (November 14, 1958): 5, suggests TM was still in Canada in November 1958. The paper reported that Morton had been involved in a car accident and his show had been postponed by two weeks.

36. BL, quoted from BL, interview by RW, ORAL TRC 6124/25, NLA, October 12, 2010.

37. John Edwards, annotated comments provided by the JEMF, accompanying John Edwards, discography, *The Yodelling Boundary Rider, Tex Morton: A Discography*, Southern Folklife Collection, Wilson Library, University of North Carolina, Chapel Hill, NC. Provided courtesy of the John Edwards Foundation; Fred Hoeptner, email to AS, September 17, 2017.

38. John Edwards, annotated comment in John Edwards, discography, *The Yodelling Boundary Rider, Tex Morton: A Discography*, Southern Folklife Collection, Wilson Library, University of North Carolina, Chapel Hill, NC. Provided courtesy of the John Edwards Foundation.

39. TM, photographs of Boys' Town concert, dated 1958, PTM Collection, NLA.

40. Letterhead on stationery used by TM, PTM Collection, NLA.

41. "Gene Autry's Melody Ranch," *Wikipedia*, accessed April 5, 2022, at: https://en.wikipedia.org/wiki/Gene_Autry%27s_Melody_Ranch; Pat Ware, "Tex Morton's Triumphant Return To Australia," *Tempo and Television Magazine* (January-February 1959): 5-6.

42. Richard (Dick) Hill to AS, letter, February 10, 1990.

43. PB email to AS, 20 June 2017.

44. Gordon Spittle, *TMS* (Auckland: GWS Publications 2008): 87. *Blood On The Rio Grande* does not appear in recognized Gene Autry filmographies, eg in Holly George-Warren, *Public Cowboy no. 1 The Life and Times of Gene Autry* (New York: Oxford University Press, 2007): 382–85.

45. "Gene Autry filmography," *Wikipedia*, accessed April 5, 2022, at: https://en.wikipedia.org/wiki/Gene_Autry_filmography.

46. Marva Felchin (Director, Libraries and Archives of the Autry Museum of the American West), email to AS, December 8, 2017; Gene Autry Museum to AS, letter, n.d. ca. 1990s.

47. "The Fabulous Tex Morton," *Tempo & Television Magazine* (January-February 1959): 7; Gordon Spittle, *TMS* (Auckland: GWS Publications, 2008): 87.

48. EW. *CMA*, 2 (Sydney: Angus and Robertson Publishers, 1983): 21.

49. EW *CMA*, 2 (Sydney: Angus and Robertson Publishers, 1983): 23.

50. Gordon Spittle, *TMS*, (Auckland: GWS Publications,2008): 86.

51. John E. Reed, photograph of Tex Morton, cited, and caption text, quoted in *TWS*, contributor Gordon Spittle (Auckland: GWS Publications), 86. The writer of the caption text for the photograph is undocumented in this book; "John E. Reed Hollywood Glamour," The New Found Photography, accessed April 6, 2022, at: http://thenewfoundphotography.blogspot.com/2009/07/john-e-reed-hollywood-glamour.html.

52. Gordon Spittle, *TMS* (Auckland: GWS Publications, 2008): 87.

53. Ibid.; "Gunsmoke (1955–1975) Full Cast & Crew," *IMDb*, accessed April 6, 2022, at: http://www.imdb.com/title/tt0047736/fullcredits/.

54. "One Man Show will be at National Tonight," Launceston *Examiner* (November 20, 1959), PTM Collection, NLA.

55. "Sergeant Preston of the Yukon (TV series)," *Wikipedia*, accessed April 6, 2022, at: https://en.wikipedia.org/wiki/Sergeant_Preston_of_the_Yukon_(TV_series)

56. "Sergeant Preston," *IMDb*, accessed April 6, 2022, at: https://www.imdb.com/find?q=Sergeant+Preston&ref_=nv_sr_sm.

57. Gordon Spittle, *TMS* (Auckland: GWS Publications, 2008): 58–59, 87; "The Fabulous Tex Morton." *Tempo & Television Magazine* (January-February 1959): 7.

58. List of guests on the Steve Allen Show, *tv.com*, accessed May 2017, at: http://www.tv.com/shows/the-steve-allen-show/episodes/. This link is now not active.

59. "The Ed Sullivan Show," *IMDb*, accessed April 6, 2022, at: https://www.imdb.com/title/tt0040053/.

60. *The Last Ride Of Tex Morton*, documentary, DVD, Attitude Productions, 2001.

61. David Smith to AS, letter, October 19, 1989.

62. TM, resume for The Bolt/Williams Agency, n.d., PTM Collection, NLA.

63. *Arsenic and Old Lace*, Google Books accessed April 12, 2022, at: https://books.google.com.au/books?id=y_IRgM7FD9YC&printsec=frontcover&dq=Arsenic+And+Old+Lace&hl=en&sa=X&ved=0ahUKEwje7v-Ii7XUAhVLvbwKHeBnAsQQ6AEIJjAA#v=onepage&q=Arsenic%20And%20Old%20Lace&f=false.

64. "Strange Cargo," *IMDb*, accessed April 12, 2022, at: http://www.imdb.com/title/tt0033105/.

65. TM, resume for The Bolt/Williams Agency, n.d., PTM Collection, NLA.

66. "Annie Oakley (TV series)," *Wikipedia*, accessed April 12, 2022, at: https://en.wikipedia.org/wiki/Annie_Oakley_(TV_series).

67. "Circus Boy Full Cast & Crew," *IMDb*, accessed July 12, 2022, at: http://www.imdb.com/title/tt0048855/fullcredits?ref_=tt_cl_sm#cast.

68. Janet Lorenz, (National Film Information Service, Academy Foundation, to AS, letter, November 6, 1990; "Tex Morton" (obituary), *Variety* Magazine (July 27): 19.

69. TM, copy of Australian resume, PTM Collection, NLA.

70. "Lux Videom Theatre," *Wikipedia*, accessed April 12, 2022, at: https://en.wikipedia.org/wiki/Lux_Video_Theatre.

71. Gordon Spittle, *TMS* (Auckland: GWS Publications, 2008): 87.

72. Television guide, November 14, 1958, PTM Collection, NLA (the year was based on the date of Friday November 14, which corresponds to the year 1958); "Lux Playhouse," *CTVA- The Classic TV Archive*, accessed April 15, 2022, at: http://ctva.biz/US/Anthology/LuxPlayhouse.htm CPTM Collection, NLA.

73. CM, "I Made Good Without Knowing It," *EM Magazine* (July 26, 1967); Ron Randell, reference for TM, July 22, 1958, PTM Collection, NLA.

74. Gordon Spittle, *TMS* (Auckland: GWS Publications, 2008): 87.

75. "Peter Finch," *Wikipedia*, accessed April 12, 2022, at: https://en.wikipedia.org/wiki/Peter_Finch.

76. "Errol Flynn," *Wikipedia*, accessed April 12, 2022, at: https://en.wikipedia.org/wiki/Errol_Flynn.

Chapter 16

1. KM, telephone conversation with AS, June 7, 2017.
2. "Legend of show biz began long career as street busker," Historical feature about TM, Sydney *Daily Mirror* (September 28, 1983): 56.
3. "Prettiest Smoky Mountain Boy" cited in "June Webb," *Wikipedia*, accessed April 25, 2022, at: https://en.wikipedia.org/wiki/June_Webb.
4. Pete Kirby to AS, letter, January 30, 1996. (Kirby was Acuff's Dobro player.) Frankie Moore's name was spelled as "More" on the official program; promotional advertisement for the Wilburn Brothers, PTM Collection, NLA.
5. "Roy Acuff C & W Show," *Music Maker Magazine* (March 1959), 2; "Folk Talent & Tunes," *Billboard Magazine* (February 16, 1959): 18.
6. Peggy McCloud and Mike McCloud, *Bashful Brother Oswald: That's The Truth If I've Ever Told It* (Madison, Tennessee: privately published by B.R. & Euneta Kirby, 1994): 82, gave the tour dates as February 19 (arrival) to April 26 (departure).
7. "The Fabulous Tex Morton," *Tempo & Television Magazine* (January-February 1959): 7.
8. "Ray Brown Reports on the Roy Acuff Show in Sydney," *CWS Magazine* (April-May-June 1959): 24.
9. TM's claim to have appeared on The Grand Ole Opry cited from "Television Parade", *Australian Women's Weekly* (March 11, 1959): 50 and "Tex Morton," *Australian Country Music Hall of Fame*, accessed April 26, 2022, at: https://ehive.com/collections/200851/objects/1461088/tex-morton; Bob Pinson to AS, letter ca. 1990. Pinson wrote that he had searched the Opry archives but could find no mention of TM.
10. *Grand Ole Opry Tour* booklet, 1959, PTM Collection, NLA.
11. "Ray Brown Reports on the Roy Acuff Show in Sydney," *CWS Magazine* (April-May-June 1959): 24.
12. Alexander Macdonald, "Night at the Grand Ole Opry," *Weekend Magazine* (March 8, 1959): 24.
13. "Alexander John Macdonald (1916–1973)," in *Australian Dictionary of Biography, Vol. 15*, accessed June 2017, at: https://adb.anu.edu.au/biography/macdonald-alexander-john-10926.
14. Elizabeth Schlappi, *Roy Acuff: The Smoky Mountain Boy* (Gretna: Pelican, 1978): 244.
15. "Grand Ole Opry A Grand Ole Flop," *Tempo & Television Magazine* (February-March-April 1959): 22.
16. "The Grand Ole (Fl)Opry ... or ... Who Goofed It," *CWS Magazine* (April—May-June 1959): 1.
17. Ibid.
18. "The Grand Ole Opry Stadium Show," *Tempo & Television Magazine* (February-April 1959): 29.

19. Money loss figure cited in Graeme Smith, 2005, *Singing Australian: A History of Folk and Country Music*. (Melbourne: Pluto Press 2005): 95; "Acuff Show Folds 'no support,'" *Music Maker Magazine* (April 1959): 3; Ray Brown, "Country & Western Music," *Music Maker Magazine* (July 1960): 33. £10 000 = $20 000.

20. Athol McCoy, interview by HC, September 9, 1989.

21. Johnny Ashcroft, cited from PB, email to AS, May 26, 2020.

22. EW, "Memo—Mr Acuff," *CWS Magazine* (April-May-June 1959): 27.

23. HC, email to AS, June 10, 2017.

24. TM, interview by Jim Branford, 5AN-Adelaide, ca. 1981. A tape of the interview was provided by Mike O'Malley for AS, 1991.

25. Buck Carson, telephone conversation with AS, June 26, 2019. Carson stated that Morton seemed proud that he had "fired a millionaire," although he wasn't promoting the show in the first place.

26. Pete Kirby to AS, letter, January 30, 1996; June Webb, *Facebook* message to AS, 2011.

27. Pete Kirby to AS, letter, January 30, 1996; Athol McCoy, interview by HC, September 9, 1989.

28. Athol McCoy, quoted from Athol McCoy with AS, telephone conversation, February 6, 1994.

29. Undocumented attribution, Gayle Dean Wardlow. *Facebook* post, June 30, 2020.

30. Max Ellis, "Country Music Capital Meets Music City", June 2002, accessed April 12, 2022, at: http://www.historyofcountrymusic.com.au/cmcmmc.html.

31. Max Ellis, telephone conversation with AS, April 27, 2020.

32. Elizabeth Schlappi, *Roy Acuff: The Smoky Mountain Boy* (Gretna: Pelican, 1978): 244.

33. TM, interview with Jim Branford, 5AN (Adelaide), ca. 1981. Recording provided by Mike O'Malley for AS, 1991.

34. Elizabeth Schlappi, *Roy Acuff: The Smoky Mountain Boy* (Gretna: Pelican, 1978): 243–44; Gayel Pitchford, *Fiddler of the Opry: The Howdy Forrester Story* (Tehachapi: Viewpoint Press, 2007): 87.

35. Alan Stoker of the Country Music Foundation thought that the *Open House* shows were made to compete with the well-known Albert Gannaway television shows of the 1950s. Acuff, he thought, had refused to appear on the Gannaway shows because he wasn't going to be paid sufficiently. "The quality [of the *Open House* shows was not very good and Acuff lost money on them when few stations aired them," (Alan Stoker, *Facebook* comment, April 17, 2020).

36. "'Open House' Big Success Overseas," *Australian Women's Weekly* (October 21, 1959): 60. £700 000 = $1 400 000.

37. Advertisement for TM show, Launceston *Examiner* (October 20, 1959).

38. "One-man show will be at National tonight," Launceston *Examiner* (October 20, 1959); "25 Years of International Fund-Raising," Launceston *Examiner* (October 13, 1959).

39. "A Message from St. Giles," PTM Collection, NLA. Terms such as "crippled children" to describe disabilities have not been used in Australia, officially, for decades. Launceston *Examiner* (September 30, 1959); Launceston *Examiner* (September 17, 1959).

40. "Australian Broadcasting Commission," *The Canberra Times* (October 7, 1959): 15.
41. "Tex Morton Here To Benefit Intellectually Handicapped Children," *Wanganui Herald* (April 7, 1960); "New School for Handicapped," *Press* (August 3, 1960): 7; "Sharpshooter Lights Target," *Evening Post* (June 15, 1960): 25, PTM Collection, NLA.
42. Article about TM, unidentified newspaper, n.d., PTM Collection, NLA.
43. Morton's show takings, cited from article clipping, unidentified newspaper (probably Tasmanian), n.d., PTM Collection, NLA.
44. "Tex Morton Show Proves Highly Popular," Dunedin *Evening Star* (September 2, 1960), PTM Collection, NLA. £800 = $1600; £1400 = $2800.
45. "'Tex' Morton Provides Versatile Entertainment", *Press* (July 19, 1960): 17.
46. "Tex Morton Returns After Ten Years," unidentified, newspaper, n.d., PTM Collection, NLA.
47. Ossi Kohi incident, cited from "Search Directions Under Hypnosis" and "Mystery is solved in trance," unidentified newspapers, n.d., PTM Collection, NLA.
48. Advertisement, Penrith *Nepean Times* (March 9, 1961): 10.
49. Advertisement, *The Canberra Times* (October 12, 1961): 19; "Around Canberra with a Camera," *The Canberra Times* (October 16, 1961): 8.
50. TM, recording artist, *Tex Morton Looks Back*, Festival label, Festival FL-31,152.
51. Otto Gray and His Oklahoma Cowboys, recording artists, "Cat Came Back," Panachord label, Panachord 12126.
52. Hal Saunders to AS, letter, July 22, 1990. TM, recording artist, *Tex Morton Looks Back*, Festival long-play album, Festival FL-7257/FL-31,152; £100 = $200.
53. TM, recording artist, *The Tex Morton Story*, Festival label, Festival FL 7093.
54. Archie Green, *Only A Miner: Studies in Recorded Coal-Mining Songs* (Chicago: University of Illinois Press, 1972): 118.
55. Hal Saunders to PB, letter, August 30, 1989.
56. "Turntable Talk," *The Biz Magazine* (December 19, 1962): 11; TM, *The Versatile Tex Morton*, Festival label, Festival FL-30,935.
57. TM, *Tex Morton Looks Back*, Festival label, Festival FL-31,152.
58. Hal Saunders to AS, letter, July 22, 1990.
59. EW, "Eric Watson Reports From NSW," *CWS Magazine* (October-November-December 1959): 24.
60. TM, recording artist, *The Sentimental Bloke By C.J. Dennis* Festival label FL-30,092/3; TM, recording artist, *Tex Morton Reads Banjo Paterson, Festival label* , Festival FL-30,876/7.
61. Hal Saunders to AS, letter, July 22, 1990.
62. Record reviews, *Australian Women's Weekly* (October 31, 1962): 7.
63. Record reviews, *Australian Women's Weekly* (September 6, 1961): 9.
64. KM, telephone conversation with AS, June 7, 2017.
65. Hal Saunders to AS, letter, July 22, 1990.
66. JM to AS, letter, October 14, 1990.
67. Hal Saunders to AS, letter, July 22, 1990. £100 = $200.
68. Ibid. £250 = $500.

69. Ibid.

70. "Hal Saunders Quits Festival," *Billboard Magazine* (July 31, 1965): 26.

71. Hal Saunders to AS, letter, August 30, 1989.

72. The distance is between 48 kilometers and 64 kilometers.

73. Hal Saunders to AS, letter, July 22, 1990.

74. TM, recording artist, "Kevin Barrie" [sic], Festival long-play album *The Versatile Tex Morton*, Festival label, Festival FL 30,935.

75. Charlie Moore, recording artist, "Rebel Soldier", *The Original Rebel Soldier*, Rebel Records label, Rebel REB-1662. Hank Locklin recorded "Kevin Barry" on the long-play album, *Irish Songs, Country Style*, RCA label, LPM-2801, in 1964.

76. Neville Pellitt, *A Country Voice 55+ Years on Air* (privately published, Golden Square: Moonlight Publishing): 45.

Chapter 17

1. CM and other journalists, interviews by AS, July 17, 1990.

2. "Hypnotist Shows His Power," Hong Kong *South China Morning Post* (June 14, 1962): 4, PTM Collection, NLA.

3. Unidentified Hong Kong newspaper clipping, n.d., PTM Collection, NLA.

4. Ibid.

5. "The Great Morton Captive Audience Applauds Skill," Hong Kong *South China Morning Post*, n.d, PTM Collection, NLA.

6. Five meters = 5 yards (15 feet).

7. Frank Crook, "The tale of a lazy oyster eater," *Daily Mirror* (May 30, 1978): 12.

8. Gordon Spittle, *TMS* (Auckland: GWS Publications, 2008): 91.

9. KM, telephone conversation with AS, November 7, 2018.

10. Hal Saunders to AS, letter, July 22, 1990.

11. "Television and Radio," *The Canberra Times* (November 22, 1963): 25; "This Week on CTC-7," *The Canberra Times* (November 18, 1963): 13.

12. KM, telephone conversation with AS, June 7, 2017.

13. KM, telephone conversation with AS, September 25, 2019.

14. KM, telephone conversation with AS, June 7, 2017.

15. "The Monaro Mall Series of special attractions," *The Canberra Times* (March 4, 1965): 30; advertisement, *The Canberra Times* (March 9, 1965): 11; advertisement, *The Canberra Times* (March 9, 1965): 7.

16. "Mall Canberra," *The Canberra Times* (March 5, 1965): 24.

17. "Second Birthday Celebrations—the theme is old fashioned values," *The Canberra Times* (March 4, 1965): 23.

18. Advertisement, Melbourne *Sun* (September 11, 1965): 21.

19. Patrick Tennison, "Morton Rides Again," *The Bulletin Magazine* (October 2, 1965): 28.

20. Tennison, "Morton Rides Again," 28.

21. TM, recording artist, *Sing Smile and Sigh*, Festival label, Festival FL-31,720.

22. *TM, recording artist, "Sing, Smile and Sigh,"* Festival label, Festival FL-31,720; TM, recording artist, *Robert 'Tex' Morton's Reading Of Ginger Mick*, Festival label, Festival FL-31,685; TM, recording artist, *The Sentiment And Humour Of Banjo Paterson, as read by Robert (Tex) Morton*, Festival label, Festival FL-31,696; TM, recording artist, *I Like Looking At Planets, Festival label, Festival* FL-31,758 (narration on Peter Scriven's *Original Tintookies* soundtrack).

23. TM, recording artist, "Tex Morton's Protest Song," Columbia (EMI) label, Columbia DO-4762. According to Trevor Day, the "Ratbag" mentioned in the song referred to Barry Hampshire, a friend of Morton's (Trevor Day to HC, letter, June 19, 1995).

24. TM, recording artist, "Tex Morton's Protest Song (Burn Another Folkie)" / "(The) Green, Green Grass of Home", EMI label, EMI DO-4762; DC, email to AS, September 7, 2021.

25. TM, recording artist, "I Got You (Right Out of My Mind)," Columbia (EMI) label, Columbia DO-8303, Morton recorded the song in 1953 as "I've Got You (Right Out Of My Mind)," Philips label, Philips P-24506-H.

26. TM, cited from liner notes to TM, recording artist, "Welcome to the Club," *Tex Morton Encores*, EMI AXIS label, AXIS 6327.

27. TM, cited from liner notes to TM, recording artist, *Tex Morton Encores*, EMI AXIS label AXIS 6327.

28. Ibid.

29. Ibid.

30. "Irma Jackson," *Wikipedia*, accessed April 18, 2022, at: https://en.wikipedia.org/wiki/Irma_Jackson.

31. Jim Bowditch to AS, letter, October 14, 1990.

32. Thirty meters = 30 yards.

33. Jim Bowditch to AS, letter, October 14, 1990.

34. TM, cited from liner notes to TM, *Tex Morton Encores*, EMI AXIS label, AXIS 6327.

35. TM, undated typewritten article, PTM Collection, NLA.

36. "Victoria Hotel, Darwin," *Wikipedia*, accessed April 10, 2022, at: https://en.wikipedia.org/wiki/Victoria_Hotel,_Darwin.

37. Athol McCoy, "King of Australia's Country Music," *Bega and District Times* (August 3, 1983): 1.

38. Athol McCoy and Eileen McCoy, interview by RW and Kevin Bradley, NLA 186493, 1993–1994.

39. TM, recording artist, "The Martins and the Coys," Regal Zonophone label, Regal Zonophone G23529.

40. Athol McCoy, quoted from Athol McCoy with HC, interview, September 9, 1989.

41. Athol McCoy, "Never Was There a Greater Showman," *Capital News* 8, no. 10 (September 1983): 4.

42. "King of Australia's Country Music," *Bega and District Times* (August 3, 1983): 1.

43. Joy McKean, *I've Been There and Back Again* (Sydney: Hachette Australia, 2011): 65.
44. Ibid.
45. CM and other journalists, interviews by AS, July 17, 1990.
46. Alan Turley, typescript of article sent to PB by Kim Lane, September 23, 2002.
47. KM, telephone conversation with AS, June 7, 2017.
48. Kevin King, telephone conversation with AS, March 24, 2019.
49. CM and other journalists, interviews by AS, July 17, 1990.
50. Buck Carson, telephone conversation with AS, August 7, 2017.
51. Buck Carson, telephone conversation with AS March 8, 2019.
52. Both sources were contacted by AS, but they have not been identified here as they wish to remain anonymous.
53. Garry Coxhead, *Facebook* message, July 28, 2017.
54. Trevor Day, telephone conversation with AS, May 6, 2019.
55. Buck Carson, telephone conversation with AS, August 7, 2017.
56. JM, "Australian Pioneer's Colourful Past," *Capital News* (July 1993): 5.
57. Kevin King, telephone conversations with AS, March 22 and 24, 2019.
58. TM cited in "John Berry," No hill-billy tag for Tex," *Sunday News* (May 19, 1968); "Tex Objects 'I'm no hillbilly,' says Tex," unidentified magazine n.d., ca. 1960s.
59. David Hardy, email to AS, July 24, 2019. Hardy wrote: "The first three EMI re-issue long-play albums—*Songs of the Outback*, *Sentimental Tex* and *Goin' Back to Texas*—were full-priced long-play albums. When these were first available, they were priced at 52/6 [about $5.25], which was a lot of money at the time and not many people could afford to buy long-play albums. *Sentimental Tex* was later issued on a budget pressing as *The Black Sheep*, with two extra tracks added from the 45-rpm extended-play *Travel By Train* (SEGO 70088)".
60. TM, *Songs of The Outback*, EMI label, EMI OSX 7631.
61. TM, recording artist, *Sentimental Tex*" EMI label EMI OSX 7749; TM, *Goin' Back To Texas*, EMI label, EMI OSX 7766; sales figures cited from DC, email to AS, August 6, 2017.
62. TM, recording artist, *The Tex Morton Regal Zonophone Collection*, 5 long-play vinyl records, EMI label, EMI EMBB 430051. The set was reissued on compact disc in 1993 on two double compact disc sets: TM, recording artist, *The Tex Morton Regal Zonophone Collection, Volume 1 (1936–1938)*, EMI label, EMI 8142022; TM, recording artist, *The Tex Morton Regal Zonophone Collection, Volume 2 (1938–1943)*, EMI label, EMI 8142052. According to EMI executive Bill Robertson, both the vinyl and compact-disc sets sold well (Bill Robertson, email to AS, June 11, 2017).
63. TM, recording artist, *You and My Old Guitar: The Original Tasman/Rodeo Recordings New Zealand 1949*, Festival double long-play vinyl records, Festival label L-45823/4; TM, recording artist, *You and My Old Guitar: The Original Tasman/Rodeo Recordings New Zealand 1949*, Festival label, Festival compact disc D 19815.
64. Radio programs reissued on the Kingfisher label: cassette tapes: *Greetings from Australia* (AUS-1); *On Air 1948 / Showtime Radio* (AUS-7); *TM On Air 1948* (AUS-8); *All*

Set and Saddled, parts 1—4 (AUS-28/29); *TM Yodelling Cowboy* (AUS-31); *TM The Lost Broadcasts of 1942* (AUS-32/33).

65. CM, "I Should Have Been a Presbyterian Minister," *EM Magazine* (July 19, 1967); CM, "I Made Good Without Knowing It," *EM Magazine* (July 26, 1967); CM, "I Had Two Trains To Call My Own," *EM* Magazine (August 2, 1967); CM, "My Mate Sold Elvis Presley," *EM Magazine* (September 9, 1967). Note: in "I Should Have Been a Presbyterian Minister," Mackay's name is spelled as "MacKay."

66. CM and other journalists, interviews with AS, July 17, 1990.

67. Ibid.

68. Ibid.

69. Malcolm Andrews, "Aussie seeks an honor for Tex," *Daily Telegraph* (city edition) (January 21, 1985).

70. Jim Oram, cited from *The Last Showman: Larry Dulhunty's Larrikin Life*, extract, sent by Oram to HC, September 15, 1993.

Chapter 18

1. "Tex Of All Trades," New Zealand *Womens Weekly* (October 2, 1967), PTM Collection, NLA.

2. "Tex Morton to Perform in Otematata," article clipping, newspaper, identified only as *Chronicle*, September 14, 1967, PTM Collection, NLA.

3. "Maria Dallas Show Fast And Bright," *Press* (September 14, 1967), PTM Collection, NLA; for a different review see "Show, Brought To Life By Maria Dallas," *Press* (September 18, 1967), in which TM was criticized for his singing and inaccurate shooting.

4. "Tex Morton—Jack Of All Trades," *Northern Advocate* (November 8, 1967), PTM Collection, NLA.

5. "Capacity Audience At Tex Morton Show", *Press* (May 29, 1960): 18; "Serenaders", *Press* (October 27, 1970): 3; "Country And Western Show Well Received," *Press* (June 11, 1968): 18.

6. "Swinging Success Of Mardi Gras," unidentified Nelson newspaper (January 6, 1969), PTM Collection, NLA.

7. Some sources give 1967 as the commencement date, but 1968 is more likely.

8. "Bryan Easte talks about 'The Country Touch,'" YouTube, accessed April 10, 2022, at: https://www.youtube.com/watch?v=hH2bGF-YoZ4.

9. Paul Trenwith, email to AS, July 30, 2017.

10. Colleen Trenwith, email to AS, June 15, 2018.

11. "Kick off your shoes . . . ," *Auckland Star* (April 13, 1968).

12. Paul Trenwith, email to AS, July 30, 2017.

13. "Bryan Easte talks about 'The Country Touch,'" YouTube, accessed April 10, 2022, at: https://www.youtube.com/watch?v=hH2bGF-YoZ4.

14. Paul Trenwith, email to AS, July 30, 2017; a 1968 stage version at Christchurch's Majestic Theatre on June 10, 1968, was reported in "Morton Returning Next Week," *Press* (June 4, 1968): 10.

15. A part of one episode is at: "Tex Morton—the Country Touch," YouTube, accessed April 18, 2022, at: https://www.youtube.com/watch?v=20sOadApark.
16. Paul Trenwith, email to AS, July 30, 2017.
17. Colleen Trenwith, email to AS, August 2, 2017.
18. Bob McClelland, "Corny But Well Done," *Auckland Star* (August 28, 1968).
19. Unidentified newspaper article, n.d., PTM Collection, NLA.
20. Unidentified newspaper article, n.d., PTM Collection, NLA
21. "Tex's Touch Just Right," *Auckland Star* (May 2, 1968).
22. TM, recording artist, *Tex Morton in New Zealand*, EMI label, SEGO 70171; sales figures cited from DC. email to AS, August 5, 2017.
23. Johnny Cash, recording artist, "A Boy Named Sue," *Johnny Cash At San Quentin*, Columbia Harmony long-play album HC 15071.
24. TM, recording artist, *Tex Morton Today*, EMI label, EMI SCXO-7933; see also "Gold in them thar LPs," *The Dominion* (March 13, 1971): 12, PTM Collection, NLA.
25. Peter Posa to HC, letter, December 12, 1995.
26. JM, "Australian Pioneer's Colourful Past," *Capital News* (July 1993): 5.
27. "Tex rides back on the mining boom," unidentified newspaper (March 5, 1971).
28. Gil Walhqist, record review, *The Sun-Herald* (December 27, 1970): 37.
29. TM, recording artist, A *Tex Morton Singalong*, EMI label, EMI SEGO-0194; sales figures cited from DC, email to AS, October 1, 2021.

Chapter 19

1. "Series' Fate Now in Balance," unidentified newspaper, n.d., PTM Collection, NLA; John Berry, "They're Movin' On," unidentified newspaper, n.d., PTM Collection, NLA. The number of series produced is not known for certain. In the first article, Easte was reported as being anxious about a third series. Paul Trenwith said three series were made, but some newspaper articles state only two series were made with TM.
2. "They're Movin' On," *New Zealand Herald* (March 28, 1970), PTM Collection, NLA.
3. "Aussie Thumbs Down to NZ Country Touch," *Lower Hutt News* (March 9, 1971), PTM Collection, NLA.
4. "Tex Morton At Home," unidentified newspaper (December 19, 1970). PTM Collection, NLA.
5. "Aussie Thumbs Down to NZ Country Touch," *Lower Hutt News* (March 9, 1971), PTM Collection, NLA; EW, *CMA, 1* (Sydney: Angus and Robertson Publishers, 1982): 24–26.
6. "Y'all Come—New Zealand country music on television 1968 to 1987," *Audioculture IWI WAIATRA*, accessed April 6, 2022, at: https://www.audioculture.co.nz/scenes/y-all-come-new-zealand-country-music-on-television-1968-to-1987.
7. Colleen Trenwith, email to AS, August 2, 2017; Paul Trenwith, email to AS, July 19, 2017.
8. Paul Trenwith, email to AS, July 30, 2017.

9. Paul Trenwith, email to AS, July 19, 2017.
10. BL, various telephone conversations to AS, 2017.
11. Paul Trenwith, email to AS, July 19, 2017.
12. 860 km = 535 miles.
13. "Dunmarra," *Australian explorer*, accessed April 6, 2022, at: https://www.australianexplorer.com/dunmarra.htm.
14. Liner notes to LP album *Tex Morton Encores*, EMI AXIS label AXIS 6327; "Barry Crump," *Wikipedia*, April 5, accessed April 10, 2022, at: https://en.wikipedia.org/wiki/Barry_Crump.
15. TM, recording artist, "Old Blue" / "Dunmarrra," Columbia (EMI) label, EMI DO-9764; DC, email to AS, March 27, 2019. Sales figures cited from from DC, email to AS, August 5, 2017.
16. Garry Coxhead, *Facebook* post, November 25, 2017. Coxhead was a very close friend of Buddy Williams.
17. Mike Burraston, cited from the article "Tex and Buddy Get Together!" *Country Music Express* 1, no. 4, April 1972: 1.
18. "Tex and Buddy Get Together!" *Country Music Express* 1, no. 4 (April 1972): 1.
19. Graham Gosper, "The fans leave Tex yodelling in the dark," unidentified newspaper (late 1972).
20. Ibid.
21. KM, telephone conversation with AS, June 7, 2017.
22. Karen Williams, telephone conversation with AS, September 12, 2017.
23. Lynette Guest, *Facebook* message, September 6, 2017; Buddy Williams, recording artist, *Aussie On My Mind*, RCA label, RCA VAL1 0136. EW, *CMA* 1 (Sydney: Angus and Robertson Publishers, 1982): 147.
24. JM, "Australian Pioneer's Colourful Past," *Capital News* (July 1993): 5.
25. TM, interview by JM, broadcast on 2TM-Tamworth, ca. 1970.
26. "A Buddy Williams Playback," *Capital News* 12, no. 12 (December 1987): 5.
27. Buddy Williams Family Get Together with Tex Morton, Sister Dorrie & The Rough Riders' Band, recording artists, "I Like Country Music," RCA label, RCA 102109 (45 single); also released on Buddy Williams & Various, recording artists, *Our Buddy—A Tribute to Buddy Williams*, (Nicholls N Dimes label VPLI 0555) in 1985, later in 1988 on EMI label AXIS 701410.
28. Lynette Guest, *Facebook* message, September 6, 2017.
29. Buck Carson, telephone conversation with AS, August 7, 2017.
30. Llewellyn Weeding, *Facebook* message, June 11, 2017.
31. Karen Williams, telephone conversation with AS, November 24, 2018.
32. Karen Williams, telephone conversation with AS, September 12, 2017.
33. Garry Coxhead, email to AS, July 28, 2017; TM, recording artist, "The Letter Edged in Black," Regal Zonophone label, Regal Zonophone G23383.
34. Lynette Guest, *Facebook* message, September 6 ,2017.
35. Slim Newton, recording artist, "The Redback on the Toilet Seat", Hadley label 7-inch

45 rpm extended play HEP 537, Hadley long-play album, Hadley label HLP 1210; "The Redback on the Toilet Seat," *Wikipedia*, accessed April 5, 2022, at: https://en.wikipedia.org/wiki/The_Redback_on_the_Toilet_Seat; David Latta, *Australian Country Music* (Sydney: Random House Australia, 1991): 13. "Redback" refers to a highly venomous spider.

36. Advertisement, Bundaberg *News-Mail*, 1972.

37. Slim Newton, telephone conversation with AS, February 12, 2018.

38. Slim Newton, letter to HC, June 2, 1995. 15 pounds = 7 kilograms.

39. Ibid.

40. Ibid.

41. Ibid.

42. Ibid.

43. KM disputes this. She said had TM been aware that Newton was in trouble, he would have assisted immediately (KM, telephone conversation with AS, October 9, 2021).

44. Slim Newton, telephone conversation with AS, February 12, 2018.

45. Slim Newton to HC, letter, June 2, 1995.

46. Slim Newton, telephone conversation with AS, February 12, 2018.

47. TM, recording artist, *Tex Morton's Australia*, Picture Records label, Picture Records PRS-001, later issued as *Tex Morton's Goondiwindi Grey*, Festival label, Festival L-36, 173; "The Goondiwindi Grey," *All Down Under*, accessed April 24, 2022, at: https://alldownunder.com/australian-music-songs/goondiwindi-grey.htm.

48. "Gunsynd," *Wikipedia*, accessed April 5, 2022, at: https://en.wikipedia.org/wiki/Gunsynd.

49. "Corn Exchange—part of Commercial Group, Statement of Significance," *NSW Government Housing and Property*, accessed April 6, 2022, at: http://www.shfa.nsw.gov.au/sydney-About_us-Heritage_role-Heritage_and_Conservation_Register.htm&objectid=154.

50. Max Ellis, email to AS, January 7, 2018.

51. Jazzer Smith, editor, *The Book of Australian Country Music 1* (Gordon: Berghouse Floyd Tuckey Publishing Group, 1984): 15.

52. "A Tribute to Tex," *History of Country Music*, accessed April 6, 2022, at: http://www.historyofcountrymusic.com.au/tributetotex.html.

53. TM, recording artist, "The Goondiwindi Grey (The Gunsynd Song)" was released as a single on Picture Records label single release PRS 001; the full album was later released as *Tex Morton's Goondiwindi Grey*, Festival label, Festival L-36,173.

54. EW, *CMA, 1* (Sydney: Angus and Robertson Publishers, 1982): 24.

55. JM, "Australian Pioneer's Colourful Past," *Capital News* (July 1993): 5.

56. Ron Hirst, cited, and John Minson, quoted, both from: John Minson, "Australian Pioneer's Colorful Life," *Capital News* (July 1993): 5.

57. Ian Hands, *Ambassadors of Country Music* (Archerfield: privately published by Ian Hands, 1984): 22.

58. Buck Carson, *Facebook* post, October 23, 2018 (edited for punctuation corrections).

59. Buck Carson, *Facebook* post, August 11, 2021 (edited for punctuation corrections).

60. Buck Carson, *Facebook* post, December 2018 (edited for punctuation corrections).
61. Trevor Day, telephone conversation with AS, May 6, 2019.
62. Johnny Heap, email to AS, December 5, 2019.
63. Terry Gordon, telephone conversation with AS, January 14, 2020.
64. Dusty Rankin, interview by RW and John Harpley, NLA Oral TRC 3388/109, 1997.
65. SPASM was an advertising agency established by John Singleton, Rob Palmer, Mike Strauss, and Dunc McAllan; "SPASM Agency", *The Dictionary of Sydney*, accessed April 19, 2022, at: https://dictionaryofsydney.org/organisation/spasm_agency.
66. "John Singleton (Australian entrepreneur)," *Wikipedia*, accessed April 7, 2022, https://en.wikipedia.org/wiki/John_Singleton_(Australian_entrepreneur).
67. Jazzer Smith, editor, *The Book of Australian Country Music 1* (Gordon: Berghouse Floyd Tuckey Publishing Group, 1984): 16; an example of the advertisement is "Where do ya get it?, YouTube, accessed April 19, 2022, at: https://www.youtube.com/watch?v=PYhjoahNqKg.
68. EW, *CMA, 1* (Sydney: Angus and Robertson Publishers, 1982): 13.
69. EW, telephone conversation with AS, early 1990s; EW, *CMA, 1* (Sydney: Angus and Robertson Publishers, 1982): 27.
70. For some reason TM consistently gave his date of birth as August 8, 1916, when it was really August 30, 1916. He deliberately told EW the incorrect date and, owing to EW's reputation, others repeated it.
71. EW, *CMA, 1* (Sydney: Angus and Robertson Publishers, 1982): 29.
72. "How Tamworth became Country Music Capital," *History of Country Music in Australia*, accessed April 19, 2022, at: https://www.historyofcountrymusic.com.au/htbcmc.html#:~:text=The%20Tamworth%20Festival%20was%20always,was%20to%20encourage%20Australian%20music.
73. Max Ellis, *Stars, Hurrahs and Golden Guitars: The Story of Tamworth, Country Music Capital* (Tamworth: Agricultural Publishers, Pty. Ltd., 2012): 56.
74. Max Ellis, *Stars, Hurrahs and Golden Guitars: The Story of Tamworth, Country Music Capital* (Tamworth: Agricultural Publishers, Pty. Ltd., 2012): 56–57.
75. Max Ellis, email to AS, August 1, 2017.
76. "Country Music Roll Of Renown," *History of Country Music in Australia,*" accessed April 4, 2022, at: http://www.historyofcountrymusic.com.au/cmroll.html; Max Ellis, *Stars, Hurrahs and Golden Guitars: The Story of Tamworth, Country Music Capital* (Tamworth: Agricultural Publishers Pty Ltd, 2012): 56–58.
77. Max Ellis, *Stars, Hurrahs and Golden Guitars: The Story of Tamworth, Country Music Capital* (Tamworth: Agricultural Publishers, Pty. Ltd., 2012): 56–57. Watson gave TM's birthday as August 8, 1916, and this was stated on the plaque, but the correct date was August 30, 1916.
78. "Country Music Roll Of Renown," *History of Country Music in Australia*, accessed April 5, 2022, at: http://www.historyofcountrymusic.com.au/cmroll.html; Max Ellis, *Stars, Hurrahs and Golden Guitars: The Story of Tamworth, Country Music Capital* (Tamworth: Agricultural Publishers Pty Ltd, 2012): 56–58.

79. "A Tribute To Tex," *History of Country Music in Australia*, accessed April 4, at: https://www.historyofcountrymusic.com.au/tributetotex.html.

80. Buck Carson telephone conversation with AS, August 7, 2017; Lorraine Pfitzner telephone conversation with AS, August 8, 2017. Lorraine Pfitzner said that while Morton was reading the inscription on his plaque, he was momentarily drenched by the sprinkler system nearby.

81. Max Ellis, *Stars, Hurrahs and Golden Guitars: The Story of Tamworth, Country Music Capital* (Tamworth: Agricultural Publishers Pty Ltd, 2012): 57.

82. JM to AS, letter, October 14, 1990.

83. *Homicide* (1964–1977) was produced by Crawford Productions for the Seven Network. "Homicide (1964–1977) Full Cast & Crew," *IMDb*, accessed April 5, 2022, at: https://www.imdb.com/title/tt0129685/fullcredits/?ref_=tt_cl_sm. TM appeared in one episode in 1975: "Tex Morton," *Wikipedia*, accessed April 20, 2022, at: https://en.wikipedia.org/wiki/Tex_Morton.

84. "Rate of Exchange Company Credits," *IMDb*, accessed April 5, 2022, at: https://www.imdb.com/title/tt1778313. TM, typewritten synopsis, PTM Collection, NLA.

85. "Matlock Police, Like Fred," *IMDb*, accessed April 5, 2022, at: http://www.imdb.com/title/tt0643811/?ref_=nm_flmg_act_7; "Matlock Police Full Cast & Crew," *IMDb*, accessed August 2017, at: http://www.imdb.com/title/tt0067408/fullcredits/; TM appeared in three episodes during 1975 and 1976: "Tex Morton," *Wikipedia*, accessed April 20, 2022, at: https://en.wikipedia.org/wiki/Tex_Morton.

86. "Glenview High, Full Cast & Crew," *IMDb*, accessed April 5, 2022, at: http://www.imdb.com/title/tt0588911/fullcredits?ref_=tt_ov_st_sm.

87. "The F.J. Holden Release Info," *IMDb*, accessed April 5, 2022, at: http://www.imdb.com/title/tt0076011/releaseinfo?ref_=ttfc_sa_.

88. "Say You Want Me," *IMBd*, accessed April 6, 2022, at: https://www.imdb.com/title/tt0402482/.

89. *The Young Doctors* (1976–1983) was produced by Reg Grundy Productions for the Nine Network; unidentified *Magazine* article, n.d; *The Young Doctors*, *IMBd*, accessed April 11, 2022, at: https://www.imdb.com/title/tt0074077/.

90. TM, curriculum vitae for Robert Morton, PTM Collection, NLA.

91. "Case for the Defence," *IMDb*, accessed April 5, 2022, at: http://www.imdb.com/title/tt0464771/?ref_=ttfc_fc_tt. Episodes in which TM appeared were: "Second Time Around," "The Man Who Died Twice," "The Family Way," "Case for the Defence" and "A Plea of Insanity".

92. Joan Morris, "Biggest-budget cop show in production," *The Canberra Times* (August 24, 1980): 10; Column by Pete Smith, *Australian Women's Weekly* (October 15, 1980): 30.

93. *Waterloo Station* (1983) was produced by Reg Grundy Productions for the Nine Network; "Meet the Characters in Nine's New Series, Waterloo Station" *TV Week Magazine* (February 5, 1983); "Waterloo Station (TV series)," *Wikipedia*, accessed April 6, 2022, at: https://en.wikipedia.org/wiki/Waterloo_Station_(TV_series).

94. "We of the Never Never," *Wikipedia*, accessed April 6, 2022, at: https://en.wikipedia

.org/wiki/We_of_the_Never_Never_(film); "The Never Never Recreated," *The Canberra Times* (October 24, 1982): 7; "Mataranka," *Australian Explorer*, accessed April 6, 2022, at: https://www.australianexplorer.com/mataranka.htm.

95. "Jeannie Gunn," *Wikipedia*, accessed April 6, 2022, at: https://en.wikipedia.org/wiki/Jeannie_Gunn.

96. Tony Barry, selected quotes and information cited from Tony Barry telephone conversation with AS, February 19, 2018; 40 km = 25 miles; 60 km = 37 miles.

97. Tony Barry, telephone conversation with AS, February 19, 2018.

98. Ibid.

99. "Life Is For The Living," *Australasian POST Magazine* (September 29, 1983): 3–4. £3000 = $6000.

100. Richard Waterhouse, "Tex Morton," *Australian Dictionary of Biography*, National Centre of Biography, Australian National University, 2012, accessed April 6, 2022, at: http://adb.anu.edu.au/biography/morton-tex-15027/text26223.

101. "Hillbilly Who Was Full of Surprises," "Lahey at Large" column in unidentified, newspaper, n.d., 1983.

102. CM, conversation with AS, July 17, 1990; "Superstar Tex Morton," Historical Feature, Sydney *Daily Telegraph* (July 23, 1991).

103. "75 classic films preserved," *NFSA*, accessed April 5, 2022, at: https://www.nfsa.gov.au/latest/deluxekodak-and-kodakatlab.

104. "Goodbye Paradise," *OZ Movies*, accessed April 6, 2022, at: https://www.ozmovies.com.au/movie/goodbye-paradise.

105. "Country Timelines—Tamworth Milestones," *History of Country Music in Australia*, accessed April 24, 2022, at: https://www.historyofcountrymusic.com.au/timeline.html.

106. SDD, interview by AS, April 30, 1989.

107. "Tex Morton—You'll Never Be Missed," YouTube, accessed April 19, 2022, at: https://www.youtube.com/watch?v=P9fQ1yk2V04. TM stated that trill yodelling involved using the back of the throat and not the tongue, implying that Williams incorrectly employed the latter technique.

108. Max Ellis, *Stars, Hurrahs and Golden Guitars: The Story of Tamworth, Country Music Capital* (Agricultural Publishers Pty Ltd, 2012): 69–70.

109. "Tex Morton dies at 66," *The Canberra Times* (July 25, 1983): 3; "Rustic Morton Nearly Sang Himself Hoarse," *Daily Telegraph*, accessed July 2019, at: https://www.dailytelegraph.com.au/rustic-morton-nearly-sang-himself-hoarse/news-story/f1ebf3b301cb39e9fc86221c4adebfd2?sv=3fa661e18775ac6c2d5d358bf5e6c87f (no longer accessible at that URL).

110. Tony Barry, telephone conversation with AS, February 19, 2018.

111. KM, telephone conversation with AS, June 7, 2017.

112. Tony Barry, quote, attributed to TM, from "Life Is For the Living," *Australasian POST Magazine* (September 29, 1983): 4.

113. Dorothy Carroll, interview by JMe, November 20, 1986.

114. KL to PB, letter, ca. 1990s or early 2000s.

115. Gordon Spittle, *TMS* (Auckland: GWS Publications, 2008): 102.

116. Tex Morton epitaph, cited in Gordon Spittle, "Tex Morton," biographical entry, accessed June 2017, at: http://www.teara.govt.nz/en/biographies/5m59/morton-tex.Gordon Spittle.

117. Photograph of TM's headstone in Nelson, findagrave.com, accessed 17 April 2022, at: https://www.findagrave.com/memorial/196246203/tex-morton.

118. Alice Cowdrey, "Theft leads to call to honour country legend," Nelson *Mail*, accessed April 6, 2022, at: http://www.stuff.co.nz/nelson-mail/news/2313062/Theft-leads-to-call-to-honor-country-legend.

119. Geoff Collett, "The Great Morton," *Geoff Collett's journalism*, accessed April 6, 2022, at: http://geoff-journalism.blogspot.com.au/2011/04/great-morton.html.

120. BL, telephone conversation with AS, July 20, 2017; Alan Turley. telephone conversation with AS, July 20, 2017.

121. AS, telephone call to the Trafalgar Centre, November 16, 2017.

122. Alan Turley, telephone conversation with AS, August 1, 2017.

123. KL to PB, letter, ca. 1990s or early 2000s.

124. Max Lash, "Development of the Rutherford Memorial," *Nelson Historical Site Journal* 6, issue 4, 2021, accessed April 11, 2022, at: https://nzetc.victoria.ac.nz/tm/scholarly/tei-NHSJ06_04-t1-body1-d6.html; "Rutherford Memorial," Te Ara Encyclopedia of New Zealand, accessed April 11, 2022, at: https://teara.govt.nz/en/photograph/29008/rutherford-memorial.

125. AS, telephone conversation with librarian, Nelson College, September 18, 2018.

126. EW, TM Medallion (number 0187) posted to AS, 1985.

127. "Making Morton Memories in Country Music Capital," *Capital News* 10, no. 13 (December 1985): 19.

128. "Bust Unveiling of Traveling Showman," *Capital News* 16, no. 8 (August 1991): 13; "Tex Morton—the legend will never die," *Northern Daily Leader* (July 24, 1991): 1.

129. Louise Radcliffe-Smith, "Tex Looks up to namesake," Melbourne *Weekly Times*, June 6, 1990.

130. "Tex Morton," *Monument Australia*, accessed April 10, 2022, at: http://monumentaustralia.org.au/themes/people/arts/display/23366-tex-morton)

Afterword

1. CM and other journalists, interviews by AS, July 17, 1990.

2. Dean Simonton, "Does Creativity Decline with Age," *Scientific American*, accessed April 11, 2022, at: https://www.scientificamerican.com/article/does-creativity-decline-with-age/.

3. Jazzer Smith. "The Tex Morton Story," *Across Country*, no 6 (February 1979): 5.

4. *The Last Ride Of Tex Morton*, DVD, (Attitude Productions / Films 2001). Although this documentary shows interesting photographs of TM, supplied to the producers by BL, it also contains numerous factual errors.

5. TM listed numerous charities he had supported over the years. An example is "25 Years of International Fund Raising," advertisement, PTM Collection, NLA.

6. Trevor Day, telephone conversation with AS, May 6, 2019.

7. TM, "No Pockets In A Shroud," PTM Collection, NLA; reproduced with permission of KM.

8. "Memory error," *Wikipedia*, accessed April 10, 2022, at: https://en.wikipedia.org/wiki/Memory_errors.

Discography

1. Morton re-recorded this song as "The Tramp's Mother" in the 1960s.

2. Around May 1936 Columbia began using new equipment from England and apparently denoted the new recording conditions with a change in the matrix preface from T to CT.

3. PB, email to AS, May 17, 2019.

4. As identified by Bob Moore, from listening to the recordings. There is a possibility that Grady Martin played lead guitar, but both Moore and Billy Garland (Hank Garland's brother) identified Hank Garland as the lead guitarist. Hank Garland did not maintain a diary of recording sessions until after 1953, so there is no written evidence of his participation in this session. At various times, Morton named Martin as lead guitarist and Billy Byrd as rhythm guitarist.

5. The correct title for this song is "Abdul Abulbul Amir."

INDEX OF SONGS AND NARRATIONS

Page numbers in **boldface** refer to the discography.

Abdulla bul-bul ameer, **279**
Across the Great Divide, 37, **255**
After the Ball, **282**
All Set and Saddled, 30, **254**
Along the Stock Route, 145, **271**
Andy's Gone with the Cattle, **289**
Anthony Considine, **281**
Are You Thinking of Me Tonight?, **270**
Aristocrat, 57–58, 65, 73, 78, 87, 215, 222, **261, 286**
As Long as Your Eyes are Blue, **283**
At the End of the Hobo's Trail. *See* End of the (Old) Hobo's Trail
Australia (a song poem), 220–21, **287**

Ballad of Ned Kelly (The), **282**
Barnacle Bill the Sailor (No. 2)/Bollocky Bill the Sailor, 37–38, 81, 161, 209, 215, **255, 267, 285**
Beautiful Queensland, 58, 87, 222, **262, 271, 286**
Beef Tea, **280**
Been There Before, **283**
Big Rock Candy Mountain(s), The, 39, **255, 271**
Bill/Billy Brink the Shearer, 51, 73, **261, 269, 282**
Billy Boy, 215, **277**
Bird in a Gilded Cage, 42, **258**
Black Sheep, The, 36, 74, 166, 220, **254, 265, 268, 271, 287**
Bob the Log, 220–21, **287**

Boko, **289**
Bonny Blue Eyes, 49, 84, **259, 269–70**
Bottle-O, **284**
Boy Named Sue, A, 221
Bullocky Bill, **289**
Bunch of Roses, A, **283**
Burn Another Folkie. *See* Tex Morton's Protest Song
Bury Me Under the Weeping Willow Tree. *See* Weeping Willow Tree
Bush Christening, A/The, 215, 220, **281, 287**
Bushrangers, The, **289**

Call of Stoush, The, **283**
Campfire Medley (Wagon Wheels, Home on the Range, Carry Me Back to the Lone Prairie), 222, **286**
Can/May I Sleep in Your Barn Tonight, Mister?, **268, 278**
Cards Are on the Table, The, 168
Carry Me Back to the Lone Prairie, 27, 222, **252, 269–70, 286**
Cat Came Back, The, 106, 202, 215, 225, **279**
Chant Pagan, 192, **276**
Chinee Luck, 222, **286**
Circus Boy, 166, **275**
Clancy of the Overflow, 192, 203, 215, **268, 269, 276, 281**
Coachman's Tale, The, **289**
Come Back to the Hills, 63
Come Back to the Valley, 63, **263, 267**

365

Conroy's Gap, **281**
Cowboy, **268**
Cowboy's Prayer, The, 192, **276**
Cream in Between, The/The Creamy, 210, 235, **284**
Cremation of Sam McGee, The, 190, 192, 203, **276**
Crime Does Not Pay, 44, 78, **259**, 267

Daddy and Home, 108, **269**
Daley's Dorg, **289**
Dan, the Yodelling Man, 24
Darwin Jailhouse Window/Jailhouse Window, 211, 215, **284–85**
Day I Left Daddy Alone, The, 51, **260**
Dear Old Sunny South by the Sea, 82
Deep in the Heart of Texas, **270–71**
Disqualified Jockey, The, **280**
Don't Go Down the Mine Dad/Dream of the Miner's Child, 203, **276**
Don't Make Me Go to Bed (and I'll Be Good)/Don't Make Me Go to Bed and I'll Be Good, 152, 220–21, **272**, **287**
Don't Say Goodbye, 65, **263**
Doreen, **280**
Dreaming With Tears in My Eyes, 44, 82, 84, **258**
Dreams of Silver (and Memories of Gold)/Dreams of Silver, 49, **259**, **277**
Dr. Hodgkisses' Gold Mine, **270**
Drinking With the Dead (The Glass on the Bar), **229**, **289**
Drover's Wife, The, 63, 166, 215, **262**, **282**. *See also* Neighbor's Wife, The
Droving Days, **281**
Duck and Fowl, **283**
Dunmarra, 224, **288**
Dying Duffer's Prayer, 44, **258**
Dying Stockman, The. *See* Wrap Me Up in My Stockwhip and Blanket

End of the (Old) Hobo's Trail, (At) The/The End of a Hobo's Trail, 16–17, 37, **251**, **255**, **282**
Everything But You. *See* (Honey, I've Got) Everything But You
Eyes of Temptation, (The)/The Eyes of Temptation, 220, **285**

Face on the Bar Room Floor, **277**
Fanny Bay Blues, 38, **255**
Father Reilly's Horse, **281**
Fireball Dan, **290**
First Surveyor, The, **281**
Flowers Never Bloom in Lonesome Valley, The/Flowers Never Bloom in Lonesome Valley, 68, **264**, **277**
Flying Doctor Poem, The, **290**
Frankie and Johnnie/Johnny, 151, 215, **269**, **272**, **278**, **290**
Freight Train Yodel, 57–58, 73, 78, 85, 143, 220, **261**, **269–70**, **286**
Frying Pan's Theology, **281**

Gallant Gentleman, A, **283**
Game, The, **283**
Ginger's Cobber, **283**
Glass on the Bar. *See* Drinking With the Dead
Goin' Back to Texas/Going Back to Texas, 24–25, **251**, **269**
Going to the Barn Dance Tonight, **267**
Good Old Days, 218, 220, **285**
Good Old Droving Days, The, 68, 73, 220, **264**, **287**
Goondiwindi Grey, The (The Gunsynd Song), 228–29, **289**
Great Australian Adjective, The, **289**
Great Calamity, The, **281**
Greatest Mistake of My Life, The, 41, **256**
Green, Green Grass of Home, (The), 209, **284**

INDEX OF SONGS AND NARRATIONS 367

Hallelujah/Halleleujah, I'm a Bum, xx, 220, **278**, **285**
Hand Me Down My Walking Cane/Hand Me Down My Walkin' Cane, 50–51, 60, **260**, **266**, **270**, **271**
Happy Yodeler/Happy Yodeller, 25–26, **251**
He Holds the Lantern (While His Mother Chops the Wood), **272**
Hitched, **280**
Hobo Bill/Hobo Bill's Last Ride, 30, 73, **267**
Holy Dan, **289**
Home on the Range, 192, 222, **276**, **286**
(Honey, I've Got) Everything But You, 60, 63, 144, **263**, **269**
How Gilbert Died, **283**
How McGinnis Went Missing, **284**
How'm I Doing, 24

I Belong to Glasgow, 203, **276**
If You Please Miss Give Me Heaven 58, **261**
I/I've Got You (Right Out of My Mind), 166–67, 209, **275**, **285**
I Left My Heart in Red River Valley, 42, **258**
I Like Country Music (I Like Mountain Music), 225, **288**
I Like Looking at Planets—The Astronomer, **284**
I Like Mountain Music, **267**. *See also* I Like Country Music
I'll Be Hanged If They're Gonna Hang Me, 49, 106, **260**, **268**, **271**
I'll Never Slip Around Again, 152, **273**
I'm Betting the Roll on Roma, **289**
I'm Dreaming Tonight of the Old Folks, 41, **256**
I'm Forever Blowing Bubbles, 158
I'm Gonna Yodel My Way to Heaven, 49, 53, **260**, **270**
In Eleven More Months and Ten More Days, 215, **278**

In Spadger's Lane, **283**
Insult, The, 16–17, **251**
In the Luggage Van Ahead/In the Baggage Coach Ahead, 63, **263**
Introduction by the Artist, **280**
Irma Jackson, 210
I've Got You (Right Out of My Mind). *See* I/I've Got You (Right Out of My Mind)
I've Known the Truth, 166–67, **275**
I've Only Loved Three Women, **269**
I Was Born in Old Wyoming. *See* Wyoming Willie

Jailhouse Window, The. *See* Darwin Jailhouse Window
Jim Carew, **281**
Johnson's Antidote, **281**
Just Because, **273**
Just Drifting Along, 28, **253**
Just Plain Folks, 58, 86, **261**, **268**

Kevin Barrie/Kevin Barry, 205, **280**
Kid, The, **280**
Kiwi Song, 166, **275**

Lasca, **289**
Last Roundup, The, 16–17, 19, **251**
Legend of the Rebel Soldier, The, 205
Letter Edged in Black, The, 12, 41, 226, **257**, **268**, **279**
Letter to the Front, A, **283**
Let the Rest of the World Go By, 50–51, **260**, **269**
Liebestraum, 46, **266**
Little Brown Jug, **282**
Little Old Church in the Valley, The, **268**
Little Sweetheart of Days Gone By, 51, **261**
Lonesome Valley Sally, 36, **254**
Lost, **284**

Mandrake, 57, 65–66, 73, 78, 80, 101, 222, 264, 271, 286
Man from Ironbark, The, 215, 281
Man from Snowy River, The, 281
Man on the Flying Trapeze, The, 282
Maori's Wool, 281
Mar, 280
Martins and the Coys, The, 42, 44, 212, 257, 271
May I Sleep in Your Barn Tonight, (Mister). *See* Can/May I Sleep in Your Barn Tonight, Mister?
Mexican Yodel, 16–17, 251
Mick Dooley's Pants, 289
Miner's Luck, 220–21, 287
Mistaken Identity, 270
Mooch O'Life, The, 280
Moonlight and Skies, 267
Mother, the Queen of my Heart, 268
Move Along Baldy, 44, 259, 269
Mulga Bill's Bicycle, 283
Murrumbidgee Jack, 49, 87, 259
My Blue Ridge Mountain Home, 41, 46, 257, 266, 268
My Daddy is Only a Picture, 152, 272
My Little Buckaroo, 268, 270
My Little Lady, 144, 151, 268, 271–72
My Mother's Tears, 39
My Old Bunkhouse Buddies, 49, 259
My Old Crippled Daddy, 44, 259
My Old Pal, 51, 269
My Sweetheart's in Love With a Swiss Mountaineer, 38, 256, 268

'Neath the Silver Willow Tree, 68, 264
Ned Kelly Song, The/Original Ned Kelly Song, The, 51, 144, 260, 269
Neighbor's Wife, The, 166–67, 215, 275. *See also* Drover's Wife, The

Old Apple Tree, The, 270
Old Blue, 224, 288
Old Boko and Me, 59, 262
Old Man Duff, 44, 84, 215, 258, 268, 279
Old Pal of my Boyhood Days, 37, 255
Old Rover/Old Rover (dedicated to a faithful friend), 59, 262, 271
Old Shep, 42, 64, 66, 77–78, 80, 101, 104, 106, 215, 217, 263, 268
Old Ship O' Mine (the Sailors' Hillbilly), 27, 74, 253
One Golden Curl, 152, 273
One Has My Name (the Other Has My Heart), 152, 272
On Kiley's Run, 283
On the Gundagai Line, 30, 73, 82, 87, 254, 269
Oregon Trail, The, 27, 252
Original Ned Kelly Song, The. *See* Ned Kelly Song, The
Over the Range, 281

Parson Joe/The Story of Parson Joe, 68, 215, 264, 277
Passing of Gundagai, 284
Pearl Diver, The, 281
Peg Leg Jack/Peg-Leg Jack, 37–38, 81, 215, 255, 268
Pilot Cove, 280
Play, The, 280
Poor Ned Kelly, 51
Prairie is a Lonesome Place at Night, The, 27, 252
Prelude, 281
Push, The, 283

Rabbits, 283
Ragtime Cowboy Joe, 27, 46, 253, 267, 269, 271
Railroad Boomer/Railroad Bum, 38, 84, 166, 167, 255, 275
Red River Valley, 41–42, 65, 143, 257, 270–71
Rio Grande, 192, 267, 276

Road to Old Man's Town, The, 283
Rock A Bye My Baby, 171
Rockin'/Rocking Alone in an Old Rocking Chair, 39, 53, 77, 143, 198, 217, 220, **256**, **268**, **270**, **286**
Rock My Cradle (Once Again), 152, **273**
Rocky Ned (the Outlaw)/Rocky Ned, 49–50, 53, 57, 73, 106, 222, **260**, **268**, **270**, **286**
Rodeo Round-up (Rocky Ned, Aristocrat, Mandrake), 222, **286**
Roll Along Covered Wagon, **267**
Rolling Stone, A, 153, **272**
Rose of Shenandoah Valley, **273**
Roundup in the Spring, The. *See* Texas in the Spring
Rover No More, 65, **264**, **270**
Rye Whiskey, 215, **279**

Sail Along Silvery Moon, 144
Saltbush Bill, **283**
Santa Claus in the Bush, **283**
Sari Bair, **283**
Satisfied Life, A, **289**
Saving Miss Mona, **270**
Sergeant Small, 23, 42, 44, 74–75, 77, 79, 80, 212, **257**
Shadow Waltz, 19
She Came Rolling Down the Mountain, 58, **261**, **268**
She'll Be Coming/Comin' Round the Mountain, 58, **271**
She Was Happy Till She Met You, **279**
Shicer, The (Moaner's Luck), 220–21, **287**
Shooting of Dan McGrew/Shooting of Dan McGrew, The (Alouette), 190, 192, **276**
Singing Soldiers, The, **283**
Sing, You Cowboy, 27, **252**, **269**
Siren, The, **280**
Sleepy Hollow, 51, **261**, **267**, **271**, **278**
Slippin' Around, 152–53, **273**

Soldier's Sweetheart, 145, 153, **271**, **282**
Soldier's Sweetheart, Part 1, 153, **272**
Soldier's Sweetheart, Part 2, 153, **272**
South American Joe, 46, **267**
Spring Song, A, **280**
Steak and Potatoes, **270**
Stockman's Last Bed, The, 59, 73, 143, **261**, **267**, **270**, **278**
Stockman's Prayer, A/Stockman's Pray'r, 153, **272–73**
Story of a Dear Old Lady, 39
Story of Mongrel Grey, **283**
Story of Parson Joe, The. *See* Parson Joe
Stoush O'Day, The, **280**
Straight Griffin, The, **283**
Strawberry Roan, The, 158
Stror'at Coot, The, **280**
Swagman's Rest, The, **281**
Swiss Sweetheart, 25–26, **251**

Take Me Back to Dream by the Old Mill Stream, 36, **254**
Teardrops in My Heart, 152, **273**
Tennessee Waltz, **276**
Texas in the Spring, 25, 46, **251**, **267**
Texas Rose, 19
Tex, Buddy and Me, 236
Tex Morton's Protest Song (Burn Another Folkie), 71, 209, 215, **284**
There Are Tear Stains on Your Letter Mother Dear, 39, **256**
There's a Bridle Hanging on the Wall, 220, **286**
There's a Gold Mine in the Sky, 144
They Cut Down the Old Pine Tree, **269**, **277**
This Cold War with You, 152, **274**
Through the Sin of a Son, 64–65, **263**, **271**
To the Boys Who Took the Count, **283**
Tramp's Mother, The, 12, 27, 144, **269**, **278**. *See also* You're Going to Leave the Old Home, Jim

Transport Man, The, 220–21, **287**
Travel by Train, 23, 49, **259**
Travelling Post Office, The, **283**
Travelling Showman, The, 92, 220–21, **287**
Treasures Untold/Treasure Untold, 151, **273**
Tumba Bloody Rumba, **290**
Tumblin' Down, 217
21st Birthday, 57, 210, **284**

Valley, the Homestead and You, The, **268**

Wabash Cannon Ball/Wabash Cannonball, 152, **274**
Wah Hoo, **266**
Waiting for a Train, 151, **273**
Waltzing Matilda, 192, 215, **268, 276**
Wandering Stockman, The, 27–28, **253, 268**
War, **283**
Wee Jeanie Hunter, 9, 215, **281**
Weeping Willow Tree (also known as Bury Me Under the Weeping Willow Tree), 41–42, 46, **257, 267–68**
Welcome to the Club, 210, **285**
When Davey Rode the Mule, **283**
When It's Night Time in Nevada, 41, **257, 267**
When My Blue Moon Turns to Gold Again, 152, **273**
When the Bloom Is on the Sage, 24, 51, 143, **261, 268, 271**
When the Cactus Is in Bloom, 64–65, 82, 84, 143, **263, 267, 270**

When You Have No One to Love You (Linda Darlin'/Linda Darling), 152, **273**
Why Should I Work?, 37, **255**
Widow Next Door, The, 57, 226, **288**
Wild Colonial Boy, The, 221
Wrap Me Up in My Stockwhip and Blanket (The Dying Stockman)/Wrap Me Up with My Stockwhip and Blanket/Wrap Me Up in my Tarpaulin Jacket, 24, 27–28, 59, 73, 76, 87, **253, 268, 270, 277**
Wreck on the Southern Old 97, 2
Wrong Mr. Hopkins, The, **270**
Wyoming Willie/I Was Born in Old Wyoming, 26, 46, 166–67, **252, 266, 268, 270–71, 275**

Yellow Rose of Texas, The, 41, **257, 271**
Yodelling Bag Man, The/Yodelling Bagman, The, 21, 23, 29, **253, 267**
Yodelling Cowboy/Yodeling Cowboy, **269**
You and My Old Guitar, 151, **268, 272, 277**
You'll Never Be Missed, 59, 153, 192, **236, 262, 276**
Young Man from the Country, **281**
Young Pat Maloney, 44, 83, **258, 281**
You Only Have One Mother, 36–37, 74, **254**
You're Going to Leave the Old Home, Jim (also recorded as The Tramp's Mother), 26, **252**

GENERAL INDEX

2BL-Sydney, 24, 30
2CN-Canberra, 201
2CY-Canberra, 201
2FC-Sydney, 40
2GB-Sydney, 46
2KY-Sydney, 23–24, 29, 33, 52, 74
2KY Radio Trials (Talent Quest), 24, 29
2SM-Sydney, 148
2TM-Tamworth, 96, 221, 232
2UW-Sydney, 144
3AW-Melbourne, 50, 107
4BH-Brisbane, **266**
5AN-Adelaide, 200
7EX-Launceston, 201

Abbott and Costello, 174
ABC (Australian Broadcasting Commission/Corporation), xx, xxi, 23–24, 52, 200–201, 213, 234
ABC Dance Band, 29–30, 39, 59
Aboriginal artists. *See* Indigenous Australians
Aboriginals and hypnotism, 179
Academy Foundation (Hollywood), 195
Acuff, Roy, 152–53, 163, 197–201, 211, 218
Addie Cantwell's Dancing Academy (Brisbane), 54
Adelaide (South Australia), xix, 30–31, 68, 99, 199–200
Adler, Larry, 29, 32
Agar, Dan, 144, **267, 269**
Aitken, George, 148
Akenson, James, xiv
Alaska (USA), 174, 213

Alice Springs (Northern Territory), 212, 224
Allans Music, 107, 109
Allen, Steve, 194–95,
All Set and Saddled (radio programs), 143–44, **269–71**
Aluminium records. *See* Speak-O-Phone discs
American Society for Clinical and Experimental Hypnosis (SCEH), 183
American Society of Clinical Hypnosis (ASCH), 183
Anderson, Lance, **247**
Andrews Sisters, 60
Annie Oakley (television series), 195
Apollo Theater (New York), 175
ARC. *See* Australian Record Company
Arctic Circle, 172, 188
Aristocrat (horse), 57, 66
Armstrong, Lillian (Lil) Hardin, 83
Armstrong, Louis, 83
Arnaz, Desi, 193
Arnold, Eddy, 152
Arsenic and Old Lace, 195
Ashcroft, Johnny, 199
Ashton's Circus, 98–99, 202
Astor Studios (New Zealand), 150, **273**
Attwater, Gordon, 50
Auckland (New Zealand), 154, 218–19, **272–73, 285**; Auckland Show, 19; "Country Touch" filmed in, 218–19; in Morton's early years, 15–16, 37; Ralph Peer visit, 147; in Tasman recordings, 150–51, **272–73**

Australasia, x, xix, 69, 147–48, 217, 229, 232–33, 239, 242, 246
Australian Broadcasting Commission. *See* ABC
Australian bush ballad. *See* Bush ballad
Australian Dictionary of Biography, 5
Australian Hill-Billies, 28–29
Australian Hillbilly Club, 108–9
Australian Hotel (Brisbane), 54
Australian Performing Right Association (APRA), 229
Australian Record Company (ARC), 55, 148, **272**, **274**
"Australia's Singing Stockman," 147
Autry, Gene, 41–42, 76, 144, 147, 152, 158–59, 171, 193–94

Balaam, Dolores, xiii, 153
Ball, Lucille, 193
Banes, Tex, xiii, 107–9
Bargo, Billy, 66, 93–94
Barnier, Amanda, 186
Barret, Joe, 13
Barret, Ray, 236
Barrie (Canada), 161
Barrie, Ian, 192, **275**
Barrie, Kevin. *See* Barry, Kevin
Barry, Kevin, 205
Barry, Tony, xiii, 234–35, 237
Batchelor, Norbert, xiii, 23
Bear Family label, 44, 82, 151, **274**
Bedogni, Lyndsay, **286**
Behind the Legend (television production), 234
Bellamy (television series), 234
Bernstein, Morey, 182
Bibby, Lionel, 34–35, 91
Bickerton, John, 111
"Big Bang of Country Music," 1, 2, 4
Big Show, The (movie), 42
Billboard (magazine), 36, 53, 100, 174, 183, 198

Bishop's School (Nelson), 10
Blinkhorn, Smilin' Billy, xiv, 51, 56, 58, 80, 85
Blitner, Donald, 235
Blood on the Rio Grande (fictitious movie), 159, 193
Bloom, Harry, 40
Blue Moon Palais (Brisbane), 54
Bluett, Fred, 63
Bluff (New Zealand), 18–19
Blyth, Ann, 158
Bond, Johnny, 152
Bonishea, Ray, 13
Bonners Ferry (USA), 160
Booth, Edwin, 1
Boston (USA), 171, 183
Boswell, Leo, 42
Boundary rider (definition), xix, 16
Bourke, Chris, xiv, 151
Bowditch, Jim, xiii, 210–11
Boyer, Charles, 194
Boxing, 22, 85, 96–97, 104, 198
Bradfield, Johnny, 150, **273**
Bradley, Owen, 165, **275**
Braemar, Walter, 154
Braid, James, 184
Brandon (Canada), 176
Breaking Point (television movie), 234
Brewster, Teddy, 195
"Bridey Murphy," 182. *See also* Hypnotic regression
Bridge, Dave, **288**
Brisbane (Queensland), xix, 99–100, 116, 170, 199, 204, 227, 230, **266**; birth of twins in, 66–67; Brisbane Exhibition, 99, 116; entertainment in, 54, 59; mentioned in song, 38; in Morton's early years, 20–22
Brisbane, Marjorie Frederica. *See* Morton, Marjorie (wife)
Bristol (USA), 1, 148
British Medical Association, 183
Brooks, Lawrence, 48

Brother Jonathan (Jonathan Delaun Heaton), 50–51
Brown, Derren, 183
Brown, Joe E, 176
Brown, Milton, 58
Brown, Ray, 198
Brumley, Ken, 188
Bryant, Johnny, 48
Bryden-Brown, John, 200–201
Buckjumping, xix, 47, 57, 65, 93, 95, 101, 103, 146, 216; songs about, 49–50, 57, 65, 222; in Wild West rodeos, 88–91, 93, 95, 98, 117, 225, 228
"Buckle bunnies," 117
Burgis, Peter, xiii, 5, 187, 215, 291
Burnette, Bernie, xiii, 70–71
Burraston, Mike, 105, 169, 187, 224–25
Burrows, Don, 211, 284
Bush ballad, x, 3, 28, 51, 56, 76, 86–87, 102, 109, 229, 244
Bust in Centennial Park. *See* Memorials to Tex Morton
Byrd, Jerry, 165, **275**

Calder, Dave, **286**
Calgary (Canada), 160, 162
Calgary Range Riders. *See* Hilton, Dixie Bill
Calgary Stampede, 160–61
California Café (Sydney), 65
Cameron, Al, 42
Campbell, George, 150, **273**
Camp Rockhampton. *See* Frontline Carnival, Tex Morton's
Canberra (Australian Capital Territory), xix, 98, 201–2, 208, 239, **251**
Cantrell, Dudley, 36, 40, 109
Caribbean, 161–62, 176
Carlisle, Cliff, 3, 65
Carlson, Neville, 15
Carlson, Violet, 48
Carnegie Hall, 191–92, **275–76**

Carr, Dick (Reginald Blyth), xiii–xiv, 35, 46–47, 60, 64, 69, 93, 212, **260**, **263–64**, **266–69**, **271–72**
Carr, Michael, 27, 37, 75, 242
Carroll, Bruce, 48, 59–60, 155
Carroll, Dorothy ("Sister Dorrie") divorce, 155; "floozy," 150; and Morton, 34, 35, 48, 59–62, 67–69, 94–95, 97–99, 106, 113–14, 116–17, 143–44, 146–47, 150–51, 154–56, 226, 237, 244; recordings, 63–65, 78–79, 144–45, 151–53, 225–27, **262–69**, **271–74**, **288**
Carroll, Roger, 59, 62, 155
Carson, Buck, xiv, 214, 230
Carter, Anita, 169
Carter, Mother Maybelle, 169
Carter, Wilf, 56, 108, 152, 160, 171
Carter Family, 41, 58, 148, 152, 168–69
Carver, Doc, 1
Case for the Defence (television series), 234
Castle Recording Studio, 165
Central School (Nelson), 10, 14
CFOR (radio station, Canada), 160
CFOS (radio station, Canada), 161
Channel Nine (TCN Nine) television (Sydney), 200–201
Charities: Dude Ranch, 146–47; Jaycees, 201, 217; Lions Club, 201; New Zealand, 201–2; Police Boys' Club, 201; Rotary, 201; St Giles, 201
Charles, Hedley, xiii, **247**
Charters Towers, 54
"Charters Towers" (horse), 65–66
Chatto, Ron, 202
Chicago (USA), 174
Chief Little Wolf, 146
Child support case, 114–16
Circus Boy (television series), 195
CJVI (radio station, Canada), 160
CKIB (radio station, Canada), 160
Cleburne, Eric, xiv, 45, 151
Clifton (USA), 174

Coffey, Kevin, xiv, 88
Cohen, Len, 218, **286**
Cohen, Mickey, 159
Colman, Peter, xiv, 104
Coltman, Tut, 14
Columbia Graphophone Company, xviii, 30, 244, **248**, **251–66** (as "Columbia Studios"), 292; Arch Kerr and, 54–56, 58, 68–70; Morton's contract with, 30; Morton' recordings with, 22, 24–27, 29, 36, 38–39, 41–44, 58, 63–64, 66, 70, 72–87
Columbia Records, USA, 165–67, **275**
Comic books. *See* Tex Morton comics
Commodore Apartments/Flats, 110–11, 115
Como, Perry, 220
Contract, recording (with Columbia Graphophone), 30
Cooley, Spade, 160
Cossacks, Russian, 21
Coughlan, Frank, 49
Country Touch (television series), 218–20, 223, 228, 244, **286**
Country Touch Singers, **287**
Courtney, Vince, 37, 63, 65
Covered Wagon shows, 45–46, **266**
Cox, Marion, 51
Coxhead, Garry, xiv, 214, 226
Crawford, Allan/Alan, 148
Crawford, Joan, 195
Craydon, Letty, 39
Crisp, David, xiii, xv, 5, 39, 80, 153, **247**
Croft, Tex, xiv, 104, 201
Crook, Frank, 207
Crosby, Bing, 80, 194
Crumit, Frank, 28, 151
Crump, Barry, 224
Curran, Tom, 93
Curtin, John, 89

Dalhart, Vernon, ix-x, 2–3, 13, 41, 63, 74, 81, 241–42
Dallas, Maria, 217

Darrell, Johnny, 209
Darwin (Northern Territory), xix, 38, 210–12
Darwin Catholic Hall, 210
Darwin Jail, 38 (Fannie Bay), 211
Davidson, Jim, 29, 30, 39–41, 59, 85
Davis, Gussie, 63
Davis, Oscar, 163–64, 189, 197
Davis Jr, Sammy, 174
Dawson, Smoky, xi, xiv, 3, 24–25, 35, 53, 56, 66–67, 70, 76, 88, 100, 103, 110, 113, 149, 158–59, 163, 233, 236
Day, Trevor, xiv, 37, 72, 214, 231
Dead Easy (television production), 234
Dean, Eddie, 152
Dean, Jimmy, 105
Decatur (USA), 162
Dell, Gordon, 103–4
Dennis, CJ, 203, 221, **279–80**
Denny, Jim, 163
Depression, Great (1929-), 9, 42, 54, 76, 86, 217, 245
Dignam, Arthur, 234
Divorce, Bruce and Dorothy Carroll, 155; Tex and Marjorie Morton, 34, 67
Doctorate. *See* PhD
Doyle, Dorothy Ellen, 110–14
Doyle, John, 111–12
Dragnet (television series), 193
Drake Hotel (Los Angeles), 159
Drinking. *See under* Morton, Tex
Drunk-driving (DUI) charge, 117–18
Dude Ranch. *See* Tex Morton Dude Ranch, The
Dulhunty, Larry, 65–66, 106, 229
Duncan, Gwen, 93–94
Dunmarra (Northern Territory), 224
Dunne, John, 148
Dusty, Slim, x, xiv, 2, 57, 80, 92, 100, 105, 209, 211, 214, 219, 229, 244; and Arch Kerr, 56; and bush ballads, 3, 28, 76, 86–87, 102; friendship with Morton,

92, 212–14; and Hamilton County
    Bluegrass Band, 224–25; influenced by
    Morton, 4, 72, 85, 100, 103, 219, 232, 242
Dyer, Bob, 42, 52

Easte, Bryan, 218, 223
Eastgate, Mildred (mother's maiden
    name). *See* Lane, Mildred
Ed Sullivan Show (television program), 195
Edwards, John, 26, 64, 151, 193, **263**
Ellis, Max, xiv, 49, 200, 232, 236
Ellul, Joe, xiv, 95
Elsey Station (Northern Territory), 234
England, xvii, 7, 38, 42, 55, 61, 89, 165, 176,
    195
Erickson, Milton, 183
Escott, Colin, xiv, 164
Evansville (USA), 175, 186
Everybody's Magazine. See *Tex Morton
    Story, The* (magazine articles)

"Father of Australian/Australasian country
    music," x, 69, 82, 233, 238, 239, 242
Featherstone, Lisa, xiv, 110, 113
Fegan, Dudley, 148
Festival Records, 192, 202–3, 205, 229,
    275–83
Field, Shirley, 162
Fields, Gracie, 41
Finch, Peter, 40, 195–96
FJ Holden, The (movie), 234
Fleming's Food Stores, 198
Flin Flon (Canada), 190
Flower, Horace, 27–28
Floyd, Elzie, 42
Flynn, Errol, 35–36, 196
"Focs'l" apartments, 32
Foley, Red, 64, 168
Folger, Billy (Cecil Smith), 152
Fonteyn, Margot, 189
Forbes (New South Wales), 60
Fort William (Canada), 176

Foster, Alfie, 21
Fraley, Pat, 50–52, 78–79, 151, 158, **260**
France, 176
Francis, "Bushman" Bill, 93–94
Frank, J. L. *See* King, Pee Wee
Franquin (Frank Quinn), 154
Fredini, Leon, 93–94
Fridolin (Gratien Galenas), 170
Frontline Carnival, Tex Morton's, 97
Funerals: of son Bernard, 157; of Tex
    Morton, xi, 238

Gable, Clark, 195
Gaieties, The, 16, 19
Gambling, 97, 117
Game of Hate, A (television program), 196
Garland, Hank, 165, **275**
Garling, "Uncle Rus," 24
Gear, Robert (Bob), xiv, 13
Geraghty, Bob, 245
Gesu Theatre (Montreal), 170
Gibson guitars, 25, 107
Gielgud, John, 189
Gill, Brian, 96
Gill, Jack, 91, 93
Gill, Kitty, 93
Gill, Stan, 91, 96
Girls of the Golden West, 36
Gish, Lillian, 189
Glenview High (television series), 234
Goodbye Paradise (movie), 236
Goondiwindi (Queensland), 66
Goondiwindi Grey (Gunsynd, horse), 229
Gordon, Terry, xiv, 231
Grade, Lew, 176
Grafton (New South Wales), 29, 40
Grand Ole Opry Tour (Australia), 197–200
Gray, Otto, 88, 202
Grayson, Kathryn, 196
Green, Archie, 203
Greenway, John, 82, 193
Grieve, Ray, xiv, 45

GTV6-Ballarat, 215
Guadalcanal, 152, 168
Guest, Lynette, xiv, 226, **288**
Guitar, Gibson. *See* Gibson guitars
Guitars, Tex Morton, 85, 107–9
Gunn, Kevin, 85
Gunsmoke (television series), 194
Gypsy spells, 213

Haggard, Merle, 210
Halls Creek (Western Australia), 212
Hamilton (Canada), 161, 175
Hamilton County Bluegrass Band (HCBB), 218, 220, 223, 225, **286**
Ham radio, 95, 187, 192, 225, 235
Ham radio licences and call signs, 192
Hands of Fame, 155, 233
Happy Chappies, 51
Harbor Bridge. *See* Sydney Harbor Bridge
Harbor ferries (Sydney), 23, 30, 33
Hardy, David, xiii, 5, 151, **247**
Harris, Charles, 58
Harris, Gilbert (Gil), xiv, 13
Harrisburg (USA), 162
Hatch Poster Collection, 162
Hatfield and McCoy dispute, 42
Hawaii, 155, 176, 198
Hawaiian Club, 47, 107, 109
Hawaiian music, 1, 13, 30, 41, 46, 83, 151
Hawking Brothers, 152
Hawkins, Hawkshaw, 160
Hayes, Evie, 48
HCBB. *See* Hamilton County Bluegrass Band
Healey, Noel, 224
Heap, Johnny, xiv, 231
Hebert, Marjolaine, 190
Helms, Don, 163–64
Hicks, Jenny, 90–92, 104, 117
Hill, Dick, xiv, 193
Hill, George/Hill Family, 226–27

Hill Billies (British group), 27, 37, 42, 49, 65, 73
Hilton, Dixie Bill, 38, 159–61, 164, 176
Hindermyer, Harvey, 51
Hirst, Ron, 229
Hobart (Tasmania), xix, 118, 212
Hoeptner, Fred, 169, 193
Hokitika (New Zealand), 8, 154
Hollywood (Los Angeles), x, 35–36, 89–92, 94, 99, 102, 152, 158–60, 163, 193–96
Hollywood Plaza Hotel (Los Angeles), 159–60, 163
Homan, Bill, 12–13
Homicide (television series), 234
Hong Kong, 186, 204, 207–8
Hoosier Hot Shots, 42
Hope, Bob, 194
Horton, Johnny, 165
Howard, Fred, 51
Howarth, Dan, 19–21
Howatt, Alan, 12–13, 20
Hughes, Billy, 32
Hypnotic regression, 182
Hypnotism: and Hank Williams, 164; post-hypnotic suggestion, 173, 207; and reincarnation, 182; selecting subjects for, 181, 185–86; stage hypnotism, xi, 8, 153–54, 160, 167–91, 202, 206–8, 210, 212, 242–43

Indigenous Australians, xx, 2, 66, 85, 93, 179, 210–11, 234–35
Institute of Hypnotherapy. *See* Toronto Institute of Hypnotherapy
Invercargill (New Zealand), 19
Ipswich (Queensland), 54, 230
Iredale, Robert, 192, 204, **275**

Jacaranda Festival, 29
Jackson, Tommy, 165–66, **275**
Jamaica, 161, 176
Jeffs, Will, 150–51, **273**

GENERAL INDEX 377

Jim Davidson's ABC Dance Band. *See* Davidson, Jim
Jolson, Al, 189
Jones, Grandpa, 160
Jones, Tom, 209
Joseph, Hugh, 159, 161, 167
Journal of Hypnotism, 183–84

Kahi, Tommy, 151, **273**
Katherine (Northern Territory), 212
Kaye, Danny, 190
Keene, Laura, 1
Kelly, Ned, xix, 6, 51, 70
Kelly, Orry George, 159
Kelly, Sam, 93
Kennedy, Jimmy, 27, 76, 242
Kerr, Arch, 39, 54–56, 58, 63–64, 66, 68–70, 76, 80, 87, 159, 243
King, Kevin, xiv, 106, 214, **288**
King, Pee Wee, xiv, 4, 159, 162, 169
King Kong Nightclub (Hong Kong), 207
King of Australian Country Music (Slim Dusty), 4, 85, 103
King of Country Music (Roy Acuff), 197
Kings Cross (Sydney), 44, 47, 110
Kings Head Hotel (Sydney), 216, 238
Kingston (Jamaica), 177
Kingston, Damien, xiv, 83–84
Kinloch, Al, 64–65, 68, **263–64, 266–67, 268–69, 271–72**
Kipling, Rudyard, 191–92, 195
Kirby, Pete (Bashful Brother Oswald), xiv, 200
Kitching, Ken, **288**
Kitimat (Canada), 188–89
Kohi, Ossi, 202
KWKH-Shreveport, 163

L. *See* Likeability Index
Lamb, Arthur, 42
Lane, Barbara (sister), xiii, 5, 22, 159, 190–91, 237–38; early life, 8–10; memories of Tex Morton and her family, 9–11, 22, 33–34, 48, 68, 102, 114, 150, 171, 175–76, 180, 182, 196; touring with Tex Morton, 159, 175–76, 188, 190–91; working in Hollywood, 188, 193
Lane, Bernard (father), 8–9, 14, 19, 34, 68, 114, 175–76, 238, 243–45; career 10; fictitious background, 10, 33; influence on Tex Morton, 8, 10; marriage, 8
Lane, Don, 213
Lane, Frankie, 174
Lane, John William (grandfather), 9
Lane, Kim (brother), xiii, 5, 8, 12, 18, 33–34, 62, 93, 99, 147, 178, 237–39
Lane, Mildred (mother), 8 (maiden name), 10, 19, 23, 34, 37, 68, 150, 171, 175–76, 238, 243–45
Lane, Rex (brother), xiii, 5, 8–9, 15, 18, 33, 237
Lane, Robert William. *See under* Morton, Tex
Lang, Fred, 161, 190
Lassie (television series), 193
Latona, Peter, 239–40
Lauder, Harry, 189
Laughton, Charles, 159, 190
Laughton, Herb, 85
Launceston (Tasmania), 117, 201
Lavater, Louis Isidor, 59
Law, Don, 165–66
Laws, Aussie, 216
Layne, Bert, 51
Lennon Brothers's Wild West Show, 50
Leonard, Art (Len Maurice), ix, 3, 38–39, 41–42
Lethbridge (Canada), 160
Lewis, Jerry, 194
Lewis, Jerry Lee, 209
Likeability Index (L), 77–79
Lindsay, Reg, xiv, 100, 148, 211

378 GENERAL INDEX

Lister, Weldon ("Big Bill"), 163
Liverpool (England), 176
London (Canada), 172
London (England), 176
Los Angeles, 10, 35, 171, 174, 179–80; Morton's arrival in (1950), 158–59; Morton's phoning Ron Wills, from 159; Morton's return to (1958/59), 193, 195; in Palo Alto University, 178; in UCLA, 168, 179. *See also* Hollywood (Los Angeles)
Los Angeles Institute of Hypnotherapy and Hypnoanalysis, 180
Louisiana, 152, 163,
Louisiana Hayride (radio program), 163–64
Louisville (USA), 162
Lurline (ship), 10
Luther, Frank, 2, 13, 25, 37, 41, 44, 74, 81
Lux TV Playhouse, 195–96
Lyons, Joseph (Joe), 32, 40

Mac and Bob. *See* McFarland and Gardner
Macdonald, Alexander, 198–99
Mackay (Queensland), 21–22, 94, 106, 212
Mackay, Colin, xiv, 7, 10, 15, 43, 50, 62, 65–66, 91, 113–14, 191, 213; admiration of Morton, 242, 245; *Everybody's Magazine* articles, 216; skepticism of some of Morton's claims, 66, 214, 216; *This is Your Life* (television program), 114
Macquarie Broadcasting Network, 45
Mafia, 213
Mahoney, Will, 48
Maintenance case. *See* Child support case
Maitai River, 7, 9
Majestic Theatre (Adelaide), 68
Malone, Bill, xi, 4
Managers. *See* Davis, Oscar; Scott, Bill; Reid, J. Ian
Manchester Robertson Alison's Ltd. building. *See* Walking blindfolded on building parapets
Mandrake (horse), 65–66, 98

Manly (Sydney), 223, 230, 238
Manly Hotel (Sydney), 214
"Marilyn," 190, 193. *See also* "Wolf Girl"
Marks, Herbie, 64, **263–64, 266–68, 269,** 271–72
Marsden Cemetery (Nelson), 238
Marshall, Herbert, 194
Martin, Dean, 194, 220
Martin, Joan, 67
Martin, Ron, **288**
Marvin, Frankie, 2, 44, 49, 63, 74, 81
Marvin, Johnny, 49
Massacre on the River (fictitious movie), 159
Mataranka (Northern Territory), 234
Matlock Police (television series), 234
Maurice, Len. *See* Leonard, Art
Mazor, Barry, xi, xiv, 4, 82
McBride, Dickie, 41
McCleod, Kid, 93, 226
McClintock, Harry, xx, 39
McConville, Thorpe, 49–50, 88
McCormack, Johnny, 93
McCoy, Athol, xiv, 39, 52–53, 200, 209, 211–12
McCoy, Tim, 90
McFarland and Gardner, 41, 51, 58
McGill University (Montreal), xiv, 178–81, 182, 186, 241
McKay's store (Nelson), 14
McKean, Joy (Joy Kirkpatrick), xiv, 212–13, 224
McMichen, Clayton, 51
McNamara, Tim, 148
Meeting (television production), 234
Melbourne (Victoria), xix, 40, 67, 96, 110, 116, 199, 204, 239; Australian Hillbilly Club in, 107–9; radio stations in, 24, 50; Tivoli shows in, 31, 59; touring shows, in 16, 19, 208–9; Wild West Rodeo in, 94, 98–99
Melody Ranch (radio show), 193–94
Melrose, George, 53, 98–99

Memorials to Tex Morton: bust in Centennial Park, Tamworth, 239–40; Hands of Fame, 233; memorial in Nelson, 238–39; Roll of Renown, 232–33, 242
Memorial to Ernest Rutherford, Nelson, 239
Memorization, 4, 153, 160, 171, 174–75, 186–87, 190, 201, 206, 242
Meredith, John, xiv, 53, 65
Mesmer, Franz, 181, 184
Microphone technique, 45, 94, 96, 106, 173–74, 187, 214
Milgate, Detective Inspector Oswald, 111
Miller, Bob, 39, 63
Miller, Roger, 166
Mills Brothers, 24, 32
Minson, John, xiv, 70, 170, 200, 221, 225, 229, 233
Mitchum, Robert, 194
Moncrieff, Gladys, 29, 39–40, 85
"Montana Bill," 10
Montez, Lola, 1
Montgomery (USA), 163
Montgomery, Melba, 197
Montreal (Canada), 159, 161, 167, 170–72, 174, 178–80, 188, 195
Montreal Expo (1967), 212
Montreal Studio and Drama Club, 195
Moore, Bob, xiv, 165
Moore, Kittra, xiv, 166
Moore, Frankie, 197
Morgan, Benny, 13
Morton, Bernard (father), 8–10, 14, 20, 33, 66, 68, 114, 238, 243, 244–45
Morton, Bob (son), 66–68, 114–16, 146, 156–57
Morton, Kath (partner), xi, 5, 61, 182, 197, 204, 214, 219, 223, 225, 227, 230, 239, 245; and Morton's death, 237; and Morton's shooting act, 208, 212
Morton, Marjorie (wife), xi, 5, 43, 52, 59, 66–68, 98, 110, 237, 244; marriage and honeymoon, 32–34; rape case, 110, 112–14; seeks child support, 114–16; and Sister Dorrie, 60, 67; touring with Morton, 34, 48, 93, 114; and twins, 66–68, 146, 155–57
Mortons and McCoys, 211–12
Mortons Garage (Waihi), 15
Morton, Tex: academic qualifications, 17–80, 189, 216; arrests, 21, 43, 110, 117; in Australia 1970s, 197–206, 223–40; in Australia, early tours, 19–23; birth, 8, 232; busking license, 21; in Canada (1950–1958), 160–62, 169–82, 186, 188, 191; cars, 47, 60, 62, 67, 69, 95, 100, 117, 205; children, attitude towards, 61, 92–93, 96, 106, 147, 156, 201–2, 244; clothes, 16, 102; death, 237; drinking, 21–22, 35, 105, 113, 115, 117–18, 154, 158, 188, 200, 204, 211, 214, 227, 235; Dude Ranch, 145–47; in the Far East, 207–8; final concert at Tamworth, 236–37; ham radio, 8, 95, 187, 192, 225, 234; leaving Columbia Graphophone, 68–70, 243; leaving home, 7, 14–16, 244; marriage, 33–34; memorial to, 238–40; migrating to Australia, 18–20; monologues (*see* Narrations); name change from Robert William Lane to "Tex Morton," 14–16, 68, 116; name change to "The Yodelling Cowboy," 24; name change to "The Yodelling Boundary Rider," 26; in Nashville (*see* Nashville); in New Zealand 1949 to 1950, 150–54, **273–74**; in New Zealand 1960s, 105, 147, 201–2, 217–21; in North America, 158–96; old people, attitude towards, 61, 147; political views, 182; record sales, xvi, 30, 73–81; religious views, 182; Roll of Renown, 232, 242; schooling, 10–12; and Wild West Rodeos (see Wild West Rodeo, Tex Morton's)
Morven (Queensland), 212
Mount Isa (Queensland), 212
Mratinich, Veronica, 76

380 GENERAL INDEX

Munting, Jack, 201
Murphy, Bridey, 182. *See also* Hypnotic regression

Narrations, 4, 59, 145, 153, 192, 203–4, 209, 220, **275–77**, **283–84**
Nashville (USA), x-xi, 4, 162–63, 165–69, 174–75, 200, 209–10, 215, 232, **275**
Nathan, Barbara, 181
National Guild of Hypnotists (NGH), 183
Neil, Jocelyn, xi, 2, 4
Nelson (Canada), 160
Nelson (New Zealand), xi, 28, 33–34, 68, 116, 179, 213, 217, 239; Morton's early years, in 7–12, 18; Morton's departing Nelson, 14–15; Morton's funeral in, 238; Morton's grave, in 238; Morton's monument in, 233; Morton's musicianship in, 12–13; Morton's returning to Nelson at various times in his career, 19, 33–34, 150, 217; Nelson College, schooling at (*see* Nelson College)
Nelson, Gene, 174
Nelson, James, 41
Nelson College (Nelson) xiv, 11–12, 175, 239
Neville Carlson's Revue, 15
Newton, Ernie, 165, **275**
Newton, Ralph Ernest (Slim), xiv, 226–28, 230
Newton, Robert, 194
New York (USA), 25, 44, 75, 161, 175, 183, 191, **276**
Nicholson's Music, 85, 109
North, Rexford L., 183
Norton, Elliott, 174
Noumea, 213
Now and Then (television production), 234
Nullarbor Plain, 99

Oakley, Annie, 195
O'Daniel, W Lee, 58, **262**
OKeh record label, 164, 167, 189
Old Bush Songs (anthology), 28, 59
Olstad, Rod, xiv, 161, 190
Open House. See Roy Acuff's Open House
Oram, James (Jim), 216
Orchante, Tommy, 105
Orillia (Canada), 161
Owen Sound (Canada), 161

Pagewood Studios (Sydney), 45, **266**
Palo Alto University (USA), 178–79
Paris, Mike and Comber, Chris (authors), 4, 82
Parsons, Gordon, xii, 76, 214
Pasadena Playhouse, 195
Paterson, A. B. ("Banjo"), 28, 59, 86, 190–92, 195, 203–4, 209, 215, 220, **280**, **283**
Pat Sheridan Quintet, 188
Payne, George, xiv, 26, 148
Payne, Rex, 59
Peach, Noel, 150
Peer, Monique, 147
Peer, Ralph, 1, 147–48, 150–51, 153, 158–59, 166
Pellitt, Neville, xiv, 104, 206
Penrith (New South Wales), 145, 147
Percy, Dr., 112
Perth (Western Australia), xix, 38, 91, 99, 155
PhD, 175, 178–80, 183–84, 189, 216, 231, 246
Philippines, 207–8
Philips records, 167, **289**
Picture Records, 229
Pine Ridge Boys, 152
Pinson, Bob, xiv, 162, 164
"Pinto Pete," 3
Platt, Robert, 191, **247**
Portage la Prairie (Canada), 176
Porterfield, Nolan, xiv, 4, 25, 145
Posa, Peter, xiv, 220–21, **286**

Presenting Robert Morton (television series), 215
Presley, Elvis, 163, 165, 174
Princess Theatre (Melbourne), 208
Puckett, Riley, 51
Pugh, Ronnie, xiv, 165
Punch McGregor, Angela, 234
Pyrmont (Sydney), 202, **275, 277–81**, **283–84, 288**

"Queen of the Road" (caravan), 95
Quirindi (New South Wales), 42–43

Racism, 235
Radio programs, xiii, 3–4, 8, 16, 18, 23, 26, 29, 40, 43, 86, 89, 108, 147–48, 163, 168, 212–13, 221, 223, 231, **266–71**; "All Set and Saddled," 143–45; "Dixie" Bill Hilton, 160–61; by hypnosis, 172, 176–77; Los Angeles programs, 193–96; by Morton, 23–24, 32, 34, 43, 50–52, 95–96, 100, 102, 191, 195, 201, 212–13, 215; by Morton and Harry Thompson, 40, 45–46
Radio salesman, Morton's occupation as, 19
Randell, Ronnie, 196
Ranger, Shorty, 148
Rankin, Dusty, 77, 231
Ransom, Wally, 150
Rape case, 98, 110–14
Ray, Johnnie, 174
Raymond, George, 64, **263, 288**
Recitations. *See* Narrations
Redshaw, Leo, 13
Reed, George. *See* Raymond, George
Reed, John E, 194
Reeves, Goebel, 12–13, 17, 25–27, 37–39, 56, 75–76, 82, 169, 192, 203, 241
Reeves, Jim, 165
Regal Zonophone label, xiii, 26, 36, 44, 63, 69, 166, 203, 215, 218
Regal Zonophone recordings, 72–87, **251–66**; number of recordings, 44; origins of songs in, 72–76; sales of, 75, 80–81; themes, 78–79
Reid, J. Ian, 189
Rene, Roy, 30–31
Renmark (South Australia), 212
Ricketts, Dorothy. *See* Carroll, Dorothy
Ringbolting, 20
Ritter, Tex, 160, 194
Roadhouse (television production), 234
Robert (Tex) Morton's Reading of Ginger Mick (vinyl album), 209, **283**
Robert, Whitey, 48
Robinson, Reg, 64
Robison, Carson, 51, 74–75, 81, 169, 192, 241–42
Rockhampton (Queensland), 21–22, 97
Rocky Ned (horse), 49–50
Rodeo label, 55, 148, **272–74**
Rodgers, Jimmie, x, 3, 24, 44, 56, 76, 86, 108, 160, 198; and the "Big Bang of Country Music," 1, 148; as influence on Australian country music, 2, 82; as influence on Morton, ix, 3–4, 12–13, 16, 25, 30, 37–38, 51, 65, 73, 81, 144–45, 151, 203, 232, 241–42
Roll of Renown (Tamworth), 232, 242
Roosevelt, Teddy. *See* Brewster, Teddy
Rose, Fred, 152
Rose, Lionel, 85
Roughriders/Rough Riders band, 64–65, 68–69, 78–79, 83–84, 94, 144–45, 150, 226, **263–69, 271, 288**
Roy Acuff's Open House (television programs), 200–201
Royal Alexandra Theatre (Toronto), 171, 189
Royal North Shore Hospital (Sydney), 237
Royalties, recording, 30, 40
Rumble, John, xiv, 166
Russell (Canada), 190
Russell, Tony, xiv, 76, 83, 87
Rutherford, Ernest, 11–12, 239

Sales figures. *See under* Regal Zonophone recordings
Santo, Syd, 85
Satherley, Art, 165
Saunders, Hal, xiv, 35, 45, 153, 192, 202–5, 208, 242
Savage, Jack, 39
Say You Want Me (television movie). *See Breaking Point*
Schlappi, Elizabeth, 197, 199
Schlue, Mary, xiv, 106
Scott, Bill, 52–53, 56, 70–71, 89, 92, 96, 99
Scott, Norm. *See* Singing Stockmen, The
Seal, Graham, xiv, 28, 86
Sears Roebuck, 175
Sentimental Bloke, The (vinyl album), 203–4, **279**
Sentimentality in recordings, 2, 17, 37, 39, 41, 44, 49, 55, 76–79, 143–44, 152, 221
Sentimental Tex (vinyl album), 215, **265**
Sentiment and Humour of Banjo Paterson, as read by Robert (Tex) Morton (vinyl album), 209, **283**
Sergeant Preston of The Yukon (television series), 194
Service, Robert, 190–92
Sevesi, Bill, 151, 273
Seville Theatre (Montreal), 172, 174
Shakespeare, William, 153, 195
Shalfoon, Epi, 14
Shand, Ron, 39
Sharp, Tommy, 64
Sharpshooting, 33–35, 40, 60–62, 89, 93–96, 98, 114, 150, 161–62, 174, 176, 188–91, 205, 207–8, 212
Shegog, Kevin, 209
Shelton Brothers, 36
"Shorty." *See* Agar, Dan
Showboat cruises, 30. *See also* Harbor ferries
Shreveport (USA), 152, 163–64
Silvers, Phil, 174
Simmons, Richard, 194
Sinatra, Frank, 48, 153
Sing, Smile and Sigh (vinyl album), 209, **281**
Singapore, 207
Singing Stockmen, The, 41
Singleton, John, 231
Sir George Williams College (Montreal), 179, 182
Sister Dorrie. *See* Carroll, Dorothy
Skinner, Dick, 117
Skuthorpe, Lance Jr, 57, 59, 89, 90–91, 98, 110–13, 117, 146
Skuthorpe, Lance Sr, 57, 88, 90–91
Skuthorpe, Violet (sister of Lance Jr), 57, 89, 90
"Slippery," 65
Small, Sergeant William James, 42–43
Smith, Cecil. *See* Folger, Billy
Smith, Ethel, 170
Smoky Mountain Boys. *See* Acuff, Roy
Snow, Hank, 168–69, 198, 213
Snow, Minnie, 169
Society for Clinical and Experimental Hypnosis (SCEH). *See* American Society for Clinical and Experimental Hypnosis
Songbooks, 85, 109
Songs of the Outback (vinyl album), 215, **265**
Sons of Fun, 68
Sons of the Pioneers, 152
Sorlie, George, 21
Southern Music Publishing, 148, 150–51
Speak-O-Phone discs, 16, 19, 37, **251**
Spittle, Gordon, xiv, xv
Springfield (USA), 162, 188
Steiner, Stephen, 180
Stephens, Joyce, xiv, 154, 172
Stewart, Alan, 211
Steyne Hotel (Sydney), 214
Stir (movie), 234, 236
St Johns (Canada), 170, 186
St Philips Church of England (Sydney), 33

Strange Cargo (movie), 195
Stratford on Avon, 176
Summons/subpoena to appear in court, 96, 115, 216
Surfers Paradise (Queensland), 245
Swanson, Allan, 214
Sydney (Canada), 175
Sydney (New South Wales), xix, 30, 32–35, 40, 44, 46–48, 50, 52–54, 58–60, 65, 67, 74, 89–90, 94, 100–101, 107, 109–10, 115–16, 145, 147, 154, 156, 167, 175, 189, 200, 202, 204–5, 211, 213–14, 216, 223–24, 229–30, 234; in broadcasting on radio, 23–25, 29–30, 33, 40, 45–46, 144, 148; and Columbia Graphophone, 24–25; in death, 237–39; Dude Ranch, near, 145, 147; early destination for Morton, 18–20, 22–25; in Grand Ole Opry show, 197–99; in marriage, 33; Ralph Peer in, 147–48, 153; as recording center, 13, **251–73, 276–85, 288–89**; in revues, 34; Rodeo Records in, 151; in "Showboat Cruises," 30–31; and twins, 156; and Wild West shows, 94, 100
Sydney Harbor Bridge, 20, 23
Sydney Morning Herald, 33
Sydney Stadium, 198

Tamworth (New South Wales), 96, 155, 221, 224–25, 232–33, 236, 239, 242
Tamworth Centenary Show (1972), 224
Tasmania, xix, 46, 52–53, 83, 89, 99, 105, 117–18, 171, 194, 201, 211
Tasman label. *See* Rodeo label
Tauber, Richard, 38
Taylor, Gerry, 170, 186
Taylor, Jim, 24
TCN9, 200–201, 213
Telegram sent to Buddy Williams, 71
Television, 114, 159, 171, 190, 193–97, 200–201, 208, 213, 215, 218, 223–25, 227–29, 231, 233–34, 243–44

Tennison, Patrick, 209
Tex Morton comics, 109
Tex Morton Dude Ranch, The, 68, 145–47
Tex Morton guitars. *See* Guitars, Tex Morton
Tex Morton Home Study Course (instruction manual), 108
Tex Morton in New Zealand (vinyl album), 220, **285–86**
Tex Morton Looks Back (vinyl album), 202–3, **278**
Tex Morton Memorial Association, 239–40
Tex Morton posthypnotic climax, 173
Tex Morton Reads Banjo Paterson (vinyl album), 203, **280–81**
Tex Morton's Australia (vinyl album), 228–29, 233, 242, **288–89**
Tex Morton's Goondiwindi Grey. See *Tex Morton's Australia* (vinyl album)
Tex Morton Singalong, A (vinyl album), 222, **286**
Tex Morton Story (vinyl album), 203, **275–76**
Tex Morton Story, The (magazine articles), 216
Tex Morton Today (vinyl album), 220–21, **286–87**
Theatre Royal (Brisbane), 59
Thomas, Wilfrid, 100, 195
Thompson, Harry, 29, 39, 41, 45, 78–79, **253, 257, 266**
Thoms, Shirley, 63, 66, 76
Thornhill, Elizabeth, 32
Thornton, Barry, 212
Thornton, James, 27
Tighe, Virginia. *See* "Bridey Murphy"
Tillman, Floyd, 152
Tin Pan Alley, 27, 75, 242
Tivoli theatres/Tivoli revues, 29–31, 48, 59, 63
Tokyo (Japan), 207
Top Hat night club (Canada), 180

384 GENERAL INDEX

Toronto (Canada), 161, 164, 171–72, 174–75, 180, 189
Toronto Institute of Hypnotherapy, 180
Torrani, Harry, 12–13, 17, 25, 81, 241
Townsville (Queensland), 22, 93–94
Trafalgar Center (Nelson), 239
Travis, Merle, 160
Trenwith, Colleen, xiv, 218–19, **286, 288**
Trenwith, Paul, xiv, 218–19, 224, **286**
Tribe, Ivan, xi, 4
Trocadero (Brisbane), 54, 59
Tudawali, Robert, 211
Tulane Hotel. *See* Castle Recording Studio
Turley, Alan, xiv, 179, 213, 238
Twins (Bernard and Bob, sons), 66–68, 114–16, 146, 155–57, 244
Tyler, Tim, 24–25, 49, 55

UCLA (University of California, Los Angeles campus), xiv, 168, 179
Ulverstone (Tasmania), 211
United States Army (US 41st Infantry Division), 97
University of California. *See* UCLA
Untouchables, The (television series), 193

Vancouver (Canada), 160, 171
Van Loewe, Leon, 154,
Versatile Tex Morton, The (vinyl album), 203, **278**
Victoria Hotel (Darwin), 211
Vietnam, 57, 210, 226
Vincent, Nat, 51, 148, 158
Von Tilzer, Harry, 42

Wagoner, Porter, 209
Wahlquist, Gil, 167, 221
Waihi (New Zealand), 15, 19, 37
Wakely, Jimmy, 152
Walker, Billy, 164
Walking blindfolded on building parapets, 170

Wallace, George, 147
Wallis, Tom, 64, **263–64, 266–69, 271–72**
Walt Disney studios, 195
WAMPAS (Western Association of Motion Picture Advertisers), 52
Wandong (Victoria), **290**
Waterloo Station (television series), 234
Watson, Eric, xiv-xv, 29, 72, 85, 162, 194, 203, 220, 229, 231, 239
Watts, Terence, 185
Webb, June, xiv, 197, 200
Wedman, Les, 171
Weems, Ted, 42
Welles, Orson, 189
We of the Never Never (movie), 234, 236
West, Harry, 108
West, Mae, 189
Western University (USA), 179
Where d'yer get it (advertising slogan), 231
Whip cracking, 88, 91, 93, 96, 98, 170, 188, 210–11, 242
White, Jack, 211
Whiting, Margaret, 152,
Why Be Serious show, 34, 48, 59
Wikara, Buddy, 47, 107–8, 110, 115, 147–48
Wilburn Brothers, 197
Wild West Rodeo, Tex Morton's, 47, 60, 65–66, 69, 80, 86, 88–93, 100–106, 114, 146, 169, 172, 191, 202, 212, 221; 1940, 93–94; 1941, 94–95; 1942, 96–97; 1943, 97; 1944, 97–98; 1945, 98; 1946, 98; 1947, 99; 1948, 99–100; 1949, 100; unsavory aspects of, 103–5
Williams, Andy, 220
Williams, Buddy, xiv, 2, 80, 214, 224, 227, 233, 242; influenced by Morton, 4, 72, 76, 85, 88, 226, 232, 242; recording with Columbia, 56, 66, 70, 80; recording with Morton, 225; reuniting with Morton, 224–25; rivalry with Morton, 58, 71, 80, 209, 214, 236; and sentimentality, 77; and telegram from Morton, 71

Williams, Hank, x-xi, 86, 152, 161–64, 168, 231
Williams, Harry, 85
Williams, Karen, xii, 71, 225–26, **288**
Wills, Bob, 58
Wills, Ron, xiv, 55–56, 64, 68–70, 159, 161, 167
Winters, Arthur, 65, 93
Wirth's Circus, 14, 18, 93, 96
Wisemans Ferry (New South Wales), 145
With Tex Morton (television series), 215
Witt, Freddy, 38
Wolfe, Charles, 6
"Wolf Girl," 161, 189–91, 193, 237

Wonthaggi (Victoria) incident, 103–4
Wood and Sons (Nelson, New Zealand), 14

Yandell, Paul, 165
Yellowknife (Canada), 172
Yodeling, 26, 46, 55–56, 76, 85, 162, 236; Arch Kerr, and, 55, 70; by Gil Harris, 13; by Goebel Reeves, 25–26, 38, 82; by Harry Torrani, 12, 13, 17, 81; by Jimmie Rodgers, 1, 3, 13, 81, 83; by Tex Morton, 8, 15–17, 19, 21, 23–27, 29–30, 37–41, 48, 60, 64–65, 68, 70, 78, 83–85, 94, 101, 106, 143–45, 151, 160–61, 166, 174, 188, 191, 225, 233, 242
Young Doctors (television series), 234

www.ingramcontent.com/pod-product-compliance
Lightning Source LLC
Chambersburg PA
CBHW060510080526
44586CB00012B/451